LATINAS IN THE CRIMINAL JUSTICE SYSTEM

LATINA/O SOCIOLOGY SERIES
General Editors: Pierrette Hondagneu-Sotelo and Victor M. Rios

Family Secrets: Stories of Incest and Sexual Violence in Mexico
Gloria González-López

Deported: Immigrant Policing, Disposable Labor, and Global Capitalism
Tanya Maria Golash-Boza

From Deportation to Prison: The Politics of Immigration Enforcement in Post-Civil Rights America
Patrisia Macías-Rojas

Latina Teachers: Creating Careers and Guarding Culture
Glenda M. Flores

Citizens but Not Americans: Race and Belonging among Latino Millennials
Nilda Flores-González

Immigrants Under Threat: Risk and Resistance in Deportation Nation
Greg Prieto

Kids at Work: Latinx Families Selling Food on the Streets of Los Angeles
Emir Estrada

Organizing While Undocumented: Immigrant Youth's Political Activism under the Law
Kevin Escudero

Front of the House, Back of the House: Race and Inequality in the Lives of Restaurant Workers
Eli Revelle Yano Wilson

Building a Better Chicago: Race and Community Resistance to Urban Redevelopment
Teresa Irene Gonzales

South Central Dreams: Finding Home and Building Community in South L.A.
Pierrette Hondagneu-Sotelo and Manuel Pastor

Latinas in the Criminal Justice System: Victims, Targets, and Offenders
Edited by Vera Lopez and Lisa Pasko

Latinas in the Criminal Justice System

Victims, Targets, and Offenders

Edited by
Vera Lopez *and* Lisa Pasko

NEW YORK UNIVERSITY PRESS
New York

NEW YORK UNIVERSITY PRESS
New York
www.nyupress.org

© 2021 by New York University
All rights reserved

References to Internet websites (URLs) were accurate at the time of writing. Neither the author nor New York University Press is responsible for URLs that may have expired or changed since the manuscript was prepared.

Library of Congress Cataloging-in-Publication Data
Names: Lopez, Vera, 1971– editor. | Pasko, Lisa, editor.
Title: Latinas in the criminal justice system : victims, targets, and offenders / edited by Vera Lopez and Lisa Pasko.
Description: New York : New York University Press, [2021] | Series: Latina/o sociology series | Includes bibliographical references and index.
Identifiers: LCCN 2021009002 | ISBN 9781479804634 (hardcover) | ISBN 9781479891962 (paperback) | ISBN 9781479806324 (ebook) | ISBN 9781479804641 (ebook other)
Subjects: LCSH: Criminal justice, Administration of—United States. | Discrimination in criminal justice administration—United States. | Discrimination in law enforcement—United States. | Hispanic American women—Crimes against. | Female offenders—United States. | Women immigrants—United States.
Classification: LCC HV9950 .L37 2021 | DDC 364.3/7408968073—dc23
LC record available at https://lccn.loc.gov/2021009002

New York University Press books are printed on acid-free paper, and their binding materials are chosen for strength and durability. We strive to use environmentally responsible suppliers and materials to the greatest extent possible in publishing our books.

Manufactured in the United States of America

10 9 8 7 6 5 4 3 2 1

Also available as an ebook

CONTENTS

Introduction   1
   Vera Lopez and Lisa Pasko

PART I. VICTIMIZATION TO OFFENDING: BLURRING THE BOUNDARIES

1. Entre Mujeres Platicamos: The Role of Informal Social Networks among Latina Survivors of Intimate Partner Violence   19
   Sujey Vega, Alesha Durfee, and Jill Messing

2. Latina Interpersonal Victimization: The Importance of Sexual Orientation   42
   Lindsay Kahle and Anthony Peguero

3. Nondisclosure of IPV Victimization among Disadvantaged Mexican American Young Adult Women   60
   Alice Cepeda, Esmeralda Ramirez, Jessica Frankeberger, Kathryn M. Nowotny, and Avelardo Valdez

PART II. LATINA OFFENDERS FROM COURT TO CORRECTIONAL INVOLVEMENT

4. Demasiados Problemas: A Focus on Gender, Ethnicity, and Juvenile Diversion Programming   83
   Lisa Pasko and Jean Denious

5. On the Run and In/Out of the System: Understanding Latina Girls in a Southern California Barrio   102
   Jerry Flores, Xuan Santos, and Ariana Ochoa Camacho

6. The Correlates and Consequences of Maternal Efficacy among Imprisoned Women   126
   Holly Foster and Chantrey J. Murphy

PART III. IMMIGRATION ENFORCEMENT, CRIMMIGRATION, AND THE DEPORTATION MACHINE

7. No Solamente Porque Soy Mujer: A Transnational Intersectional Framework for Understanding Latin American Women's Experiences with Crimmigration   151
   Katie Dingeman and William Estuardo Rosales

8. Masking Punitive Practices: Latina Immigrants' Experiences in the U.S. Detention Complex — 182
Cecilia Menjívar, Andrea Gómez Cervantes, and William G. Staples

9. Adriana and Esther: Experiences of Formerly Incarcerated Migrant Women Deportees — 209
Martha Escobar

10. Young Women's and Girls' Experiences in the Facilitation of Migrant Smuggling — 237
Gabriella Sanchez

PART IV. COMMUNITY PROGRAMMING FOR SYSTEM-IMPACTED LATINAS

11. From the Streets to the Halls of Higher Education: The Case of an Undocumented Latina on the Margins of the Justice System — 259
Lisa M. Martinez

12. Maternal Racial and Ethnic Strategies as a Protective Factor against Delinquency among Latina Girls: An Exploratory Study — 280
Veronica E. Cano

13. Mi Hermana's Keeper: Empowering Latina Youth to Improve Services That Prevent Juvenile Justice System Involvement — 300
DeAna Swan, Johanna Creswell Báez, and Diandrea Garza

14. Xinachtli: A Healing-Informed, Gendered, and Culturally Responsive Approach with System-Involved Latinas — 315
Sara Haskie-Mendoza, Josephine V. Serrata, Heriberto Escamilla, and Christian Jaimes

Conclusion — 333
Vera Lopez and Lisa Pasko

About the Contributors — 339

About the Editors — 349

Index — 351

Introduction

VERA LOPEZ AND LISA PASKO

At court, I just had an ugly argument with the prosecutor because he was very aggressive. I thought. Yeah? What happened was I am a really strong person in order to take the crushing words he told me. Because from the beginning he yelled. I do not know if this is the way that the prosecutors treat people because I had never been in a court. He began to yell and ask why I was fighting in order to stay in this country. That I should take all my things and leave. And later he told me regarding my eldest son, I don't remember well what he said, but he told me "Your son is not important to me, what is important to me is American citizens."
—Juana

This quote is from Juana, a Mexican woman who had immigrated to a small mountain community in Colorado in order to seek better economic opportunities for her family. While working at a hotel as a member of the housekeeping staff, Juana was caught up in an immigration raid whereby local law enforcement asked Juana's employers for her documentation papers. Upon discovering that Juana's documentation was falsified, the officers arrested and detained her for "falsification of papers." As indicated by Juana's narrative, the prosecutor assigned to her case said that because Juana and her son were not U.S. citizens, he did not care about them. Although the prosecutor's message was clear, Latinas in the United States often receive both covert and overt messages from the media, politicians, and others that they do not belong in the United States. Latinas receive messages that they are "ni de aquí, ni de allá" (neither from here, nor from there), regardless of on what side of the U.S.-Mexico border they were born.

The U.S. juvenile justice, criminal justice, and immigration enforcement systems (hereafter referred to as U.S. criminal justice systems) play a large role in the "othering" of Latinas, like Juana, who are unfortunate enough to become ensnared within them. Despite their involvement with these systems, Latinas' experiences have rarely been considered in the criminological literature (Lopez & Pasko, 2017; for notable exceptions, see Díaz-Cotto, 2006; Schaffner, 2008). Most criminological research to date has continued to focus on either Latino men or (white) women in general, glossing over the lives and experiences of Latina girls and women. Such approaches are problematic "because examining and describing women's experiences independently from race, ethnicity, class, sexual orientation, age, and other aspects of identity creates a distinct female voice that often ignores the experiences of those on the margins" (O'Neal & Beckman, 2017, p. 644).

The purpose of *Latinas in the Criminal Justice System* is to remedy this deficit and to underscore the experiences, backgrounds, and struggles of system-impacted Latinas. In this volume, we elevate these often ignored and invisible voices, as we share research about Latina girls' and women's experiences with victimization, law violations, and systems of surveillance and punishment. This volume does not focus on Latinas who work as justice professionals, nor does it make intergender comparisons. Although we recognize and acknowledge that system-impacted Latinas share overlapping experiences and confront similar barriers as Latino boys and men and women in general, their experiences with the U.S. legal systems should be viewed through an intersectional lens that centers their experiences. By relying on an intersectional lens, *Latinas in the Criminal Justice System* avoids essentializing system-impacted Latinas or viewing their experiences primarily through a singular, reductionist cultural lens (which often leads to stereotyping and victim blaming).

As this book demonstrates, the girls and women whose lives are changed by the labels "victim," "offender," and "undocumented immigrant" often struggle with "multiple marginality" in that their gender, race, class, and legal status have placed them at the social and economic periphery of society. Understanding the lives and choices of Latina girls and women who find themselves in the U.S. criminal justice systems also requires a bigger understanding of the contexts within which their "law-violating" behavior is rooted. There are important links between Latina girls' and women's problems and their system involvement—an involvement that often delivers powerful impacts, furthering their legal, court, and correctional troubles. It is because of this, that we aptly named our volume *Latinas in the Criminal Justice System: Victims, Targets, and Offenders*, for even when Latina women are victims of violence or crossing the U.S.-Mexico border, they often fear a system response that will treat and target them as criminals.

As a project of social justice, *Latinas in the Criminal Justice System* addresses how ethnicity, gender, class, sexuality, legal status, and/or carceral status shape the perceptions, interactions, and experiences of Latinas within the U.S. criminal justice systems. The chapters throughout this volume use different methodologies and ways of knowing to understand Latinas' involvement with these systems; however, most of the chapters center the voices of Latinas themselves. Consistent with Chicana feminist epistemologies, we value and accept Latinas' realities as the foundation of knowledge about their experiences (Bernal, 1998; Calderón, Bernal, Huber, Malagón, & Vélez, 2012). By spotlighting the voices and experiences of Latina girls and women, we provide them with a forum to tell their stories, share their experiences, and speak their truths to the researchers, policy makers, and practitioners who will read this volume. When they share their fears of police, experiences with discrimination, feelings of injustice, and oppression by systems of social control, we do not question their realities but rather accept their truths. Specifically, *Latinas in the Criminal Justice System* examines how Latina "victims" of interpersonal violence view their interactions with police officers and other system actors; how Latina girls and women experience the juvenile and criminal justice systems as "offenders"; and how undocumented Latina women experience the U.S. "crimmigration" system while recognizing that these labels are neither clear-cut nor mutually exclusive and that their use varies by whose perspectives are being privileged.

What We Know about System-Impacted Latinas

Understanding the extent of Latinas' involvement in these systems is challenging because of the lack of data on Latinas/os in national databases.[1] Even when ethnicity data are collected, they are rarely disaggregated by gender, which limits our knowledge of the "true" extent of Latina girls' and women's involvement in the U.S. criminal justice systems. Further, national estimates do not account for state and local variations. States with larger populations of Latinas/os (e.g., California, Texas, Arizona, New York) no doubt have proportionately more Latina girls and women involved in the U.S. criminal justice systems than national estimates indicate (Eppler-Epstein, Gurvis, & King, 2016). Finally, certain women such as those who are undocumented may be less likely to participate in surveys (Massey & Capoferro, 2004).[2] With these caveats in mind, we present a broad overview about what is known about the extent of Latina girls and women's involvement in the U.S. criminal justice systems.

LATINAS AND INTERPERSONAL PARTNER VIOLENCE. *Latinas in the Criminal Justice System* focuses on Latina "victims" of interpersonal partner violence (IPV) and their perceptions of and help-seeking experiences with law enforcement and formal social services. The prevalence of IPV (sexual violence, physical violence, and/or stalking) among Latina women, as with other women, is high. National Intimate Partner and Sexual Violence Survey estimates based on 2010–2012 data indicate that approximately 35 percent of Latina women have experienced IPV in their lifetime; however, IPV rates ranged from 31.4 percent to 61.6 percent among Latinas across the twenty-one states included in this study (Smith et al., 2017).[3] In general, though, Latina women report lower rates of IPV than women of other racial/ethnic groups.

LATINA GIRLS AND WOMEN IN THE JUVENILE AND CRIMINAL JUSTICE SYSTEMS. In the juvenile justice system, Latina girls accounted for 17 percent of all delinquency cases in juvenile court in 2015, which is lower than their proportion (23 percent) of the general female youth population in the United States (Ehrmann, Hyland, & Puzzanchera, 2019).[4] In 2018, Latina girls were referred most often to juvenile court for person offenses (34.7 percent), followed by property offenses (25.8 percent), public order offenses (24.8 percent), and drug offenses (14.8 percent; Sickmund, Sladky, Kang, & Puzzanchera, 2019). Although further breakdowns for each of these offenses by race and ethnicity are unavailable, it is likely that most of the person and property offenses committed by Latina girls are for simple assaults and larceny-theft offenses, as this is generally true for the female delinquency caseload in general. Detention, adjudication, and placement rates for cases involving Latina girls are higher for Latina girls than for Black and white girls (Ehrmann et al., 2019). Latina women are more likely than white women to be incarcerated in jails and prisons (Carson & Golinelli, 2014) and are incarcerated at 1.3 times the rate of white women (Sentencing Project, 2019). While Black women are still disproportionately represented in U.S. jails and prisons, their rate of imprisonment decreased by 53 percent from 2000 to 2015, while the rates of imprisonment for white women and Latinas increased by 44 percent and 12 percent, respectively (Sentencing Project, 2018).

LATINA WOMEN AND IMMIGRATION. Historically, most of the migration flows across the southern border of the United States have been due to Mexican men coming to the United States to work in the agricultural sector (Rosenblum & Brick, 2011). Over the past two decades, the migration flow to the United States has diversified. While immigrants from Mexico continue to cross the U.S.-Mexico border, most immigrants today are from El Salvador, Guatemala, and Honduras (Rosenblum & Brick, 2011). The majority of these immigrants are less educated and poorer than other immigrants and other U.S.-born Latinos (Noe-Bustamante & Flores, 2019). Women and children also make up a higher proportion of today's migration flow than in decades past. They are migrating to the United States to escape violence in their home countries and with the hope of better economic opportunities as well as for gendered reasons such as domestic violence and sexual abuse (see chapter 7).

Why We Edited This Book

Disheartened by the lack of published research specific to system-impacted Latinas' perspectives and experiences, we decided to develop an edited volume focused on Latinas' experiences within the U.S. criminal justice systems. In 2018, we reached out to respected scholars in the field and posted a general call for those interested in contributing to a special edited volume on system-impacted Latinas. We strongly encouraged contributing authors to adopt an intersectional perspective that moved beyond an "add Latinas and stir" approach to critically consider how ethnicity, gender, class, legal status, sexuality, and carceral status shape the perceptions, interactions, and experiences of Latinas within the U.S. criminal justice systems.

Unlike the editors of other academic volumes, we thought it important to include the voices, experiences, and perspectives of both academic scholars as well as practitioners who work directly in the community on behalf of and in collaboration with system-impacted Latinas. Several contributors have firsthand experience as formerly system-impacted Latinas/os; others either have worked or are currently working directly with system-impacted Latinas; and still others actively advocate on behalf of many of the girls and women whose experiences and narratives are presented in this volume.

Although we did not specifically encourage contributors to adopt a critical stance, most of the research presented in this volume is critical of the carceral state's role in the lives of system-impacted Latinas. The carceral state is defined as the use of prison logics that go beyond the walls of the prison to structure how the state and its institutional and organizational actors interact with individuals deemed "undesirables" who are disproportionately defined as people of Color and/or poor people (Martensen, 2020). These carceral logics influence the targeting, surveillance, and control and punishment of individuals whose actions are classified (or socially constructed) as criminal. The role of the carceral state is a central theme that runs through many of the chapters in this volume. *Latinas in the Criminal Justice System*'s biggest contributions to the criminological literature are the great depth as well as nuance that many of our contributors placed on system-impacted Latina girls' and women's experiences as shaped by intersecting social identities and positions while also keeping a critical lens on how various legal systems based on carceral logics respond to them.

Importance of Intersectional Perspectives

Intersectionality "focuses on simultaneity, attends to within group differences, and rejects 'single-axis' categories that falsely universalize the experiences or needs of a select few as representative of all group members" (May, 2015, p. 23). Although feminist scholars of Color have been doing intersectional research since the 1960s, the term "intersectionality" was first coined by legal scholar Kimberlé Crenshaw in the early 1990s when she argued that an exclusive focus on either gender or race risked disappearing the perspectives, experiences, and needs of Black women (Crenshaw, 1990; Garcia, 2016; Potter, 2015). Feeling misunderstood by both the Chicano movement and the women's movement, Chicana feminist scholars have made similar claims about the importance of considering how Latinas' intersecting identities shape their experiences (Baca Zinn & Zambrana, 2019; Hurtado, 2020). For Chicana and other Latina feminists, this means recognizing that Latina women "belong to more than one oppressed group and that through understanding the intersection of how these different social categories (sexuality, class, race, ethnicity, gender, physical ableness) intersect in contextually specific situations," Latinas' multiple oppressions can be understood (Hurtado, 2020, p. 28).

Gloria Anzaldúa's concept of the borderlands has been instrumental in Chicana and Latina feminist research. Anzaldúa posited that "ideas about borderlands are complex, have multiple meanings, and represent social spaces in which 'races' conflict and 'otherness' are formed" (Baca Zinn & Zambrana, 2019, p. 684). The borderlands can be both physical such as the Southwest border between Mexico and Texas as well as nonphysical but still very much real. They are "spaces that are safe and unsafe, distinguishing *us* from *them*, as well as places of identification, of feeling 'in between' cultures, languages, or places" (Baca Zinn & Zambrana, 2019, p. 684). These feelings of otherness do not arise in isolation but are interwoven into the fabric of this nation's colonial history.

Despite Latinas/os being in the United States since before its inception, they continue to confront messages that they are "the other," are different / less than, and do not belong. These messages reinforce existing U.S. power dynamics that oppress Latinas/os and other people of Color. Power can be overt and coercive as well as hidden and insidious (Roscigno, 2011). Unlike overt power, coercive power is where "agendas are set, biases are mobilized, and non-decision making ensures that hierarchies remain intact." This more insidious form of power is deeply entrenched within the social fabric of our society and is not "easily observable and measurable," which makes it easy to deny (Roscigno, 2011, p. 355). Power is manifested and reinforced via representational images, policies and practices, intersubjective judgments, and experiential domains of power (see Núñez, 2014).

Representational images or what Patricia Hill Collins refers to as "controlling images" of Latinas serve to justify societal forms of gendered racialized oppression (Collins, 2002; Núñez, 2014). Such images include stereotypical media representations (e.g., Latinas as hypersexual and submissive to men—Hurtado, 2020; Latinas as gangsters—Yosso, 2002) and discriminative narratives (e.g., Latina immigrant women have "anchor babies" to take advantage of U.S. benefits; Chavez, 2013) that position Latinas as deviant, criminal, and the other (Slakoff, 2020). Moreover, even when Latinas are "victims" of crime, they are more likely than white women to be portrayed by the news media as "risk takers and bad women" whose victimization is "normalized through descriptions of their unsafe environments" (Slakoff & Brennan, 2019, p. 488). Representational images are intricately linked to oppressive policies and procedures. Those who have negative representations or social constructions and weak power (e.g., criminals, drug users, immigrants, gang members) are more likely to be disadvantaged and oppressed than other groups because politicians and other decision makers are less likely to advocate on their behalf (Schneider & Ingram, 1993). As a result, discriminatory policies and practices are enacted that disproportionately criminalize the actions and behaviors of stigmatized groups (e.g., punitive policies toward Latino youth—Durán, 2009, Rios, 2007, punitive immigration policies—Armenta, 2017).

Representational images and practices and policies shape individuals' assumptions about targeted groups and micro-level interactions. Núñez refers to these assumptions and interactions as the intersubjective domain of power wherein "individual level judgments" of "others" shape interpersonal interactions. A juvenile court judge relying on stereotypes of Latina teens as hypersexual when making decisions about whether they should be placed on probation or in detention is an example of how power can be manifested within the intersubjective domain (Pasko & Lopez, 2018).

The experiential domain of power focuses on how individuals "process, reconcile, and/or internalize both positive and negative messages." Power relations are maintained when Latinas and other people of Color internalize negative messages about themselves (Feagin & Cobas, 2008; Pyke, 2010). It is important to emphasize that individuals can resist such messages as well. At its core, intersectional research is "not neutral" but rather a tool that can be used to dismantle inequalities. In order to address inequalities, careful attention must be focused on addressing entrenched societal power dynamics that serve to privilege some at the expense of others. Through their own words, we learn about how Latina girls and women feel victimized by the state even when calling upon state actors for support, how frustrated they feel when trying to navigate the immigration court system when they do not understand the language, and how they believe the various justice systems are discriminatory and anything but *just*.

A Word about Language

We have intentionally adopted certain wording and made certain editorial decisions as a means of signaling our commitment to social justice. Consistent with other feminist scholars of Color (Hurtado, 2020; Hurtado & Sinha, 2016; Potter, 2015), we use the term "people of Color" to refer to Latinos/as, Asians / Asian Americans, Native Americans, and Black people, all of whom are racialized groups in the United States. Like feminist scholars Aida Hurtado and Mrinal Sinha (2016), we capitalize "Black" to denote and acknowledge the history and the racial identity of Black Americans. We do not capitalize "white" because "it refers not to one ethnic group or to specific ethnic groups but to many" (Hurtado & Sinha, 2016, p. 2). In this volume, we use the descriptor "white" to signify non-Latina/o whites.

Although we (the editors) use the term "Latinas" throughout this volume, we acknowledge that it is a social construction and applies to a large number of girls and women with varying ethnicities, races, national origins, generation statuses, and classed social positions. We chose "Latinas" over "Hispanics" because the latter is "viewed by many as emphasizing European heritage while ignoring the population's Indigenous and African roots" (Hurtado & Sinha, 2016, p. 5). Thus, in this volume we use the term "Hispanic" only when citing research reports that use this label in their discussion of Latina/o issues. Many of our contributing authors also used the term "Latina," while others used "Latinx." By and large, "Latina" was the most popular identifier used by our contributors. Nevertheless, we recognize the problems associated with this term, especially considering the different social positions and experiences of

Latina/o ethnic subgroups. With that said, it should be emphasized that the majority of the chapters in this volume focus on Mexican-origin and Central American Latinas living in the United States. This was not intentional but instead reflects the current state of the criminological and sociological literatures on system-impacted Latinas.

We also want to clarify that we (the editors) use the terms "system-impacted" and "system-involved." The term "system-impacted" is a closer representation of how many of the girls and women whose narratives are shared in this volume experience their interactions and involvement with the U.S. criminal justice systems and denotes existing power dynamics in which the overarching carceral state has power and control over girls and women of Color in ways that are rarely viewed as helpful or positive in the United States. The term "system-involved" is more neutral and is commonly used in the criminological literature to denote an association with the U.S. criminal justice systems.

Overview of *Latinas in the Criminal Justice System*

Latinas in the Criminal Justice System is divided into four sections specific to major issues impacting system-impacted Latinas. The first section examines how the boundaries between "victims" and "offenders" are often blurred on the basis of Latina girls' and women's sexualities, legal status, and past histories of drug use and criminal justice involvement; the second section focuses more specifically on Latinas' experiences once they enter either the juvenile justice or criminal justice system as "offenders"; the next section considers how undocumented Latina immigrant girls and women experience the U.S. "crimmigration" system; and the final section highlights the importance of community-based alternatives that are culturally and gender responsive to address the needs of system-impacted Latina girls. Arranging the book in this way allows us to highlight and investigate the ways in which Latinas perceive and interact with the U.S. criminal justice systems primarily as "victims," "offenders," and/or undocumented immigrants while recognizing that overlaps exist across all three of these social categories based on how any particular group is socially constructed in a given time and place.

Part I: Victimization to Offending: Blurring the Boundaries

The line between victims and offenders is often blurred. This is why the first section is so important. Women whose stories do not fit the blameless, passive, and nonviolent "good women" narrative are especially vulnerable to unsympathetic responses from criminal justice actors and social service providers (Miller, 2018). Research specific to IPV indicates that Latina women—particularly those who do not fit the "good victim" narrative by virtue of their intersecting social identities and locations—often feel like others (i.e., law enforcement, social service providers) do not take their victimization seriously. Worse, as poignantly illustrated by Sujey Vega and colleagues' and Alice Cepeda and colleagues' chapters, they fear being further criminalized if they are undocumented and/or have previous histories of drug and criminal justice involvement. Girls and women of Color, particularly those who identify as bisexual, lesbian, or transgender women are not only at risk for victimization but also less likely to have their stories shared, acknowledged, and validated. As illustrated in Lindsay Kahle and Anthony Peguero's chapter, more research on LGBQ Latina girls' victimization experiences is needed, especially since victimization is a risk factor for girls' involvement in the juvenile justice system.

Part II: Latina Offenders from Court to Correctional Involvement

The three chapters in this section focus on Latina "offenders" once they enter the juvenile and criminal justice systems. Lisa Pasko and Jean Denious employed a mix-methods approach to examine differences between court-involved Latina and white girls in Colorado in terms of adverse childhood experiences, offense histories, and attitudes toward probation officers and services. Jerry Flores and colleagues delved more deeply into how system-impacted Latina girls experience the juvenile justice system as an overarching system of control and surveillance. In the final chapter of this section, Holly Foster and Chantrey J. Murphy investigated the correlates and consequences of maternal efficacy among incarcerated Latina mothers in a federal prison. Foster and Murphy argue that prisons should build upon maternal efficacy as a strength by developing and supporting programs and opportunities for women in prison that can promote broader feelings of efficacy that may be generally beneficial but even more salient when relationships with children have been severed.

Part III: Immigration Enforcement, Crimmigration, and the Deportation Machine

The third section focuses on law enforcement, crimmigration, and the deportation of Latina migrants caught up in the U.S. criminal justice and immigration systems. Although many of the women whose stories are presented in this section are not U.S. citizens, they are the "victims" of increased U.S. law enforcement and detention, even when they are seeking asylum.[5] As will become clear from reading the chapters in this section, the U.S.-Mexico border is not clear-cut but rather a nebulous region where migrants risk their lives in the "hopes of a better life." Katie Dingeman and William Estuardo Rosales discuss how the merging of the U.S. criminal justice and immigration systems has impacted women migrants' premigration experiences as well as their experiences during apprehension, detention, and removal proceedings. Cecilia Menjívar, Andrea Gómez Cervantes, and William Staples provide an in-depth examination of how women migrants from Latin America are "processed" in the U.S. immigration system. Martha Escobar illustrates how two Mexican women—Adriana and Esther—experienced the U.S. crimmigration system as well as how their social positionality shaped their experiences. In the final chapter of this section, Gabriella Sanchez provides the reader with a rare behind-the-scenes look at the role that young women and girls play in the migrant smuggling trade along the U.S.-Mexico border.

Part IV: Community Programming for System-Impacted Latinas

Over the past several decades, researchers, practitioners, and activists have called for more gender and culturally responsive community-based programming for system-impacted Latina girls and women. The four chapters in this section provide recommendations for developing intersectional programmatic efforts as well as poignant illustrations of how such programming can benefit system-impacted Latinas. Central to each of these chapters is the role that culture plays in young Latinas' lives. Instead of a cultural-deficit approach, all four chapters recognize the value of cultural values as a strength, while also acknowledging the challenges that stem from living within what Gloria Anzaldúa refers to as the borderlands (Anzaldúa, 1987). Lisa Martinez employs a case study approach to illustrate how culturally responsive community-based programming can prevent Latina teens from becoming further involved in delinquency. Veronica Cano examines how acculturation-related stressors (e.g., acting as language and cultural brokers for parents, negotiating two different sets of gendered expectations) and discrimination impact system-impacted Latina girls and explores how maternal racial and ethnic strategies can foster girls' positive ethnic identity—a known protective factor against delinquency. DeAna Swan, Johanna Creswell Báez, and Diandrea Garza from Southwest Key introduce the readers to the Mi Hermana's Keeper Toolkit, a research-grounded resource developed for community-based organizations interested in developing and implementing gender and culturally responsive programming for system-impacted Latinas. In the final chapter of this section, by Sara Haskie-Mendoza and colleagues, we learn about the Xinachtli program, a powerful example of how the Mi Hermana's Keeper Toolkit's recommendations can be successfully implemented by and within the community.

Conclusion

As the various chapters in this edited volume illustrate, Latinas who interact with and are involved in the U.S. legal systems are not a homogenous group. They vary in terms of age, sexuality, class, nationality, legal status, and delinquent/criminal background. Yet as the chapters illustrate, whether Latinas are victims of interpersonal violence in need of help, migrant women applying for asylum, or girls and women with histories of drug use and crime, most of them do not report positive interactions with state actors. Even more disturbing, they often view their experiences with the various U.S. criminal justice systems as harmful, traumatic, and to be avoided at all costs. Even when they are clearly "victims," they feel like offenders and fear removal of their children by the state, being deported (or having their partners deported), or being blamed and even criminalized for their own victimization. Yet there is cause for hope. Assessing the culture and conditions of Latina girls' and women's system involvement, *Latinas in the Criminal Justice System* also presents legal reforms, community mobilization efforts, and gender-sensitive alternatives to incarceration that have been developed in recent years to bring greater justice and equity to system-impacted Latinas. We hope that researchers, practitioners, activists, policy makers, and students will find this edited volume and the practice and policy implications included within each chapter useful in their own efforts to advocate and fight for justice. To use the words of Chicana feminist scholar Gloria Anzaldúa, we do this work because it matters, *Vale la pena!*

NOTES

1 Latinos in general are not counted in some national and state-level datasets. In 2016, the Urban Institute conducted a survey of criminal justice data to determine how many states collected ethnicity data across five categories: arrests, probation, prison population, prison population by offense, and parole. Of the states, 75 percent regularly and recently reported data by ethnicity on at least one of the five measures, but only 39 percent did so for two or more measures. Thirteen states collected no ethnicity data, and only one (Alaska) collected ethnicity data across all five categories.
2 See Massey and Capoferro (2004) for more information on methodological challenges related to surveying members of migrant populations.
3 National Violence Against Women Survey results indicate that 34.4 percent of Hispanic women reported victimization in their lifetime.
4 National estimates of juvenile court data are developed by the National Juvenile Court Data archive project, which is funded by the Office of Juvenile Justice and Delinquency Prevention. Black girls accounted for 35 percent of the female delinquency caseload but only 15 percent of the U.S. female youth population. White girls accounted for 46 percent of the female delinquency cases in juvenile court but 55 percent of the U.S. female youth population.
5 We use the term "victims" to denote our stance that these women are "victims" of the U.S. immigration enforcement system but acknowledge that others might disagree with this conceptualization.

REFERENCES

Anzaldúa, G. (1987). *Borderlands/La frontera* (Vol. 3). San Francisco: Aunt Lute Books.
Armenta, A. (2017). Racializing crimmigration: Structural racism, colorblindness, and the institutional production of immigrant criminality. *Sociology of Race and Ethnicity, 3,* 82–95.

Baca Zinn, M., & Zambrana, R. E. (2019). Chicanas/Latinas advance intersectional thought and practice. *Gender & Society, 33*, 677–701.

Bernal, D. D. (1998). Using a Chicana feminist epistemology in educational research. *Harvard Educational Review, 68*, 555–583.

Calderón, D., Bernal, D. D., Huber, L. P., Malagón, M., & Vélez, V. N. (2012). A Chicana feminist epistemology revisited: Cultivating ideas a generation later. *Harvard Educational Review, 82*, 513–539.

Carson, E. A., & Golinelli, D. (2014). *Prisoners in 2014*. Washington, DC: Bureau of Justice Statistics.

Chavez, L. (2013). *The Latino threat: Constructing immigrants, citizens, and the nation*. Stanford, CA: Stanford University Press.

Collins, P. H. (2002). *Black feminist thought: Knowledge, consciousness, and the politics of empowerment*. New York: Routledge.

Crenshaw, K. (1990). Mapping the margins: Intersectionality, identity politics, and violence against women of Color. *Stanford Law Review, 43*, 1241–1299.

Díaz-Cotto, J. (2006). *Chicana lives and criminal justice: Voices from el barrio*. Austin: University of Texas Press.

Durán, R. J. (2009). Legitimated oppression: Inner-city Mexican American experiences with police gang enforcement. *Journal of Contemporary Ethnography, 38*, 143–168.

Ehrmann, S., Hyland, N., & Puzzanchera, C. M. (2019). Girls in the juvenile justice system. U.S. Department of Justice, Office of Juvenile Justice and Delinquency Prevention. https://ojjdp.ojp.gov.

Eppler-Epstein, S., Gurvis, A., & King, R. (2016). *The alarming lack of data on Latinos in the criminal justice system*. Washington, DC: Urban Institute.

Feagin, J. R., & Cobas, J. A. (2008). Latinos/as and white racial frame: The procrustean bed of assimilation. *Sociological Inquiry, 78*, 39–53.

Garcia, L. (2016). Intersectionality. *Kalfou, 3*(1), 102–106.

Hurtado, A. (2020). *Intersectional Chicana feminisms: Sitios y lenguas*. Tucson: University of Arizona Press.

Hurtado, A., & Sinha, M. (2016). *Beyond machismo: Intersectional Latino masculinities*. Austin: University of Texas Press.

Lopez, V., & Pasko, L. (2017). Bringing Latinas to the forefront: Latina girls, women, and the justice system. *Feminist Criminology, 12*, 195–198.

Martensen, K. M. (2020). Review of carceral state studies and application. *Sociology Compass, 14*, e12801.

Massey, D. S., & Capoferro, C. (2004). Measuring undocumented migration. *International Migration Review, 38*, 1075–1102.

May, V. M. (2015). *Pursuing intersectionality, unsettling dominant imaginaries*. New York: Routledge.

Miller, S. L. (2018). *Journeys: Resilience and growth for survivors of intimate partner abuse*. Berkeley: University of California Press.

Noe-Bustamante, L., & Flores, A. (2019). Facts on Latinos in the U.S. Pew Research Center. https://www.pewresearch.org.

Núñez, A. M. (2014). Advancing an intersectionality framework in higher education: Power and Latino postsecondary opportunity. In M. B. Paulsen (Ed.), *Higher education: Handbook of theory and research* (pp. 33–92). Berlin: Springer.

O'Neal, E. N., & Beckman, L. O. (2017). Intersections of race, ethnicity, and gender: Reframing knowledge surrounding barriers to social services among Latina intimate partner violence victims. *Violence Against Women, 23*, 643–665.

Pasko, L., & Lopez, V. (2018). The Latina penalty: Juvenile correctional attitudes toward the Latina juvenile offender. *Journal of Ethnicity in Criminal Justice, 16*, 272–291.

Potter, H. (2015). *Intersectionality and criminology: Disrupting and revolutionizing studies of crime*. New York: Routledge.

Pyke, K. D. (2010). What is internalized racial oppression and why don't we study it? Acknowledging racism's hidden injuries. *Sociological Perspectives, 53*, 551–572.

Rios, V. M. (2007). The hypercriminalization of Black and Latino male youth in the era of mass incarceration. In In M. Marable, K. Middlemass, & I. Steinberg (Eds.), *Racializing justice, disenfranchising lives* (pp. 17–33). New York: Palgrave Macmillan.

Roscigno, V. J. (2011). Power, revisited. *Social Forces, 90*, 349–374.

Rosenblum, M. R., & Brick, K. (2011). US immigration policy and Mexican/Central American migration flows. Washington, DC: Migration Policy Institute. www.migrationpolicy.org.

Schaffner, L. (2008). Latinas in U.S. juvenile detention: Turning adversity to advantage. *Latino Studies, 6*, 116–136.

Schneider, A., & Ingram, H. (1993). Social construction of target populations: Implications for politics and policy. *American Political Science Review, 87*, 334–347.

Sentencing Project. (2018). Incarcerated women and girls, 1980–2016. www.sentencingproject.org.

Sentencing Project. (2019). Incarcerated women and girls. www.sentencingproject.org.

Sickmund, M., Sladky, T. J., Kang, W., & Puzzanchera, C. (2019). Easy access to the census of juveniles in residential placement. U.S. Department of Justice, Office of Juvenile Justice and Delinquency Prevention. www.ojjdp.gov.

Slakoff, D. C. (2020). The representation of women and girls of Color in United States crime news. *Sociology Compass, 14*, e12741.

Slakoff, D. C., & Brennan, P. K. (2019). The differential representation of Latina and Black female victims in front-page news stories: A qualitative document analysis. *Feminist Criminology, 14*, 488–516.

Smith, S. G., Chen, J., Basile, K. C., Gilbert, L. K., Merrick, M. T., Patel, N., Walling, M., & Jain, A. (2017). The National Intimate Partner and Sexual Violence Survey (NISVS): 2010–2012 state report. Atlanta: National Center for Injury Prevention and Control, Centers for Disease Control and Prevention. www.cdc.gov.

Yosso, T. J. (2002). Critical race media literacy: Challenging deficit discourse about Chicanas/os. *Journal of Popular Film and Television, 30*, 52–62.

PART I

Victimization to Offending

Blurring the Boundaries

1

Entre Mujeres Platicamos

The Role of Informal Social Networks among Latina Survivors of Intimate Partner Violence

SUJEY VEGA, ALESHA DURFEE, AND JILL MESSING

I was crying. I was telling her what happened. She was like,
"You need to go to domestic violence shelter. Do you not
understand that?"
—Soledad

Approximately 37 percent of Hispanic women in the United States will experience intimate partner violence (IPV) during their lifetimes (Black et al., 2011) and face a choice like Soledad's. Latina IPV survivors are confronted with complicated situations—they often endure immigration fears, language barriers, lower socioeconomic conditions, and distrust of police in addition to abuse. Formal help-seeking options may not provide adequate resources to address these situations, and sometimes they inadvertently present barriers to safety. Thus, in response to their victimization, Latinas often use informal resource networks, such as family, friends, and neighbors, to connect to formal aid or as resources for assistance. After her victimization, Soledad chose to confide in her neighbor, who listened, provided temporary refuge, and pled with Soledad to flee. Eventually Soledad went to a shelter and received the resources she needed to leave her abuser. At the time of the interview, Soledad was still living at the shelter but was safe.

In this chapter, we analyze how Latinas use social networks to access resources and gain knowledge necessary for survival when an intimate partner abuses them. We do this through the analysis of twenty-seven interviews conducted with immigrant and nonimmigrant Latina IPV survivors. By attending to what worked for them and recognizing the efficacy of their survival strategies, we can design better intervention efforts for Latina survivors. We also discuss the impact that immigration, immigration policy, and isolation have on social networks and help-seeking options. In doing so, we highlight the crucial role that close female friends and "linkpersons" play in intervening and providing survivors with survival strategies. We conclude with a description of the necessary steps suggested by interviewees for improving and expanding the resources available to survivors and explain how *promotora* programs can prepare linkpersons to work in communities. By acknowledging how social networks undergird Latina resiliency and coping mechanisms, future outreach models can incorporate these organic survival strategies into their repertoire of services.

Formal and Informal Resources for Latina Survivors

Barriers to Formal Avenues of Aid

Latina survivors face substantial barriers to formal avenues of aid, like social and medical services and police intervention. Discriminatory policing strategies, coupled with social isolation, distrust of courts, fears of deportation, language barriers, limited economic resources, and lack of employment, complicate Latina women's decision making in abusive relationships (Acevedo, 2000; Bauer, Rodriguez, Quiroga, & Flores-Ortiz, 2000; Erez, Adelman, & Gregory, 2009; Lipsky, Caetano, Field, & Larkin, 2006; Menjívar & Salcido, 2002; Reina, Lohman, & Maldonado, 2014; Rizo & Macy, 2011; Sabina, Cuevas, & Schally, 2012). For immigrant Latina survivors, institutional and structural inequalities exacerbate their already vulnerable positions and contribute to the power and control exerted by abusers (Erez et al., 2009; Menjívar & Salcido, 2002; Raj & Silverman, 2002). When compared with nonimmigrant women, immigrant women report greater perceived risks and barriers to leaving abusive relationships (Amanor-Boadu et al., 2012), and undocumented immigrants increasingly mistrust and fear state officials (Villalón, 2010; Vishnuvajjala, 2012). Abusers use these fears as a mechanism of control and rely on further isolation to prevent survivors from seeking help (Ammar, Orloff, Dutton, & Aguilar-Hass, 2005; O'Neal & Beckman, 2017; Reina et al., 2014; Roditti, Schultz, Gillette, & de la Rosa, 2010).

Latinas who are legal residents, naturalized citizens, and/or U.S.-born citizens may also face systemic barriers to accessing resources due to the "ripple effects" of anti-immigrant legislation (O'Leary & Sanchez, 2011). As a result, Latina IPV survivors (immigrant, naturalized, and native born) find it difficult to access resources intended to ameliorate the violence that they experience. Additionally, because Latino families may exist in mixed-status households (where some members are undocumented and others are legal residents), it is important to include the experiences of survivors who identify as undocumented immigrants, legal resident/citizens, and U.S.-born Latinas to identify the multiple ways that immigration status plays into their help-seeking decisions (O'Leary & Sanchez, 2011).

The Importance of Informal Resource Networks

Although Latinas are less likely to use formal resources than are non-Latinas (Rizo & Macy, 2011), research indicates they are apt at utilizing informal support networks (Brabeck & Guzman, 2009; Kyriakakis, 2014; Menjívar & Salcido, 2002; Ocampo, Shelley, & Jaycox, 2007; Roditti et al., 2010). Their "everyday resistance strategies," though "less visible, less organized, and less recognizable," can be effective at creating opportunities for survival (Delgado Bernal, 2001, p. 626)—and are precisely where more analysis should take place. Research and practice should shift from deficit models to strength-based approaches highlighting current resiliency strategies (Roditti et al., 2010). For Latinas, informal networks are often critical coping mechanisms to combat loneliness, depression, anxiety, and violence (Ayón & Naddy, 2013; Menjívar & Bejarano, 2004).

Latina survivors often use female friends to provide emotional and material aid via the culturally familiar roles of *comadre* (co-mother) and/or *hermana* (sister). These terms translate culturally as deeply close friends (through familial relationships or friendships) and are recognized through formal and informal religious practices. Comadres can be formal Catholic godmothers or informal "mother-friends" who function as confidants, provide advice, and are willing to intervene. Hermanas can be actual sisters, deep co-mother friends, or, for non-Catholic Latinas, members of one's congregation. This coethnic best friendship is important to women who do not have close relatives nearby and "consciously adopt each other as family" (Herrera, 2011, p. 51). This "sisterhood serves as a support system . . . to sustain themselves against racialized and sexualized constructions of Chicana women created by the dominant culture" (Herrera, 2011, p. 61).

These sisterhoods are especially important for immigrant Latina women when transitioning from a deeply social Latin American community to one of isolation, which can lead to alienation and mental health issues like anxiety and depression (Nogales, 2012). In response to experiences tied to immigration status, racism, sexism, working-class experiences, and familial expectations to provide for kin on both sides of the border, Latinas hunger for a social network—a comadre—that provides a shared experience and gives strength to survive. "A comadre is your best friend—the person you call for help in the middle of the night. A comadre acts as a lay psychotherapist. She is an empowering healer . . . a comadre helps women to empower themselves. She helps women to build their strengths, reclaim their voice, and develop resilience" (Comas-Diaz, 2013, pp. 69–70).

There is a deep attachment between women who connect in this way; these "woman-to-woman . . . networks" create situations where women can inform other women about community resources (Menjívar, 2002, p. 452). This sisterhood bond, or *hermandad*, serves as a support mechanism for Latina women to help them combat bouts of loneliness or depression, the barrage of attacks they face from abusive partners, and/or social antagonism fueled by race, class, immigration, and gender. Moreover, these social networks provide critical brokers of information, or "linkpersons," who link friends and families with critical services in the community (Ayón & Naddy, 2013; Valle & Bensussen, 1985).

While Latina/o social networks provide crucial roles as sources of assistance, the literature on these networks often focuses on the measurable material exchange of financial resources, informal lending, employment leads, and general upward mobility (Calzada, Tamis-LeMonda, & Yoshikawa, 2013; Garcia, 2005; Juffer, 2008; Krause & Hayward, 2014; Vélez-Ibáñez, 2010; Williams & De Mola, 2007). Yet social networks can provide both emotional and instrumental support and serve to repudiate violence within families (Wright & Benson, 2010). These linkpersons are often the first individual a survivor turns to (Ammar et al., 2005;

Kyriakakis, 2014; Liang, Goodman, Tummala-Narra, & Weintraub, 2005; Menjívar & Bejarano, 2004; Pitts, 2014).

While linkpersons can bridge the gap between informal and formal resources, they may not be well equipped to assist IPV survivors. Survivors may receive conflicting or detrimental advice, family members can side with abusers, and/or survivors may feel shame in revealing abuse (Acevedo, 2000; Ammar et al., 2005; Kyriakakis, 2014; Menjívar, 2000; Roditti et al., 2010; Wright & Benson, 2010). Supportive family and friends may not have access to accurate information about legal, social, medical, and other resources (Ocampo et al., 2007). Thus, the purpose of our chapter is to examine the ways in which Latina survivors use informal social networks—including talking and sharing with linkpersons or comadres—in their attempts to achieve safety.

Methods

We analyze interviews conducted in 2013 with twenty-seven Latina-identified IPV survivors residing in nine domestic violence shelters in the U.S. Southwest. These semistructured interviews ranged in length from 29 to 100 minutes ($M = 42.65$ minutes) and focused on help seeking in response to IPV. Survivors could opt for an interview in Spanish ($n = 13$) or English ($n = 14$). A graduate student (native speaker of Spanish) conducted interviews with Spanish-speaking participants. All interviews were audio-recorded and transcribed in their original language; Spanish interviews were translated into English by a transcription service and checked by the first author. All names used in this chapter are pseudonyms.

We used grounded theory (centering the voices and experiences of the research participants) to develop specific codes and NVivo for coding. Initial broad-brush coding explored whether local and state-based anti-immigrant legislation created barriers to protection orders (POs) for Latina survivors. Parent-level nodes consisted of whether a survivor sought a PO and how they received information about POs. First-level coding marked formal help-seeking strategies, including calling the police, disclosing abuse to health professionals, assistance from victim advocates, and attempts to obtain or the receipt of a PO. As these were coded, evidence of informal networks became apparent. Latina survivors relied heavily on their informal social networks to link them to formal aid. Codes were then adjusted to include advice from informal resources (friends, families, neighbors, strangers, church, or coworkers) prior to or in lieu of calling police, whom a survivor spoke to about their abuse, and whether they provided a point person for formal resources. Once this coding began, the transcripts revealed how informal social networks also hindered survivor safety. For instance, the presence of unsupportive family or friends sometimes normalized abuse and increased feelings of despair. In these cases, gendered expectations and pressures to preserve the marriage resulted in self-silencing to maintain family harmony. Additionally, survivors noted that their abuser purposefully isolated them from informal networks that could provide refuge. Thus, our analysis included codes capturing whether informal social networks assisted and/or hindered survivors.

Results

Participants

As shown in Table 1.1, twenty-six (96 percent) participants identified exclusively as Latina (Hispanic, Mexican, Cuban, Dominican, or Puerto Rican) and one (4 percent) identified as multiracial (Latina and Black). Although those of each nationality experience their presence in the United States differently, we grouped these women into a collective Latina-identified label. This is due, in large part, to the way that all Spanish speakers and their descendants have been legislatively identified and treated in anti-immigrant legislation across the United States (Androff et al., 2011; Magaña & Lee, 2013; Szkupinski Quiroga, 2013). In particular, the political environment surrounding this study included denigrating rhetoric and actions by local police agencies to report any parties of a crime (perpetrators and victims) to Immigration and Customs Enforcement (ICE). In other scenarios, IPV survivors feared the role of the Department of Child Safety (DCS) to take away children from undocumented and resident/citizen survivors (Vega, 2014). Fifteen survivors (56 percent) reported that they were residents/citizens, and twelve women (44 percent) reported that they were undocumented. We use the term "resident/citizen Latinas" to recognize the limits of a word like "documented," which does not disaggregate among

TABLE 1.1. Sociodemographic Characteristics of Interviewees

Variable	Total % (n)
Survivor race/ethnicity	
Exclusively Latina	96 (26)
Latina and Black	4 (1)
Survivor citizenship status	
U.S. citizen/LPR*	56 (15)
Undocumented/other	44 (12)
Survivor age (M, SD)	31.7 (8.7)
Abuser age (M, SD)	34.3 (8.8)
Survivor has children under 18	
Yes	89 (25)
No	11 (2)
Number of children (M, SD)	2.3 (1.7)
Abuser is biological father of at least one child	96 (24)
Survivor economic self-sufficiency	
Survivor currently employed	
Yes	11 (3)
No	89 (24)
Survivor employed before entering shelter	
Yes	52 (14)
No	48 (13)
Survivor education level	
Less than high school	44 (12)
High school or GED	26 (7)
More than high school	30 (8)

*Legal Permanent Resident
Note: $N = 27$. Values are percentage and n, unless otherwise indicated.

the spectrum of legal residency options. Similarly, a more complicated identifier than "undocumented" would recognize survivors who are in transition or have conditional residency while their Violence Against Women Act (VAWA) visa application is being reviewed (Salcido, 2011). Unfortunately, for this study we did not collect additional information beyond a Latina survivor's "undocumented" status. Thus, we grouped the residents/citizens into one category to recognize their relatively more stable position in the United States, placing undocumented survivors in another category to account for their increased vulnerability.

The survivors, on average, were younger than their abusers (31.7 vs. 34.3 years), were less likely to be U.S. citizens or legal permanent residents (55 percent, $n = 15$) than their abusers (63 percent, $n = 17$), and were more likely to be undocumented (44 percent, $n = 12$) than their abusers (37 percent, $n = 10$). The majority of the interviewed survivors had relationship ties with their abusers that made legal help seeking more complicated and made a complete separation from their abusers difficult. Almost all survivors (89 percent, $n = 25$) had at least one child under the age of eighteen, and nearly all of the abusers were the biological parent of at least one of those children (96 percent, $n = 24$). Only three of the twenty-seven interviewees (11 percent) were currently employed, though 14 (57 percent) had been employed prior to entering shelter. Almost half (44 percent, $n = 12$) of the women did not have a high school degree, seven (26 percent) had a high school or GED degree, and eight (30 percent) had additional education.

Existing and Denied Informal Networks

SEVERED AND INACCESSIBLE NETWORKS. Latina survivors in this study (especially undocumented survivors) viewed the perceived risks of contacting the police or reaching out to formal resources as detrimental given their immigration status or previous negative police encounters. As shown in Table 1.2, only 22 percent of Latina survivors called the police. When they did call, Latinas felt that police did not consistently provide needed information about safety options.

Concha said that when she called the police, they simply warned the abuser, "You have to get under control. . . . They didn't give me anything like a report or anything." Ana was clear that the police would be less helpful than her own informal networks: "I was better off calling the guys that lived down the street than I was calling the police department."

Josefa stated that the police actually hurt her chances of getting POs by not doing a full investigation: "[Courts] ask for too much proof and sometimes you can't get it because [police] . . . do not take photos of you; they don't want to because they see you're Hispanic, the racism, and all that. Sometimes the police don't want to help and you do not have this

TABLE 1.2. Formal and Informal Forms of Assistance Sought by Latina Survivors

	Total % (n)
Formal networks	
Police	22 (6)
Community organization	15 (4)
Medical staff/doctor	11 (3)
Church	22 (6)
Children's school	7 (2)
Informal networks	
Friend	44 (12)
Family	63 (17)
Neighbor	33 (9)
Coworker	19 (5)
Stranger	7 (2)

Note: $N = 27$.

proof and they [courts] ... deny you an order of protection." Survivors also shared that the police created more danger for them. Trinidad recalled that when an officer found her, "He [the officer] noticed the bruise on my arm; he checked it and the officer wrote the report, took me back home. He took me home, and he talked to [abuser], and I paid the price for that, too. ... The report was made but there was never any follow through or anything with it."

Survivors who found the police unhelpful or who felt that they were in greater danger because of police contact were subsequently hesitant to call or never called the police again. This is especially troubling given the increased shift of governmental funding for IPV prevention and intervention to police and the criminal justice system (Messing, Becerra, Ward-Lasher, & Androff, 2015). Rocio, another survivor, recalled how a detective forced her to stay in the state where the abuse had happened while her abuser was prosecuted. "[The detective] would tell me that if I left the state he would arrest me, so I felt really harassed by him. ... If I had to go through that all over again I would not say another word to him. I would rather flee without talking to police." In this case, a policy intended to "protect" the victim through prosecution jeopardized

TABLE 1.3. Levels of Isolation Expressed by Latina Survivors

	Total % (*n*)
Survivor expressed isolation from any social network	78 (21)
Survivor felt severed from family	33 (9)
Abuser had social network of his own that reinforced his power and abuse	56 (15)
Survivor had social network of her own to resist abuse	52 (14)
Survivor expressed her social network was critical to her survival	78 (21)

Note: *N* = 27.

survivor safety and caused emotional and psychological distress. Eventually Rocio did flee the state and was not arrested, but the detective's determined efforts to prosecute her abuser left Rocio feeling scared of both her abuser and the police.

Survivors described informal networks as more willing and able to help than formal networks. Informal social networks were so important that, when their social networks were severed through isolation and geopolitical boundaries, survivors were left without any assistance to help them in fleeing abuse and they faced isolation and despair. As shown in Table 1.3, of the twenty-seven Latina survivors interviewed, twenty-one (78 percent) reported feeling alone or isolated and/or did not have a social network at the time of their abuse. Survivors expressed how this loneliness altered their safety options; many felt they had no choice but to stay. For example, Petra had no one in the United States and felt she could not confide in her family back in Mexico because "in Mexico, it's . . . not very common . . . to say that there's domestic violence. . . . And it's the embarrassment, the fear." Unwilling to burden her family in Mexico and afraid of the shame a disclosure might bring, Petra remained in the relationship.

In other cases, geographical distance made an impact for survivors who did not have friends or family in their immediate reach. For instance, Margarita lacked support nearby: "I didn't have anywhere to go, that's why I was always there [in home]. If I had somewhere to go to, well I would have left and I would have gotten a protection order, but well I didn't know anything. I would say to myself, where should I go, who should I tell? It was really hard." Although Margarita had a sister in the United States, she was over a thousand miles away. The physical distance between them made Margarita feel alone and isolated. That Margarita was undocumented and did not trust the police exacerbated these feelings. Sandra also felt isolated: "I don't have nowhere to live; I don't have nobody out here." Though Sandra had legal residency, the lack of connection to a social network made her feel helpless. She had no one to provide her housing options or a safer place "to live," even temporarily. Of the respondents, 33 percent ($n = 9$) noted that they were severed from family during the abuse, leaving them with no one to turn to. Similar to Sandra, Dolores noted, "I have no family, no friends out here." The desperation of feeling disconnected from family was also present in Teresa's response: "There were times that we would fight and argue and I would feel like, closed in. . . . And what am I gonna do? Where am I gonna go? Who am I gonna go with?" Unfamiliarity with local resources and fear of the consequences of seeking formal help increased feelings of isolation that were compounded by the lack of familial support.

Immigration legislation and tactics of legal violence affect the safety of survivors (Menjívar, 2013). Survivors had to be willing to confront linguistic, cultural, and immigration barriers to even begin the process of seeking formal assistance—and if survivors were undocumented, the combination of not having someone to turn to and the fear of deportation limited their help seeking. Nine survivors stated that their immigration status deterred them from contacting police. For instance, Angelica feared state-based immigration enforcement laws: "I became scared that they would see my [lowers voice] documentation. That's the reason. Truthfully, because of that. That's the reason I didn't call . . . because of that. [Before the law] the police wouldn't . . . ask so many questions." Angelica was not the only survivor to reference how state-based legislation halted her formal help seeking. Margarita shared, "They ask you for ID for everything here, the state . . . is a very harsh state. They are very demanding, especially for immigrants who don't have IDs, they are a little racist. A little? I mean, too [racist]." Angelica, Margarita, and other survivors were likely to depend on social networks for information or to provide respite from an abusive partner because they were fearful of formal resources and concerned about their immigration status.

Undocumented immigrant survivors feared calling the police or obtaining a PO because of their status. A survivor who both lacked a social network and was undocumented faced particular structural and social barriers in seeking safety. Socially, they lacked someone to turn to. Structurally, they feared formal services who may collude with ICE officials. If a social network was present, those individuals often echoed survivors' fears. Sandra had a local social network, but it was primarily her abusive partner's friends. These friends reinforced her apprehension toward police and social services. Sandra recalled believing she had no rights because of her status: "Because we are illegal here, they don't give you the help you need. . . . Or they ask for . . . documents that you can't provide . . . and more than anything they, people close to him would tell me I shouldn't call them, that it wasn't an option to call the police, because the police cause harm instead of helping you." Other undocumented survivors also expressed that fear of deportation was a major deterrent to contacting police or filing for a PO. News and other stories spread among social networks about collaborations between police and ICE increased these fears.

Abusers used the vulnerability of citizenship status as a form of control. Undocumented survivors "think that they don't have anywhere to live, they think that they don't have anywhere to go because they're undocumented" (Viki). When survivors did contact formal services, abusers would use their citizenship status to deny them access to those resources. As one survivor noted, "I told 911 . . . I needed the agents to speak Spanish. They told me that that was fine and when they got there they didn't speak it. . . . I don't know what they talked about, the only thing when I came out my husband said 'No, nothing happened . . . everything is calm.'" As Viki's abuser was English dominant and had full citizenship, his privilege gave him authority with the police, who she felt sided with him and never ensured that she was safe.

Abusive partners also purposefully denied survivors access to social networks. As shown in Table 1.3, fifteen Latinas (56 percent) reported that their abusers had a support network that reinforced his control. By limiting the survivors' networks, abusers controlled information about survivors' rights and resources and obstructed safety options. For example, Soledad's abuser moved her to a rural area where only he had friends and family. She explained that her abuser would threaten her by saying he might not kill her, "but somebody else might. It's scary, because all his family and friends that he knows that are out there, they have weapons. They have guns." Soledad understood that her abuser's power extended to his friends with guns and that they could harm her if she resisted or left. Abusers created an atmosphere of constant surveillance. Beatriz's abuser moved her to an area where only he had a social network. "He would always drive me, or his cousins and his family live out there, so they would come take me wherever I needed to go." This reliance on her abuser and/or his network left Beatriz completely dependent and limited her ability to seek help or disclose abuse. Importantly, both Soledad and Beatriz were resident/citizen Latinas. Even without the fear of deportation and with greater geographic mobility, they still felt their abuser used distance and isolation from their social networks to reinforce abuse. Though they were legally free to leave their homes, they reported feeling "like a hostage" or "incarcerated."

Migration and movement often compounded this control mechanism. Survivors said their abusers took advantage of geopolitical borders and physical distance to separate them from friends and kin. Lorena's abuser moved her away from friends in San Antonio to control her. Similarly, Eva's abuser (like Soledad's) isolated her from her social network and used her isolation to threaten her life: "You don't have nobody [here] ... I could kill you and nobody would know." In both cases, Latina resident/citizen survivors felt their abusers intentionally eliminated their access to a social network to undermine their ability to seek support.

ROLE OF SOCIAL NETWORKS AND INFORMAL LINKPERSONS. The previous section described the detrimental impact of isolation and severed social networks for Latina survivors, who found themselves alone and without assistance. In contrast, informal linkpersons often provided survivors with sanctuary, advice, and comfort in ways that surpassed formal help-seeking avenues. These interactions often confirmed that abuse had occurred and led survivors to evaluate their options. Of Latina survivors, 78 percent ($n = 21$) said their informal networks of friends, neighbors, and coworkers were critical to their survival by providing direct mechanisms of escape and/or connections to formal resources. And 63 percent ($n = 17$) of the interviewed survivors reached out to informal networks prior to calling police or seeking shelter, indicating the importance of these social networks. Though they eventually used formal supports, this happened after contact with and advice from informal social networks.

Some social networks were also described as unhelpful and even abusive. Family members (especially mothers-in-law) excused and justified violence and were sometimes abusive themselves. As Dolores recalled, "My husband's mother was violent with me . . . that was the straw that broke the camel's back . . . she ended up choking me because my husband wanted to take my son." For Dolores, this confrontation provided the catalyst to leave her abuser. Only two survivors (7 percent) said their abusers' family was helpful in leaving—and both were the sisters of male abusers. These sisters knew the potential harm their brothers could inflict. Dolores's sister-in-law screamed at her own parents after one physical altercation, saying "look at what's happening . . . we need to help her." Though Dolores appreciated the intervention, it did not convince the abuser's parents that there was a problem. With few options, Dolores remained in the abusive relationship.

Survivors (44 percent, $n = 12$) said that friends were helpful in providing aid, shelter, useful advice, and/or emotional and moral support. Indeed, friends were listed at a frequency twice that of police for providing assistance (see Table 1.2). Female friends, in particular, provided a *comadrazgo* ("sister of the heart") bond for survivors who had no kin nearby. As Valeria (an undocumented Latina) recalled, "I didn't have family, I only had my friend who I fled to on several occasions. Every time he hit me or we would fight, I would go to her house, and I would stay a week or three to four days." Only two interviewees (7 percent) said they had male friends on whom they could rely for help.

Even when survivors used formal resources, they relied on informal social networks for advice, for direct material and/or emotional assistance, and for help in locating other formal resources. For immigrants, these networks lessened the pain of nostalgia and assisted in countless ways with navigating a world that was socially and linguistically foreign. Consuelo saw a phone number for help. At first, she hesitated, but "I talked to my friend and she said, 'Do it, because what he is doing to you is unbearable.'" Consuelo then called and got information about the shelter she was staying in during the interview.

Sometimes a longing to talk to someone they trusted compelled survivors to use long-distance social networks. Mari Luz found a domestic violence shelter through a female friend several states away, saying, "I didn't even know places like this [shelter] existed until a friend of mine in [another state] called me." Importantly, Mari Luz was a resident/citizen and therefore had more confidence in maneuvering interstate connections. In contrast, Margarita did not "have anywhere to go" and felt too far from family in Mexico and in the United States. For her, the lack of a social network in the immediate vicinity, in combination with her undocumented status, made her feel isolated, and were it not for the medical staff at a clinic she would not have known about shelters in the area.

When neither friends nor families were around, survivors relied on neighbors to provide help in desperate situations (33 percent, $n = 9$; see Table 1.2). Some survivors had established relationships with their neighbors, but others knew them only through casual greetings. Regardless of the level of intimacy, their desperation led survivors to reach out. For instance, Noemi remembered one particularly tense encounter with her abuser when her neighbor took the children so they would not have to witness the abuse: "He'd just start throwing things, and yelling and screaming. One of the ladies next door was really nice, and she would let the kids go over there." However, subtle and important differences emerged between the ways Latina survivors referenced aid from friends versus neighbors. Friends (usually other women) were trusted for intimate conversations and advice and were more valued, and the ways in which they talked about them reflected an extended kinship pattern associated with Latin American comadres (female friendships). These friends had names in survivors' stories, were spoken of reverentially, and knew more about daily battles and private altercations. In contrast, neighbors lacked names—they were *el vecino* (the neighbor) or "one of the ladies next door"—and the level of trust with them was different. Neighbors intervened as a result of particular, public escalations in the abuse. Lizette recalled that a neighbor witnessed her abuse "and she told me 'this dude's crazy . . . I'm telling you one thing, even if you don't have documents, you have rights.'"

English-dominant neighbors were sometimes intimidating to undocumented Latinas with little command of English, and abusers sometimes used their linguistic seclusion as a control mechanism. As a Spanish speaker and undocumented immigrant, Lizette distrusted police intervention. When her neighbor suggested she call police, Lizette replied, "The police doesn't do anything." Her neighbor said, "It doesn't matter, we are going to call, I do have papers." Although she did not speak Spanish, the neighbor tried to communicate vital information about rights to Lizette—who was savvy enough to know her neighbor's citizenship and status as an Anglo woman was useful. Lizette recalled strategically maneuvering her body during the last abusive encounter so that her neighbors would witness the violence: "I don't speak English but the neighbors liked me, they were gringos [Anglos] . . . and I wanted them to see him go inside my house and hit me—I wasn't that dumb." Lizette distrusted that the police would "do anything" if she called and perhaps feared that her undocumented status would impact her negatively. She made sure her abuser was seen by her English-speaking Anglo neighbors, who she felt could contact police more productively and safely.

Latina survivors, especially those with prior experiences with the police, knew the value of language and race/ethnicity when calling police. Twenty survivors (74 percent) shared experiences where police were unsupportive or provided little to no resources. For Lizette, having an Anglo English-speaking neighbor bear witness to the abuse brought validity to her claims and provided protection in ways that her brown-skinned, undocumented, monolingual body did not. After her neighbor called the police, Lizette still feared that she would not be believed and/or that police would not help her because she lacked papers and the linguistic capacity to explain the abuse that she suffered. Her "gringo" neighbors came to her aid, lent credibility to her case, and drove her to a domestic violence shelter. Other survivors told of neighbors who opened their door to provide sanctuary, provided rides to shelters, called the police, and/or allowed survivors to use their phone. Griselda's male neighbor offered to drive her to a shelter. "He didn't speak Spanish, but he told my daughters that he'd serve as a witness of the domestic violence [my abuser] put me through." In another case, a neighbor who had little interaction with a survivor let her stay the night in a room to avoid an abusive partner.

Whether friends or neighbors intervened, it was clear that other survivors were a resource to those seeking assistance. They knew the signs of despair and turmoil and formed a connection with survivors who felt otherwise helpless. Latinas recalled how important these linkpersons were for them and wanted to extend this assistance to other survivors. Berta advocated for public IPV education, including the distribution of pamphlets in places inaccessible to abusers, because "if one person hears about it, while another person misses [it] . . . the first will say

'You know what, this is what I heard.'" For Berta, it was also important to provide more avenues for linkpersons to intervene. Survivors knew that they owed their current sense of safety to friends, neighbors, and linkpersons. They felt they had a responsibility to share the information they now knew with those currently in abusive relationships. Eight survivors (30 percent) asked to receive further information and pamphlets for survivors "because one never knows. Perhaps other people might need it beyond me" (Carmen). Clara stated that she no longer needed the pamphlets but took them anyway "because there might be somebody who might need that one day, and I'll be able to have some type of knowledge." Margarita felt strongly that classes and information needed to be available for the community. "For them to know they can get a protection order no matter what situation they are in . . . maybe it doesn't specifically help you or is directed toward you, but if you know someone who's passing [through it] you can tell them 'You know what? You can do this; you don't have to stand by idly.' . . . Knowing how to tell them they don't have to have a legal status." Margarita was also adamant that other undocumented Latinas should have access to life-saving information about IPV and resources. Survivors were grateful for their newfound knowledge and wanted to find ways to promote options for formal and informal assistance.

Conclusion

This chapter has explored the voices of Latina IPV survivors to understand the importance of informal support networks—especially linkpersons—in providing survival strategies, accessing resources, and achieving safety. Survivors are often isolated or severed from their support networks by abusers; in our study, Latina survivors reported that their abusers utilized isolation as a mechanism of control. While abusers generally use this tactic (Stark, 2007), the consequences of seclusion are exacerbated for Latina survivors who often rely on ethnic social networks for their emotional and material needs. Abusers cut off survivors from information, threatened them with physical and legal violence, and kept them from having contact with social networks. Consistent with previous research, survivors in this study hesitated to call police because they felt police intervention would not "solve anything," they feared it might exacerbate the abuse, and they were suspicious of deportation procedures (Akers & Kaukinen, 2009; Coulter, Kuehnle, Byers, & Alfonso, 1999; Ingram, 2007; Johnson, 2007; Kugel et al., 2009; Lipsky et al., 2006; Menjívar & Bejarano, 2004; Pitts, 2014).

When traditional formal options are unavailable, the importance of informal resources increases exponentially. Wong and colleagues suggest that "there is an urgent need to design strategies and interventions specific to the unmet needs of immigrants to reduce their depressive symptoms and enhance their social support" (2013, p. 2197), and deep listening to the survivors' narratives analyzed here can help us replicate their successful strategies. The importance of social networks and linkpersons was a consistent theme among survivors in this study. Social networks among Latino communities provide not just emotional stability but also safety against violence (Wright & Benson, 2010), and the survivors in this study emphasized the importance of linkpersons, friends, neighbors, and others as avenues of information. Although resident and citizen Latinas heavily relied on their existing social networks as a survival mechanism, these networks were especially critical for undocumented immigrants. For some, their fear of the state rivaled their fear of their abusers. The precariousness associated with being undocumented—intersected with the lack of English proficiency, little to no work skills, and geographic isolation—made Latinas feel trapped. The presence of a trusted friend to assure them of specific organizations or shelters provided much-needed security in an otherwise dangerously isolated situation. Without the linkpersons in their networks, these survivors may have remained in an unsafe intimate relationship.

Policy and Practice Implications

In this study, survivors illustrated how the expression *entre mujeres platicamos* ("between women we talk") is crucial for understanding the survival strategies of Latinas (Kyriakakis, 2014). Latinas expressed their willingness to be the talkers and sharers of knowledge. Those with social networks present expressed getting useful information from individuals who had personal experience in the process of leaving an abusive relationship. Indeed, survivors said they could assist others in the future, as they now knew how to navigate the system. We suggest creating community-centered programs to train lay advocates, as this is where Latinas are most likely to get help (friends and neighbors) (Wilcox, 2000). Modeled after promotora programs, this approach utilizes informal social networks to match needs in a community with lay-trained individuals who can refer friends and family to formal services. Of the survivors in our study, 30 percent relayed their interests in taking the knowledge they learned while in shelter and sharing it with others currently experiencing IPV. In this regard, women knew they might be promotoras, or bridge the community to specific resources, and comadres whom others rely on for comfort and advice.

Promotora programs could provide friends and neighbors with information about survivors' rights, safety strategies, and formal resources available. Holding community workshops and training promotoras would utilize existing relationships and social networks to spread vital information about IPV and resources. However, outreach to IPV survivors is difficult, in part because of the shame involved in disclosure. Therefore, promotora training targeted toward educating "friends helping friends," or comadre promotoras, may entice more women to participate and reduce stigma because this model relies on creating trust and "sisters-of-the-heart" bonds that disrupt the idea of silence and move someone toward safety. Moreover, working with women in shelters willing to lead promotora training through *platicas* ("talks") could also serve to empower survivors in ways that utilize their strength and resiliency for their communities. Because they are culturally familiar with the community, promotoras can help establish spaces of confidentiality and aid where they are most needed. Churches, for example, were noted by six participants (22 percent) as spaces where they met linkpersons who provided critical information. Though religious institutions can also serve to pressure survivors to stay in abusive relationships, promotoras can help establish trust and provide alternative narratives of support toward safety.

Creating opportunities for communal knowledge and safe *mujerista* spaces can help women feel empowered and want to disseminate this knowledge to each other (Fitts & McClure, 2015). Overall, it is through the amplification of survivors' voices and the replication of their strength in surviving and healing from abusive relationships that we can best design and implement prevention and intervention programs that can help Latina IPV survivors achieve safety and serenity in their everyday lives.

REFERENCES

Acevedo, M. J. (2000). Battered immigrant Mexican women's perspectives regarding abuse and help-seeking. *Journal of Multicultural Social Work, 8*, 243–282.

Akers, C., & Kaukinen, C. (2009). The police reporting behavior of intimate partner violence victims. *Journal of Family Violence, 24*, 159–171.

Amanor-Boadu, Y., Messing, J. T., Stith, S. M., Anderson, J. R., O'Sullivan, C., & Campbell, J. C. (2012). Immigrant and non-immigrant women: Factors that predict leaving an abusive relationship. *Violence Against Women, 18*, 611–633.

Ammar, N. H., Orloff, L. E., Dutton, M. A., & Aguilar-Hass, G. (2005). Calls to police and police response: A case study of Latina immigrant women in the USA. *International Journal of Police Science & Management, 7*, 230–244.

Androff, D. K., Ayón, C., Becerra, D., Gurrolla, M., Salas, L., Krysik, J., & Segal, E. (2011). U.S. immigration policy and immigrant children's well-being: The impact of policy shifts. *Journal of Sociology & Social Welfare, 38*, 77–98.

Ayón, C., & Naddy, M. B. G. (2013). Latino immigrant families' social support networks. *Journal of Community Psychology, 41*, 359–377.

Bauer, H. M., Rodriguez, M. A., Quiroga, S. S., & Flores-Ortiz, Y. G. (2000). Barriers to health care for abused Latina and Asian immigrant women. *Journal of Health Care for the Poor and Underserved, 11*, 33–44.

Black, M. C., Basile, K. C., Breiding, M. J., Smith, S. G., Walters, M. L., Merrick, M. T., & Stevens, M. R. (2011). *National Intimate Partner and Sexual Violence Survey.* Atlanta: Centers for Disease Control and Prevention.

Brabeck, K. M., & Guzman, M. R. (2009). Exploring Mexican-origin intimate partner abuse survivors' help-seeking within their sociocultural contexts. *Violence and Victims, 24*, 817–832.

Calzada, E. J., Tamis-LeMonda, C. S., & Yoshikawa, H. (2013). Familismo in Mexican and Dominican families from low-income, urban communities. *Journal of Family Issues, 34*, 1696–1724.

Comas-Diaz, L. (2013). "Comadres: The healing power of a female bond." *Women & Therapy 36*, 62–75.

Coulter, M. L., Kuehnle, K., Byers, R., & Alfonso, M. (1999). Police-reporting behavior and victim-police interactions as described by women in a domestic violence shelter. *Journal of Interpersonal Violence, 14*, 1290–1298.

Delgado Bernal, D. (2001). Learning and living pedagogies of the home: The mestiza consciousness of Chicana students. *International Journal of Qualitative Studies in Education, 14*, 623–629.

Erez, E., Adelman, M., & Gregory, C. (2009). Intersections of immigration and domestic violence: Voices of battered immigrant women. *Feminist Criminology, 4*, 32–56.

Fitts, S., & McClure, G. (2015). Building social capital in hightown: The role of confianza in Latina immigrants' social networks in the new south. *Anthropology & Education Quarterly, 46*, 295-311.

Garcia, C. (2005). Buscando trabajo: Social networking among immigrants from Mexico to the United States. *Hispanic Journal of Behavioral Sciences, 27*, 3-22.

Herrera, C. (2011). Comadres: Female friendship in Denise Chavez's "Loving Pedro Infante." *Confluencia, 27*, 51-62.

Ingram, E. M. (2007). A comparison of help seeking between Latino and non-Latino victims of intimate partner violence. *Violence Against Women, 13*, 159-171.

Johnson, I. M. (2007). Victims' perceptions of police response to domestic violence incidents. *Journal of Criminal Justice, 35*, 498-510.

Juffer, J. (2008). Hybrid faiths: Latino protestants find a home among the Dutch Reformed in Iowa. *Latino Studies, 6*, 290-312.

Krause, N., & Hayward, R. D. (2014). Ethnic religious social support, religious commitment, and health among older Mexican Americans. *Journal of Social and Personal Relationships, 31*, 352-365.

Kugel, C., Retzlaff, C., Hopfer, S., Lawson, D. M., Daley, E., Drewes, C., & Freedman, S. (2009). Familias con voz: Community survey results from an intimate partner violence (IPV) prevention project with migrant workers. *Journal of Family Violence, 24*(8), 649-660.

Kyriakakis, S. (2014). Mexican immigrant women reaching out: The role of informal networks in the process of seeking help for intimate partner violence. *Violence Against Women, 20*, 1097-1116.

Liang, B., Goodman, L., Tummala-Narra, P., & Weintraub, S. (2005). A theoretical framework for understanding help-seeking processes among survivors of intimate partner violence. *American Journal of Community Psychology, 36*, 71-84.

Lipsky, S., Caetano, R., Field, C. A., & Larkin, G. L. (2006). The role of intimate partner violence, race, and ethnicity in help-seeking behaviors. *Ethnicity & Health, 11*, 81-100.

Magaña, L., & Lee, E. (2013). *Latino politics and Arizona's Immigration Law SB 1070*. New York: Springer.

Menjívar, C. (2000). *Fragmented ties: Salvadoran immigrant networks in America*. Berkeley: University of California Press.

Menjívar, C. (2002). The ties that heal: Guatemalan immigrant women's networks and medical treatment. *International Migration Review, 36*, 437-466.

Menjívar, C. (2013). Central American immigrant workers and legal violence in Phoenix, Arizona. *Latino Studies, 11*, 228-252.

Menjívar, C., & Bejarano, C. (2004). Latino immigrants' perceptions of crime and police authorities in the United States: A case study from the Phoenix metropolitan area. *Ethnic and Racial Studies, 27*, 120-148.

Menjívar, C., & Salcido, O. (2002). Immigrant women and domestic violence: Common experiences in different countries. *Gender & Society, 16*, 898-920.

Messing, J. T., Becerra, D., Ward-Lasher, A. W., & Androff, D. (2015). Latinas perceptions of law enforcement: Fear of deportation, crime reporting & trust in the system. *Affilia, 30*, 328–340.

Nogales, A. (2012). A heart-to-heart connection. In A. V. Lopez (Ed.), *Count on me: Tales of sisterhoods and fierce friendships* (pp. 189–202). New York: Altria Press.

Ocampo, B. W., Shelley, G. A., & Jaycox, L. H. (2007). Latino teens talk about help seeking and help giving in relation to dating violence. *Violence Against Women, 13*, 172–189.

O'Leary, A. O., & Sanchez, A. (2011). Anti-immigrant Arizona: Ripple effects and mixed immigration status households under "policies of attrition" considered. *Journal of Borderlands Studies, 26*, 115–133.

O'Neal, E. N., & Beckman, L. O. (2017). Intersections of race, ethnicity, and gender: Reframing knowledge surrounding barriers to social services among Latina intimate partner violence victims. *Violence Against Women, 23*, 643–665.

Pitts, K. M. (2014). Latina immigrants, interpersonal violence, and the decision to report to police. *Journal of Interpersonal Violence, 29*, 1661–1678.

Raj, A., & Silverman, J. (2002). Violence against immigrant women: The roles of culture, context, and legal immigrant status on intimate partner violence. *Violence Against Women, 8*, 367–398.

Reina, A. S., Lohman, B. J., & Maldonado, M. M. (2014). "He said they'd deport me": Domestic violence help-seeking practices among Latina immigrants. *Journal of Interpersonal Violence, 29*, 593–615.

Rizo, C. F., & Macy, R. J. (2011). Help seeking and barriers of Hispanic partner violence survivors: A systematic review of the literature. *Aggression and Violent Behavior, 16*, 250–264.

Roditti, M., Schultz, P., Gillette, M., & de la Rosa, I. (2010). Resiliency and social support networks in a population of Mexican American intimate partner violence survivors. *Families in Society, 91*, 248–256.

Sabina, C., Cuevas, C. A., & Schally, J. L. (2012). The cultural influences on help-seeking among a national sample of victimized Latino women. *American Journal of Community Psychology, 49*, 347–363.

Salcido, M. O. (2011). "Wolves" or "blessing"? Victims'/survivors' perspectives on the criminal justice system. Doctoral dissertation, Arizona State University.

Stark, E. (2007). *Coercive control: How men entrap women in personal life*. New York: Oxford University Press.

Szkupinski Quiroga, S. (2013). Vamos a aguantar: Reflections on how Arizona's SB 1070 has affected one community. *Latino Studies, 11*, 580–586.

Valle, R., & Bensussen, G. (1985). Hispanic social networks, social support and mental health. In W. A. Vega & M. R. Miranda (Eds.), *Stress and Hispanic mental health: Relating research to service delivery* (pp. 147–173). Bethesda, MD: National Institute of Mental Health.

Vega, S. (2014). Crimmigration at the crossroads of America or how divisive politics tarnish the Heartland. In A. R. Ackerman & R. Furman (Eds.), *The criminaliza-*

tion of immigration: Contexts and consequences (pp. 75–88). Durham, NC: Carolina Academic Press.

Vélez-Ibáñez, C. G. (2010). *An impossible living in a transborder world: Culture, confianza, and economy of Mexican-Origin populations.* Tucson: University of Arizona Press.

Villalón, R. (2010). *Violence against Latina immigrants: Citizenship, inequality, and community.* New York: New York University Press.

Vishnuvajjala, R. (2012). Insecure communities: How an immigration enforcement program encourages battered women to stay silent. *Boston College Journal of Law & Social Justice, 32*(1), 185–213.

Wilcox, P. (2000). "Me mother's bank and me nanan's, you know, support!": Women who left domestic violence in England and issues of informal support. *Women's Studies International Forum, 23,* 35–47.

Williams, P. J., & De Mola, P. F. L. (2007). Religion and social capital among Mexican immigrants in southwest Florida. *Latino Studies, 5,* 233–253.

Wong, J. Y. H., Tiwari, A., Fong, D. Y. T., Yuen, K. H., Humphreys, J., & Bullock, L. (2013). Intimate partner violence, depressive symptoms, and immigration status: Does existing advocacy intervention work on abused immigrant women in the Chinese community? *Journal of Interpersonal Violence, 28,* 2181–2202.

Wright, E. M., & Benson, M. L. (2010). Immigration and intimate partner violence: Exploring the immigrant paradox. *Social Problems, 57,* 480–503.

2

Latina Interpersonal Victimization

The Importance of Sexual Orientation

LINDSAY KAHLE AND ANTHONY PEGUERO

Interpersonal victimization against youth and adolescents is a major public health and safety concern in the United States. With Latina/o/x youth and adolescents representing the largest segment of girls of Color, a growing number of studies have concentrated on Latina girls' experiences and exposure to violence and interpersonal victimization. Evidence indicates that Latina girls are at increased risk of being bullied, experiencing dating violence, and suffering sexual assault (Lopez, 2017a; Madriz, 1997; Romero, Wiggs, Valencia, & Bauman, 2013; Shekarkhar & Peguero, 2011). However, research that focuses on the victimization experiences of lesbian, gay, bisexual, or questioning (LGBQ) Latina girls remains limited.

This chapter remedies such paucity in the literature research through an examination of the role of sexual orientation in association with bullying, dating violence, and sexual assault among Latina girls. It utilizes data from the 2013 Youth Risk Behavior Surveillance System (YRBSS) to investigate whether experiences of interpersonal victimization differ for LGBQ Latina and heterosexual Latina girls and shows how LGBQ Latina girls are at relatively increased risk of victimization. This chapter concludes with a discussion of the importance of understanding the intersection of gender, race, ethnicity, and sexual minority status with victimization.

Latina Interpersonal Victimization

The effect of interpersonal victimization is damaging for youth and adolescent development (Finkelhor, 2008; Flores, 2016; Rojas-Gaona, Hong, & Peguero, 2016). Because youth and adolescents have limited mental capacity (compared to adults) and are less able to defend and protect themselves than adults, all forms of interpersonal victimization may result in long-lasting emotional, mental, and physical injury (Finkelhor, 2008; Flores, 2016; Rojas-Gaona et al., 2016). Although interpersonal victimization is a serious social problem that continues to receive well-deserved research and resources, most of that attention focuses on exploring boys' interpersonal victimization while leaving girls' interpersonal victimization in the background (Crenshaw, Ocen, & Nanda, 2015; Lopez, 2003, 2017a; Lopez, Chesney-Lind, & Foley, 2012; Popp & Peguero, 2011; Popp, Peguero, Day, & Kahle, 2014). Indeed, girls face a variety of detrimental experiences through their school, community, family, and peer interactions, including physical, sexual, and psychological abuse (Crenshaw et al., 2015; Flores, 2016; Garcia, 2009; Lopez, 2017a), which are associated with higher incidences of depression, lack of school retention, substance abuse, early parenthood, delinquency, and involvement in both the juvenile justice and the criminal justice systems (Crenshaw et al., 2015; Flores, 2016; Lopez, 2017a; Shekarkhar & Peguero, 2011; Woodford, Paceley, Kulick, & Hong, 2015). Research that investigates the intersection of race, ethnicity, gender, and interpersonal victimization suggests that girls of Color often experience an increased susceptibility to interpersonal violence (Crenshaw et al., 2015; Cuevas, Sabina, & Milloshi, 2012).

Research has shown that Latina girls have increased experiences with dating violence (Lopez, 2017b; Lopez et al., 2012; Madriz, 1997; Sabina, Cuevas, & Lannen, 2014). Whereas some studies indicate that sexual assault rates for Latina girls may be lower than what their white counterparts experience, other research has demonstrated that Latina girls may have higher rates of such victimization but, instead, decline to report (Cuevas, Bell, & Sabina, 2014). This may be due to fear, shame, connection to the perpetrator, and/or the dismissal of such accusations by officials who assume Latina girls to be promiscuous (Cuevas et al., 2012; Cuevas et al., 2014; Madriz, 1997; Postmus, 2015; Romero et al., 2013; Sabina et al., 2014).

The Significance of Sexual Orientation and Identity

Overall, research suggests that disparities in types and prevalence of youth violence exist, especially among LGBQ youth (Kahle, 2020;

Katz-Wise & Hyde, 2012; Langenderfer-Magruder, Walls, Whitfield, Brown, & Barrett, 2016; Rivers, 2011). LGBQ youth report marginally higher levels of physical and emotional violence and injury than do heterosexual youth (Kahle, 2020; Katz-Wise & Hyde, 2012; Langenderfer-Magruder et al., 2016; Rivers, 2011). In particular, LGBQ youth experience higher levels of violence and threats of violence while at school, are more likely to report feeling unsafe at school, and are also at increased risk for dating violence and sexual violence (Kahle, 2020; Katz-Wise & Hyde, 2012; Langenderfer-Magruder et al., 2016; Rivers, 2011). There is also a social and cultural narrative within the research literature that "overwhelmingly [focuses] on violence involving hate crimes and bullying, while ignoring the fact that vulnerable youth also may be at increased risk of violence in their dating relationships" (Dank, Lachman, Zweig, & Yahner, 2014, p. 846). Research on dating violence and sexual assault tends to focus less on sexual minority youth, thus ignoring the possible short- and long-term effects of these types of victimization in sexual minority youth (Dank et al., 2014; Peterson & Panfil, 2014; Woodford et al., 2015). However, studies have demonstrated that LGBQ girls experience higher rates of social aggression, physical and cyberbullying, and sexual harassment at school as well as increased risk of dating violence and sexual assault (Edwards, 2018; Gemberling et al., 2015; Kahle, 2020; Katz-Wise & Hyde, 2012; Pascoe, 2011). The specific school experiences, challenges, and victimization confronting LGBQ girls of Color remain understudied.

The Current Study

Given the paucity of research on LGBQ Latina girls' victimization, two main research questions drove this study. First, what are the distinctions between LGBQ Latina girls and heterosexual Latina girls in terms of the prevalence of victimization (i.e., school victimization, dating violence, and sexual assault)? Second, does identifying as LGBQ increase the likelihood of Latina girls' victimization? The current study addresses these two questions by utilizing 2013 YRBSS data to investigate the vulnerabilities of interpersonal victimization for LGBQ Latina girls.

Methods

YRBSS was developed by the Centers for Disease Control and Prevention (CDC) in 1990 in order to monitor health risk behaviors that contribute to causes of death, disability, and social problems among youth living in the United States. Risky behaviors often emerge during childhood and adolescence; thus, the YRBSS was designed to determine the prevalence, co-occurrences, and change in patterns of health risk behaviors (CDC, 2014a, 2014b). Additionally, the YRBSS also compares these data across geographic locations and among different subpopulations of youth.

The YRBSS includes school-based surveys from national, state, territorial, tribal, and local schools. The surveys (self-report questionnaires distributed in classrooms) are collected every two years, and the representative sample targets students in ninth through twelfth grades. While the nationwide school surveys are conducted by the CDC, the state, territorial, tribal, and local school surveys are conducted by departments of health and education. Overall, the surveys provide data representative of mostly public high school students across the United States (Kann et al., 2014).

This project utilized data from the 2013 YRBSS, which, until recently, had the most state, district, and territorial participation in asking at least one of two questions pertaining to sexual orientation. After eliminating all states that did not include sexual orientation questions, four states were selected that adequately included all variables of interest: Connecticut (n = 198), Florida (n = 909), Illinois (n = 523), and North Carolina (n = 96). The total sample for the analysis included 1,726 (268 sexual minority) Latina youth.

This research was intended to focus on Latina youth, more specifically those identifying as lesbian, gay, bisexual, or questioning. Therefore, *Latina* was a composite variable, computed using a response of 1 to the dichotomized variables of female (0 = not female, 1= female) and Latina (0 = not Latina, 1= Latina). It was then used as a filter variable for the analyses.

Sexual orientation encompasses three different conceptual dimensions: (1) self-identification, (2) sexual behavior, and (3) sexual attraction

(Sexual Minority Assessment Research Team, 2009). In this study, sexual orientation was used as a measure of self-identification, in which respondents were asked, "Which of the following best describes you?" Response items included (1) heterosexual (or "straight"), (2) gay or lesbian, (3) bisexual, and (4) not sure. Additionally, the CDC (2016) defines sexual minority youth as those who identify as gay, lesbian, or bisexual or who have sexual contact with persons of the same or both sexes. Thus, *sexual minorities* is used as a categorical variable representing all self-identified sexual orientations in this study other than heterosexual (or "straight"). Similar to research by Mustanski, Van Wagenen, Birkett, Eyster, and Corliss (2014), responses were then dichotomized as *sexual minorities* (gay or lesbian, bisexual, and questioning youth) or *not sexual minorities* (heterosexual or "straight").

This study analyzes different forms of interpersonal victimization as dependent variables, including different forms of bullying (electronic, physical, and sexual orientation), dating violence (sexual, physical, or psychological violence occurring within the context of a dating relationship), and sexual assault (forceful kissing, touching, or sexual intercourse). All responses were dichotomized into yes/no responses. Last, this project employed several controls. Research demonstrates that additional student characteristics are also associated with victimization, namely, age (Espelage & Horne, 2008), weight (Farhart, Iannotti, & Simons-Morton, 2010; Wang, Iannotti, & Luk, 2010), misbehavior (Kahle, 2020; Peguero, 2008), mental health, and geographic location (Guerra & Williams, 2010). Therefore, this study controlled for these potential confounders.

Analytic Strategy

This research expands investigations of the intersection of race, ethnicity, and gender within victimization by focusing on Latina LGBQ girls specifically. Table 2.1 presents descriptive and victimization data for the 268 girls in the study. Next, the study uses binary logistic regression (Field, 2009) in order to estimate the likelihood of school victimization, dating violence victimization, and sexual assault victimization in Latina LGBQ girls. These findings are presented in Table 2.2.

TABLE 2.1. Descriptive Statistics for Latina Youth

	N	M	SD
Sexual minority	268	0.16	0.362
Victimization			
Traditional bullying	1,726	0.18	0.383
Electronic bullying	1,726	0.14	0.345
Sexual orientation bullying	1,726	0.07	0.262
Dating violence	1,726	0.07	0.258
Sexual assault	1,726	0.10	0.304
Controls			
Grade	1,726	10.43	1.105
Weight	1,726	2.25	0.671
Misbehavior	1,726	0.03	0.158
Mental health	1,726	0.29	0.453
Florida	909	0.53	0.499
Illinois	523	0.30	0.460
North Carolina	96	0.06	0.229

Results

Table 2.1 presents the descriptive statistics for Latina youth in the study. A small proportion (although higher than the national average) of Latina girls identified as LGBQ (16 percent). Overall, Latina girls did report experiencing traditional bullying (18 percent), electronic bullying (14 percent), sexual orientation bullying (7 percent), dating violence (7 percent), and sexual assault (10 percent). In terms of controls, there is a relatively even distribution across grade levels ($M = 10.43$, $SD = 1.105$). The average perception of weight among Latina girls was just above "average" ($M = 2.25$, $SD = 0.671$), while a very small proportion of Latina girls reported engaging in misbehavior (3 percent) and a higher proportion of Latina girls reported poor mental health (29 percent). In terms of distribution across geographic location, the majority of Latina girls resided in Florida (53 percent), followed by Illinois (30 percent), Connecticut (11 percent), and North Carolina (6 percent).

TABLE 2.2A. Logistic Regression of Victimization in Latina Youth

	Traditional Bullying			Electronic Bullying			Sexual Orientation Bullying		
	β	Exp (B)	SE	β	Exp (B)	SE	β	Exp (B)	SE
Sexual minorities	0.501	1.650***	0.161	0.673	1.961***	0.17	1.854	6.384***	0.205
Controls									
Grade	−0.282	0.754***	0.061	−0.092	0.912	0.066	−0.376	0.686***	0.096
Weight	0.279	1.322*	0.097	−0.058	0.944	0.105	0.285	1.330	0.149
Misbehavior	1.417	4.125***	0.323	1.666	5.289***	0.323	1.103	3.013*	0.389
Mental health	0.349	1.418*	0.137	0.364	1.439*	0.150	0.412	1.510*	0.208
Florida	−0.317	0.728	0.196	−0.372	0.689	0.216	−0.503	0.604*	0.250
Illinois	−0.206	0.814	0.210	−0.130	0.878	0.228	−2.088	0.124***	0.378
North Carolina	−0.259	0.772	0.322	−0.519	0.595	0.387	−0.162	0.850	0.411
χ^2		76.425			59.679			165.971	
Log likelihood		1539.612			1324.975			746.285	
Nagelkerke R^2		.071			.062			.223	
Constant	0.731	2.078	0.665	−0.816	0.442	0.727	0.63	1.878	1.039

*$p \leq .05$. ***$p \leq .001$.

The logistic regression results for probability of victimization are presented in Table 2.2. As the results suggest, LGBQ Latina girls are more likely to experience traditional bullying than are heterosexual Latina girls, Exp(B) = 1.650, $p \leq .001$. In addition, grade, weight, misbehavior, and mental health are also related to traditional school bullying. As a student's grade level increases, the likelihood of traditional bullying decreases, Exp(B) = 0.754, $p \leq .001$. In turn, as student perceptions of weight increase, so does the likelihood of traditional bullying, Exp(B) = 1.322, $p \leq .05$, and as involvement in misbehavior increases, the likelihood of traditional bullying does as well, Exp(B) = 4.125, $p \leq .001$,. As a student's poor mental health increases, so does the likelihood of traditional bullying, Exp(B) = 1.418, $p \leq .05$.

LGBQ Latina girls are also more likely than heterosexual Latina girls to experience electronic bullying, Exp(B) = 1.961, $p \leq .001$, and sexual orientation bullying, Exp(B) = 6.384, $p \leq .001$. In terms of controls, misbehavior and poor mental health are related to electronic school bullying, whereas grade, misbehavior, mental health, and geographic location are related to sexual orientation bullying. Furthermore, LGBQ

TABLE 2.2B. Logistic Regression of Victimization in Latina Youth

	Dating Violence			Sexual Assault		
	β	Exp (B)	SE	β	Exp (B)	SE
Sexual minorities	1.267	3.549***	0.207	0.738	2.092***	0.189
Controls						
Grade	0.150	1.162	0.089	−0.084	0.920	0.074
Weight	0.024	1.024	0.143	0.212	1.236	0.121
Misbehavior	2.041	7.699***	0.348	−0.015	0.985	0.486
Mental health	0.402	1.495*	0.203	−0.026	0.974	0.176
Florida	−0.184	0.832	0.293	−0.444	0.641	0.236
Illinois	−0.450	0.638	0.325	−0.372	0.689	0.253
North Carolina	0.477	1.612	0.431	0.097	1.101	0.356
χ^2		82.801			26.284	
Log likelihood		809.123			1119.446	
Nagelkerke R^2		.116			.031	
Constant	−4.564	0.010***	1.014	−1.590	0.204	0.822

*$p \leq .05$. ***$p \leq .001$.

Latina girls are more likely than heterosexual Latina girls to experience dating violence, $\text{Exp}(B) = 3.549$, $p \leq .001$, with misbehavior and poor mental health also serving as predictors. Finally, LGBQ Latina girls are more likely than heterosexual Latina girls to experience sexual assault, $\text{Exp}(B) = 2.092$, $p \leq .001$. Interestingly, none of the controls are related to sexual assault victimization.

Conclusion

This research bridges a critical gap in studies of the vulnerability of Latina girls and the significance of sexual orientation in victimization. Several studies across the social sciences confirm that both Latina girls and LGBQ youth (Cuevas et al., 2012; Dank et al., 2014; Eaton, Davis, & Barrios, 2007; Eaton et al., 2006; Edwards et al., 2015; Kahle, 2020) are at increased risk for interpersonal victimization, but few specifically focus on the experiences of LGBQ Latina girls. This study finds that while a small proportion of the overall sample of Latina youth identify as sexual minorities, those who do are at increased risk for various types of victimization. Thus, this study confirms the importance of considering the intersection of gender, race, ethnicity, and sexual orientation when addressing experiences with interpersonal victimization.

Latina Interpersonal Victimization

Although this study focused only on Latina girls, comparisons between Latinas and other youth should be noted. The Latina girls in our sample self-reported slightly lower levels of bullying and average levels of dating violence and sexual assault in comparison to national averages. For example, in comparison to over 20 percent of students reporting incidents of bullying (CDC, 2013), 18 percent of Latina girls experienced traditional bullying, 14 percent experienced electronic bullying, and 7 percent experienced bullying based on actual or perceived sexual orientation. In terms of dating violence, 7 percent of Latina girls reported that someone they were dating or going out with physically hurt them on purpose, in comparison to national averages of 10 to 33 percent (Eaton et al., 2006; Eaton et al., 2007; Howard, Wang, & Yan, 2007). Finally, about 10 percent of Latina girls were forced into unwanted sexual contact. These findings are comparable to those of Finkelhor, Turner, Ormrod, Hamby, and Kracke (2009), who found that by the age of seventeen, the lifetime prevalence of sexual victimization is about 9.8 percent for girls.

LGBQ Latina Interpersonal Victimization

While the post–World War II work of Alfred Kinsey estimated the LGBQ population in the United States to be around 10 percent, contemporary studies suggest that right around 3 percent of adults identify as LGBQ (Gates, 2011). The estimate for teens identifying as LGBQ, on the other hand, is higher. According to previous reports and studies that used 2013 and 2015 YRBSS data, about 7.5 percent (Kann et al., 2011) to 11.2 percent (Kahle, 2020; Kann et al., 2014) of ninth through twelfth graders identified as LGBQ. In the current study, the number of Latina girls identifying as LGBQ is even higher at about 16 percent of the sample. Because the logistical models of this study show that identifying as LGBQ puts Latina girls at significant risk for various types of interpersonal victimization, the sheer proportion of those identifying as such makes intervention efforts that consider sexual orientation more urgent.

In terms of identity and risk associated with interpersonal victimization, considering sexual orientation—in addition to race, ethnicity, and gender—presents a more vibrant picture than that presented in earlier studies. The current study confirms that LGBQ youth experience higher levels of physical and emotional violence, particularly while at school and in terms of dating violence and sexual assault (Kahle, 2020; Katz-Wise & Hyde, 2012; Langenderfer-Magruder et al., 2016; Rivers, 2011). Results also corroborate findings from previous research studies, which indicate that sexual minority youth are twice as likely to experience bullying while at school (Kosciw, Diaz & Greytak, 2007; Massachusetts Department of Education, 2004). Latina girls who identified as LGBQ were 1.7 times more likely to experience traditional bullying, 2 times more likely to experience electronic bullying, and 6.4 times more likely to experience bullying based on sexual orientation. With regard to dating violence and sexual assault, this study aligns with those that show that girls and sexual minorities are more at risk for all types of dating violence and sexual assault (Dank et al., 2014; Edwards, 2018; Edwards et al., 2015; Edwards & Sylaska, 2013; Gemberling et al., 2015; Gillum, & DiFulvio, 2012; Katz-Wise & Hyde, 2012). LGBQ Latina girls are 3.5 times more likely to experience dating violence and 2 times more likely to experience sexual assault than heterosexual Latina girls. Other characteristics were also associated with interpersonal victimization. Results suggest that grade level is associated with traditional and sexual orientation bullying victimization (Espelage & Horne, 2008). As students grow older, they are about 25 percent less likely to report experiencing traditional bullying and about 32 percent less likely to report experiencing sexual orientation bullying. While studies find that weight is also associated with victimization (Farhart et al., 2010; Wang et al., 2010), this study finds that as a student's weight increases, the likelihood of victimization increases by 1.3 times for traditional bullying only. While a small proportion of Latina girls engaged in misbehavior, these results strongly align with previous studies that show its association with victimization (Kahle, 2020; Peguero, 2008). In fact, Latina girls who engaged in misbehavior were 4.1 times more likely to experience traditionally bullying victimization, 5.3 times more likely to experience electronic bullying victimization, 3 times more likely to experience sexual orientation bullying, and 7.7 times more likely to experience dating violence.

Very few studies, if any, test mental health as a control variable. This study found that 29 percent of Latina girls reported feelings of depression and suicidality. Poor mental health was also significantly associated with interpersonal victimization in Latina LGBQ girls, where those experiencing it were 1.4 to 1.5 times more likely to report traditional, electronic, and sexual orientation bullying victimization as well as dating violence. Finally, geographic location was also significantly associated with interpersonal victimization (Guerra & Williams, 2010). Students in Florida were 40 percent less likely to report sexual orientation bullying victimization, and students in Illinois were 88 percent less likely to report sexual orientation bullying victimization.

The Importance of Considering Intersectionality

The concept of the intersectionality of gender, race, ethnicity, and sexual orientation is crucial to the growing body of research on youth and adolescent violence and victimization. As Collins (2004) argues, it is important for scholars to keep race, ethnicity, class, gender, sexuality, and age "in dialogue with one another" when crafting antiracism and antiviolence initiatives. Additionally, Crenshaw (1989) warns against "single axis frameworks" of conceptualization as they marginalize those who experience discrimination in multiple ways. Indeed, this study confirms Crenshaw's call to action and supports her framework as well as those of others who have exemplified the fundamental associations between violence, race, ethnicity, gender, and now sexual orientation (Burgess-Proctor, 2006; Crenshaw et al., 2015; Peguero & Popp, 2012; Potter, 2015).

In Crenshaw's (1991) discussion of identity politics, she highlights how this theorization often ignores intragroup (within-group) differences: "Within the context of violence against women, this elision of difference in identity politics is problematic, fundamentally because the violence that many women experience is often shaped by other dimensions of their identities, such as race and class" (p. 1242). Results from this study support this claim by highlighting intragroup differences within Latina girls. Not only are girls, or Latina girls, at increased risk for victimization, but Latina girls who specifically identify as LGBQ have especially high risk of victimization. In this case, sexual orientation adds a specific layer of risk to Latina girls' identities.

Overall, these results highlight how discrimination (i.e., victimization) can be experienced in multiple ways across multiple and intersecting dimensions of identity. It is the residual effects of such victimization, however, that add additional value to using this framework. For example, Irvine, Wilber, and Canfield (2017) highlight that, in addition to victimization, LGBQ youth are more likely to experience family rejection, run away from home, be homeless, have higher levels of child welfare involvement, and engage in survival crimes. This ongoing mistreatment and stigma can create what Garnette, Irvine, Reyes, and Wilber (2011) call a "pipeline" from the home to the juvenile justice system. Furthermore, Irvine and Canfield (2016) describe that a specific "pathway" exists for LGBQ and non-gender-conforming and trans youth, extending from family rejection to the child welfare system, homelessness, survival crimes, and the juvenile justice system. In consideration of this study's findings, research, theory, and practice must consider the supplementary role that sexual orientation plays in addition to race, ethnicity and gender, in terms of both victimization rates and the possible long-term consequences for adolescents.

Potential Implications for LGBQ Latina Girls' Justice System Involvement

According to this study's findings, it is clear that LGBQ Latina girls have increased vulnerability of being a victim of violence; therefore, this increased likelihood of victimization has potential implications for LGBQ Latina girls' justice system involvement. It has been well established that the relationship between victimization and offending is symbiotic. In this regard, it is also evident that the history of abuse and related trauma as well as victimization can place girls, especially racial and ethnic minorities, on a path of juvenile and criminal justice involvement (Cuevas et al., 2014; Lopez & Nuño, 2016). Youth victimization appears to precede engagement in violent behavior rather than vice versa; moreover, victimization is often established as a risk factor for drug use and future delinquent behavior (Cuevas et al., 2014; Cuevas, Finkelhor, Turner, & Ormrod, 2007). Although this relationship between victimization, offending, and juvenile and criminal justice involvement is well established, research also highlights that race, ethnicity and sexual orientation confound girls' vulnerability to the detrimental consequence of victimization and juvenile justice involvement.

It has been argued that the victimization of marginalized girls, such as racial and ethnic minority and LGBQ girls, is often minimalized or dismissed by justice and school authorities (Irvine, 2010; Lopez & Nuño, 2016). Studies have reported that authorities have perceptions that racial and ethnic minority girls' tolerance for violence is higher and believe that violence and victimization are daily aspects of their experiences (Cuevas et al., 2014; Juvonen & Graham, 2014). As a result, the attention and concern that justice and school authorities have for white girls' exposure to violence and victimization are relatively higher in comparison to the victimization of racial and ethnic minority girls (Cuevas et al., 2014; Juvonen & Graham, 2014). This pattern of dismissing the trauma or injury associated with the victimization of racial and ethnic minority youth is paralleled for LGBQ girls (Garnette et al., 2011; Irvine, 2010; Irvine & Canfield, 2016). To confound the complexities for LGBQ girls of Color, research also indicates LGBQ girls of Color often run away from home or out-of-home placement to escape negative treatment such as physical, sexual, and emotional abuse (Garnette et al., 2011; Irvine, 2010; Irvine & Canfield, 2016). As a consequence, LGBQ girls of Color have increased odds of justice system involvement.

Practice and Policy Implications

Breaking this cycle is complicated, but research suggests that several policy implications and practices can be made. For example, Irvine (2010) highlights that juvenile justice professionals must acknowledge the reality that about 15 percent of justice-involved youth identify as LGBQ and gender-nonconforming. By overcoming this invisibility, professionals can then follow several practices to reduce issues facing LGBQ and gender-nonconforming youth in the system, including policy development, training, development of family crisis protocols, community-based collaborations, alternatives to detention, and consistent data analysis of the issue. Additionally, Garnette et al. (2011) highlight that the juvenile justice system must create an entire culture of inclusivity by implementing policies that prohibit discrimination and promote equitable treatment as well as specifically training juvenile justice professionals (i.e., probation officers, judges, public defenders, district attorneys, and community organizations) about the specific needs of LGBT youth and how they can be addressed.

This study contributes additional evidence to the importance of centering the vulnerabilities of women and girls of Color, especially those identifying as LGBQ, toward being victims of interpersonal violence as well as receiving social and policy attention in terms of addressing their injury (Burgess-Proctor, 2006; Crenshaw et al., 2015; Potter, 2015). Program and policy initiatives should continue highlighting the importance of gender-responsive programming, albeit not ignoring how deeply systemic racism and heterosexism are embedded in our society. Yes, it is a fact that racial and ethnic minorities, women and girls, and sexual minorities are disproportionately at risk for interpersonal victimization. However, we can gain important understanding and headway in reducing these issues by no longer crosscutting these axes of identity and instead acknowledge the unique severity and policy needs of youth who reside at these intersections.

REFERENCES

Burgess-Proctor, A. (2006). Intersections of race, class, gender, and crime: Future directions for feminist criminology. *Feminist Criminology, 1*, 27–47.

Centers for Disease Control and Prevention. (2013). *Youth violence*. Atlanta: Centers for Disease Control and Prevention.

Centers for Disease Control and Prevention. (2014a). 2013 YRBS data user's guide. Atlanta: Centers for Disease Control and Prevention.

Centers for Disease Control and Prevention. (2014b). Web-Based Injury Statistics Query and Reporting System (WISQARS). Atlanta: Centers for Disease Control and Prevention, National Center for Injury Prevention and Control.

Centers for Disease Control and Prevention. (2016). *Sexual identity, sex of sexual contacts, and health-related behaviors among students in grades 9–12—United States and selected sites, 2015*. Atlanta: Centers for Disease Control and Prevention.

Collins, P. H. (2004). *Black sexual politics: African Americans, gender, and the new racism*. New York: Routledge.

Crenshaw, K. (1989). Demarginalizing the intersection of race and sex. *University of Chicago Legal Forum, 1989*, 139–168.

Crenshaw, K. (1991). Mapping the margins: Intersectionality, identity politics, and violence against women of Color. *Stanford Law Review, 43*, 1241–1299.

Crenshaw, K., Ocen, P. A., & Nanda, J. (2015). *Black girls matter: Pushed out, over policed and unprotected*. New York: African American Policy Forum, Center for Intersectionality and Social Policy Studies.

Cuevas, C. A., Bell, K. A., & Sabina, C. (2014). Victimization, psychological distress, and help seeking: Disentangling the relationship for Latina victims. *Psychology of Violence, 4*, 196–209.

Cuevas, C. A., Finkelhor, D., Turner H. A., & Ormrod, R. K. (2007). Juvenile delinquency and victimization: A theoretical typology. *Journal of Interpersonal Violence, 22*, 1581–1602.

Cuevas, C. A., Sabina, C., & Milloshi, R. (2012). Interpersonal victimization among a national sample of Latino women. *Violence Against Women, 18*, 377–403.

Dank, M., Lachman, P., Zweig, J., & Yahner, J. (2014). Dating violence experiences of lesbian, gay, bisexual, and transgender youth. *Journal of Youth and Adolescence, 43*, 846–857.

Eaton, D. K., Davis, K. S., & Barrios, L. (2007). Associations of dating violence victimization with lifetime participation, co-occurrence, and early initiation of risk behaviors among U.S. high school adolescents. *Journal of Interpersonal Violence, 22*, 585–602.

Eaton, D. K., Kann, L., Kinchen, S., Ross, J., Hawkins, J., Harris, W. A., et al. (2006). Youth risk behavior surveillance—United States, 2005. *CDC Morbidity and Mortality Weekly Report, 55*(SS-5), 1–108.

Edwards, K. M. (2018). Incidence and outcomes of dating violence victimization among high school youth: The role of gender and sexual orientation. *Journal of Interpersonal Violence, 33*, 1472–1490.

Edwards, K. M., & Sylaska, K. M. (2013). The perpetration of intimate partner violence among LGBTQ college students: The role of minority stress. *Journal of Youth and Adolescence, 42*, 1721–1731.

Edwards, K. M., Sylaska, K. M., Barry, J. E., Moynihan, M. M., Banyard, V. L., Cohn, E. S., Walsh, W. A., & Ward, S. K. (2015). Physical dating violence, sexual violence, and unwanted pursuit victimization: A comparison of incidence rates among sexual-minority and heterosexual college students. *Journal of Interpersonal Violence, 30*, 580–600.

Espelage, D. L., & Horne, A. (2008). School violence and bullying prevention: From research based explanations to empirically based solutions. In S. Brown & R. Lent (Eds.), *Handbook of counseling psychology* (4th ed., pp. 588–606). Hoboken, NJ: John Wiley.

Farhart, T., Iannotti, R. J., & Simons-Morton, B. G. (2010). Overweight, obesity, youth, and health-risk behaviors. *American Journal of Preventive Medicine, 38*, 258–267.

Field, A. P. (2009). *Discovering statistics using SPSS* (3rd ed.). Thousand Oaks, CA: Sage.

Finkelhor, D. (2008). *Childhood victimization: Violence, crime, and abuse in the lives of young people.* New York: Oxford University Press.

Finkelhor, D., Turner, H., Ormrod, R., Hamby, S., & Kracke, K. (2009). *Children's exposure to violence: A comprehensive national survey* (NCJ 227744). Washington, DC: U.S. Department of Justice, Office of Justice Programs.

Flores, J. (2016). *Caught up: Girls, surveillance, and wraparound incarceration*. Berkeley: University of California Press.

Garcia, L. (2009). "Now why do you want to know about that?" Heteronormativity, sexism and racism in the sexual (mis)education of Latina youth. *Gender & Society, 23*, 520–541.

Garnette, L., Irvine, A., Reyes, C., & Wilber, S. (2011). Lesbian, gay, bisexual and transgender (LGBT) youth and the juvenile justice system. In F. T. Sherman & F. H. Jacobs (Eds.), *Juvenile justice: Advancing research, policy, and practice* (pp. 156–173). Hoboken, NJ: John Wiley.

Gates, G. J. (2011). How many people are lesbian, gay, bisexual and transgender? UCLA School of Law, Williams Institute. https://williamsinstitute.law.ucla.edu.

Gemberling, T. M., Cramer, R. J., Miller, R. S., Stroud, C. H., Noland, R. M., & Graham, J. (2015). Lesbian, gay, and bisexual identity as a moderator of relationship functioning after sexual assault. *Journal of Interpersonal Violence, 30*, 3431–3452.

Gillum, T. L., & DiFulvio, G. (2012). "There's so much at stake": Sexual minority youth discuss dating violence. *Violence Against Women, 18*, 725–745.

Guerra, N., & Williams, K. (2010). Implementing bullying prevention in diverse settings: Geographic, economic and cultural influences. In E. Vernberg & B. Biggs (Eds.), *Preventing and treating bullying victimization* (pp. 319–336). New York: Oxford University Press.

Howard, D. E., Wang, M. Q., & Yan, F. (2007). Psychosocial factors associated with reports of dating violence among U.S. adolescent females. *Adolescence, 42*, 311–324.

Irvine, A. (2010). "We've had three of them": Addressing the invisibility of lesbian, gay, bisexual and trans-gender youth in the juvenile justice system. *Columbia Journal of Gender and Law, 19*, 675–701.

Irvine, A., & Canfield, A. (2016). The overrepresentation of lesbian, gay, bisexual, questioning, gender nonconforming and transgender youth within the child welfare to juvenile justice crossover population. *Journal of Gender, Social Policy & the Law, 24*, 243–261.

Irvine, A., Wilber, S., & Canfield, A. (2017). *Lesbian, gay, bisexual, questioning, and/or gender nonconforming and transgender girls and boys in the California juvenile justice system: A practice guide*. San Francisco: National Center for Lesbian Rights.

Juvonen, J., & Graham, S. (2014). Bullying in schools: The power of bullies and the plight of victims. *Annual Review of Psychology, 65*, 159–185.

Kahle, L. L. (2020). Are sexual minorities more at risk? Bullying victimization among lesbian, gay, bisexual, and questioning youth. *Journal of Interpersonal Violence, 35*, 4960–4978.

Kann, L., Kinchen, S., Shanklin, S., Flint, K., Hawkins, J., Harris, W., & Zaza, S. (2014). Youth risk behavior surveillance—United States, 2013 (Surveillance Summary No. 4). Atlanta: Centers for Disease Control and Prevention.

Kann, L., Olsen, E., McManus, T., Kinchen, S., Chyen, D., Harris, W., & Wechsler, H. (2011). Sexual identity, sex of sexual contacts, and health-risk behaviors among students in grades 9–12, youth risk behavior surveillance, selected sites, United States, 2001–2009. Atlanta: Centers for Disease Control and Prevention.

Katz-Wise, S. L., & Hyde, J. S. (2012). Victimization experiences of lesbian, gay, and bisexual individuals: A meta-analysis. *Journal of Sex Research, 49*, 142–167.

Kosciw, J., Diaz, E., & Greytak, E. (2007). *The 2007 National School Climate Survey: The experiences of lesbian, gay, bisexual and transgender youth in our nation's schools.* New York: Gay, Lesbian & Straight Education Network.

Langenderfer-Magruder, L., Walls, N., Whitfield, D. L., Brown, S. M., & Barrett, C. M. (2016). Partner violence victimization among lesbian, gay, bisexual, transgender, and queer youth: Associations among risk factors. *Child and Adolescent Social Work Journal, 33*, 55–68.

Lopez, N. (2003). *Hopeful girls, troubled boys: Race and gender disparity in urban education.* New York: Routledge.

Lopez, V. (2017a). *Complicated lives: Girls, parents, drugs, and juvenile justice.* New Brunswick, NJ: Rutgers University Press.

Lopez, V. (2017b). Love is a battlefield: Mexican American girls' strategies for avoiding players. *Youth & Society, 49*, 23–45.

Lopez, V., Chesney-Lind, M., & Foley, J. (2012). Relationship power, control, and dating violence among drug-involved Latina girls. *Violence Against Women, 18*, 681–690.

Lopez, V., & Nuño, L. (2016). Latina and African-American girls in the juvenile justice system: Needs, problems, and solutions. *Sociology Compass, 10*, 24–37.

Madriz, E. (1997). Latina teenagers: Victimization, identity, and fear of crime. *Social Justice, 24*, 39–55.

Massachusetts Department of Education. (2004). 2003 Massachusetts Youth Risk Behavior Survey results. Boston: Massachusetts Department of Education.

Muschert, G. W., Henry, S., Bracy, N. L., & Peguero, A. A. (2013). *Responding to school violence: Confronting the Columbine effect.* Boulder, CO: Lynne Rienner.

Mustanski, B., Van Wagenen, A., Birkett, M., Eyster, S., & Corliss, H. L. (2014). Identifying sexual orientation health disparities in adolescents: Analysis of pooled data from the Youth Risk Behavior Survey, 2005 and 2007. *American Journal of Public Health, 104*, 211–217.

Pascoe, C. J. (2011). *Dude, you're a fag: Masculinity and sexuality in high school.* Berkeley: University of California Press.

Peguero, A. A. (2008). Bullying victimization and extracurricular activity. *Journal of School Violence, 7*, 71–85.

Peguero, A. A., & Popp, A. M. (2012). Youth violence at school and the intersection of gender, race, and ethnicity. *Journal of Criminal Justice, 40*, 1–9.

Peterson, D., & Panfil, V. (2014). Introduction: Reducing invisibility. In D. Peterson & V. Panfil (Eds.), *Handbook of LGBT communities, crime, and justice* (pp. 3–14). New York: Springer.

Popp, A. M., & Peguero, A. A. (2011). Routine activities and victimization at school: The significance of gender. *Journal of Interpersonal Violence, 26*, 2413–2436.

Popp, A. M., Peguero, A. A., Day, K. R., & Kahle, L. L. (2014). Gender, bullying victimization, and education. *Violence & Victims, 29*, 843–856.
Postmus, J. L. (2015). Women from different ethnic groups and their experiences with victimization and seeking help. *Violence Against Women, 21*, 376–393.
Potter, H. (2015). *Intersectionality and criminology: Disrupting and revolutionizing studies of crime.* New York: Routledge.
Rivers, I. (2011). *Homophobic bullying: Research and theoretical perspectives.* New York: Oxford University Press.
Rojas-Gaona, C., Hong, J. S., & Peguero, A. A. (2016). The significance of race/ethnicity in adolescent violence: A decade of review, 2005–2015. *Journal of Criminal Justice, 46*, 137–147.
Romero, A. J., Wiggs, C. B., Valencia, C., & Bauman, S. (2013). Latina teen suicide and bullying. *Hispanic Journal of Behavioral Sciences, 35*, 159–173.
Sabina, C., Cuevas, C. A., & Lannen, E. (2014). The likelihood of Latino women to seek help in response to interpersonal victimization: An examination of individual, interpersonal and sociocultural influences. *Psychosocial Intervention, 23*, 95–103.
Sexual Minority Assessment Research Team. (2009). *Best practices for asking questions about sexual orientation on surveys.* Los Angeles: Williams Institute.
Shekarkhar, Z., & Peguero, A. A. (2011). Latina exposure to violence at school. *Justice Policy Journal, 8*, 2–26.
Wang, J., Iannotti, R. J., & Luk, J. W. (2010). Bullying victimization among underweight and overweight U.S. youth: Differential associations for boys and girls. *Journal of Adolescent Health, 47*, 99–101.
Woodford, M., Paceley, M. S., Kulick, A., & Hong, J. S. (2015). The LGBQ social climate matters: Policies, protests, and placards and psychological wellbeing among LGBQ emerging adults. *Journal of Gay & Lesbian Social Services, 27*, 116–141.

3

Nondisclosure of IPV Victimization among Disadvantaged Mexican American Young Adult Women

ALICE CEPEDA, ESMERALDA RAMIREZ, JESSICA FRANKEBERGER, KATHRYN M. NOWOTNY, AND AVELARDO VALDEZ

When we first met Cindy in 2000, she was fifteen years old, living with her mother and two siblings in a Westside public housing unit in San Antonio. She had been dating her boyfriend for only two months when their first violent confrontation occurred.

> Me and my boyfriend got in an argument because he said I was playing him. We had been going out for like about two months already, and his last girlfriend told him that I was dating another guy. He went to my house and told me "Who the hell are you talking to?" I go, "Well, why are you still talking to that other bitch?" He goes, "because she has my baby." I told him, "You don't have to be with me anymore." That's when he pushed me. I go "Well, I don't want to fucking be with you." He slapped me and I started crying. He then punched me in my eye and gave me a black eye. (Valdez, 2007, p. 127)

When we relocated Cindy, she was thirty-two years of age, had five children (of whom she had custody of only one), and had a past history of injecting heroin. The following account reflects Cindy's sustained experiences of violence victimization with one of four partners she had been with since we last interviewed her as an adolescent:

> He was very abusive to me. Look at the scar on my face. You know why he did that? I was in the living room watching TV and he said he heard me whispering with his brother. He grabbed me by the hair and dragged me to the room. I'll never forget that day. There was a glass cup. He threw it at me and it shattered all over my face. I didn't realize I was bleeding

until afterward, this was hanging down (motioning to the scar on the right part of her cheekbone). He didn't let me go to the hospital 'cause he knew he was gonna get in trouble. All the scars I have are from him. He used to strap tie me and beat me. He was real jealous.

Cindy's case study reflects an age-graded life course victimization pathway that initiates with dating violence during adolescence and continues into young adulthood with additional experiences of intimate partner violence (IPV). Cindy's case is not unique. Approximately one in four women in the United States experiences severe physical violence at the hands of an intimate partner. All too often, the social and physical consequences of IPV and victimization continue to impact women across the life span (Niolon et al., 2017). For Latina women, and in particular poor Latina women living in disadvantaged communities, the experiences of IPV often go underreported and understudied. This chapter provides primary data from a sample of young adult Mexican American women who are part of an ongoing longitudinal study (Proyecto SALTO—San Antonio Latina Trajectory Outcomes) documenting the long-term health outcomes of partner violence among adolescent females as they transition into adulthood. Specifically, presented here are the women's stories, perceptions, and attitudes associated with decisions not to disclose the violence and how these decisions are fueled by a plethora of factors that are unique to these marginalized women.

Nondisclosure of IPV Victimization in Minority Communities: An Intersectional Perspective

The context of women's lives, including the violence they have experienced and their previous experiences with the police, affects their intentions to use the criminal justice system (Fleury-Steiner, Bybee, Sullivan, Belknap, & Melton, 2006). In general, living in a neighborhood characterized by high levels of social disorganization is associated with greater exposure to violence (Butcher, Galanek, Kretschmar, & Flannery, 2015). For example, using longitudinal data and controlling for a host of individual-level factors, Benson, Fox, DeMaris, and Van Wyk (2003) found that neighborhood economic disadvantage, neighborhood residential instability, male employment instability, and subjective financial strain influence the likelihood of violence against women in intimate relationships. For communities of Color in the United States, neighborhood disadvantage is the product of larger sociohistorical processes of racial inequality and residential segregation (Valdez & Cepeda, 2008; Williams & Collins, 2001).

This is particularly consequential for women and girls who are involved in crime and have histories of incarceration. Feminist pathways theory asserts that female criminality is largely survival-based and tied to a constellation of factors including experiencing trauma and living in poverty (Belknap & Holsinger, 2006; Chesney-Lind, 1989; Wattanaporn & Holtfreter, 2014). Overall, women who are involved in the criminal justice system report extensive histories of sexual and physical violence with consequent mental health and substance abuse problems (McDaniels-Wilson & Belknap, 2008; Nowotny, Belknap, Lynch, & DeHart, 2014). The criminalization of women's trauma experiences contributes to women's decisions to not report victimization to law enforcement for fear of further incurring criminal justice sanctions (Burgess-Proctor, 2012).

The Current Study

In this study, we apply an intersectional perspective to nondisclosure of IPV victimization among U.S.-born young adult Latina women. We examine how multiple minority statuses contribute to underreporting of chronic victimization experiences. These stigmatized statuses are conceptualized as overlapping and include victim, racial/ethnic, and gender minority statuses. We also examine how stigmatized behavior-related statuses (criminal and drug user) influence women's decisions not to seek out formal support. The current study adds to the growing knowledge of IPV among Latinas by examining Mexican American women's experiences, perceptions, and attitudes toward nondisclosure of abuse and the distinct factors reducing the likelihood of reporting to police. The lives of these women when they were adolescents are the focus of the book titled *Mexican American Girls and Gang Violence: Beyond Risk* (Valdez, 2007). Documented are these young girls' involvement in behaviors such as drug use, crime, risky sexual behavior, and dating violence in isolated community settings that place them beyond risk when compared to girls in more conventional settings. In this chapter, we use a qualitative approach to examine the nature and circumstances associated with not reporting more recent incidents of IPV victimization among these same girls, but now as young adults.

Methods

This research is based on data collected through a National Institute on Drug Abuse–funded study (Proyecto SALTO) examining the long-term health outcomes of drug use and IPV among a cohort of Mexican American women in San Antonio, Texas. The current project follows up with and adds to the original cohort of 150 women who were interviewed as adolescents between 1999 and 2001 (Valdez, 2007). The ongoing study employed a concurrent mixed-method (CMM) nested longitudinal cohort design, which included the collection of biological, survey, and qualitative data. Data from the original sample collected over fifteen years ago served as time 1 (adolescence); time 2 data were collected using the Natural History Interview (NHI) technique (Hser, Hoffman, Grella, & Anglin, 2001; Hser, Huang, Chou, & Anglin, 2007) covering the fifteen-year retrospective period; and current (past year) data at the time of the most recent interview serve as time 3.

Data for the current analysis comes from qualitative data collected during the course of the administration of the NHI to a sample of 175 women who had completed follow-up surveys to date as well as ethnographic interviews with a subset of 27 women from the larger sample. One of the themes that emerged from the NHI part of the study was the reporting of abuse to local police; therefore, the ethnographic portion of our study focused on eliciting more information about this theme. Specifically, the ethnographic interviews captured text narratives that place women's experiences within a situational context that generates insights into meanings, perceptions, and beliefs of disclosing victimization. An NVivo database consisting of transcripts from the qualitative NHI data and ethnographic interviews was used for the analysis.

Analysis

The ethnographic data analysis involved four inductive strategies that proceeded sequentially (LeCompte & Schensul, 1999; Ragin, 1999; Strauss & Corbin, 1990). The first strategy, item-level analysis, implemented a form of unrestricted initial coding consisting of line-by-line reading to identify item codes. A constant-comparison analytic process was conducted whereby codes were compared within and across interviews. Next, a pattern-level analysis was conducted to establish linkages among the item codes and develop potential categories. Third, a structural-level analysis involved organizing relationships among patterns of the data into themes associated with types of nondisclosure. Last, interpretation consisted of defining the types and specific variations that distinguished the relationship processes that shaped patterns of nondisclosure for the female participants.

Community Context

The San Antonio population in 2010 was estimated to be 1.3 million, with more than 50 percent of Mexican descent (DeNavas-Walt, Proctor, & Smith, 2010) and primarily composed of second- and third-generation Mexican Americans. The metropolitan San Antonio area ranks the highest in residential income segregation among the thirty largest metropolitan areas in the United States (Fry & Taylor, 2012). The sample for this study was recruited from neighborhoods in San Antonio characterized by a high concentration of poverty, adult criminality, drug markets, and delinquent behavior. The Economic Innovation Group developed the distressed communities index, an inequality indicator at the zip code level (Economic Innovation Group, 2017). Not only does San Antonio rank in the top ten cities with the largest (proportion) number of people living in distressed zip codes (percentage of adults without high school degrees, housing vacancy, adults not working, poverty, and median income ratio), but the city also has the highest level of spatial inequality between zip codes. For example, the least distressed zip code in San Antonio has a distress score of 0.5, contrasted with a score of 97.8 for the most distressed zip codes. The latter zip code encompasses the setting for the present study.

Characteristics of the Study Sample

Of the 175 women interviewed to date, most are relatively young (mean age = 33), with a mean educational level of tenth grade. Approximately 29 percent of the sample reported currently being unemployed, and

46 percent reported a history of evictions. On average, the participants had three children, with over 40 percent reporting being married or cohabitating. Close to 80 percent of the sample reported a history of IPV victimization. On average, the women who reported IPV victimization had been in a violent relationship for about nine years. Of these women, 19 percent reported a history of seeing a doctor or needing hospitalization as a result of a violent incident. Thirty-seven percent of the sample also reported a minimum of one of their children witnessing violence at home. Table 3.1 reflects the disproportionate rates of incarceration and lifetime drug use prevalence for this sample of women. Over 60 percent of the women had an incarceration history, with 65 percent reporting that they had been convicted of a felony (mean age of first felony = 22.9). Given the nested aspect of the study design, the qualitative sampling strategy ensures that the ethnographic sample does not differ substantively from the overall sample with regard to key sociodemographic and IPV victimization characteristics.

Findings

Decisions for Nondisclosure of IPV

During the course of our study, the women described numerous victimization incidents, but rarely mentioned calling police or seeking out other types of formal help-seeking behaviors; however, they did speak extensively about their decisions and motivations for not disclosing their physical victimization.

LOYALTY TO PARTNER. A prominent theme that emerged from the interviews is not reporting partners as perpetrators of IPV because of feelings of love or loyalty to the men. Parents and friends of these women often were aware of the abuse and attempted to persuade women to leave their partners. Jennifer, a thirty-two-year-old housewife with four children, described her reluctance to leave her ex-boyfriend. They stayed together for years despite the physical violence she endured and despite her mother's encouragement to leave. "My mom, she would try to keep me away from him and tell me he wasn't no good and stuff, and I wouldn't listen, and I would just stay." A single mother of five children and home health care provider, Lucretia described staying with an abusive boyfriend despite her family and friends' misgivings. When discussing injuries incurred during an argument with her partner, Leticia said,

TABLE 3.1. Sociodemographic Characteristics of Women Interviewed to Date

	M	SD	Frequency (%)
Age	33.13	2.21	
Highest education level completed	10.98	1.98	
Marital status			
Single			36.0
Separated/divorced/widowed			13.7
Married/cohabitating			44.6
Children			
Number of children	3.34	1.74	
Unemployed			28.6
History of eviction			46.4
Lifetime IPV victimization			78.9
Years in violent relationships	8.75	5.12	
IPV doctor/hospital visit			18.7
Reports of child witnessing IPV			37.7
Incarceration history			
Ever incarcerated (Y/N)			63.6
Felony conviction			64.5
# of felonies	2.30	1.91	
Times incarcerated for 30+ days	1.94	2.65	
0 times			62.3
1 time			12.6
2+ times			25.7
Lifetime drug use			
Marijuana			88.9
Sedatives/hypnotics			35.3
Methamphetamines			33.5
Methadone			24.6
Crack/cocaine			21.7
Noninjecting heroin			41.8
Prescription opiates			22.2
Injection drug use			29.4

Note: $N = 175$.

"I did tell my family about it. It was really bad. They wanted me to press charges, but I didn't want to. Cause I loved him a lot. And I just didn't want to. I didn't want him to go to jail or anything."

Strong emotional ties to their partners make it particularly difficult for these women to report incidents of domestic violence to law enforcement. Many women who call the police to report an abusive partner eventually report having a change of heart after the incident. Amy, age thirty-one, described how she stood up to her long-term partner after he was abusive to her and her daughters. She called the police, but he hid and returned later to the house apologetic and crying. She stated that her daughters "felt bad" so she allowed him to come back into the house, but told him to leave them alone. Her reluctance to pursue further legal charges was related to the emotional ties she had to him. These strong emotional ties prevent many women's ability to break the cycle of IPV.

SOCIAL AMBIVALENCE AND AVERSION. Women also expressed ambivalence about reporting their partners' violent abuse and involving law enforcement or other governmental entities. This ambivalence and aversion were often related to patterns of distrust toward police within their neighborhoods. Sarah, a thirty-three-year-old HIV-positive former sex worker who has lived on the Westside of San Antonio her entire life described an argument with a former partner that escalated into physical violence. She said, "Nobody could stop us or wanted to call the cops. Nobody going to fucking say anything around there. Let them fight all they want." Iris, also a former sex worker who now lives with a partner in these same Westside neighborhoods, echoed this sentiment when she explained why she did not report former partners for physically abusing her. She shared a story about a former partner beating her up after finding out that she began prostituting herself. When asked why she did not report him to the police, she replied, "I just wouldn't do that. You don't call the cops, you know what I mean?"

In some cases, this ambivalence can be directly tied to the women's past experiences. Jennifer, a thirty-two-year-old housewife with four children, described witnessing violent altercations between her parents during her childhood.

> Sometimes when my mom and my dad would fight, my mom would call me and put me in front of her, so my dad wouldn't hit her. I remember I

used to call the police, but I would get in trouble. I would go under the table and put the phone under there, and I would call the police and hang up when I'd see them coming. But when the police came, they would tell them their daughter was playing with the phone and accidentally called the cops.

Though her instinct at a young age was to call the police to protect her mother from her father, Jennifer's mother reinforced the idea that calling the police was a mistake. These examples reflect the social ambivalence and aversion women have in reporting their victimization to the police, a perception that is embedded into the social fabric of this community.

FEAR OF RETALIATION. Women also expressed fear of further retaliation from their partner as a reason for not reporting violent incidents to the police. Carla is a thirty-three-year-old single mother who makes ends meet with part-time work and social services assistance. She was in a long-term relationship with an older man who over the years had subjected her to a constant series of beatings. These beatings were especially violent when he was intoxicated or high. When asked what her partner would have done if she had reported his abuse to the police, Carla said, "He would have tracked me down and killed me." The relationship ended when her boyfriend was arrested and incarcerated on a homicide charge. Carla described continuing to live in fear even though her boyfriend was incarcerated. Now that he has been released, these fears have intensified. She said, "I am now really scared of him, afraid that he will be looking for me. Maybe kill me or he'll pay someone to do it for him."

In other cases, women expressed fearing for not only their own safety but also the safety of their loved ones. Cynthia, thirty-three years old, spent fifteen years as a daily injection heroin user. At the time of our interview, she was in a methadone maintenance program in an attempt to maintain custody of her daughter. Although Cynthia was in a stable long-term relationship and working her first job at the time of the interview, her previous relationships were often violent and volatile. Cynthia lived in particular fear of one ex-partner, who had tried to stab her while she was at her mother's house. "I was, like, call the ambulance, Julien stabbed me. And I told Julien to leave because my mom called the cops. And she called them and said to them, 'I need you to send the ambulance cause my daughter's boyfriend stabbed her.' And I was like, 'Mom don't tell them that, just tell them to send an ambulance and that I'm stabbed.'" After the EMS and police arrived, Cynthia did not tell them what really happened and told her mother to not say anything. "I didn't tell them that it was him that stabbed me. I told my mom you don't know nothing. That's the first thing I told her before I left. The cops are going to ask them what happened, you tell them you don't know nothing. You tell them that I just walked in like that, you don't know." After Cynthia was released from the hospital and returned to her mother's house, her boyfriend was waiting for her. Despite her mother's protests, Cynthia left with him. It was not until several days later, when they started arguing again, that she questioned her decision.

> And then, I'm just there and I'm like, "What am I doing?" My mom got mad because I left with him. And I was, like, "Hell no, this dude's going to end up killing me." He already stabbed me, punctured my lung. And I was, like, what . . . what am I looking for? What am I waiting for? And I was, like, "Nah, I can't do this, like, I can't." And so I left, yeah. I left. And I didn't turn back.

Though she never reported his abuse to law enforcement, Cynthia was able to leave the relationship before more harm was done.

Rosemary, a thirty-two-year-old restaurant manager, described leaving the father of her children, recounting the night she left him for good after he forced her into the car and then drove around aimlessly for hours. During this long drive, Rosemary said her partner regularly punched and slapped her. She shared how she finally escaped: "It's night. We're, like, headed towards the country. I'm so scared, like, oh my god what is this guy going to do to me? At a gas station, I go to the bathroom, and I stay in there, and I don't come out because I'm literally afraid. I stay in the store. I call my mom to come pick me up. I was so scared. I thought he was going to kill me."

Like Cynthia, rather than involving law enforcement to end the abusive relationship, Rosemary protected herself by leaving her partner. Also like Cynthia, this was possible only with the help of her family, specifically her mother. Fortunately, in both of these cases the former partners did not retaliate.

Some women expressed other ways of engaging law enforcement in order to protect themselves and/or their family, but without reporting their partner's abuse directly. Margie was scared that her abusive partner would hurt her parents and siblings, with whom she was living. Her then boyfriend was a suspect in a murder investigation, and the police questioned her about him. For a while she refused to cooperate with the cops, until her boyfriend threatened her family. She described making this decision: "I was so scared of him that I thought he would do something to my family, I really did. That's when I got the courage, like, you know, I don't want my family to die because of something I didn't do. So, I just reported him to the police. I needed to say something. I didn't want him to kill my family." Similar to Cynthia and Rosemary, Margie found an alternative method of protection. Though she never reported her boyfriend to law enforcement for the violence he inflicted on her, she did let the police know where they could find him for the homicide charge. This ultimately led to his arrest and imprisonment and Margie's peace of mind and safety.

Confounding Factors Contributing to Nonreporting

Motivating women's decisions are the negative perceptions of law enforcement and the criminal justice system. As in many disadvantaged low-income communities that are subjected to hyperpolicing by law enforcement, citizens in these communities view these institutional entities as highly discriminating and repressive. In particular, older adolescents and young adults are subjected to aggressive law enforcement tactics and special gang and drug police units (Durán, 2013; Rios & Vigil, 2017). As a result, residents living in Mexican American communities may be highly suspicious of law enforcement and are less likely to turn to them for public safety. It is within this social and public context that women in this study live.

UNWANTED INSTITUTIONAL CONTACT. Many of the women reported not calling police because they feared criminal justice consequences for themselves. A large proportion of women in this study had criminal records (see Table 3.1). At the time of the interview, many either were under some type of court supervision (parole, probation, warrants, etc.) or had been under some type of court supervision in the past. They feared calling the police could bring unwanted attention to their own legal status.

Bianca is a thirty-five-year-old small business owner and mother of two whose fifteen-year marriage has been characterized by highly abusive arguments, physical violence, affairs (by both parties), divorce, and remarriage. Her husband reported her to the police for IPV, but she never reported him even though he was far more violent. When probed as to why she did not involve police, Bianca stated, "I've never really wanted to call the cops because I know it messes up my record whenever a call to the cops is made." Bianca did not want the police involved because she feared reporting her abuse would have a negative effect on her police record, even though she was the victim. This is a belief that is sustained by her previous negative experiences with the police. At the end of the interview, she expressed her frustration: "It just pisses me off, like, he can do that to me."

Aside from fearing criminal justice consequences for themselves and their partners, women did not report their victimization due to a fear of additional negative consequences for their families. For instance, calling the police on an abusive partner exposes their home life to further scrutiny by other social service agencies such as Child Protective Services (CPS). Ruby, a pregnant thirty-six-year-old home health care provider, directly attributed her reporting of IPV to the loss of custody of her five children: "CPS got involved in my life. I was with an abusive boyfriend, the father of my kids. He was abusive [to me] and the children. CPS got called. They drug tested me. I would smoke a lot of weed around that time and they drug tested me. So, I was tested positive, and they took my kids away. I guess that's what they do." Although CPS was called because of the IPV occurring in the home, ultimately it was Ruby's use of marijuana that led to her children being taken away. This reflects the paradoxical nature of these women's victimization within the context of existing drug laws.

Another unintended consequence that results from calling the cops is arrest or incarceration for the women experiencing the abuse. In many cases, this is because the women fight back and defend themselves. Rather than being a victim, these women are treated as offenders. Lisa, a disabled, divorced mother of two, described the aftermath of a violent incident with her partner, which resulted in the police being called. "So,

I fought back, like, you don't do that to me. Cops get called, they go, 'Did you hit him back?' I didn't lie, I said 'Yes I did, because he went at me.' I started explaining to [the cop], you know this is self-defense. They said they had to take us both to jail."

April, a street-level dealer of marijuana, methamphetamine, and heroin, described an arrest for what she considered self-defense during an argument with her common-law husband: "We were drinking. I told him we need to stop, he wanted to keep going, so we threw it down [continued to drink heavy]. We ended up in a fight. We hit each other, but he hurt me. [The police were called.] I didn't press charges, but he did. He tried to drop it and couldn't. I went straight to jail."

Women who have criminal records or current warrants are faced with the possibility of being arrested if police are involved. Although women seek out law enforcement for help and protection, the focal point can shift from their victimization to their own perpetration or past criminal charges. Valerie is a homeless injection drug user in methadone maintenance. Her status as both a homeless woman and a person with a history of drug use made her highly vulnerable to law enforcement. She described their involvement after being called to the scene of a fight with her female partner: "We were at this bus stop, and I got upset because she was taking pills, and we were trying to clean up. I was yelling at her, and she didn't like it, and she just swung at me. I fell and that's when the cops got there and arrested both of us. Mine was for tickets; hers was for a warrant."

Lily, a thirty-five-year-old mother of four who works as a general manager for a fast-food restaurant, also described her own arrest after calling the police during a violent incident with a former partner: "I mean he didn't really, like, beat me up, but he pushed [me], pulled my hair, and you know punched me. And it was funny because I called the cops, and I ended up in jail because I had a misdemeanor for stealing. I had a warrant. I ended up going to jail for that and not him. I was, like, I'm the one going to jail when I called the cops!"

Decisions relating to disclosure of abuse to law enforcement often require women to balance the pros of calling the police with the cons of potential negative consequences such as CPS involvement, arrests, and incarceration. These negative consequences act as impediments to disclose victimization, especially for those who come from disadvantaged and criminal or drug use backgrounds.

NOT WORTH IT TO REPORT. While many women did not report their IPV experiences to law enforcement, many others discussed experiences in which the police, when called, never showed up or did not intervene. For example, Kelly, a thirty-four-year-old diabetic with two kids, described a violent incident in which her partner was beating her outside their apartment. The cops, who showed up, did nothing. "He [her partner] beat the crap outta me outside when I didn't want to be with him no more. Literally left me black and blue. He was so violent. Outside, everybody was looking, and the [other people] wouldn't even do nothing 'cause he had a gun. . . . And [I] called the cops, and the cops didn't do nothing about it. Nothing. The cops would pass by and nothing." Kelly also shared what the police said after being repeatedly called out to her sister's house for reports of domestic violence: "I have a sister, and her baby's dad, he's violent too. And [the police] said that they're just so sick of them. They're just sick of my sister calling them, and she still continues to stay with him. So that's why the police don't listen to her. They get tired of going back and going back. And she's still with the same fucking guy." According to Kelly, law enforcement has explicitly told her sister that there is a limit to the amount of support they will provide to women who remain in long-term, physically abusive relationships.

Women often expressed frustration about how little happens to perpetrators even when they do report IPV to the police. For instance, Melody, a thirty-one-year-old with five kids, described what happened after she called police after a violent fight between her and her former partner: "We was at court, like, two months ago, and he won it. They got him [arrested] for the highest charge but it got dismissed. And I was, like, I want it on his record for when he does it [violent assault] the next time with somebody else. But, they took it off anyway." Although her relationship with this man is over, Melody expressed frustration at the criminal justice system's lack of ability to protect her and this man's future romantic partners. Such experiences led some women to doubt if there was any benefit in reporting IPV experiences to law enforcement. For instance, Stephanie, a thirty-two-year-old single mother of two, questioned the benefits of calling police. She said that "on San Antonio's Westside it takes at least forty-five minutes for a cop to get there, so you're already dead or something by the time they get there." Stephanie's sentiment was shared by many of the women in the study, who would rather risk their safety than bother to call and wait for the police who may let the male perpetrator go free and potentially arrest them instead.

Conclusion

Overall, our findings highlight the intersectional nature and complexity of factors contributing to the underreporting of IPV victimization among young adult Latina women with histories of drug use and criminal justice involvement living in disadvantaged communities. For a large proportion of the women who were the focus of this chapter, partner violence victimization has been a sustained, oftentimes chronic, and distressing experience in their short life trajectories. In attempting to understand these women's persistent IPV victimization, we focused on the motivations and decision-making processes by which reports to police oftentimes were never made. The women in our study reported several reasons for not calling police, including being loyal to their partners, believing that the police would not help, and wanting to avoid extra surveillance from law enforcement and other agencies (e.g., child protective services) given their involvement or prior history of stigmatized behaviors (drug use, crime and incarceration histories).

Findings from our study complement those of national population studies that have documented personal privacy, protecting the offender, and fear of reprisal as reasons for not disclosing IPV victimization (Montalvo-Liendo, 2009; Reaves, 2017). Our results also support previous findings with Latinas that attribute a lack of police reporting to the nature of the "private matter" and potential negative effects on family (Ackerman & Love, 2014). Our findings go beyond these population-based studies to illustrate the nature and context in which these women's decisions are made that attenuate and exacerbate the continued abuse occurring in partner relationships within these communities. For instance, the stories depict how fear is the source for many of these women's decisions to not report their partners' abuse. We captured a glimpse into the subjective nature of the incidents that make the fear they feel for themselves and their loved ones real and beyond the detached checked boxes of surveys. These results add to the existing research documenting the distinct role fear plays in influencing Latinas' (immigrant and nonimmigrant) unwillingness to report violent partner victimization to police (Menjívar & Salcido, 2002; Messing, Becerra, Ward-Lasher, & Androff, 2015).

Our findings also suggest that nondisclosure is strongly related to the skepticism and negative perceptions women have of the police and criminal justice system. These perceptions are multifaceted and shaped by the intersectional status of this population as poor Mexican American women with previous arrest histories (criminal and drug possession charges). IPV victimization was a prolonged occurrence in the lives of many of the women in our sample. Characterizing their nonreporting as "not worth it to report it" is understandable given that many of the women reported unsuccessful contacts with police in the past. The women reported that their partners rarely experienced legal ramifications for their violent actions. These past experiences resulted in a perception, on the part of many of the women in the sample, that the criminal justice system cannot be relied upon or trusted when dealing with an abusive partner.

We also documented a dual-victim phenomenon that has rarely been addressed in the IPV literature (Lee, 2015). Women had strong beliefs that reporting their victimization would result only in unsolicited contact with law enforcement and/or child protective services. Due to extensive histories with these institutions, women preferred not to report or disclose their violent victimization because they feared that they or their children could end up in the system again. This results in a cycle of victimization fueled by the women's multiplicity of stigmatized statuses that are often overlooked when considering the low rates of reporting among Latinas (Alvarez, Davidson, Fleming, & Glass, 2016; Lopez, 2017).

Previous research has attributed decisions to not disclose abuse to informal and formal resources to be associated with Latino cultural factors, including family values, women's gender roles, and fear of blame (Kennedy & Prock, 2018; Klevens, 2007). However, women's IPV nondisclosure cannot be reduced to a traditional gendered, lower class stereotype of dependency on men and subordination to them (Valdez, Kaplan, & Cepeda, 2000). One of the most intriguing findings of these young women when they were adolescents (Cepeda & Valdez, 2003; Valdez, 2007) was the alternative normative course they followed that did not adhere to a moral prescription for timing of sex, childbearing, and engagement in criminal and delinquent behavior, similarly documented in other low-socioeconomic female populations (Erickson, 2010). In conducting this study, we observed how these women continue to exhibit autonomy that has rarely been documented with Latinas who are often stereotyped as being submissive and subordinate to men. Collectively, nonreporting for these women may not be associated with submissiveness and subordination to men; instead, it may be a survival mechanism in an ethnic community that clearly imposes gender, class, and structural barriers for victimized women. This autonomy however is "paradoxical" because it comes with the ambiguity these women feel in placing a value on maintaining relationships with abusive men and the overwhelming chronic stress and detrimental mental and physical health consequences. A value of maintaining interpersonal partner relationships and bonds to children has similarly been documented among young adult Mexican American persistent male offenders in these same communities (Valdez, Nowotny, Zhao, & Cepeda, 2018).

Practice and Policy Implications

Results have important implications in identifying women who are at the highest risk for not reporting IPV victimization. Findings can inform policies and give insight into critical points of intervention that require more tailored responses to these women and their children, which considers women's intersecting social positions and identities and the disadvantaged contexts in which their victimization occurs. Moreover, it is worth noting that distal interventions aimed at justice reinvestment programs and improving economic conditions and community policing strategies in the Westside of San Antonio would go a long way toward addressing the upstream factors associated with violence against women in intimate partner relationships (Brown, Cunneen, Schwartz, Stubbs, & Young, 2016; Pew Charitable Trust, 2018). According to Tucker and Cadora (2003, p. 2), "The goal of justice reinvestment is to redirect some portion of the $54 billion America now spends on prisons to rebuilding the human resources and physical infrastructure—the schools, healthcare facilities, parks, and public spaces—of neighborhoods devastated by high levels of incarceration." Investing in the physical infrastructure of historically marginalized communities (Valdez & Cepeda, 2008; Williams & Collins, 2001) can improve social and human capital, thereby reducing racial and class inequalities and the harms caused by mass incarceration (Brown et al., 2016; Clear, 2009). This strategy can go a long way toward reducing violence against women and alleviating the negative consequences of reporting violence to law enforcement.

REFERENCES

Ackerman, J., & Love, T. P. (2014). Ethnic group differences in police notification about intimate partner violence. *Violence Against Women, 20*, 162–185.

Alvarez, C. P., Davidson, P. M., Fleming, C., & Glass, N. E. (2016). Elements of effective interventions for addressing intimate partner violence in Latina women: A systematic review. *PLOS ONE, 11*, e0160518.

Belknap, J., & Holsinger, K. (2006). The gendered nature of risk factors for delinquency. *Feminist Criminology, 1*, 48–71.

Benson, M. L., Fox, G. L., DeMaris, A., & Van Wyk, J. (2003). Neighborhood disadvantage, individual economic distress and violence against women in intimate relationships. *Journal of Quantitative Criminology, 19*, 207–235.

Brown, D., Cunneen, C., Schwartz, M., Stubbs, J., & Young, C. (2016). Justice reinvestment: A response to mass incarceration and racial disparity In *Justice reinvestment: Winding back imprisonment* (pp. 17–53). London: Palgrave Macmillan.

Burgess-Proctor, A. (2012). Pathways of victimization and resistance: Toward a feminist theory of battered women's help-seeking. *Justice Quarterly, 29*, 309–346.

Butcher, F., Galanek, J. D., Kretschmar, J. M., & Flannery, D. J. (2015). The impact of neighborhood disorganization on neighborhood exposure to violence, trauma symptoms, and social relationships among at-risk youth. *Social Science & Medicine, 146*, 300–306.

Cepeda, A., & Valdez, A. (2003). Risk behaviors among young Mexican American gang-associated females: Sexual relations, partying, substance use, and crime. *Journal of Adolescent Research, 18*, 90–106.

Chesney-Lind, M. (1989). Girls' crime and woman's place: Toward a feminist model of female delinquency. *Crime & Delinquency, 35*, 5–29.

Clear, T. R. (2009). *Imprisoning communities: How mass incarceration makes disadvantaged neighborhoods worse.* New York: Oxford University Press.

DeNavas-Walt, C., Proctor, B. D., & Smith, J. C. (2010). *Current population reports: Income, poverty, and health insurance coverage in the United States, 2009.* Washington, DC: U.S. Census Bureau.

Durán, R. (2013). *Gang life in two cities: An insider's journey.* New York: Columbia University Press.

Economic Innovation Group. (2017). Distressed communities index. http://eig.org/dci.

Erickson, P. I. (2010). *Latina adolescent childbearing in East Los Angeles.* Austin: University of Texas Press.

Fleury-Steiner, R. E., Bybee, D., Sullivan, C. M., Belknap, J., & Melton, H. C. (2006). Contextual factors impacting battered women's intentions to reuse the criminal legal system. *Journal of Community Psychology, 34*, 327–342.

Fry, R., & Taylor, P. (2012). The rise of residential segregation by income. Pew Research Center. https://sph.umd.edu.

Hser, Y.-I., Hoffman, V., Grella, C. E., & Anglin, M. D. (2001). A 33-year follow-up of narcotics addicts. *Archives of General Psychiatry, 58*, 503–508.

Hser, Y.-I., Huang, D., Chou, C.-P., & Anglin, M. D. (2007). Trajectories of heroin addiction: Growth mixture modeling results based on a 33-year follow-up study. *Evaluation Review, 31*, 548–563.

Kennedy, A. C., & Prock, K. A. (2018). "I still feel like I am not normal": A review of the role of stigma and stigmatization among female survivors of child sexual abuse, sexual assault, and intimate partner violence. *Trauma, Violence, & Abuse, 19*, 512–527.

Klevens, J. (2007). *An overview of intimate partner violence among Latinos*. Thousand Oaks, CA: Sage.

LeCompte, M. D., & Schensul, J. J. (1999). *Designing and conducting ethnographic research* (Vol. 1). New York: Rowman Altamira.

Lee, T. (2015). Child welfare practice in domestic violence cases in New York City: Problems for poor women of Color. *Women, Gender, and Families of Color, 3*, 58–87.

Lopez, D. (2017). High intimate partner violence rates among Latinas in Bushwick: A literature review. *21st Century Social Justice, 4*, 5.

McDaniels-Wilson, C., & Belknap, J. (2008). The extensive sexual violation and sexual abuse histories of incarcerated women. *Violence Against Women, 14*, 1090–1127.

Menjívar, C., & Salcido, O. (2002). Immigrant women and domestic violence: Common experiences in different countries. *Gender & Society, 16*, 898–920.

Messing, J. T., Becerra, D., Ward-Lasher, A., & Androff, D. K. (2015). Latinas' perceptions of law enforcement: Fear of deportation, crime reporting, and trust in the system. *Affilia, 30*, 328–340.

Montalvo-Liendo, N. (2009). Cross-cultural factors in disclosure of intimate partner violence: An integrated review. *Journal of Advanced Nursing, 65*, 20–34.

Niolon, P. H., Kearns, M., Dills, J., Rambo, K., Irving, S., Armstead, T., & Gilbert, L. (2017). Preventing intimate partner violence across the lifespan: A technical package of programs, policies, and practices (0160939687). Atlanta: Centers for Disease Control and Prevention.

Nowotny, K. M., Belknap, J., Lynch, S., & DeHart, D. (2014). Risk profile and treatment needs of women in jail with co-occurring serious mental illness and substance use disorders. *Women Health, 54*, 781–795.

Pew Charitable Trust. (2018). 35 states reform criminal justice policies through justice reinvestment: Legislative action aims to increase public safety return on corrections spending. www.pewtrusts.org.

Ragin, C. C. (1999). The distinctiveness of case-oriented research. *Health Services Research, 34*(5 pt. 2), 1137–1151.

Reaves, B. A. (2017). Police response to domestic violence, 2006–2015 (NCJ 250231). Washington, DC: U.S. Department of Justice, Bureau of Justice Statistics.

Rios, V. M., & Vigil, J. D. (2017). *Human targets: Schools, police, and the criminalization of Latino youth*. Chicago: University of Chicago Press.

Strauss, A., & Corbin, J. M. (1990). *Basics of qualitative research: Grounded theory procedures and techniques*: Thousand Oaks, CA: Sage.

Tucker, S. B., & Cadora, E. (2003). Justice reinvestment. *Ideas for an Open Society, 3*, 2–7.

Valdez, A. (2007). *Mexican American girls and gang violence: Beyond risk*. New York: Springer.

Valdez, A., & Cepeda, A. (2008). The relationship of ecological containment and heroin practices. In Y. F. Thomas, D. Richardson, & I. Cheung (Eds.), *Geography and drug addiction* (pp. 159–173). Dordrecht: Springer.

Valdez, A., Kaplan, C. D., & Cepeda, A. (2000). The process of paradoxical autonomy and survival in the heroin careers of Mexican American women. *Contemporary Drug Problems, 27*, 189–212.

Valdez, A., Nowotny, K. M., Zhao, Q.-W., & Cepeda, A. (2018). Interpersonal partner relationships, bonds to children, and informal social control among persistent male offenders. *Social Problems, 66*, 468–483.

Wattanaporn, K. A., & Holtfreter, K. (2014). The impact of feminist pathways research on gender-responsive policy and practice. *Feminist Criminology, 9*, 191–207.

Williams, D. R., & Collins, C. (2001). Racial residential segregation: A fundamental cause of racial disparities in health. *Public Health Reports, 116*, 404–416.

PART II

Latina Offenders from Court to Correctional Involvement

4

Demasiados Problemas

A Focus on Gender, Ethnicity, and Juvenile Diversion Programming

LISA PASKO AND JEAN DENIOUS

Before the mid-1970s, most formal discussions of juvenile offenders and juvenile court did not include specific inquiry into girls' lives. Today, however, female juvenile offenders are no longer invisible and have become one of the fastest growing segments of the juvenile justice system. Girls have become an increasing proportion of arrests, court referrals, adjudications, and commitments over the past three decades (Chesney-Lind & Pasko, 2013; Federal Bureau of Investigation, 2018; Sickmund, Sladky, & Kang, 2015). In particular, the number of girls placed in residential facilities for committing a person offense has more than tripled in the past thirty years (Chesney-Lind & Pasko, 2013; Sickmund et al., 2015). These findings have led scholars to examine girls' pathways to offending, the justice system they experience, and the rationale behind the decisions made for them (e.g., Bloom, Owen, Deschenes, & Rosenbaum, 2002; Chesney-Lind & Shelden, 2014; Mallicoat, 2007; Pasko, 2010, 2011).

Indeed, research has shown that girls in trouble with the law experience a vast set of interconnected difficulties, from problems resulting from childhood trauma and abuse to struggles with self-worth, stress, and anger (to name a few, Belknap, 2014; Belknap & Holsinger, 2006; Bloom et al., 2002; Chesney-Lind & Pasko, 2013; DeHart & Moran, 2015; Miller & Mullins, 2009). Girl offenders are more likely than their male counterparts to experience disrupted families, to have problematic romantic relationships, and to lack education about substance abuse and chemical dependency (Acoca & Dedel, 1998; Artz, Blais, & Nicholson,

2000; Bergen, Martin, Richardson, Allison, & Roeger, 2004; Giordano, 2010; Leve & Chamberlain, 2004; Schaffner, 2006). As the "pathways" perspective illustrates, such stressors and struggles precipitate coping and escape strategies that often result in status offending and low-level delinquency (Acoca & Dedel, 1998; Chesney-Lind & Pasko, 2013; Miller & Mullins, 2009). Such theories also underscore female juvenile offenders' high rates of coexisting mental health (in particular, depression) and substance abuse disorders (Bailey & McCloskey, 2005; Fishbein, Miller, Winn, & Dakof, 2009; Liu, 2004; Pasko & Chesney-Lind, 2010; Schaffner, 2006; Teplin et al., 2006; Widom, 1995; Zahn, 2009).

Despite increased focus on girls in the justice system, girls of Color and the court and correctional decisions made about and for them remain an area neglected and fairly scarce in the field of criminal or juvenile justice. Indeed, girls' experiences within the juvenile justice system—particularly those of girls of Color—can further exacerbate pathways factors leading to their arrests. As the introduction to this volume noted, the visibility of Latina girls is increasingly apparent and yet neglected in research.

Given girls' increased participation in juvenile justice and the confounding problems created by inadequate understanding and treatment of them by the system, research that further explicates gender and ethnic differences in girls' pathways toward criminal activities as well as the institutional response to them is needed. This chapter rectifies this deficit through an examination of Latina and white girls' experiences inside and outside the justice system. This chapter examines pathways toward delinquency and court involvement and diversion programming. It also investigates the social stressors (family, school, peer, and romantic attachments) leading to delinquency as well as the girls' reactions to their justice involvement. This chapter concludes with policy recommendations for gender- and culturally-sensitive programming.

Methods

This chapter uses a multimethod approach in order to represent girls from every level of the justice system: from those in diversion (not filed in court) to adjudicated female youth on probation to girls with histories of secure confinement. The data utilized in the first section result from information collected by juvenile diversion programs in one western U.S. state. In this state, funding is administered to eligible juvenile diversion programs that meet the criteria of providing pre-file diversion to youth, ages ten to seventeen, who have been arrested for the first time for a district-level offense. Historically, the state's funding has encompassed over twenty programs across fifteen judicial districts, with programs based either in the community or in district attorney's (DA) offices and varying considerably in the range and types of services provided. The dataset derived from these programs consist of 9,146 (95.6 percent) youth who were screened at intake and then accepted into a diversion program, from 2011 to 2015. Just over half (51.3 percent) of the youth were referred to diversion pre-file, with about one-third (33.2 percent) referred at pre-adjudication and 15.5 percent post-adjudication (i.e., deferred sentence or as a condition of probation). Youth were referred primarily from a DA's Office (67.3 percent), with referrals also coming from the district court judge (14.2 percent) and district court probation (12.9 percent). The remaining referrals came from police/sheriff's offices (4.9 percent) or another diversion program. All analyses in this chapter are derived from the accumulated dataset, which includes 3,274 girls (36 percent of the overall sample) and 1,061 Latina girls (11.7 percent of the overall sample, and 32 percent of all girls in the sample) who were arrested and referred to one of the state-funded diversion programs.

As part of the overall evaluation, program staff (e.g., case managers) collected and documented background and process data on each youth as part of their formal intake and exit processes. Intake data, collected at the point at which the youth entered the program, included information on youth background and demographics as well as basic information about the type of offense, program referral source, and referral or adjudication status. Underscored in this chapter are school status and disciplinary history, prior police contact, level and type of offense, and charge leading to arrest. Exit data, documented at the point at which the youth completed the program, included information on services received by the youth, whether the youth successfully completed or not, and if new charges were filed *during* the youth's participation in diversion. Chi-square analysis was used to assess differences in descriptive background factors; logistic regression was used to predict categorical outcomes (e.g., recidivism).

To assess the long-term outcomes, recidivism data (a filing or filings for a new offense, criminal, misdemeanor, or juvenile delinquency, up to one year after they exited the program) were also collected through cooperation with the state's division of criminal justice. It is important to note the uneven distribution of youth across programs. Programs ranged considerably in size, with the two largest programs accounting for approximately one-third (33.0 percent) of the youth in this sample, the next six largest programs also accounting for nearly one-third (32.6 percent) of youth, and the remainder of the sample (34.4 percent) distributed across the remaining fourteen programs.

Coming from the same western state, the data in the second part of this chapter include questionnaire research ($n = 151$) from participants in a gender-specific intervention program and in-depth interviews with fifteen of its participants (nine Latina and six white, non-Latina). The survey part of the data included questions pertaining to demographics, arrest records, school performance, family background and stressors, community dynamics, mental health, violence exposure and behavior, and gang involvement. Although not purposeful in design to capture a diverse sample, 64 Latina girls and 87 white, non-Latina girls completed the questionnaires. All of the girls had been referred to court. They varied, however, in their experiences with court and corrections, ranging from first-time offenders referred by teen court ($n = 98$) to formal adjudication and probation only ($n = 35$) to probation with some previous experience in secure confinement, such as detention ($n = 18$).

For the interviews, girls were mostly recruited ($n = 13$) from the questionnaire sample, with help from the program staff. Two were referred from outside this sample, as they had previously completed the program (but not the questionnaire). Of the fifteen, nine had experience with formal adjudication and (Latina $n = 7$; white $n = 2$). So as to gather participants' interpretations of their experiences and expressions of their life narratives and in order to attenuate preconceived notions about girl offenders' lives, intensive interviewing with a broad, open-ended instrument was the method chosen (see Charmaz & Belgrave, 2003). Girls were asked open-ended inquiries into interpretations of their significant childhood to contemporary experiences and prompted intermittently to discuss family structures and relationships, neighborhood and community dynamics, school participation, significant relationships, sexual behavior, drug use, criminal behavior including violence, mental and physical health, and social/justice system involvement. Several of the girls also gave follow-up interviews. Extensive notes were taken during the interviews, and all but five interviews were audiotaped as well. After recording notes and doing transcriptions, the first author and her research assistant worked independently in their coding to ensure incisive thematic analysis, meeting biweekly to review notes, read through transcripts, and compare codes.

The following sections show the various backgrounds, pathway factors, and diversion program success for Latina and white system-involved girls. First, the programming data are presented, followed by the questionnaire and interview research, with ethnic similarities and differences unpacked.

Results

In looking at first-time female offenders, several statistically significant differences emerge between Latina and white girls. Latina diversion participants were significantly more likely than their white counterparts to have been suspended in the past year (Latina females—19.8 percent, white females—10.8 percent), $\chi^2(1) = 40.72$, and to have a lower average age of first police contact, 13.8 years old for Latina girls versus 14.3 years old for white girls. White females and Latinas differed significantly as well in terms of prior offenses, $\chi^2(5) = 19.00, p = .002$. Latinas were more likely to have a misdemeanor charge, while white girls were more likely to have a petty charge (misdemeanor charges—68.5 percent of Latina females vs. 61.6 percent of white females; petty charges—17.2 percent of Latinas vs. 22.9 percent of white females). Latina and white females also differed significantly from each other on type of charge, $\chi^2(5) = 98.66$, $p < .001$, with higher percentages of person charges among Latina females (41.0 percent vs. 26.0 percent for white females) and higher percentages of drug charges among white females (24.6 percent vs. 12.6 percent for Latinas). A closer look at the offenses revealed that disorderly conduct and person offenses were much more common for Latinas than for white females.

TABLE 4.1. Statistically Significant Differences between Latina and White Girls in Diversion

Characteristic	Latina (n = 1,061)	White (n = 1,635)
School suspension*	19.8%	10.8%
Age of first police contact*	$M = 13.8$	$M = 14.3$
Misdemeanor**	68.5%	61.6%
Petty charge**	17.2%	22.9%
Person offenses*	41.0%	26.0%
Drug charges*	12.6%	24.6%
Disorderly conduct*	11.9%	2.9%

*$p < .001$. **$p < .002$.

Moreover, once participants entered the program, several attributes were assessed, including intentions to engage in risky behaviors as well as level of self-esteem. Latina females had significantly lower risky behavioral intentions scores at baseline, compared to white females ($p = .017$). Latina females also had marginally significantly higher reports of self-esteem at baseline, compared to white females ($p = .056$). In terms of program completion and recidivism, Latinas had a slightly higher rate of successful completion than white females, 90.8 percent versus 88.3 percent, respectively, however this difference fell short of statistical significance. Despite these background and offense distinctions, there was no difference in the rate of recidivism between Latinas (10.1 percent) and white females (10.5 percent).

The second part of this project took a deeper dive into the lives of system-involved girls who participated in an intervention program. Table 4.2 summarizes their backgrounds. Overall, theft charges were the most frequent offense for both white and Latina girls, while both also faced drug charges. Latina girls were arrested significantly more often for person offenses, whereas white girls were arrested for status offense (e.g., curfew violations, truancy) more often. Additionally, Latina and white girls experienced similarities in several family and community factors. They both had issues with housing insecurity and frequent moves (over three-fourths of respondents), although the overwhelming majority did live with one or more parents (i.e., instead of foster care or extended family). Most also reported that (at least one) parent had employment, although over half of the girls reported chronic medical/mental health problems in their immediate families. Several statistically significant differences did emerge. Latina girls reported witnessing violence in their homes or communities, having a gang-involved family member, having a parent with substance abuse issues, and having someone important jailed, more often than white girls reported.

In the areas of mental health, Latina and white girls similarly expressed feelings of loneliness as well as feelings of self-respect and

TABLE 4.2. Backgrounds of White and Latina Juvenile Offenders

	White ($n = 87$)	Latina ($n = 64$)
Arrests		
Assault (simple)*	19.5%	39.1%
Theft	72.4%	62.5%
Drugs	15.7%	21.9%
Status offenses*	46.0%	31.2%
Family and community background		
Housing insecure	86.2%	78.1%
Parents have trouble finding/keeping work	35.6%	34.4%
Has witnessed violence in the home*	47.1%	75.0%
Family or friends are gang-involved*	5.7%	31.3%
Lives with one or more parent	81.6%	84.4%
Parent has drug or alcohol problem*	43.7%	32.8%
Family member has chronic health issue	57.1%	59.3%
Someone important to them has been to jail*	26.4%	70.3%
Has witnessed violence in the community*	67.8%	82.8%
Mental and emotional health		
Frequent sadness/loneliness	83.9%	87.5%
Can't stop thinking about something bad that happened to them*	56.3%	70.3%
Has self-respect/self-worth	79.3%	84.4%
School		
Got into a fight at school*	35.6%	71.9%
Dropped from school*	37.9%	46.8%
Qualified for free or reduced lunch*	41.4%	59.4%

*χ^2, $p < .01$.

self-worth. However, Latina girls reported more frequent thoughts on prior trauma than did white girls ("cannot stop thinking about something bad that happened to me"). Latina girls also reported differences with white girls at school, in terms of fighting, dropping out, and qualifying for free or reduced lunch.

The interviews with girls explicate the reasons for the similarities and differences in the girls' responses. The girls shared how relationships in their lives can lead to feelings of loneliness and sadness, how family can provide sites of both strain and support, how community dynamics can amplify exposure to violence and victimization, and how school can be a place of success as well as stress, failure, and fights. The interviews also showed how all of these contexts and processes are situated in ethnic and gendered structures.

Family and Relationships

Overall, the presence of myriad forms of deprivation and oppression were apparent in girls' narratives. Housing instability, poverty, stressful fighting, drug and alcohol abuse, broken attachments to caregivers, and physical and mental health problems were strong memories for many of the interviewees. For Latina girls, this seemed particularly true, with the majority qualifying for free or reduced lunch, moving frequently, witnessing violence within the household, dealing with a physically ill or mentally compromised family member, experiencing policing and justice surveillance, and/or having someone they loved jailed recently. As one Latina interviewee (age sixteen) noted, "We've moved around a lot, especially after Dad went away [to jail]."

Experiences of violence in the home and consequent child protection services and justice interventions were common memories among interviewees. Additionally, the majority of Latina girls felt they could not speak openly about the problems their families experienced and were frequently worried about detection and inspection of their families' problems. Having limited memories of accessing a private health care system for mental health and/or drug treatment, they felt it was their responsibility to shoulder such secrecy: "We just don't talk about those things. It's no one's business" (Latina, sixteen). White girls expressed their parents' drug and alcohol use more openly and more often, often using medicalizing language:

> My mom went away for a while when I was younger. I didn't understand it then but it was because she needed drug treatment. (white girl, eighteen)

> I always sort of wished someone would find out how much my mom drinks and how she can be a hypocrite like that. She gets all upset if I smoke pot, but then how many times I've had to, you know, pick her up and help her when she has had too much to drink. (white girl, sixteen)

> My mom has a disease and that is what can be tough. (white girl, sixteen)

Other interviewees explained that while family was of primary importance to them, they felt overwhelmed by the responsibilities placed on them for caretaking of younger siblings, extended families, and general household care. When interviewees discussed their conversations and interactions within their families, they often would share how their families needed them for instrumental reasons, but otherwise discarded (or "did not have time for") their opinions and emotional reactions, often leading them to feel weak, difficult, unwanted, and inconvenient. Wishing to be alleviated from such duties, girls' desire for a "normal" life often conflicted with such socioeconomic demands of the household. Latina girls reported feeling this way more often ($n = 6$), especially those whose parents were of "uncertain" status ($n = 3$). This also translated into compromised bonds and developing disconnection with parents at times, while simultaneously feeling like a disappointment and failure to the family:

> I would do anything for my parents. . . . But sometimes they don't . . . understand. They are from a different place, I feel, although I know they love me and want to provide everything for me. I just feel like sometimes, I wish I could just not have to be around to do so much and then not fight about that. (Latina, seventeen)

> My parents work all the time and aren't around a lot so that means I have to be there for my sisters. (Latina, sixteen)

I just want to be like my other friends and do what they do and go out and stuff, not have to always be doing something. I feel like I always have to be doing something for someone else. I don't think my mom and dad get that. (Latina, eighteen)

I feel like I have been a disappointment to my family. (Latina, seventeen)

Strained connections with their mothers, pain of absent fathers, and their resistance to feelings of inferiority also contributed to girls' assaults in the home, with younger siblings or mothers as victims. For example, one interviewee (Latina, eighteen)—whose early childhood was marked by her father's chronic unemployment and alcohol abuse and her mother's absence as she worked two jobs—eventually initiated a physical fight with her mother. Molested by her father starting at age five, she and her younger brother were removed temporarily to foster care, and her father was subsequently arrested, convicted, and incarcerated for the sex offense against her. After "unhelpful" therapy ("I don't remember it doing anything for us") and returning to her mother's home, she began breaking curfew, smoking, drinking, and ditching school by age eleven and was arrested for shoplifting when she was twelve. "When we went back to live with [her mother], I never listened to her. I hated her." The verbal contest between them, blaming her mother for her father's actions and absence, culminated into violence: "I do blame my mom. I know she works a lot and I speak English and she doesn't really, so we don't talk much, but I just think if she were, I don't know, just did something different for me, I would be okay, it would be better. I just think that if she made different choices my life would be different and it's unfair to put it all on my dad."

Community and School

Community dynamics also varied for Latina and white girls, although the majority have witnessed some form of violence. Latina girls reported early memories with police contact while out in the neighborhood ($n = 4$) and first contact while at home ($n = 5$), whereas white girls' ($n = 4$) first memories with police were with their own arrest ($n = 3$) or a call to their homes ($n = 3$). Additionally, all but one of the Latina girls in the interview part of this study reported witnessing community violence, and nearly two-thirds knew someone in a gang. This exposure to criminality and violence often amplified girls' fears of being victimized as well as their needs to display toughness and bravado ("must be tough"; Latina, eighteen).

> Just the other week I saw a guy get beat up. Happens a lot. (Latina, seventeen)

> It can be scary at times. (Latina, sixteen)

> I don't like to talk about it [gang friends]. It's just the way it is. (Latina, sixteen)

> Lots of bad stuff happen around me, but I'm strong. I can do it. (Latina, eighteen)

However, both Latina and white girls expressed that they would feel their greatest unease or lack of safety while waiting for the bus or walking home from or being at school.

> I have seen stuff on the bus, but generally, just fights at school. Or drugs or stuff like that. (white girl, eighteen)

> I have seen lots of fights, my brothers that one time, and in the park when that shooting happened. It's all around. (Latina, eighteen)

> I feel scared at times, 'cause I've seen things. (Latina, eighteen)

Navigation of the school environment was also a highly problematic area of interviewees' lives. Fewer than half were earning or had earned passing grades; only half had expectations of going on to further education, and six had histories of suspension or expulsions. Despite a range of academic abilities, school was marginalizing for them. The majority of interviewees reported positive experiences in early elementary school—teachers appeared invested in them and cared about them, classmates were friends, and they had a certain ease in scholastic work. As girls moved through middle and high school, they felt the perception of them changed, as if they were no longer deserving of positive attention but rather of suspicion and surveillance. In these middle and high school years, interviewees felt characterizations of them experienced in their households ("manipulative," "dramatic," "difficult") became impressed upon them in the school environment as well. For Latina girls in this study, they also reported feeling judged as "lazy," and "untrustworthy," often an unworthy time commitment from the teachers:

> Teachers used to like us and care about us. Now, they just want to get rid of me because I make problems. (Latina, seventeen)

> I got into it with this girl who kept texting [rumors] about me and we got into it in class so the teacher sent us to the principal's office and when we both tried to explain our sides, he got tired of us and told us it was over, he was done with it, and told us to stop and leave. So we did, but it didn't stop, and then the next week, she grabbed my hair in the bathroom and cut it, so I hit her and now I'm here [court-ordered program]. But they knew about it. They didn't care. It's like, just catch 'em fighting so we can get kicked out. (Latina, fifteen)

Girls in this study did report tremendous conflict with other girls ($n = 19$), often actively avoiding friendships with other girls and hanging out exclusively with a male peer group or male romantic partner. Their entrance into "boy world" was not liberating for them, however. They felt boys often used them sexually or promoted girl-on-girl fights as a way of settling their own conflicts or as a form of entertainment. Similar to their attachments in their homes, the quality of their relationships also produced volatility, with girls simultaneously speaking boastfully about how boyfriends were their best friends as well as a great source of pain, disloyalty, and betrayal. Such continuous conflicts at home, in the community, and at school often caused both Latina and white girls to express despair, sadness, and loneliness, and perseveration on bad things that have happened; this applied more often for white girls. This may be due partly to the fact that white girls had more experience with private counseling and thinking about their mental health and personal feelings in such ways. It is also partly due to the fact that they reported being left physically alone more often—having fewer extended family members as part of their lives and having fewer neighborhood associations and school friends, whether positive or negative:

> I feel lonely a lot. I'm alone a lot. (white girl, seventeen)

> No, I'm not alone, but I do get stressed and feel bad for what I am doing to everyone. (Latina, sixteen)

> Who would want my life? (white girl, eighteen)

> I've never really had a best [girl] friend, and I don't get along with my mom much. I'd like to have a better relationship with my mom. We just don't communicate like we should. I would say yeah, I do feel lonely at times. (white girl, seventeen)

> Right now, I'm on a couch and wonder where we [she and infant son] will sleep next. [My family] is having a time with it [having baby]. So I do feel alone. (Latina, eighteen)

With an absence of close confidantes and difficulty forming bonds with peers, mentors, and trusting adults, white interviewees were often left feeling like they were constantly dealing with a lot of pain:

> Being a girl sucks. It's tough. You have to put up with so much bullshit, from other girls but just from people, in general. (white girl, nineteen)

> I know people do care about me. I wish they could see why I am the way I am, like what's really inside and then I am not in it this way by choice. (white girl, eighteen)

Experiences with the Juvenile Justice System

Unsurprisingly, girls encountered similar characterizations, judgments, and frustration once they entered the justice system, ranging from feelings of unfair arrests and exaggerated responses by school administrators to absent or ineffective intervention, constant judgment, and complicated relationships with case managers and probation officers, who sometimes shared nearby office space with their guidance counselors and school nurses. Additionally, when programming or counseling was offered or mandated by the court, interviewees felt suspicious and defiant with such services. Moreover, girls were reluctant to plead responsible because they wanted to avoid consequences, punishment, and added surveillance in their lives. However, such refusal to "take responsibility for their choices" for offenses was perceived by the interviewees as evidence of inherent flaws in their character: undeserving, irresponsible, and difficult. As one interviewee (white, fifteen) explained, "I feel like I have to take responsibility for everything but no one was responsible for me."

Moreover, several girls felt that their probation officers felt annoyed by them and thought they were a nuisance. This seemed predominantly true for Latinas ($n = 3$), whereas white girls, still frustrated by their correctional status, more frequently saw their probation officers ($n = 3$) as caring and attentive. Indeed, one white interviewee mentioned that her PO was a close confidante, taking her to a doctor's appointment and being available by phone often. She also explained, "I can tell that she [probation officer] hates it when I leave her long [voicemail] messages, but she ends up laughing about it with me. I know she wants me to do well. I don't want to disappoint her."

Conversely, Latina girls felt that their probation officers were not in a position to be helpful since they did not speak Spanish (for parents) nor understand "where I am coming from with my family, often recommending distance from family or friends considered 'undesirables'" (Latina, eighteen). They also did not appreciate the constraints that transportation or cost of programs had on families, according to several Latina girls interviewed:

> I was on my way [to court-ordered program] when this guy at the bus stop . . . well, he wasn't a good guy and my mom said I didn't have to go back to the program because it wasn't safe, but my PO said I had to and I'd have to find another way to get there, but I couldn't. So, it was like I was getting into more trouble just because I didn't want to be hurt and my mom didn't drive. (Latina, seventeen)

> My mom and dad don't get how they have to pay for things [with court] and it is not . . . like, we can only afford basic sort of stuff, so I don't know

how to handle costs, you know, and [PO] doesn't get it. It's like everyone is in trouble because I got caught [shoplifting] and that make me feel bad. (Latina, sixteen)

I stay quiet when I am around her [PO]. I won't cause problems that way. (Latina, sixteen)

My PO just acts annoyed with me all the time. (Latina, eighteen)

Conclusion

This chapter has illustrated key differences and similarities in Latina and white girls' pathways to delinquency and court involvement. As the first section of results showed, Latina girls were more likely than white girls to have a history of suspension, to be younger at first police contact, and to be charged with a person offense and disorderly contact. However, Latina girls were less likely to be charged with a drug offense and less likely to be assessed as having risky intentions. Indeed, Latina girls reported higher self-esteem and slightly higher program completion rates.

What emerges from the questionnaire and interview data is that these system-involved girls navigate challenging environments in their homes, communities, and schools, often exposed to multistructural disadvantages, such as housing insecurity, police surveillance, and violence/victimization; and this seemed more pronounced for Latina girls. Likewise, Latina girls also reported more issues with school retention and fights at school, whereas white girls expressed (more openly) issues with parents' drug and alcohol problems as well as being alone in dealing with such problems. Involvement in the juvenile justice system, too, felt challenging because of stressors at home and lack of funds to complete court-ordered requirements, although white girls showed more affinity and trust in their probation officers.

Policy and Practice Implications

This chapter has also shown that Latina girls are not identical in backgrounds, needs, experiences, and program services as their non-Hispanic, white counterparts. Yet their recidivism was low, their completion was high, and their resilience was likely. Diversion, indeed, seemed to work. As such, programs should be continually scrutinized to guarantee that they are serving as genuine alternatives to girls' incarceration rather than simply extending the social control of girls. There is a tendency for programs serving girls to become security oriented in response to girls' propensity to run away. A component of successful programming for girls must be advocacy as well as an appreciation for the multidecade effort to decarcerate youth and the difficulties that arose with such efforts.

What also emerges from this study is an evident policy implication. Schools (and other welfare and health service systems) are in need of revision and repair in order to adequately address system-involved girls' lives and needs, especially in terms of recognizing risks, understanding what is behind their delinquency, and offering trauma-informed care as well as real opportunities to address structural dislocation and disadvantage. We recognize that this might be a somewhat geographic-specific recommendation. In the United States, however, many districts remain focused on identifying and punishing delinquent girls, and officials often refuse to address the problems of these multiple failing systems. The content of gender-specific (or girl-sensitive) programs formed within the juvenile justice system requires special attention since the family court has a long history of paternalism and policing of girls' behavior without sensitive, nuanced, girl-centered approaches (Davidson, Pasko, & Chesney-Lind, 2011; Tracy, Kempf-Leonard, & Abramoske-James, 2009). Programming for this population often fails to offer girls spaces, experiences, and relationships that will move them away from criminogenic and violent pathways. While not apologizing for them or reducing them to victims of life circumstances, programming must address the obstacles that are presented by girls' perceptions of judgment and unfairness, with this being especially true for girls of Color. Indeed, programming needs to be culturally sensitive as well as incorporate diverse and inclusive staff who can dismantle stereotypical assumptions. For example, white girls in this study reported having more connection and trust with their probation officers. It is not a coincidence that all of the probation officers were white.

Indeed, scholarship on life histories of girls in trouble with the law has found that their "troubles" often went unnoticed and untreated by those charged to care for them. For example, Schaffner (2006) maintains that many girls in her study reported that their emotional conditions were overlooked by parents, justice professionals, and mental health practitioners. Instead, their coping strategies were often regarded by the court as evidence of their inability to take responsibility for their actions and of their propensity to be manipulative, hysterical, and in need of protection (see also Baines, 1997; Bond-Maupin, Bond-Maupin, & Leisenring, 2002; Gaarder, Rodriguez, & Zatz, 2004; Pasko, 2010). Interestingly, Schaffner (2006) also concludes that "being listened to" was the resource that girls most often requested (see also Davidson et al., 2011).

It is also imperative that research on female juvenile offenders further interrogate early entry points into the juvenile justice system and recommend policy and programming components to better serve girls' needs. Indeed, the picture becomes bleaker when programs that address Latina girls' cultural needs are examined. According to the Pew Research Center (2006), more than one out of five Latino youth fail to speak English with proficiency; an even higher percentage of their parents do not speak English well. Despite the obvious need for bilingual services, most juvenile justice settings are ill equipped to meet the linguistic needs of this population. This can have dire consequences when it comes to placement decisions and access to mental health treatment (Vera Institute of Justice, 2012). As previously mentioned, community-based programs for justice-involved girls sometimes fail to recognize stressors associated with transportation, safety, and costs of attending the program—all of which can explain noncompletion of this element of probation requirements and are stressors more often reported by Latina girls. Indeed, officials leading program development and its implementation need to acknowledge the developmental hurdles girls manage during their everyday lives; recognize their needs for healthy emotional attachment with caregivers, friends, and teachers; embrace diversity and inclusivity; break ethnic stereotypes; and recognize and amplify girls' perceived openings for change and resiliency.

REFERENCES

Acoca, L., & Dedel, K. (1998). *No place to hide: Understanding and meeting the needs of girls in the California justice system*. San Francisco: National Council on Crime and Delinquency.

Artz, S., Blais, M., & Nicholson, D. (2000). Developing girls' custody units. Unpublished report.

Bailey, J., & McCloskey, L. (2005). Pathways to adolescent substance use among sexually abused girls. *Journal of Abnormal Child Psychology, 33*, 39–54.

Baines, M. (1997). Mad, bad, or angry? *Youth Studies Australia, 16*, 19–24.

Belknap, J. (2014). *The invisible woman* (3rd ed.). Belmont, CA: Wadsworth.

Belknap, J., & Holsinger, K. (2006). The gendered nature of risk factors for delinquency. *Feminist Criminology, 1*, 48–71.

Bergen, H., Martin, G., Richardson, A., Allison, S., & Roeger, L. (2004). Sexual abuse, antisocial behaviour and substance use: Gender differences in young community adolescents. *Australian and New Zealand Journal of Psychiatry, 38*, 34–41.

Bloom, B., Owen, B., Deschenes, E. P., & Rosenbaum, J. (2002). Improving juvenile justice for females: A statewide assessment for California. *Crime & Delinquency, 48*, 526–552.

Bond-Maupin, L., Bond-Maupin, J. R., & Leisenring, A. (2002). Girls' delinquency and the justice implications of intake workers' perspectives. *Women & Criminal Justice, 13*, 51–77.

Charmaz, K., & Belgrave, L. L. (2003). Qualitative interviewing and grounded theory analysis. In J. Gubrium (Ed.), *Sage handbook of interview research: The complexity of the craft* (pp. 347–363). Thousand Oaks, CA: Sage.

Chesney-Lind, M., & Pasko, L. (2013). *The female offender* (3rd ed.). Thousand Oaks, CA: Sage.

Chesney-Lind, M., & Shelden, R. G. (2014). *Girls, delinquency, and juvenile justice* (3rd ed.). Belmont, CA: Wadsworth.

Davidson, J. T., Pasko, L., & Chesney-Lind, M. (2011). "She's way too good to lose": An evaluation of Honolulu's girls court. *Women & Criminal Justice, 21*, 308–327.

DeHart, D., & Moran, R. (2015). Poly-victimization among girls in the justice system: Trajectories of risk and associations to juvenile offending. *Violence Against Women, 21*, 291–312.

Federal Bureau of Investigation. (2018). *Uniform Crime Reports, 2017*. Washington, DC: Department of Justice.

Fishbein, D., Miller, S., Winn, D., & Dakof, G. (2009). Biopsychological factors, gender, and delinquency. In M. Zahn (Ed.), *The delinquent girl* (pp. 84–106). Philadelphia: Temple University Press.

Gaarder, E., Rodriguez, N., & Zatz, M. S. (2004). Criers, liars, and manipulators: Probation officers' views of girls. *Justice Quarterly, 21*, 547–578.

Giordano, P. (2010). *Legacies of crime: A follow-up of the children of highly delinquent girls and boys*. New York: Cambridge University Press.

Leve, L., & Chamberlain, P. (2004). Female juvenile offenders: Defining an early-onset pathway for delinquency. *Journal of Child and Family Studies, 13*, 439–452.

Liu, R. (2004). The conditional effects of gender and delinquency on the relationship between emotional distress and suicidal ideation or attempt among youth. *Journal of Adolescent Research, 19*, 698–715.

Lopez, V., & Nuno, L. (2016). Latina and African American girls in the juvenile justice system: Needs, problems, and solutions. *Sociology Compass, 10*, 24–37.

Mallicoat, S. (2007). Gendered justice: Attributional differences between males and females in the juvenile courts. *Feminist Criminology, 2*, 4–30.

Miller, J., & Mullins, C. (2009). Feminist theories of girls' delinquency. In M. Zahn (Ed.), *The delinquent girl* (pp. 50–83). Philadelphia: Temple University Press.

Pasko, L. (2010). Damaged daughters: The history of girls' sexuality and the juvenile justice system. *Journal of Criminal Law and Criminology, 100*, 1099–1130.

Pasko, L. (2011). Setting the record "straight": Girls, sexuality, and the juvenile correctional system. *Social Justice, 37*, 7–26.

Pasko, L., & Chesney-Lind, M. (2010). Under lock and key: Trauma, marginalization, and girls' juvenile justice involvement. *Justice Research and Policy, 12*, 25–49.

Pasko, L., & Lopez, V. (2018). The Latina penalty: Juvenile court and correctional attitudes toward the Latina juvenile offender. *Journal of Ethnicity in Criminal Justice, 16*, 272–291.

Pew Research Center. (2006). Table 19: Language spoken at home and English-speaking ability by age, race, and ethnicity. Statistical portrait of Latinos in the United States. Washington, DC: Pew Research Center.

Schaffner, L. (2006). *Girls in trouble with the law*. New Brunswick, NJ: Rutgers University Press.

Sickmund, M., Sladky, A., & Kang, W. (2015). Easy access to juvenile court statistics: 1985–2005. National Center for Juvenile Justice. http://ojjdp.ncjrs.gov.

Teplin, L., Abram, K., McClelland, G., Mericle, A., Dulcan, M., & Washburn, J. (2006). *Psychiatric disorders of youth in detention*. Washington, DC: Office of Justice Programs.

Tracy, P., Kempf-Leonard, K., & Abramoske-James, S. (2009). Gender differences in delinquency and juvenile justice processing. *Crime & Delinquency, 55*, 171–215.

Vera Institute of Justice. (2012). If parents don't speak English well, will their kids get locked up? Language barriers and disproportionate minority contact in the juvenile justice system. Annie E. Casey Foundation. www.aecf.org.

Widom, C. (1995). *Victims of childhood sexual abuse—Later criminal consequences*. Washington, DC: Office of Juvenile Justice and Delinquency Prevention.

Zahn, M. (2009). *The delinquent girl*. Philadelphia: Temple University Press.

5

On the Run and In/Out of the System

Understanding Latina Girls in a Southern California Barrio

JERRY FLORES, XUAN SANTOS, AND
ARIANA OCHOA CAMACHO

The practice of "going on the run" is part of the fugitive and law enforcement lexicon that describes how both men and women attempt to avoid detection, evade and resist authorities, and avoid punishment by the court and subsequent incarceration (Goffman, 2009). Increasingly affected by community and family disruption, young Latinas, especially those "on the run," face gendered and racialized struggles while on the streets as well as the criminalization that comes along with the expansion of the justice system and zero-tolerance school policies (Davis, 2003; Díaz-Cotto, 2006; Morín, 2013; Olgin, 2010; Schaffner, 2008). However, mainstream criminological thought often lacks an inclusive understanding about surveillance and incarceration experiences from young Latinas' perspectives. Most feminist scholarship and research on young women of Color often overlook Latinas in particular (e.g., Díaz-Cotto, 2006). This chapter remedies such paucity and adds to our understanding of how the justice system affects communities of Color. It also challenges the Black-white binary often found in academic literature by highlighting the gendered, socioeconomic, and racialized challenges young system-involved Latinas experience. In doing so, this chapter provides insight about a group that is popularly imagined unidimensionally as "bad girls" who behave "badly" and whose actions are often divorced from larger discussions of inequality.

This chapter describes the experiences of Latinas on the run in a small Latino barrio in Southern California. We show how interlocking structures motivate and prompt these young women to evade contact with the very institutions and cultural forces that shape their constrained options. Drawing on two years of ethnographic research, we respond to the following questions: First, how do legal entanglements in their community affect young Latinas on the run? Second, how are these young people's lives affected by the structural arrangements, institutions, and social barriers they confront? Last, how do Latina youth describe the strategies and negotiations they make while they run? As we discuss in the following sections, Latinas on the run must negotiate a unique set of challenges, which are inextricably tied to their ethnicity, class, gender, and sexuality as well as the legacy of marginalization within their neighborhood.

Intersecting Identities and Criminalization

Interlocking structural arrangements are salient within the criminal justice system and often operate to keep men and women of Color in subordinated and marginalized positions (Alexander, 2010; Ocen, 2013). Several significant works have illustrated the ways systems of surveillance and formal social control are racialized, gendered, and heteronormative. For example, Miller's (2008) analysis of seventy-five urban Black adolescents (forty-five boys and thirty girls) with delinquent track records from various poor and crime-ridden neighborhoods in St. Louis, Missouri, showed how such youth experience frequent heightened and routinized gendered violence. Revealing that girls are harassed and experienced unreported sexual violence by men, Miller found that neighborhood violence was interwoven with class, gender, and racial oppression. Furthermore, the community was not responsive to girls' struggles, and schools did not take gendered violence seriously, with girls often blamed for their own victimization.

In his influential work, Victor Rios (2011) discussed the often-criminalized lives of Black and Latino male youth in Oakland, California. Rios's work highlights how masculinity instilled in young men a hypermasculine outcome in order to earn respect from community peers, who often deny them such dignity. The young adults were often hypercriminalized by what Rios calls the Youth Control Complex, an interlocking web of social institutions (the police, schools, the community for example) that systematically treats everyday marginalized youth behavior (and survival strategies) as deviant. Altogether, his work (Rios,

2006, 2011) addresses gender performativity among Latino men and their experiences with such scrutiny.

Indeed, Goffman also illustrated similar processes in her ethnographic study of young Black men in inner-city Philadelphia and how they dealt with police, the courts, and the probation and parole departments. Goffman (2009) argued that for these young men, their "illegal or semilegal status instilled an overriding fear of capture" (p. 340). This fear comes along with being suspicious of close friends and family in addition to avoiding institutions, places, and locations where they once turned for support. The consequence "is a complex interactive system in which ghetto residents become caught in constraining legal entanglements" (Goffman, 2009, p. 340).

Additionally, Brewer and Heitzeg (2008) argue that in order to understand systemic oppression within the criminal justice system and the prison-industrial complex, scholars must take on an intersectional analysis that incorporates "Black and Third World people, working-class people, older people, women, gay/lesbians, and physically challenged people" (p. 641). Understanding Latinas' experiences on the run requires such an intersectional approach that not only underscores girls' identities, interactions, and negotiations but also interrogates the effects of different institutions and the ways in which they interlock to shape Latinas experiences on the run.

California Juvenile Probation and El Valle Detention Center

In California, the juvenile justice system is intended to rehabilitate youthful offenders through community-based corrections and secure confinement (California Legislative Office [CLO], 2007). After minors are arrested, law enforcement agents take them to juvenile halls, managed by county probation departments. Youth placed in secure detention by the probation department may then be referred to adult court by the district attorney or be placed on formal probation, informal probation, house arrest, group housing, or a combination of these upon their release.

County probation departments supervise 97 percent of all juveniles in the California criminal justice system.[1] To give a sense of the scale of the number of young people under discussion, 222,512 underage individuals were arrested in California in 2005, roughly the size of a medium city (CLO, 2007). After arrest, 87 percent of these young people were referred to local probation departments, with the vast majority of these arrested juveniles eventually ending up on some type of community supervision (Rios, 2011). Given that people, including youth, can be stopped, searched, and drug tested by any law enforcement agents at any time without their consent (see Alexander, 2010), many of these juveniles end up rearrested, many times for violating the requirements of their probation (Chesney-Lind & Pasko, 2013).

Once youth are on formal probation, they must fulfill various demands to avoid a return to secure detention. For example, they are required to meet with their probation officer regularly. During these visits, they are frequently drug tested, with positive results earning detention. Youth on probation are also required to keep a passing grade point average, avoid excessive school absences, and keep to a curfew established by their probation officer. Some youth on probation are also prohibited from spending time in certain parts of the city or with particular individuals. Still other youth on probation are prevented from interacting with or wearing clothing associated with gangs. These so-called gang restrictions are typically doled out to Latina/o youth (Lopez-Aguado, 2016; Rios, 2006, 2011). Finally, youth are restricted from committing new crimes or having any further contact with criminal justice agents. Engaging in any restricted behavior results in a probation violation, which means that the youth is rearrested and taken to a detention center by the assigned probation officer. For the youth in this study, this means returning to El Valle Detention Center.

The county where El Valle is located is situated forty miles outside of Los Angeles, California.[2] The history of this barrio is similar to that of many Latino communities in Southern California. When under the control of the Mexican government, this community was used largely for agriculture and to raise cattle (Almaguer, 2009; Glenn, 2004). During this time, there was a large landed Mexican aristocracy that controlled the region (Almaguer, 2009; Glenn, 2004). After the signing of the Treaty of Guadalupe Hidalgo in 1848, when large parts of the Southwest came under the control of the U.S. government, this community continued to be an agricultural town (Almaguer, 2009). After this transition, a large encroachment of white settlers began to systematically disfranchise Latinos in order to take over these fertile lands. Similarly, white Americans began establishing their dominance, seized political power, and isolated Latinos into unwanted and underresourced parts of the city, often with the support of local authorities (Almaguer, 2009; Glenn, 2004). During the 1940s and 1960s, a large population of Latinos and newly arrived Mexicans revitalized the community and were able to recover some of their economic power (Almaguer, 2009; Calavita, 1992; Glenn, 2004). However, in the era of neoliberal economic policies and the subsequent end of well-paid factory work, El Valle became a challenging place to live. The drop in living-wage jobs, the increase in heroin and methamphetamine trafficking and addiction, the rise of mass policing and incarceration, and the peak in gang violence in Southern California further hurt the community in the 1980s. This coupled with the continued de facto and de jure discrimination of Latinos in the city completely devastated El Valle. These events left a ballooning gang and drug problem with no resources to address these issues, along with an expanding California prison system that seemed to envelope whole families and neighborhoods. Today, in a county of two hundred thousand individuals, three-quarters Latino, El Valle's residents are majority migrant workers, are working poor, or live below the poverty line. This historical and economic context is extremely important for the youth in our study; it directly shapes the experiences of young women on the run, as it engenders the specific conditions of race and class through which they lived gendered lives.

El Valle Juvenile Detention Facility and Legacy Community School

This study is based on research conducted at two locations. The first is El Valle Juvenile Detention Center. This newer juvenile detention center was built on fifty acres in the past twenty years and can hold upward of four hundred youth. Young people in this detention center are segregated by sex. Approximately 90 percent of the youth in this facility are boys, amounting to forty young women housed daily. The girls reside in one unit and are segregated from the boys. The girls' unit is divided into House 1 and House 2. House 1 holds juveniles who have not been adjudicated or who will reside in the facility fewer than thirty days. House

2 houses all other girls. Each cell in the facility can hold up to four people. The unit is connected to a recreational yard and central communal space called a day room, where the girls eat and interact with each other. Most of the youth incarcerated here are Latinas and were arrested for nonviolent drug-related offenses.

The second field site is Legacy Community School. Initially the first author planned to focus the research solely on El Valle Juvenile Detention Center. However, during fieldwork he met an educational administrator who connected him with the school. Shortly after visiting Legacy, the first author discovered multidimensional economic and administrative ties between the school and El Valle. He also noticed that the same youth who attended Legacy were often incarcerated at El Valle. Accordingly, he expanded the study to incorporate Legacy. This school serves sixth through twelve grade and is less than five miles from El Valle. The number of students served by Legacy usually hovers around a hundred fifty, even though its capacity is for three hundred students. For most students, this is their final stop in California public schools. Students also go to Legacy when they are expelled from other schools for violent offenses. Like El Valle, Legacy schools more Latino students and more students who are working class or poor, in comparison to other continuation schools (at Legacy, 80 percent of students are Latino and at least 66 percent are classified by school officials as "socioeconomically disadvantaged"). Additionally, Legacy contains more students struggling academically—92 percent of the students here are not proficient in math or English, and 15 percent have been diagnosed with a learning disability. Legacy offers no Advanced Placement courses, and no student has ever met the requirements to enter any of the four-year California public universities. At some point, a large portion of students at Legacy had contact with the juvenile justice system either in the form of secure detention or with supervision in their communities.

In Legacy, unlike other schools, there is a steady flow of incoming and outgoing youth from El Valle. Even if students are not on formal (court-mandated) probation when enrolling at Legacy, it is school policy to put them in contact with a probation agent. This school almost exclusively enrolls students who have been previously incarcerated at El Valle or similar juvenile detention facilities. This milieu creates additional scrutiny for its youth beyond any required by law or as part of a rehabilitation process.

Methods

Over twenty-four months, the first author conducted ethnographic research at El Valle Juvenile Detention Center and Legacy Community School. This investigation began through volunteer work in the educational program found within the detention center. During this time, the first author served as a tutor for young women in this detention center and later volunteered at Legacy in the same role, eventually securing permission to conduct research in these facilities. Doing fieldwork as a researcher and educational volunteer at El Valle Juvenile Detention Center (2009–2011) and at Legacy Community School (2010–2011), the first author conducted participant observation for approximately two years and gathered five hundred pages of single-spaced notes before conducting interviews or collecting additional data. This allowed him to restructure the initial research design to address the issues that appeared most at both field sites, notably the violence that exists at every stage of young women's lives and their negative experiences in the community. Once the first author reached the saturation point using field notes, he began conducting interviews.[3] During the participant observation stage, the significance of young women's experiences on the run emerged.

After collecting these preliminary data, forty-four in-depth, semistructured interviews with thirty-three different incarcerated girls were completed. The first author conducted all preliminary interviews inside secure detention. He also conducted focus groups and individual follow-up interviews at Legacy. Each formal interview lasted between one and three hours, with most lasting about an hour and a half, and all were conducted inside an empty soundproof interview room that teachers, counselors, and probation officers use to meet with incarcerated youth. All research in this study was approved by the institutional review board and received consent/assent by the interviewees, their parents, and/or their guardians.

Field notes and interviews were transcribed verbatim, with special attention paid to how youth in these settings discussed their experiences at home, at school, in detention, and in the community school. Our

TABLE 5.1. Sample Demographics

Name	Age	Race	Times Previously Incarcerated	Age First Incarcerated
Alexis	14	Latina	7	12
Amber	18	Latina	2	18
Anita	15	Asian	2	14
Aracely	19	Latina	19	13
Denise	17	Latina	5	14
Diana	17	Latina	6	14
Feliz	17	Latina	5	16
Jackie	15	Latina	4	14
Mari	15	Latina	5	14
Mariana	16	Latina	2	14
Maribel	18	Latina	—	15
Martha	17	Latina	—	—
Payasa	17	Latina	19	13
Rasta	15	White	6	13
Ray	17	Latina	—	14
Sandra	15	Latina	8	13
Virginia	16	Latina	1	13

analysis included a thorough examination of "negative cases" or alternative explanations. When we were confronted with a negative case, we addressed it in the text or incorporated it into the larger analysis. Looking for alternative explanations in this research ultimately strengthened our findings. This method of analyzing ethnographic data follows the process described in Emerson, Fretz, and Shaw (1995).

The phrase "on the run" or a discussion about being on the run appeared fifty-six different times during the coding process. This phrase emerged in field notes on twenty-two occasions and in interviews thirty-four times. In total seventeen different girls mentioned being on the run out of the thirty-three included in the study (see Table 5.1 for demographic information). The seventeen young people who discussed being on the run all described resonant themes with only slight variations. In other words, of the young women included in this study, seventeen discussed being on the run and had strikingly similar experiences.[4]

Latinas on the Run

In Goffman's research (2009, 2014), most of her participants went on the run for minor infractions, such as delinquent court fines, failure to appear in court, or probation or parole violations. These minor infractions led to warrants for young men's arrest. Similarly, most of the young women in this study went on the run for minor infractions. Unlike the people in Goffman's study, all of these young people were on probation. Thus, any actual or perceived infraction could lead to future arrest. This was exacerbated by the fact that these young women could be arrested for status offenses (such as truancy or curfew violations) given their juvenile probation status. Most of the reasons for going on the run were the same in both studies: to avoid arrest and subsequent incarceration. Even if going on the run was a relatively straightforward response to the immediate threat of incarceration, the decision-making process involved was complex.

Like Goffman's (2014) participants, young women in this study developed a set of strategies where they avoided routines, developed a hyperawareness of the police and avoided anywhere they might interact with law enforcement agents. These strategies also involved being prepared to run from police immediately and in any situation. They often participated in a complicated cost-benefit analysis before actually leaving. Within a series of minutes or seconds, these young people must engage in a process whereby they ask themselves if enduring the multiple challenges of being on the run is better than returning to secure confinement.

This was the first step our participants took in going on the run. During an interview, fourteen-year-old Alexis described how she decided to go on the run:

> Um, we were blazin' it [smoking marijuana], and I took the best hit ever, and then I turn around and Mr. Paul [principal] is right there. I had the smoke in my mouth, and I was like fuck. And then . . . I quickly gave . . . the piece [pipe] and the lighter to my friend and then I look[ed] at Mr. Paul who was just standing there, and that's when he said, "I think these girls are smoking dope." Then I couldn't hold it in any longer, and then I just started coughing and a bunch of smoke came out, and I was

like, "Oh my God." I had just walked away. I was like, "Okay, I'm not a part of this. Maybe you didn't see me." And then, um, he took my homegirls, and they were walking, and then one of them still had my piece and my lighter and she's like, "Here Alexis," right in front of his face. So then he brought me along and then I was like, "I'm gonna book it right now, guys. I can't get locked up." I always think I'm gonna come back in here for some reason, and I don't want to. So, then I was like, "I'm gonna book it right now. Anybody down?" And then Linda's like, "I'll book it with you. I'll book it with you." We ran and we were under this tunnel for like five hours.

Instead of getting caught and being sent to detention, Alexis ran and hid under a freeway underpass for five hours. She proceeded to stay on the run for several months. Alexis made this very serious decision within seconds of her former principal confronting her.

Martha, a seventeen-year-old third-generation Latina, faced a similar dilemma. This excerpt shows the intricacies in such decision making.

A Latina probation officer walked into the courtyard and approached Martha. The officer was dressed in black army fatigues and wore a utility belt that holds pepper spray, handcuffs, and other tools. Her dark glasses obscured her eyes. She asked Martha if she was ready to test. Martha replied, "I can't. I just went." The probation officer looks at her, and asked, "When can you go?" Martha replied, "I am not sure. I just went," and the officer walked away and said nothing. . . . When the officer left, Martha walked up to the first author and said, "Fuck. I'm going to get locked up. I smoked weed and did some coke yesterday. I smoke hella shit [meth] too. I'm a get busted. I'm fucked! What should I do?"

Thinking about options and looking down at her shoes, Martha generated a worried look and stated, "And I just got this stupid tattoo on my chest. I was drunk when I got it and it looks stupid. I can't wear any shirts anymore. I want to have it removed . . . get in trouble for that. What should I do?" Martha then lifted her sweater to show the undecipherable cursive writing on the middle of her chest. She told the first author the phrase spelled out the name of a local gang with which she is associated, and since her probation terms include a gang restriction that forbids her from associating with gangs or wearing gang paraphernalia, her new tattoo will no doubt earn her another probation violation.

Martha was able to delay her drug test, but it was inevitable that she would have to test soon. Given the drugs she took over the weekend, the test would likely be positive. She was left with a serious dilemma: should she leave and face several days, weeks, or months on the run, or should she test and go back to El Valle? Martha, unlike Alexis, decided to stay and face the consequences of testing positive. Her decision was not simple and entailed a tremendous amount of psychological and emotional stress.

These excerpts demonstrate the tricky and difficult decision-making processes these youth must engage in when deciding to go on the run. They are even more compelling when we consider the young ages of these two women, the short time frame to contemplate their choices, and the very real consequences of going on the run. Many young women in this study decided to go on the run after weighing the odds of receiving a probation violation. For example, they would run before taking a drug test they felt would be positive or right after a fight in the community or a disagreement with group home staff or a resident. After fighting with their parents or being asked to leave by their guardians, young people in this study also went on the run.

Getting Kicked Out

Young women in our study often reported being kicked out of their homes for violating gendered and culturally specific norms of behavior in the eyes of their guardians, and this often led to their decision to leave. Girls who violated heteronormative expectations—stayed out late, had premarital sex, or used drugs and alcohol—commonly found themselves in trouble at home. Diana, for example, initially started getting in trouble in the eighth grade: "I started dating . . . and my mom did not approve cause I was with a girl. And my mom, she doesn't go to church or nothing, she is not religious. She just didn't condone it." As Diana continued dating her girlfriend, this created tension between her and her mother. Ironically, her mother runs a group home for girls, and she used her insider knowledge of the placement and justice system to punish Diana or to have her placed in secure detention. For example, she kicked Diana out of the house and then told law enforcement officials that she ran away. Eventually, Diana decided that going on the run was preferable to going home, fighting with her mom, and getting subsequently arrested.

The young women in this project were also kicked out of their homes for experimenting with drugs, occasionally their parents treating them as "throwaways." Fifteen-year-old Mari said, "I ended up getting high on meth and spent one night away from my house. And I was afraid to go back because I did not want to get locked up. [Now] my mom does not want me back." Similarly, other young women would go on the run after fighting with their parents about dating, becoming pregnant at an early age, sneaking out at night, running away for short periods, or expressing their sexuality in overt ways. Conservative Latino cultural ideals can command that young women remain chaste until marriage, be submissive, and show deference to authority figures (Dietrich, 1998; Garcia, 2012). Garcia (2012) poignantly addresses how these ideals of Latina femininity are stereotypical, outdated, and erroneous. Still, some young girls continue to be held to these standards at home. The experiences of Diana and other young women in the study demonstrate how parents can kick or push out young Latina women for violating gendered and culturally specific expectations, instead of actual injury or harm caused by them.

After leaving home, most young women could not return easily and were forced to avoid institutions like home, group homes, community centers, and school. Due to their involvement with the juvenile justice system and their probation status, youth in this study were often issued a probation violation and a warrant upon leaving their homes. This meant that returning to the previously mentioned institutions would most often lead to an arrest and subsequent incarceration. Similar to men on the run (Goffman, 2014), these young women systematically devised strategies of avoidance. For example, seventeen-year-old Payasa said, "I can honestly say I haven't been to school since I was in eighth grade... [because] I was, um, always on the run." Similarly, fifteen-year-old Jackie discussed avoiding school in this field note:

> Jackie says she has been out [on the run] for three months and another girl says she's [on the run] for six months. Someone asked Jackie what

school she went to when she was on the "outs" [in the community] and she replied, "I didn't go to school. I was on the run. I'm not going to get caught up at school." Young women like Jackie avoid educational institutions because of their close linkages and collaborations with the criminal justice system.

Although the youth in our study were aware that they would face arrest, some attempted to return temporarily for survival reasons: clothes, food, hygiene supplies, or a hot shower. For the most part, returning to these institutions did not go well. Diana discussed her experiences returning home after being on the run:

> I came back . . . [after] I was kicked out, and I said [to my mom], "Oh, I came back . . . I wanna stay home again. I'm a take a shower." And then she put her hand up like "No!" and I said, "What are you doing. I'm 'a get in my room." And she is like "that's not your room, no more." I was like, "I need to get my clothes and stuff" and then she was just like, "No!" and I kinda pushed her hand away, and she pushed me back, and we fought. [She called the police and I was arrested.] And in the report, it says that she was afraid.

Her attempt to return home for fulfillment of her basic needs created conflict with her family and resulted in her mother calling the police. Diana made a calculated risk in the face of limited options to deal with this conflict with her mother.

Jackie, Diana, and Payasa all discussed a key component of being on the run. For young people with a probation violation and an arrest warrant, returning to places like home and school was not an option. Jackie and Payasa discussed how they avoided school in order to prevent being "caught up" or arrested for attempting to attend class. Indeed, Diana's excerpt demonstrates the dangers of attempting to return home after being on the run. Simply returning home for a shower and clothes resulted in a fight with her mother, a probation violation, a new criminal charge, and a return to El Valle.

While these excerpts focus on avoiding school and home, the young people in this research also used the same rationale for avoiding any institutions where there was the potential of encountering a law enforcement agent or an adult who might call the authorities. Payasa, for example, had been arrested nineteen times, and most of these arrests were related to her being on the run. Given this, Payasa and other girls like her avoided multiple institutions like school, group homes, and community centers for fear of arrest. While doing so, they missed out on potentially positive services and support. Given these circumstances, young Latina women often stayed on the run for extended periods and were exposed to multiple (and constant) forms of gendered violence.

Negotiating the Streets

Once young women went on the run, they made a slew of difficult choices related to finding shelter. Finding somewhere to stay was by far one of the most dangerous activities to negotiate for young women while on the run. It presented various barriers and exposed these young women to physical, psychological, and sexual violence. This part of being on the run also included the constant negotiation of their relationships with men and the threat of sexual assault and exploitation, which is commonplace for young women when contrasted to the experiences of young men. For most young women, the first step to finding somewhere to stay was getting a ride. Getting a ride for these young women was important, but problematic.

Given the general urban sprawl that is found in Southern California, mass transit was often inaccessible for the young women in this study. Thus, they depended on partners, ex-partners, friends, or acquaintances to pick them up after leaving their place of residence. Having a fast and semidependable ride made the difference between being arrested and avoiding the authorities. While youth often depended on these individuals to help pick them up, these acquaintances were usually unreliable or did not have access to their own transportation. The girls in our study reported waiting hours for a ride, having their partners steal a car to pick them up, or being told, "No, I won't pick you up." Given the general unreliability of people in their lives and their lack of family ties, the young women often attempted to find a random ride. This often included flagging down cars often driven by men.

Sandra, a fifteen-year-old third-generation Latina, discussed the process of getting a ride:

> I ran away with my homegirl [friend] and we ran onto the freeway. She was wearing nice clothes so she was trying to get a ride [waving her arms] . . . so we finally got a ride [to another city] from him, and she told the guy "if you take us home we will give you weed" and she gave him a sack of weed and her number [in case] she needed another ride.

For young women like Sandra, the simple act of finding a ride to a friend's house or to another city can be complicated. Young women who could not find a ride were often forced to choose between staying somewhere unsafe, facing the threat of sexual assault, getting arrested, or attempting to flag random cars. They often targeted cars driven by men and attempted to use their sexuality to negotiate a ride. Sandra and her friend made the extreme choice of jumping on a busy interstate freeway to find a ride to a city forty miles away. The promise of marijuana and alcohol satisfied the person who gave them a ride. However, young women also exchanged various forms of sexual contact or the promise of sex in order to acquire transportation.

In these examples, we can begin to see how gender, a historically segregated Latino community with little resources, and constant police surveillance interact to structure the experiences of young Latinas on the run in distinct and more challenging ways compared to those of young men. Moreover, the experiences of these young women are complicated when compared to those of other girls, whose communities may have better transportation, infrastructure, and resources. Getting a ride also exposed young women to potential sexual violence. Once youth relocated to somewhere safe from detection by authorities, they then had the difficult task of finding somewhere to stay. Most of the young people in this study attempted to stay with friends, distant family members, or a romantic partner. Initially, staying with friends worked well. Girls found a safe haven and were able to reduce their potential contacts with the criminal justice system by staying indoors. While these arrangements worked initially, they did not last long. Often, the young women in this study started drinking and consuming drugs in excess. This led to fights with their friends or partners and an increasingly chaotic living situation. Substance abuse and "partying" attracted older men with questionable motives to girls' new homes. Substance abuse also contributed to increasingly abusive treatment from romantic partners. This dynamic provoked fear and anxiety for girls about their vulnerability to sexual assault or an unwanted relationship. For example, eighteen-year-old Maribel describes staying with a friend while on the run:

> I was, like, fifteen and a half. I was living with my friend Alex. We had our own studio pretty much because her mom was the manager [of an apartment complex], so her mom wouldn't care if we had parties every night. And she [Alex] met this guy that lived across the way from us. He was, like, thirtysomething years old, and they started dating, and he moved in with us, and he introduced us to meth. And we were just sitting, like, in the apartment there, and he wouldn't let us go anywhere, he wouldn't let us, like, talk to anybody. He just had us trapped in there and, like, you know controlled us with drugs and stuff. I kinda freaked out 'cause I realized what was happening, and I just left. I didn't know where to go. I was homeless . . . I was homeless. My mom didn't want me back either.

The process that Maribel describes is a common one for young women on the run. Sandra provides another instance of the challenges of staying with friends. Like other youth in the study, Sandra began staying with a friend (and ex-partner) as well as his mother.

Sandra started dating her friend again and began a regular sexual relationship. At first things worked well, but then they started smoking methamphetamine and marijuana. Her partner started using heroin. She recounts one vivid incident with her partner:

> Well, I went to [my] friend's house for a while, but he's, like, worse than [I expected]. He was like, "Here is a sack [of meth] smoke. Smoke your life away." He's all smoked out too . . . all heroined out, he was just gone. [And I wanted to go] but . . . he's like, "You can't leave, you can't leave!" And I was like, "Okay, yes I can." He's like, "No, no, you can't!" And then he's like, "If you leave just watch what happens."

From the interview with Sandra, it was not clear if her partner initially coerced her into the relationship. When she attempted to leave, her partner refused to let her go and threatened physical violence. This was exacerbated by this man's status: he was older and a well-connected drug dealer in the community. Given her warrant and status on the run,

Sandra could not reach out to law enforcement for help without being taken into custody.

Youth often attempted to stay with female friends (often other young women) because they felt this would provide a relatively safe place and reduce their likelihood of experiencing sexual violence. Despite this, similar issues related to drug use, attraction of older, abusive men to the home, and the potential for sexual victimization still occurred. Given this, young women sometimes chose to stay and temporarily exchange sex for drugs and shelter. Most of them eventually tired of the arrangement, fled, and attempted to live on the streets. While young women attempted to avoid this pattern and these situations by moving to different friends' houses, the outcome was usually the same. Sandra, like Maribel, eventually left and attempted to negotiate the streets of El Valle.

Living on the Streets

For the most part living on the streets was the last option for young women on the run, as it exposed them to multiple forms of gendered and interpersonal violence. When on the streets, they slept under bridges, at bus stops, or in abandoned buildings or simply walked all night. Other young people found a family member who would let them live in a shed, storage room, or hidden area at their places of employment. These acquaintances allowed them to temporarily use their spaces, but they did not provide food, clothing, or any type of economic support. Simultaneously, young women noted how their drug consumption increased and getting drugs became the focal point of their lives. Living on the streets with no money often led young women to participate in petty theft, trade sex for drugs or money, or sell drugs. All seventeen youth mentioned the fear of sexual assault as a constant part of their realities on the run, a gendered nuance of our participants' experiences and their attempts to avoid arrest.

A small number of young women were recruited into sex work. Amber, age eighteen, initially went on the run when her mother kicked her out of the house. In Spanish (translated below), she describes how she decided to participate in sex work:

> When they kicked me out of the house, I got my own little job. I became independent.... What would you do on the streets? Being a Chicana? When

you don't have food? Let's say you have an interview. You can go to the interview and see if they might hire you? ... Or are you going to go to the homie that says "I can help you make two thousand dollars right now"? You take the two thousand because it's a sure thing. ... I would say gracias a Dios [thank God] after every job [sex work] I did because it would give me food and a room to stay in. But sometimes I am not sure if He [God] will forgive me for some of the things I did ... porqué I could not do them sober.

Amber provides a very detailed description of her decision to participate in survival sex when on the run, which were typical daily negotiations for such young women in our study (see Chesney-Lind & Pasko, 2013). She poignantly discusses how the possibility of an interview for a formal job is unrealistic when faced with her immediate material needs. From her point of view, participating in sex work was one of only a few ways to become independent and self-sufficient.

Young women on the run also face the possibility of being forced into sex work. As fifteen-year-old Rasta, kidnapped and trafficked, commented about her experiences,

> I started selling dope, and I met this ... older guy. ... I smoked with him like an idiot, and I was too high, and we went to his motel room. ... I didn't even know I was locked up till [I woke up] like five days later. I had bruises up and down on me, had scabs on my head from being hit with brass knuckles. ... I was, like, in a bathroom for six weeks straight. I couldn't sleep. I was too fucking high to do anything. They [pimp] shot me up [with heroin] and wanted to prostitute me on the streets of the city. For three months, I wasn't a person anymore.

Rasta provides an extreme example of the gendered dangers of being on the run. It is important to note that Rasta is not Latina; however, her low socioeconomic status, her outstanding warrants, and the fact that she lived in El Valle meant that she faced some of the same legal, socioeconomic, and gender-specific challenges as Latinas trying to avoid arrest. While she was only one of a handful of young women to be forced into the sex trafficking circuit and "formal" sex work, this is increasingly happening in the United States and disproportionately affects poor girls and girls of Color (Bergquist, 2015; Kotrla, 2010; Rafferty, 2016).

On average, the young women in this study were on the run between one and six months before turning themselves in to authorities. They eventually turned themselves in instead of enduring the multiple gendered, socioeconomic, and racialized challenges of being on the run as well as the constant emotional stress and fear related to their strategies, negotiations, and victimization experiences. A smaller number of young people were caught and arrested in the community for minor offenses like petty theft or breaking and entering or were picked up for soliciting or returning home. Even smaller numbers were arrested for fighting. While initially these young people went on the run to avoid being arrested, they often realized that being detained was substantially "easier" than enduring the run.

Additionally, many of these young women discussed wanting to "move on" and start "new lives"; they often could not. With a warrant out for their arrest, they could not pass a background check for employment in the formal sector, nor could they enroll in community college or secure safe housing. Girls in the study could not secure a state identification card. In other words, they could not work in the formal sector because of their criminal histories and probation status and could not go home (or to a group home) because of this same status. Paradoxically, their negotiation of this dilemma and their choice to go on the run and avoid the justice system all but guaranteed their arrest and continued involvement with this institution.

Conclusion

In this chapter, we interrogated how racial, cultural, gender, and neighborhood differences shape the lives of Latinas on the run and the various decision-making and survival strategies they employed. The young women in this study negotiated the ever-expanding "legal entanglements" of being on probation. Research on Black men on the run (and the polemical backlash) provided us with the building blocks for understanding how young Latinas experience criminalization in their respective neighborhoods. We expanded on Goffman's work by focusing on the unique and understudied experiences of young Latinas who attempted to avoid capture and detention within a working-class Latino barrio in Southern California, a community wrought with drug and sex trafficking, economic hardship, and increased police surveillance.

This chapter has highlighted how the experiences of young women on the run are shaped by intersecting structural limitations and opportunities. They were often kicked out of their homes for violating culturally prescribed expectations for Latina women and then encountered multiple gendered challenges when attempting to find transportation after fleeing their homes. Once on the street they also had to negotiate interpersonal forms of violence while attempting to avoid authorities and to find a safe space to stay. For young women, unlike men, the threat of sexual violence is a commonplace occurrence in their experiences on the run. We inform current research in this area by demonstrating how young women engage in a complex cost-benefit analysis before deciding to go on the run. This finding is significant given the young age of these youth and the short window of time they had to make this potentially life-altering decision.

Young Latinas' experiences were shaped by El Valle's lack of resources and its segregated legacy. Their unique standpoints provided us with a lens that allows us to see how gender, a historically segregated Latino community, and the constant threat police and probation presence made the experiences of Latinas on the run recognizably different from those of men. This research contributes to the growing amount of work that addresses the unique experiences of Latinas in the field of criminology and indicates how institutions, like schools and group homes, preemptively punish young people but do not offer a safe alternative to living on the streets. Furthermore, young Latinas who turn themselves in often receive little to no services for their experienced trauma on the run. When young Latinas are finally released from detention, juvenile justice authorities regularly return them to the same living situations that pushed them to go on the run in the first place, thus exacerbating a vicious cycle.

The juvenile justice system directly shapes Latinas' trajectories, but we must also consider how multiple entanglements with different institutions, such as school and the family, interlock with the juvenile justice system to engender the conditions that provoke young women to go on the run. The young Latinas in our study described a process consisting of a neighborhood and interlocking institutions like family, schools, group homes, and police that punish young people and offer little to no rehabilitative services. Added surveillance makes these young women additionally vulnerable and functionally enables external state forces to intervene readily in their lives more.

This finding is unique compared to other works related to individuals on the run. For example, Goffman (2009, 2014) argues that being a fugitive can serve as an excuse for persons to deny accountability for obligations that may have gone unfulfilled anyway. She also argues that within the context of limited opportunity and hypersurveillance you have an "interactive system in which ghetto residents become caught in constraining legal entanglements while simultaneously calling on the criminal justice system to achieve a measure of power over one another in their daily lives" (Goffman, 2009, p. 340). For our study, this was not a part of young women's experiences with the juvenile justice system. In other words, the juvenile justice system did not transform their lives but continued to work against this subaltern community (see Muniz, 2014). Those who are on the run will continue to engage in contentious resistance by fleeing the same institutions that punish them and associated agents of social control (like police and probation officers) that continue to subjugate, hypercriminalize, and incarcerate people of color, like the Latinas in our study. Researchers, teachers, parents, and criminal justice practitioners need to find ways to positively intervene in the lives of young women. Collectively we need to decriminalize survival strategies and mobilize resources for marginalized communities, like El Valle, to be successful.

There are a few key limitations in this work. First, we focused on a small group of young women in one specific location. Although significant, this qualitative study is not generalizable to all young women or all Latina women. Further study on Latinas' intersectional experiences would be key. The additional structures connected to these groups are likely to significantly shape the experiences and circumstances of being on the run. Specific focus on these might tease out more nuanced distinctions and descriptive data to better understand and address the vulnerabilities and needs of young Latina women on the run as a group.

Practice Implications

Young women like those in this study need to be able to fulfill their basic needs without fear of criminal punishment or further victimization. Having somewhere to stay is extremely important for young women

(Dietrich, 1998). This study notes that when they are on the run, things devolve for them quickly. Young women need a space in the community for emergency shelter exclusively dedicated to them. Given the gendered dangers our participants experience, they should also have access to dependable and free transportation access to resources such as shelter, social networks, and support. Finally, an outreach worker who develops contacts with young Latina women on the streets would be an ideal resource to direct young women to community resources.

As we have detailed, young women are often caught in the disciplinary forces of various institutions. Emergency caseworkers should avoid integration strategies to put youth back into the institutions, such as school or family, that contributed to their instability. The focus of such efforts should be to provide interventions at critical moments such as transitions and provide resources to establish their safe independence when appropriate. Ideally, these caseworkers can provide social and legal services for young women during their time on the run to alleviate the immediate crises and move toward stabilizing and accessing support networks while disrupting the cycle of criminalization that can further endanger young women. Instead of mandates, surveillance, and policing that exacerbate pressures, young Latina women need resources to manage the constellation of interlocking pressures on their own terms within their own contexts.

NOTES

1 California uses Youth Authority detention centers to house the other 3 percent of youth who commit more serious crimes or who struggled in local detention centers. These Youth Authority centers are directly controlled by the state.
2 This and all names used in this chapter are pseudonyms. Individual research participants chose their pseudonyms.
3 The saturation point occurs when no new or relevant information emerges. This is characterized by the same patterns of information emerging in the data (Emerson, Fretz, & Shaw, 1995).
4 This indicates the veracity and strong internal reliability of our data but is not a claim to generalize to a broader population of Latinas. This subset might indicate larger patterns for further research.

REFERENCES

Alexander, M. (2010). *The new Jim Crow: Mass incarceration in the age of colorblindness*. New York: New Press.

Almaguer, T. (2009). *Racial fault lines: The historical origins of white supremacy in California* (New ed.). Berkeley: University of California Press.

Bergquist, K. S. (2015). Criminal, victim, or ally? Examining the role of sex workers in addressing minor sex trafficking. *Affilia, 30*, 314–327.

Brewer, R. M., & Heitzeg, N. A. (2008). The racialization of crime and punishment: Criminal justice, colorblind racism, and the political economy of the prison industrial complex. *American Behavioral Scientist, 51*, 625–644.

Calavita, K. (1992). *Inside the state: The Bracero Program, immigration, and the I.N.S.* New York: Routledge.

California Legislative Office. (2007). *California's criminal justice system: A primer.* Sacramento, CA: Legislative Analyst's Office.

Chesney-Lind, M., & Pasko, L. (2013). *The female offender: Girls, women, and crime* (3rd ed.). Thousand Oaks, CA: Sage.

Davis, A. Y. (2003). *Are prisons obsolete?* Toronto: Seven Stories Press.

Díaz-Cotto, J. (2006). *Chicana lives and criminal justice: Voices from el barrio.* Austin: University of Texas Press.

Dietrich, L. C. (1998). *Chicana adolescents: Bitches, 'ho's and schoolgirls.* Westport, CT: Praeger.

Emerson, R., Fretz, R. I., & Shaw, L. L. (1995). *Writing ethnographic fieldnotes.* Chicago: University of Chicago Press.

Garcia, L. (2012). *Respect yourself, protect yourself: Latina girls and sexual identity.* New York: New York University Press.

Glenn, E. N. (2004). *Unequal freedom: How race and gender shaped American citizenship and labor.* Cambridge, MA: Harvard University Press.

Goffman, A. (2009). On the run: Wanted men in a Philadelphia ghetto. *American Sociological Review, 74*, 339–357.

Goffman, A. (2014). *On the run: Fugitive life in an American city.* Chicago: University of Chicago Press.

Kotrla, K. (2010). Domestic minor sex trafficking in the United States. *Social Work, 55*, 181–187.

Lopez-Aguado, P. (2016). "I would be a bulldog": Tracing the spillover of carceral identity. *Social Problems, 63*, 203–221.

Miller, J. (2008). *Getting played: African American girls, urban inequality, and gendered violence.* New York: New York University Press.

Morín, J. L. (2013). Latinas/os and U.S. prison: Trends and challenges. *Latino Studies, 6*, 11–34.

Muniz, A. (2014). Maintaining racial boundaries: Criminalization, neighborhood context, and the origins of gang injunctions. *Social Problems, 61*, 216–236.

Ocen, P. A. (2013). Unshackling intersectionality. *Du Bois Review, 10*, 471–483.

Olgin, V. (2010). *La pinta: Chicana/o prisoner literature, culture and politics.* Austin: University of Texas Press.

Rafferty, Y. (2016). Challenges to the rapid identification of children who have been trafficked or commercial sexual exploitation. *Child Abuse & Neglect, 52*, 158–168.

Rios, V. (2006). The hyper-criminalization of Black and Latino male youth in the era of mass incarceration. *Souls, 8*, 40–54.

Rios, V. (2011). *Punished: Policing the lives of Black and Latino boys.* New York: New York University Press.

Schaffner, L. (2008). Latinas in US juvenile detention: Turning adversity to advantage. *Latino Studies, 6*, 116–136.

6

The Correlates and Consequences of Maternal Efficacy among Imprisoned Women

HOLLY FOSTER AND CHANTREY J. MURPHY

The United States is broadly recognized as a world leader in mass incarceration, yet it is also noteworthy that it ranks eighteenth for female imprisonment rates internationally (National Resource Council [NRC], 2014; World Prison Brief, 2015). Although prisoners in the federal system constitute about 13 percent of the U.S. incarcerated population (Carson, 2018), it is a site where the war on drugs has been waged acutely (Lynch, 2016). For example, while almost half of those incarcerated in the federal system are serving time for drug offenses, this percentage is much lower (at about 15 percent) among prisoners in state facilities (Carson, 2018; Federal Bureau of Prisons, 2018). To better understand the experiences of mothers with minor children, who are the focus of this chapter, racial and ethnic patterns need to be further taken into account (Enos, 2001), as national patterns show that among federal prisoners more Latinas (63 percent) and African American women (55.2 percent) are mothers than are white women (47 percent) (Glaze & Maruschak, 2010). Finally, in keeping with trends showing there are now more Latinx prisoners in federal prisons than there has been previously (Lopez & Light, 2009; Sentencing Project, 2018), almost half of the mothers of minor children in the study featured in this chapter are Latinas. Yet despite these trends, Lopez and Pasko (2017) have observed that relatively little is known about Latinas' experiences in the criminal justice system. We begin to address this gap in research by adding new information on mothers with minor children incarcerated in a federal prison, using a comparative perspective by race and ethnicity.

Racial and ethnic disparities are widely acknowledged in both the federal and state prison systems with the dramatic overrepresentation of African American and Latinx groups compared to whites relative to each group's percentages in the national U.S. population (Carson, 2018, p. 8; NRC, 2014).[1] As Lynch (2016) argues, these patterns reveal the workings of long-standing institutionalized racism as the fallout of policies like the war on drugs. In keeping with dramatic increases in women's incarceration rates in both state and federal facilities in the United States (Kruttschnitt, 2010), there is evidence that these trends also vary somewhat by race and ethnicity. For both Latinas and white women, incarceration rates rose from 2000 to 2009 (an increase of 23 percent and 47 percent, respectively); however during the same time period, there was a drop in incarceration rates for African American women (by 31 percent) (Sentencing Project, 2018, p. 4). Yet, given disparities in the system, incarceration rates continue to show persistent racial and ethnic disparities where African American women have the highest incarceration rates (at 142 per 100,000), followed by Latinas (74 per 100,000) and then white women (50 per 100,000) (Sentencing Project, 2018, p. 5). These differentials highlight the need for an intersectional approach that attends to gender and race/ethnicity to more fully understand the lives of imprisoned women and their families (Lopez, 2017; McCall, 2005). Accordingly, we take a quantitative approach using a comparative perspective on maternal efficacy and mother-child coresidence histories to investigate the experiences of Latinas relative to those of African American and white mothers.

Maternal Race/Ethnicity and "Linked Lives": Bringing in Residential Histories

Our comparative approach is in keeping with intersectional feminist scholarship, where, as Wattanaporn and Holtfreter (2014) observe, "pathways scholarship focuses on acknowledging not only differences *between* males and females but also *within* female offenders (emphasis in original)" (p. 193). Additionally, from life course perspectives we focus on the idea of "linked lives" (Elder, 1998, p. 4), referring to the interdependent lives of family members, or in our research those of imprisoned mothers and their children. We therefore focus on how imprisoned women's linked lives may vary by race and ethnicity and how that matters for their coping resources and their children's school-related problems.

Several studies of children's living arrangements while mothers are in prison show different patterns by race and ethnicity (Enos, 2001; Foster, 2011; Foster & Hagan, 2009; Foster & Lewis, 2015; Johnson & Waldfogel, 2004). For example, in a prior analysis of the dataset we analyze here on mothers in a minimum-security federal prison, Foster and Lewis (2015) found that Latinas (88 percent) and African American mothers (87 percent) were significantly more likely than white mothers (46 percent) to have been coresident with their minor children prior to incarceration. This finding is in keeping with earlier research showing a similar pattern where 20 percent of white mothers lived with their children prior to incarceration, yet this number was much higher at 54 percent for African American women (Bresler & Lewis, 1983; Enos, 2001). Furthermore, although women in our dataset are similar in their common expectations to live with their children upon release, this was nonetheless heightened among Latina (88 percent) and African American mothers (93 percent) compared to white mothers (73 percent) (Foster & Lewis, 2015, p. 100). Our studies build on prior research to suggest that Latina mothers and African American mothers have more integrated family ties, or more tightly linked lives, before imprisonment than white mothers. Siegel's (2011) qualitative research on children of predominantly African American (74.3 percent) imprisoned and jailed mothers revealed how some were highly engaged with them beforehand whereas others were more disengaged. We build on these insights with a quantitative analysis of the influences of mother-child coresidential histories before imprisonment (i.e., as an indicator of linked lives) on maternal efficacy, net of other factors. We then investigate how maternal efficacy influences children's school problems.

Maternal Efficacy

Personal efficacy refers to one's sense that one can influence one's life situations and is supported as an effective coping resource in both community and prison samples (Bandura, 1982; Gecas, 1989; Kruttschnitt & Vuolo, 2007; Loeb, Steffensmeier, & Kassab, 2011; Turner & Roszell, 1994).[2] Even in a context where stressors known as the "pains of imprisonment" (Sykes, 1958) are acutely felt, feeling some control over everyday life can be a resource that decreases mental health problems among female inmates (i.e., feeling suicidal) (Kruttschnitt & Vuolo,

2007). Across studies, two forms of efficacy that are beneficial in prisoners' lives include "task-specific" forms (e.g., around health management) (Loeb et al., 2011) as well as more "global" perceptions of efficacy (e.g., a sense of control over day-to-day life in prison) (e.g., Kruttschnitt & Vuolo, 2007). While imprisoned women clearly face restrictions on mothering practices, Haney's (2010) ethnographic research shows how those that are intentionally reinforced are ones in accordance with institutional foci. Mothering in prison then becomes institutionally shaped and socially controlled. Yet it is also the case that mothers exert very circumscribed control, albeit to varying degrees, over at least some decisions concerning their children. One of these is where children live when mothers are arrested and incarcerated, which is a form of efficacy.

Research on parental efficacy in community studies defines it as "the degree to which the parent feels competent and confident in handling child problems" (Johnston & Mash, 1989, p. 167). Maternal efficacy scales in this area tap mothers' perceptions of being able to address difficult child behaviors in certain settings, being able to engage in effective infant care, as well as being able to breastfeed (Dennis, 2003; Sanders & Woolley, 2005; Teti & Gelfand, 1991). However, these particular forms of maternal efficacy are clearly constrained in prisons. We therefore measure maternal efficacy among imprisoned women in a more task-specific way. Women with minor children were asked about the level of control they felt they had over their children's residential placement when they were arrested.

Related to this, a study of mothers in a state prison examined maternal preferences over their children's caregivers (Poehlmann, Shlafer, Maes, & Hanneman, 2008). That research used interview data to create a variable reflecting whether the incarcerated mother felt the target child's caregiver was her own choice or not. In coding the open-ended responses, the authors found that 86 percent of mothers felt their choice of caregivers had been honored. Poehlmann and colleagues reported that many of the incarcerated mothers (55 percent) considered factors of stability or quality of care when expressing a choice about the child's placement. Their quantitative results further revealed a marginally significant association between maternal reports that the placement was her choice and child caregiver stability.

We build on this research in two ways. First, we consider how maternal-child coresidential histories may positively influence maternal efficacy at the time of arrest as recalled by mothers in prison. Second, while research on maternal and paternal incarceration has shown adverse spillover strains detrimentally influence children (Comfort, 2007; see review by Foster & Hagan, 2015; Wakefield & Wildeman, 2014), we now consider how there may also be potentially protective spillover coping influences on children. While maternal efficacy perceptions in prison are based on decisions made at the time of their arrest, we have found through qualitative data in this same study that when mothers with minor children were then asked "how do you feel about the decision on the placement of your children?," 92 percent reported being satisfied with this decision. Some women expressed they felt it was the best decision they made under the circumstances and that it made them feel relieved (Foster & Lewis, 2015, p. 102). Maternal efficacy at time of arrest therefore seems to provide imprisoned women with an ongoing degree of comfort, in keeping with how coping resources work (Turner & Roszell, 1994). We hypothesize that there will be a protective association between maternal efficacy and children's school problems among incarcerated women, indicative of a spillover coping resource.

In sum, our guiding hypotheses are as follows:

Hypothesis 1: Main Effect: Maternal coresidential histories with minor children should increase maternal efficacy at time of arrest, net of covariates.

Hypothesis 2: Residential Histories: (a) *Main Effect*: Due to racial and ethnic differences in child living arrangements when mothers are incarcerated, Latinas and African American mothers should have higher levels of maternal efficacy at time of arrest than white mothers. (b) *Mediating Hypothesis*: Maternal coresidence with minor children before imprisonment will explain associations between race and ethnicity and maternal efficacy.

Hypothesis 3: Spillover Coping Hypothesis: Maternal efficacy at time of arrest will be predictive of children's school-related problems during maternal incarceration, net of covariates.

Methods

Data

The data analyzed in this chapter are from a larger study of 201 Latina, African American, and white women who were in a minimum-security prison in 2011.[3] This group of imprisoned women includes those of different family statuses such as mothers of minor children, those with adult children, as well as those without children. After informed consent was gained, respondents completed a self-administered survey questionnaire. Respondents were recruited through posters placed at the facility as well as institutional announcements. Questionnaires took on average between thirty and forty-five minutes to complete. A pretest using this questionnaire was administered prior to conducting the full study to ensure the questions were making sense to respondents, resulting in minimal changes to the final questionnaire used in this research. The subsample analyzed here includes 101 mothers of minor children (younger than eighteen) with full data on study variables.

Measures

DEPENDENT VARIABLES. All maternal variables were self-reported in response to questions on the survey administered in 2011. Maternal efficacy over child placement at the time of their arrest was measured through the question, "How much say/choice did you have in the placement of your children?" Responses included none (0), very little (1), some (2), much/all (3).

To gauge maternal perceptions of their child's school performance, they were asked, during the past year, "has your eldest child under age 18 had trouble paying attention in school?" and "has your eldest child under age 18 had trouble getting his or her homework done?" Response options included never (1), just a few times (2), about once a week (3), almost every day (4), every day (5), don't know (6). Items with a don't know response were set to missing. A mean score of these two items based on a national study (Harris et al., 2009) was used to indicate children's level of maternal-rated school problems.

MATERNAL INDEPENDENT VARIABLES. A number of other questions asked of imprisoned women were used in the survey instrument modeled on a prior study of male and female prisoners in Texas as well as some questions based on the National Longitudinal Study of Adolescent to Adult Health (Crouch, Dyer, O'Dell, & McDonald, 1999; McClellan, Farabee, & Crouch, 1997; Mullings, Pollock, & Crouch, 2002). These include questions on maternal sociodemographics (e.g., race/ethnicity, age, education level), mother-child coresidential histories, and maternal childhood traumas. If the respondent indicated they had a child or children younger than eighteen, they were asked a series of questions about their eldest one. Mother-child residential history was measured through the question, "was she/he living with you before you were arrested this last time?" Responses were recoded to yes (1) or no (0).

Maternal childhood traumas were measured with two variables. First, economic hardship was measured with three items with the stem question, "as you were growing up, how often did you experience the following?" (1) you had no place to live; (2) you did not have enough food to eat; (3) you did not have adequate clothes to wear. Responses to each item were dichotomized to never (0) and seldom and frequently (1). Maternal experiences of sexual abuse in childhood were measured through the item, "you were sexually mistreated, abused or raped," with responses recoded into never (0) and seldom/frequently (1).

Maternal drug histories were measured with two variables. First, women were asked, "during the last 12 months, prior to being locked up, did you ever feel that you needed or were dependent on drugs or alcohol?" Responses were coded yes (1) or no (0). Second, women were asked, "what offense are you currently incarcerated for?," followed by an open-ended response space. The open-ended response was recorded verbatim and then reclassified into drug-related offenses (1) versus others (0). Although responses varied in specifying the exact drug offense for which they were imprisoned, a look at national data in 2015 indicates that the overall category records trafficking, possession, and other, where 99 percent of those in the federal system are sentenced for trafficking (Carson, 2018, p. 20).

Maternal sociodemographics included their race and ethnicity in response to the following question: "Which of the following best describes your racial or ethnic group?" Options included white (1), African American (2), Hispanic (3), Asian (4), American Indian (5), something else (6). Using this information, two dummy variables were created to indicate respondent identities as African American or Latina compared to whites. Due to small numbers in this analysis, respondents of other races and ethnicities were removed, resulting in the removal of a few cases. Mothers reported their age in years at the time of the survey. Maternal education was measured through an item from a national survey

(Harris et al., 2009): "What is the highest grade or year of school you have completed?" Response options included less than sixth grade (1), sixth grade (2), seventh grade (3), eighth grade (4), ninth grade (5), tenth grade (6), eleventh grade (7), twelfth grade (8), one year of college (9), two years of college (10), three years of college (11), four years of college (12), five years of college (13), one or more years of graduate school (14).

CHILD CONTROL VARIABLES. Mothers provided information on their child's gender and age in response to the following questions: "Is your child a boy or girl (your eldest child under age 18)?" (scored girl = 1; boy = 0) and "How old is she or he?" (years) (Crouch et al., 1999).

Analytic Plan

Descriptive statistics are discussed in the results section below and are briefly compared to institutional statistics at this facility in 2011 (see also Foster, 2012). Since participation in the Social Support Study was voluntary, this comparison gauges the representativeness of the sample to all women imprisoned at this facility. In line with quantitative intersectional scholarship, we adopt the analytic approach of "categorical complexity" where statistical patterns are compared among women in prison across racial and ethnic groups (McCall, 2005). We first analyze the means of variables included in our analyses by race and ethnicity. We then use multivariate ordinary least squares (OLS) regression analyses to test the focal hypotheses outlined above (H1 to H2a, H2b) regarding the predictors of maternal efficacy at the time of arrest and the posited mediating influences of residential histories. Finally, maternal ratings of child school problems are then regressed on maternal and child covariates to investigate spillover influences (H3). Analyses of child school problems involved fewer cases ($n = 79$) as some minor children were not yet of school age. We display the predicted results of the last analysis using the margins techniques in Stata 15 (StataCorp, 2017) as described by Long and Freese (2014).

Results

Descriptive Statistics

Regarding the racial and ethnic demographic composition of this subsample of mothers of minor children ($n = 101$), 47 percent were

Latinas, 13 percent were African Americans, and 40 percent were whites. Institutional statistics in 2011 indicated that overall 40 percent of women in this federal prison were Latinas, 18 percent were African Americans, and 40 percent were whites, with 2 percent of other race and ethnicities. Latinas are therefore more prominent and African Americans are underrepresented in this subsample of mothers of minor children than in the full institutions. However, the percentage of whites in the subsample and overall prison match. The average age of mothers in this subsample of incarcerated women with minor children was younger on average at 33.61 than the overall mean age in the prison (36). As seen in Table 6.1, mothers of minor children had on average between an eleventh and twelfth grade education, given the metric of this scale. Group comparisons indicate African American mothers had slightly higher levels of education than the other two racial and ethnic groups.

Regarding the childhood traumas that feature prominently in feminist pathways scholarship, 43 percent of mothers experienced sexual abuse in childhood, and this percentage did not vary by race and ethnicity. Overall, the average level of financial hardships and traumatic experiences in childhood was 0.7 (on a scale of 0–3) among mothers in this subsample, with the mean level slightly higher among Latinas (0.91) than whites (0.51), albeit at a marginally significant level ($p < .10$). Drug problems were also common for the vast the majority of these mothers (74 percent), but this was more so the case for whites (85 percent) than Latinas (62 percent) ($p < .05$). Furthermore, in accordance with the salience of war on drugs policies for federal prisoners, 76 percent of these mothers were convicted for a drug offense. The prevalence of drug convictions among mothers of minor children is higher (by 7 percent) than the 69 percent of women overall at this prison for this reason in 2011, but they still compose the clear majority.

As indicated in Table 6.1, Latinas (89 percent) and African American mothers (92 percent) in this subsample were more likely than whites ($p < .05$) to have been living with their minor children prior to imprisonment (see also Foster & Lewis, 2015). Regarding our second hypothesis (H2a), preliminary support is seen in these comparative descriptive statistics for differences in mean levels of maternal efficacy at time of arrest by race and ethnicity. Graphically displayed in Figure 6.1,

TABLE 6.1. Descriptive Statistics

	Full Sample (n = 101)			Subgroup Mean Comparisons			Significant Group Differences
	M	SD	Range	Whites	African Americans	Latinas	
Maternal variables							
Maternal efficacy							
Maternal perceived efficacy over child placement	2.43	1.03	0–3	2.02	3.0	2.62	W<L*; W<AA*
Residential histories							
Lived with minor child before imprisonment	0.73	—	0–1	0.49	0.92	0.89	L>W*; AA>W*
Childhood traumas							
Economic hardships in childhood	0.70	1.13	0–3	0.51	0.58	0.91	L>W†
Sexual abuse in childhood	0.43	—	0–1	0.41	0.33	0.45	
Drug involvement							
Drug problems before imprisonment	0.74	—	0–1	0.85	0.50	0.62	W>L*; W>AA*
Pathways to prison							
Incarcerated for drug offense	0.76	—	0–1	0.78	0.67	0.77	
Sociodemographics							
African Americans[a]	0.13	—	0–1				
Latinas	0.47	—	0–1				
Age (years)	33.61	6.28	22–54	35	32	33.02	
Education level	7.83	2.33	3–14	8.05	9.08	7.38	AA>W†; AA>L*
Child variables							
Minor child's age	11.75	4.47	1–17	11.68	11	12.21	
Minor child's gender (female = 1)	0.44	—	0–1	0.44	0.42	0.45	
Maternal perceived levels of child's school problems (n = 79)	1.96	1.05	1–5	2.23	1.73	1.86	

Note: Reference group: aNon-Hispanic Whites.

†p < .10. *p < .05.

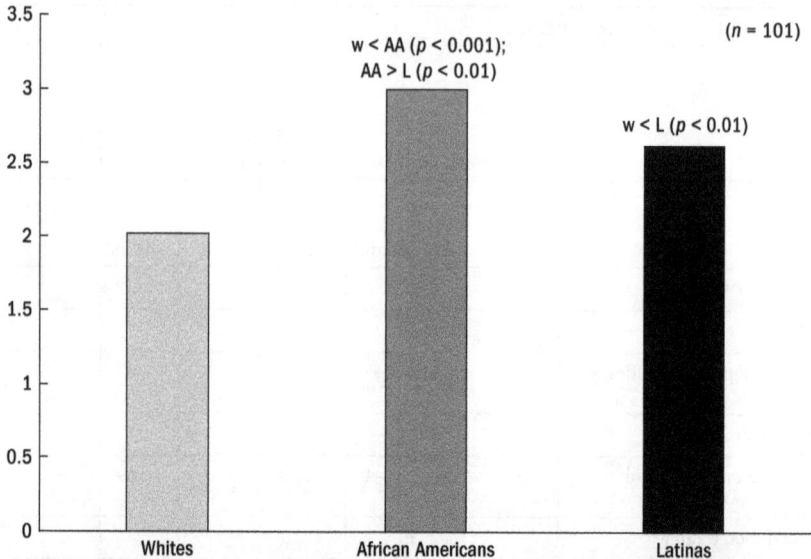

FIGURE 6.1. Perceived Efficacy over Child Placement among Incarcerated Mothers by Race and Ethnicity

based on Table 6.1, white mothers had significantly lower levels of maternal efficacy at the time of arrest (2.02) than did Latinas (2.62, $p < .05$) and African American mothers (3.0, $p < .05$).

In terms of the characteristics of the mother's eldest minor children, they were on average 11.75 years of age and about 44 percent were girls. Mothers with school-aged children ($n = 79$) perceived on average a score of 1.96 child school problems, corresponding to a frequency of occurrence about once per week. These ratings of child school problems did not vary significantly by maternal race and ethnicity. These descriptive statistics therefore indicate points of both similarity and difference among incarcerated mothers by race and ethnicity.

Multivariate Analyses

Taking control variables into account, the results of multivariate OLS regression analyses of maternal efficacy are presented in Table 6.2. As seen in column 1, and further to the descriptive statistics, both African

American ($b = .78$, $p < .05$) and Latina mothers ($b = .52$, $p < .05$) had higher levels of maternal efficacy at the time of arrest than white mothers, net of covariates. These findings are consistent with hypothesis 2a regarding the predicted racial and ethnic differences. Column 1 also shows that an older maternal age reduces maternal efficacy at the time

TABLE 6.2. OLS Regression of Maternal Efficacy on Maternal and Child Predictors

	1	2	3	Std. b
Maternal Variables				
African American[a]	.78* (.32)	.77* (.33)	.56† (.33)	.18
Latina	.52* (.22)	.54* (.22)	.32 (.23)	.16
Age (years)	−.03* (.02)	−.03 (.02)	−.03 (.02)	−.16
Education level	−.04 (.04)	−.05 (.05)	−.04 (.04)	−.09
Economic hardships in childhood	−.17† (.09)	−.17† (.09)	−.18† (.09)	−.19
Sexual abuse in childhood	−.01 (.20)	−.05 (.21)	−.04 (.19)	−.02
Drug problems before imprisonment	−.26 (.25)	−.29 (.25)	−.25 (.24)	−.10
Pathway to prison				
Incarcerated for drug offense	−.28 (.24)	−.26 (.24)	−.19 (.24)	−.02
Child variables				
Eldest minor child's age (years)		−.01 (.03)	−.01 (.03)	−.08
Eldest minor child's gender (female = 1)		−.25 (.20)	−.22 (.20)	−.03
Maternal residential history				
Lived with minor child before imprisonment			.56* (.24)	.24
Constant	4.11*** (0.80)	4.19*** (0.82)	3.63*** (0.83)	
Adjusted R^2	.14	.14	.18	
F-test	3.03**	2.59**	2.94**	

Note: Reference group: [a]Non-Hispanic Whites. $n = 101$ (b/sb).
†$p < .10$. *$p < .05$. **$p < .01$. ***$p < .001$.

of arrest ($b = -.03, p < .05$), as does economic hardships in childhood, albeit at a marginal level of statistical significance ($b = -.17, p < .10$).

In column 2 of Table 6.2, the child demographic variables of age and gender are added to the model. These variables are not predictive of maternal efficacy, and the adjusted R^2 statistic remains at 14 percent as per the model with only maternal variables. Turning to the role of residential histories in relation to maternal efficacy (H1), column 3 of Table 6.2 shows that mothers who were coresident with their children prior to imprisonment had higher levels of maternal efficacy at the time of arrest ($b = .56, p < .05$). Furthermore, the hypothesized mediating role of residential histories in explaining race and ethnic differences in maternal efficacy (H2b) is supported: the addition of the residential histories variable decreases the gap between Latinas and whites in maternal efficacy perceptions by 41 percent (from $b = .54, p < .05$ in column 2 to $b = .32, p > .10$). Residential histories also explain part of the gap between African Americans and whites in maternal efficacy by 27 percent (from $b = .77, p < .05$ to $b = .56, p < .10$). Furthermore, the addition of the residential histories variable to the models predicting maternal efficacy at the time of arrest increased the adjusted R^2 to 18 percent, explaining 4 percent more of the variation in this coping resource. Finally, in column 4 the standardized regression coefficients are presented, where the mother-child coresidential histories variable considered comparatively to other predictors has the strongest relative influence on maternal efficacy at the time of arrest among imprisoned mothers (standardized $b = .24, p < .05$).

Table 6.3 presents the results of OLS regression analyses of maternal ratings of child school problems on maternal and child covariates. As seen in Table 6.3, there are no differences by race and ethnicity in maternal predictions of children's problems at school. However, an older maternal age is protective against children's school problems ($b = -.05, p < .05$). Yet an older age of the eldest child is predictive of more school problems ($b = .08, p < .05$). Regarding the hypothesized spillover influence of incarcerated mothers' level of maternal efficacy at the time of arrest (H3), potentially working through a more positive maternal role appraisal in prison, the results show higher levels of maternal efficacy at the time of arrest over child placement are in fact protective against school problems among children ($b = -.40$,

TABLE 6.3. OLS Regression of Maternal Perceptions of Child's Problems at School on Maternal and Child Predictors

	1	Std. b
Maternal Variables		
African American[a]	−.40 (.40)	−.14
Latina	−.34 (.30)	−.17
Age (years)	−.05* (.02)	−.32*
Education level	−.002 (.05)	−.005
Economic hardships in childhood	−.01 (.12)	−.01
Sexual abuse in childhood	.27 (.25)	.13
Drug problems before imprisonment	−.20 (.27)	−.09
Pathway to prison		
Incarcerated for drug offense	−.12 (.28)	−.05
Child variables		
Eldest minor child's age (years)	.08* (.03)	.33*
Eldest minor child's gender (female = 1)	−.18 (.24)	−.09
Maternal residential history		
Lived with minor child before imprisonment	.12 (.32)	.05
Maternal efficacy		
Maternal efficacy over child placement	−.40** (.14)	−.37**
Constant	4.13*** (1.09)	
Adjusted R^2	.13	
F-test	1.98*	

Note: Reference group: [a]Non-Hispanic Whites. n = 79.
*p < .05. **p < .01. ***p < .001.

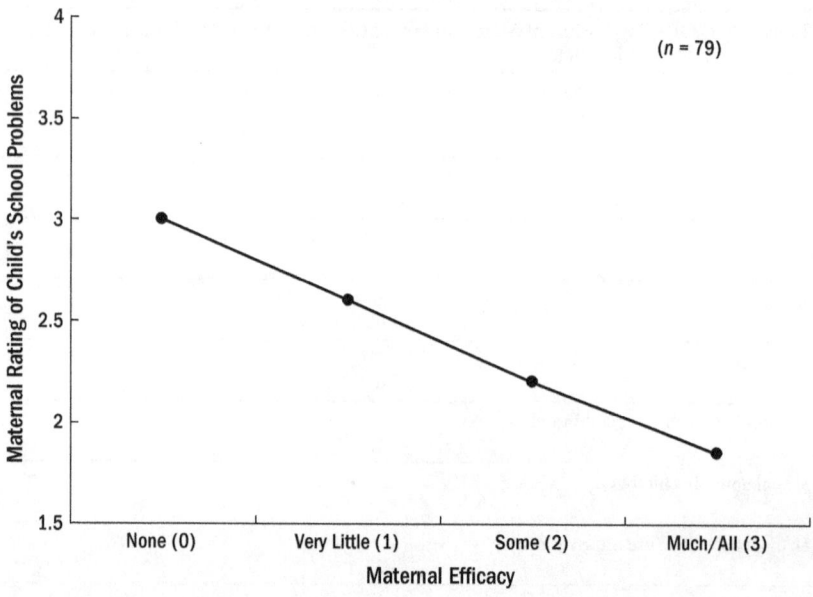

Figure 6.2. Adjusted Predictions of Mother's Perceived Problems of Child at School

$p < .001$). This result is supportive of spillover influences of maternal efficacy at time of arrest and the qualitatively expressed sense of positive maternal role appraisal while in prison for children outside of prison. The second column in Table 6.3 presenting standardized regression coefficients indicates that the influence of maternal efficacy is comparable to that of the maternal and child age variables on child school problems but is actually slightly stronger (standardized $b = -.37, p < .01$). By using the margins commands in Stata (Long & Freese, 2014), we highlight visually in Figure 6.2 the predictive influence of maternal efficacy over child placement at the time of arrest on levels of child school problems, taking covariates into account. At very low levels of maternal efficacy (0 or none), children have an adjusted prediction of having more frequent problems at school (at a score of about 3, corresponding to about once a week). These adjusted predictions of child school problems decrease linearly with every 1-unit increase in maternal efficacy perceptions. At the highest level of maternal efficacy at the time of arrest (a score of 3, or having much/all say in this decision), children are predicted to have lower levels of school problems (at just over 1.5, or between never and just a few times per week).

Conclusion

Consistent with patterns in feminist pathways scholarship in criminology, the vast majority of incarcerated women in this study have had lives of sustained disadvantages and marginalization (Lopez, 2017; Owen, Wells, & Pollock, 2017; Sharp, 2014). Most women in this study followed a drug-involved or drug-connected pathway to prison (Brennan, Breitenbach, Dieterich, Salisbury, & van Voorhis, 2012; Carbone-Lopez, Owens, & Miller, 2012; Daly, 1994; Simpson, Yahner, & Dugan, 2008). Our chapter has focused on a study of women imprisoned in a minimum-security federal prison. An important aspect of the subsample is that over half of the mothers with minor children are Latinas, and this chapter begins to illuminate their experiences in prison relative to those of African American and white mothers. While our results show similarities among women in prison, they also reveal some group-based variability in the kinds of conditions women have faced over their lifetimes. For example, Latina mothers endure slightly higher levels of economic hardship in childhood than do white mothers, but white mothers are more likely than Latina mothers to have had drug use problems before imprisonment. These comparisons by race/ethnicity among women begin to reveal structural nuances in their pathways, the issues mothers face while in prison, and how they cope.

While policies of mass incarceration need to be revisited to decrease these trends markedly, this will take time as with current rates of decarceration, meaningful reductions are estimated to take about seventy-two years to achieve (Ghandnoosh, 2019). Therefore, until that goal is met, it is vital to find ways to support women and their families already in the prison system. We do that in this chapter by investigating maternal efficacy. Our results show that mother-child coresidential histories increased maternal efficacy at the time of arrest, consistent with our first hypothesis (H1).[4] Therefore, structural living arrangements influence this coping resource. Furthermore, Latina mothers and African American mothers were more likely than white mothers to have been coresident with their children before imprisonment, net of other factors (see also Enos, 2001; Foster & Lewis, 2015). We also found that Latina and African American mothers had higher levels of maternal efficacy than did white mothers, consistent with our second hypothesis (H2a). We hypothesized that race and ethnic differences among women in maternal efficacy would be explained by their coresidential histories with children (H2b). This hypothesis was supported, showing how structural conditions facilitate maternal coping resources.

Since there are profound and enduring racial and ethnic disparities in the criminal justice system (NRC, 2014), it is vital to recognize and support the strengths of racial and ethnic minority families in coping with these adverse circumstances. An example of family strengths is the higher levels of maternal-child coresidence before imprisonment among African American and Latina mothers compared to white mothers, which is associated with maternal efficacy. This finding has broader implications for understanding how important coping resources are among prisoners. Following a logic similar to that of Turner and Marino's (1994) stress process research on the epidemiology of social support in community settings, these findings suggest that if it were not for these family strengths (i.e., the higher levels of coresidence) there would likely be lower levels of maternal efficacy in these groups. Lower maternal efficacy may in turn result in even more adverse consequences for these women and their children resulting from policies of mass imprisonment, like the war on drugs.

We also found support for our spillover coping hypothesis, where we found a negative or protective association between higher levels of maternal efficacy among incarcerated women and their perceptions of lower levels of school problems among their eldest minor child. This result is in keeping with goals of applying criminological theories like general strain theory (GST) to understand prison settings (Agnew & DeLisi, 2012). In the GST framework, maternal strains are reduced by higher levels of maternal coping resources, and therefore research on women in prison should attend to both aspects of stress and coping (Agnew, 2006). Our research shows how maternal coping resources are also beneficial for incarcerated women's children outside.

Our finding adds to Poehlmann and colleagues' (2008) research on associations between maternal perceptions that the child care arrangements were her choice and caregiver stability in her children's lives. It may be that mothers with more efficacy are supported by circumstances of caregiver stability and these factors lead to fewer problems among their children in school. Together these studies offer insights into how programmatic investments in maternal coping resources may be beneficial for children outside as well. There are therefore potentially positive spillover consequences of investing in rehabilitative efforts while women are in prison.[5]

Practice and Policy Implications

In recognizing maternal efficacy as a protective resource among women in prison with a firm structural basis, programs and policies in prison settings may be developed to further strengthen and support it. For example, programming may include working with women and their families to find ways to better include mothers in some aspects of decision making around their children, where it is feasible. Furthermore, since research shows that experiencing some degree of control in prison promotes women's mental health while incarcerated (Vuolo & Kruttschnitt, 2008) and feelings of personal efficacy aid in successful reentry efforts among prisoners returning to communities (Liem, 2016), investment in efforts to promote women's efficacy may be beneficial in both the short term and the long term. This may mean developing and supporting programs and opportunities for women in prison that can promote broader feelings of efficacy, which may be generally beneficial but even more salient when relationships with children have been severed. Essential in developing programming is that maternal or global efficacy is developed in ways that are meaningful to imprisoned women and that restore some sense of agency. In developing socially informed programming efforts in prison, the power dynamics revealed in other research in mothering from prison (Haney, 2010) must be kept in mind, and efforts need to be undertaken to ensure women feel efficacious from the inside out, rather than feeling a need to comply with imposed programming (i.e., that primarily meets institutional goals) in order to survive their sentence.

NOTES

1 Census data show that the U.S. national population is 13 percent African American, 18 percent Hispanic, and 61 percent non-Hispanic white (U.S. Census Bureau, 2019).
2 Criminologists are also broadly familiar with "collective efficacy" as a community-level resource, where residents perceive they can come together to achieve a common purpose associated with a decrease in neighborhood violence (Sampson, Raudenbush, & Earls, 1997).
3 Although 10 incarcerated women of other races and ethnicities were in the full study sample of 211 participants, they are not included in these quantitative analyses because of the small size of this group.
4 In focusing on maternal efficacy among women in prison, our one-item measure provides a step forward in offering a succinct, quantitative, task-specific measure facilitating the systematic comparisons we have provided here. However, future research should focus on developing a multi-item comprehensive scale of maternal efficacy tailored to the prison environment to more fully probe its components. With further research into the elements of maternal efficacy in this context, more effective programming can be offered.
5 More fine-grained research on the life course dynamics of maternal/child residential histories over time (i.e., before and after imprisonment) would add further information on how the intricately linked lives of prisoners and their families influence both maternal and child well-being. Furthermore, since our study uses maternal perceptions of child behavior problems, future research testing the influences of spillover coping resources from mothers to children would benefit from incorporating independent information gained through additional caregiver and teacher ratings of child behaviors.

REFERENCES

Agnew, R. (2006). *Pressured into crime: An overview of general strain theory*. Los Angeles: Roxbury.

Agnew, R., & DeLisi, M. (2012). General strain theory, the criminal justice system and beyond: Introduction to the special issue. *Journal of Criminal Justice, 40*, 174–175.

Bandura, A. (1982). Self-efficacy mechanism in human agency. *American Psychologist, 37*, 122–147.

Brennan, T., Breitenbach, M., Dieterich, W., Salisbury, E. J., & van Voorhis, P. (2012). Women's pathways to serious and habitual crime: A person-centered analysis incorporating gender responsive factors. *Criminal Justice and Behavior, 39*, 1481–1508.

Bresler, L., & Lewis, D. K. (1983). Black and white women prisoners: Differences in family ties and their programmatic implications. *Prison Journal, 63*, 116–123.

Carbone-Lopez, K., Owens, J. G., & Miller, J. (2012). Women's "storylines" of methamphetamine initiation in the Midwest. *Journal of Drug Issues, 42*, 226–246.

Carson, E. A. (2018). Prisoners in 2016 (Bureau of Justice Statistics Bulletin 25114). Washington, DC: U.S. Department of Justice, Office of Justice Programs, Bureau of Justice Statistics. www.bjs.gov.

Comfort, M. (2007). Punishment beyond the legal offender. *Annual Review of Law and Social Science, 3*, 271–296.

Crouch, B. M., Dyer, J. A., O'Dell, L. L., & McDonald, D. K. (1999). *Methodology used in the 1998 Survey of Texas Prison Inmates Male and Female Institutional Division.* Austin: Texas Commission on Drug and Alcohol Abuse.

Daly, K. (1994). *Gender, crime, and punishment.* New Haven, CT: Yale University Press.

Dennis, C. (2003). The Breastfeeding Self-Efficacy Scale: Psychometric assessment of the short form. *Journal of Obstetric, Gynecologic & Neonatal Nursing, 32*, 734–744.

Elder, G. H., Jr. (1998). The life course as developmental theory. *Child Development, 69*, 1–12.

Enos, S. (2001). *Mothering from the inside: Parenting in a women's prison.* Albany: State University of New York Press.

Federal Bureau of Prisons. (2018). Inmate statistics: Offenses. Washington, DC: Federal Bureau of Prisons. www.bop.gov.

Foster, H. (2011). Incarcerated parents and health: Investigating role inoccupancy strains by gender. *Women & Criminal Justice, 21*, 225–249.

Foster, H. (2012). The strains of maternal imprisonment: Importation and deprivation stressors for women and children. *Journal of Criminal Justice, 40*, 221–229.

Foster, H., & Hagan, J. (2009). The mass incarceration of parents in America: Issues of race/ethnicity, collateral damage to children, and prisoner reentry. *Annals of the American Academy of Political and Social Science, 623*, 179–194.

Foster, H., & Hagan, J. (2015). Punishment regimes and the multilevel effects of parental incarceration: Intergenerational, intersectional, and interinstitutional models of social inequality and systemic exclusion. *Annual Review of Sociology, 41*, 135–158.

Foster, H., & Lewis, J. (2015). Race, ethnicity and living arrangements of children of incarcerated mothers: Comparative patterns and maternal experience. In C. M. Renzetti & R. K. Bergen (Eds.), *Understanding diversity: Celebrating difference, challenging inequality* (pp. 92–106). New York: Pearson.

Gecas, V. (1989). The social psychology of self-efficacy. *Annual Review of Sociology, 15*, 291–316.

Ghandnoosh, N. (2019). *U.S. prison population trends: Massive buildup and modest decline.* Washington, DC: Sentencing Project.

Glaze, L. E., & Maruschak, L. M. (2010). Parents in prison and their minor children (Bureau of Justice Statistics Special Report 22298). Washington, DC: U.S. Department of Justice, Office of Justice Programs, Bureau of Justice Statistics.

Golash-Boza, T. (2009). The immigration industrial complex: Why we enforce immigration policies destined to fail. *Sociology Compass, 3*, 295–309.

Gómez Cervantes, A., Menjívar, C., & Staples, W. G. (2017). "Humane" immigration enforcement and Latina immigrants in the detention complex. *Feminist Criminology, 12*, 269–292.

Haney, L. A. (2010). *Offending women: Power, punishment, and the regulation of desire*. Berkeley: University of California Press.

Harris, K. M., Halpern, C. T., Whitsel, E., Hussey, J., Tabor, J., Entzel, P., & Udry, J. R. (2009). The National Longitudinal Study of Adolescent to Adult Health: Research design. University of North Carolina at Chapel Hill, Carolina Population Center. http://cpc.unc.edu.

Horowitz, S. (2015, October 6). Justice Department set to free 6,000 prisoners, largest one-time release. *Washington Post*. www.washingtonpost.com.

Johnson, E. I., & Waldfogel, J. (2004). Children of incarcerated parents: Multiple risks and children's living arrangements. In M. Patillo & D. F. Weiman (Eds.), *Imprisoning America: The social effects of mass incarceration* (pp. 97–131). New York: Russell Sage Foundation.

Johnson, K. (2017, February 28). Attorney General Jeff Sessions: "We are in danger" of rising violence. *USA Today*. www.usatoday.com.

Johnston, C., & Mash, E. J. (1989). A measure of parenting satisfaction and efficacy. *Journal of Clinical Child Psychology, 18*, 167–175.

Kruttschnitt, C. (2010). The paradox of women's imprisonment. *Daedalus, 139*, 32–42.

Kruttschnitt, C., & Vuolo, M. (2007). The cultural context of women prisoners' mental health. *Punishment and Society, 9*, 115–150.

Liem, M. (2016). *After life imprisonment: Reentry in the era of mass incarceration*. New York: New York University Press.

Light, M. T., Lopez, M. H., & Gonzalez-Barrera, A. (2014). The rise of federal immigration crimes: Pew Research Center's Hispanic Trends Project. Pew Research Center. www.pewhispanic.org.

Loeb, S. J., Steffensmeier, D., & Kassab, C. (2011). Predictors of self-efficacy and self-rated health for older male inmates. *Journal of Advanced Nursing, 67*, 811–820.

Long, J. S., & Freese, J. (2014). *Regression models for categorical dependent variables using Stata* (3rd ed.). College Station, TX: Stata Press.

Lopez, M. H., & Light, M. T. (2009). A rising share: Hispanics and federal crime. Pew Research Center. www.pewhispanic.org.

Lopez, V. (2017). *Complicated lives: Girls, parents, drugs, and juvenile justice*. New Brunswick, NJ: Rutgers University Press.

Lopez, V., & Pasko, L. (2017). Bringing Latinas to the forefront: Latina girls, women, and the justice system. *Feminist Criminology, 12*, 195–198.

Lynch, M. (2016). *Hard bargains: The coercive power of drug laws in federal court*. New York: Russell Sage Foundation.

McCall, L. (2005). The complexity of intersectionality. *Signs, 30*, 1771–1800.

McClellan, D. S., Farabee, D., & Crouch, B. M. (1997). Early victimization, drug use, and criminality: A comparison of male and female prisoners. *Criminal Justice and Behavior, 24*, 455–476.

Mullings, J., Pollock, J., & Crouch, B. (2002). Drugs and criminality: Results from the Texas Women Inmates Study. *Women & Criminal Justice, 13*(4), 69–96.

National Resource Council. (2014). *The growth of incarceration in the United States: Exploring causes and consequences* (J. Travis, B. Western, & S. Redburn, Eds.). Washington, DC: National Academies Press.

Owen, B., Wells, J., & Pollock, J. (2017). *In search of safety: Confronting inequality in women's imprisonment.* Berkeley: University of California Press.

Poehlmann, J., Shlafer, R. J., Maes, E., & Hanneman, A. (2008). Factors associated opportunities with young children's family relationships incarceration. *Family Relations, 57,* 267–280.

Sampson, R. J., Raudenbush, S. W., & Earls, F. (1997). Neighborhoods and violent crime: A multilevel study of collective efficacy. *Science, 277,* 918–924.

Sanders, M. R., & Woolley, M. L. (2005). The relationship between maternal self-efficacy and parenting practices: Implications for parent training. *Child: Care, Health and Development, 31,* 65–73.

Sentencing Project. (2017). Federal prison population will expand under new DOJ directive. www.sentencingproject.org.

Sentencing Project. (2018). Incarcerated women and girls, 1980–2016. www.sentencingproject.org.

Sharp, S. F. (2014). *Mean lives, mean laws: Oklahoma's women prisoners.* New Brunswick, NJ: Rutgers University Press.

Siegel, J. A. (2011). *Disrupted childhoods: Children of women in prison.* New Brunswick, NJ: Rutgers University Press.

Simpson, S. S., Yahner, J. L., & Dugan, L. (2008). Understanding women's pathways to jail: analysing the lives of incarcerated women. *Australian and New Zealand Journal of Criminology, 41,* 84–108.

StataCorp. (2017). Stata statistical software: Release 15. College Station, TX: StataCorp.

Sykes, G. M. (1958). *The society of captives: A study of a maximum security prison.* Princeton, NJ: Princeton University Press.

Teti, D. M., & Gelfand, D. M. (1991). Behavioral competence among mothers of infants in the first year: The mediational role of maternal self-efficacy. *Child Development, 62,* 918–929.

Turner, R. J., & Marino, F. (1994). Social support and social structure: A descriptive epidemiology. *Journal of Health and Social Behavior, 35,* 193–212.

Turner, R. J., & Roszell, P. (1994). Psychosocial resources and the stress process. In W. R. Avison & I. H. Gotlib (Eds.), *Stress and mental health: Contemporary issues and prospects for the future* (pp. 179–210). New York: Plenum.

U.S. Census Bureau. (2019). QuickFacts: United States (Table PST045217). https://census.gov.

Vuolo, M., & Kruttschnitt, C. (2008). Prisoners' adjustment, correctional officers, and context: The foreground and background of punishment in late modernity. *Law and Society Review, 42,* 307–336.

Wakefield, S., & Wildeman, C. (2014). *Children of the prison boom: Mass incarceration and the future of American inequality*. New York: Oxford University Press.

Wattanaporn, K. A., & Holtfreter, K. (2014). The impact of feminist pathways research on gender-responsive policy and practice. *Feminist Criminology, 9*, 191–207.

World Prison Brief. (2015). United States of America. www.prisonstudies.org.

PART III

Immigration Enforcement, Crimmigration, and the Deportation Machine

7

No Solamente Porque Soy Mujer

A Transnational Intersectional Framework for Understanding Latin American Women's Experiences with Crimmigration

KATIE DINGEMAN AND WILLIAM ESTUARDO ROSALES

Actions of civil disobedience have become relatively commonplace since Donald Trump's election. In a political climate wherein anti-immigrant rhetoric has become unexceptional and policies increasingly draconian, contingents of pro-immigrant activists and allies seek to make evocatively visible otherwise suppressed knowledge of people and injustices caught in the immigration enforcement system. Trump's election brought about a travel ban barring the lawful migration of people from predominantly Muslim countries, the revocation of the Deferred Action for Childhood Arrivals (DACA) policy, suspension of Temporary Protected Status (TPS), elimination of protections for asylum seekers, expansion of Customs and Border Patrol (CBP) and Immigration and Customs Enforcement (ICE), and repeated calls to build a wall between Mexico and the United States, among other measures. National and international outcry condemning these initiatives has highlighted the virtually untethered political opportunism, nativism, and state repression of the Trump era. Yet targeted communities endured mass detention and deportation long before the escalations of the Trump administration (Kanstroom, 2007).

Removals have surged since at least the mid-1990s and seem to have reached their height under Obama. Between 1995 and 2016, formal removals increased from 50,924 to 340,056 (U.S. Department of Homeland Security [DHS], 2017). Not only did removals skyrocket over this period, but deportation as a tool of social control grew to be more punitive than ever before. Scholars argue that the blame resides in the turn toward "crimmigration" (Stumpf, 2006). Starting in the 1980s, the federal social safety net dramatically declined as public services became privatized and social problems were increasingly governed through crime control (García Hernández, 2013). Formerly distinct immigration and criminal justice systems, including their bodies of law, mechanisms of enforcement, and institutions of containment, entwined to expedite the mass criminalization, detention, and deportation of migrants. Humanitarian mechanisms considered central to U.S. immigration policy (i.e., asylum, U/T/V/VAWA visas, TPS) as well as proactive measures at state and local levels (i.e., sanctuary cities, tuition and driver's licenses for the undocumented) mitigated some of the harsh effects of crimmigration. But insomuch as they represent forms of "humanitarian exceptionalism" (Fassin, 2011), they not only fail to undermine crimmigration but enhance the binary, often gendered, notions of "worthy" versus "unworthy" immigrants underpinning it.

Sociolegal researchers interested in the dynamics of crimmigration note the ways identities interact and become entangled with the deportation apparatus. Golash-Boza and Hondagneu-Sotelo (2013) argue that deportation is a gendered and racialized system of social control in which Latin American and Caribbean men have a disproportionate risk of being removed. They estimate at least 85 percent of deported people in recent years were men. Golash-Boza (2016) further contends that "immigration law enforcement has teamed up with criminal law enforcement—a collaboration that has led to . . . specific gender and racial disparities" (pp. 490–491). Though more than half of migrants to the United States are women, "migrants have entered the labor force in gendered ways . . . male immigrants labor outdoors in construction and gardening while women work indoors in childcare and housekeeping" (Golash-Boza, 2016, p. 495). Interior enforcement targets industries where men are principally located as well as jails and prisons where they are more likely to be contained. Thus, "mostly men are deported, [and] women are left to fend for themselves when their children's father is deported" (p. 498).

This argument is insightful for demonstrating how the deportation regime operates similarly to mass incarceration, affecting men and women differently in the aggregate. This perspective is further advanced in ethnographic accounts of the impact of deportation that focus mostly on men (Brotherton & Barrios, 2011; Das Gupta, 2013; Dingeman-Cerda &

Rumbaut, 2015; Drotbohm, 2015; Golash-Boza, 2015) and research highlighting the experience of being "left behind" for women and children (Capps et al., 2015; Cervantes, Ullrich, & Matthews, 2018; Dreby, 2015). Collectively this literature finds that family units experience hardship after deportation in gendered ways. Women typically suffer due to the loss of a male breadwinner and need to locate work to support children and send remittances abroad. Men struggle to survive in their countries of origin while coping with stigma, discrimination, and separation from family. This reorganization of traditional gender roles amounts to a gendered, racialized, and classed "reversal of family lives" (Drotbohm, 2015).

While useful, this gendered analysis ultimately results in a binary understanding of deportation processes: basically, "men get deported" and "women are left to fend for themselves" (Golash-Boza, 2016, p. 498). Binary logics, whether indirectly or directly intended, have the consequence of simplifying institutional and structural locations and the power dynamics inherently attached to those structures. Observing men are "deported" and women "are left behind" runs the risk of essentializing experiences by overlooking the multitude of *additional factors* interacting with race, class, and gender to shape particular experiences and outcomes. This rendering also parallels and arguably feeds into binary logics pervasive in political rhetoric and enmeshed in immigration law enforcement that reduce women to victims in need of salvation from men as likely culprits (Kagan, 2015).

This chapter crafts a *transnational intersectional framework* to examine the ways gender, class, and national origin interact with other critical and less commonly articulated factors—parental status, kinship ties, and community support—to shape the experiences of deportable Latin American migrant women. Owing to high levels of gender violence and a dearth of protections in their countries of origin, many poor Central American women and girls are entering the migratory circuit and subsequently channeled through crimmigration enforcement. We excavate the multilayered ways they are impacted as they *cross* to enter the United States, are contained in detention, and exit via political asylum or deportation. Drawing on border and crimmigration scholarship, we explicate the ways gender and state power unfold to heighten or lessen vulnerability of poor noncitizen women and girls as they interact with *specific spatial and institutional sites*. This framework demonstrates when the power of the state is apparent or latent as well as the ways situated gendered hierarchies are contested and reproduced in relation to it.

Migration in a Context of Border Reconfiguration

The hyper-restrictionism of the current era is linked to a decades-long process of rebordering, or border reconfiguration, in which the U.S. government systematically was engaged. Throughout much of U.S. history, the southern border was relatively open and indeterminate. Specific historic moments saw the assertion of state sovereignty via immigration control along racialized, classed, gendered, and other lines in ways that foreshadowed and laid the groundwork for today's mass deportation (Kanstroom, 2007).[1] Yet the border as a region to be expanded and vigilantly guarded is a relatively recent phenomenon. If we consider the border as more than a geographic site, but "a regime of security and immigration control" (Cunningham, 2009), in recent decades it has "deterritorialized and projected into the interior" (Dowling & Inda, 2013) and denationalized and expanded into Mexico. This not only reshapes borders within and beyond the United States but also shapes the sites at which migrants' identities intersect, structuring their journey.

Since the mid-1990s, the border zone was militarized purportedly to prevent terrorism, control migration, and prevent the importation of drugs and crime. Securitization of the southern border occurred along with free-trade agreements like NAFTA to control the entry of unauthorized labor with the influx of goods and materials (Nevins, 2010). A massive state-subsidized enforcement industry now bolsters 21,000 CBP agents, advanced surveillance technologies (e.g., virtual fences, drones, watchlist and database systems), and 170 interior checkpoints where legal status can be questioned and criminality is routinely policed (ACLU, 2018; Douglas & Sáenz, 2013). Such securitization efforts serve mostly political and economic purposes, giving off the appearance of border control in an era of mobility (Andreas, 2000). They also channel migrants into the most dangerous border regions, make the migratory journey more costly, and bolster the smuggling industry (Sanchez, 2015; Slack, Martínez, Lee, & Whiteford, 2016).

At the same time the national border hardened, "numerous locales across the interior of the United States . . . [transformed] into border zones of enforcement" (Inda & Dowling, 2013, p. 10) through a process sociolegal scholars dub "crimmigration" (García Hernández, 2013; Stumpf, 2006). Crimmigration can be tied to color-blind post–civil rights concessions, neoliberal reforms, and the rise of mass imprisonment as social control. It escalated in the 1990s and especially after 9/11 with the formation of DHS and its internal enforcement arm, ICE. ICE has since instituted several initiatives to "secure the homeland" and deport "all removable aliens," including Operation Endgame and the Secure Border Initiative. Such efforts were facilitated by the gross expansion of deportable offenses, criminalization of immigration violations, and initiatives like 287(g) that delegated powers traditionally reserved by the federal government to state and local actors. This is further augmented by the Criminal Alien and Secure Communities programs that identify deportable immigrants in jails and prisons (Macías-Rojas, 2017) and through raids in workplaces, residences, and near quasi-public spaces like schools and hospitals. Collectively these crimmigration initiatives help reborder the interior not so much by reducing undocumented immigration but by maintaining states of deportability—the fear of deportation—across class, race, and gendered lines (De Genova, 2002).

As U.S. borderlines have simultaneously thickened and disaggregated into the interior, they have also extended transnationally (Rosas, 2006). According to Galemba (2018, p. 10), "Mexico inaugurated Plan Sur (Southern Plan) in the summer of 2001, a few months prior to the terrorist attacks of September 11, 2001, to strengthen its southern border. Plan Sur began a shifting of the border-policing sphere from the United States–Mexico to the Mexico–Guatemala border with U.S. support." These plans were eventually superseded by "the Mérida Initiative . . . to support the purchase of military equipment and training as part of Mexico's newly declared 'war' on drugs and crime" (International Crisis Group, 2018, p. 2). In 2014, as a response to Central American migration, the United States and Mexico reignited Programa Frontera Sur to fund the militarization of Mexico's southern border. In 2017, the United States was implementing projects costing $163 million to assist Mexican authorities with surveillance, securitization, detention, and deportation operations (Isacson, Meyer, & Smith, 2017). This effort is further bolstered by campaigns to deter emigration, including radio spots in Central America and directives for Mexico to pay for a wall. Mexico now acts as a "buffer state" against immigrants, deporting more Central Americans than the United States in 2005, and as a destination for asylum seekers (International Crisis Group, 2018, p. 2). Far from protecting migrants, this extension of U.S. rebordering transnationally has increased migrant abuses along the journey, particularly along class, race, and gender lines (Smyth, 2015).

Feminization of Migration and Deportation

How are women moving through this complex and evolving terrain? Most women channeled through U.S. immigration enforcement derive from Central America, Mexico, and the Caribbean initially because of poverty, inequality, and violence associated with gangs and state repression. They also migrate for gendered reasons, including domestic and sexual abuse. The Northern Triangle is among the most violent regions in the world to be a woman according to rates of femicide, sexual assault, domestic violence, and gendered gang violence (Kids in Need of Defense, Latin American Working Group, & Women's Refugee Commission, 2017). Women's lives are more vulnerable owing to a cultural and legal climate that fails to support their rights. Most sexual and gender-based crimes are underreported and go unpunished due to social stigma and official complicity within a broader climate of political corruption and impunity. Thus, when faced with common, deathly threats of gendered violence and abuse, many women and girls migrate to the United States in search of safety (Hallock, Ruiz Soto, & Fix, 2018).

Literature on women's direct experience with crimmigration enforcement points to the gendered ways the law is constructed and enforced to treat them as potential victims in need of salvation by the United States from dangerous men. Binaries of this kind are necessarily tied to criminalization and securitization initiatives and have consequences when women seek humanitarian relief, such as visa and asylum provisions. Criminality is often the linchpin of removal decisions. Further, poor deportable migrants are not granted legal aid to fight their criminalization and deportation despite credible claims to humanitarian relief, which would more likely lead to legalization (Eagly & Shafer, 2015). There also exists widespread discretion in the allocation of relief and enforcement of immigration, such that the system operates like a "removal roulette" in which regularization is dependent on detainees' location and the type of criminal offense committed (Pedroza, 2013), in addition to intersecting axes of class, race, and gender.

Scholarship on women and crimmigration also looks at women's experiences during migration, apprehension, detention, and deportation. Women might face similar institutional processes as men once they are apprehended, but they are simultaneously less likely to be deported and, once apprehended, are made more vulnerable than men due to their status as partners and mothers and their propensity to be violated sexually (Harty, 2012). Thus, "[their] gendered status yields a contradictory impact. On the one hand, experiences of criminalization and dehumanization are worsened by [gendered treatment by] agents of the law, as well as preoccupations with the impact on their [family] (Escobar, 2016; Harty, 2012). On the other, their status as a vulnerable class . . . sometimes affords them legal aid, sympathy, and credibility denied to men" (Dingeman et al., 2017, p. 299).

Toward a Transnational Intersectional Approach

Existing literature has yet to unpack fully the ways women situated at different social locations encounter U.S. crimmigration enforcement. In this chapter, we advance an intersectional approach to understanding the disparate gendered experiences of Central American migrant women. Intersectionality complicates the relationship between the multiple social identities of individuals and the mapping of inequality and power at the group and structural/institutional levels. By moving beyond the idea that there exists one macro system of "domination," Collins argued that depending on the *context*, a person is "member of multiple dominant groups and a member of multiple subordinate groups" (Collins, 1990, p. 230). Further, specific spatial, institutional, and interactional *sites* further contextualize and reveal the power relations between the oppressor and the oppressed. Commonly referred to as the "matrix of domination" (Romero, 2008), intersectionality thus recognizes the multidimensionality and overlapping nature of oppression at the institutional level (Collins, 2000).

Intersectionality in the extant immigration literature has given visibility to varied ways social structure interacts with migrant identities to differentially impact immigration outcomes. García (2017) shows how "illegality" "unfolds" in "various institutional contexts, such as workplace, criminal justice system, education system, and healthcare setting," to further marginalize Mexican-origin women (p. 481). In considering the spatial aspect of encounters with immigration enforcement, Romero (2008) demonstrates how particular spaces of policing interact with race and class to influence "selective citizenship inspections" (pp. 139–140). Not only were physical characteristics, such as the subjects' "Mexicanness," important in the racial profiling that occurred during the Chandler Roundup, but the neighborhood spatial context, such as the low-income areas populated by Latinos, were integral in understanding who was at higher risk of being detained and possibly deported (Romero, 2008). Institutional and spatial contexts thus form *sites* of "domination and subordination" (Collins, 1993) as they intersect with racialized and classed markers of subordinated social identities, such as "illegality," to affect the inclusion and exclusion of immigrants (García, 2017; Romero, 2008).

Our intersectional analysis engages in a remapping of the situated interactions of the nation-state and migrants' lived realities at different sites *transnationally*. While intersectionality studies have considered the interaction between social identities and institutions, scholars have largely neglected the spatial and temporal dynamics of these encounters in the migration literature. The lived social identities of individuals are not only dynamic and fluid in time but, importantly for migrants, are in constant interaction with the state, particularly as they manifest through immigration law, enforcement, and spaces of migrant containment. The nature of these *sites of interaction* between the state and migrants' intersecting identities shifts in time and place. Sanchez and Zhang (2018) note that "stepped-up border enforcement and immigration controls have forced migrants and those who guide them to travel in inhospitable and remote areas" (p. 138). In this case, the nation-state produces a dynamic where statuses like gender take an increased salience, pushing "migrants' exposure to crime by necessitating long unprotected walks through the wilderness" (Brigden, 2018, p. 112). Not only does this spatial and temporal shifting of sites of migratory crossing differentially affect men and women, but women are differentially situated.

To better understand the dynamism of migrant lived realities as they intersect with spatial and institutional contexts, we account for the contested and sometimes conflicting interactions between the expanding borderlines of the nation-state and migrant identities. We contend that intersectional experiences at specific sites in the United States are predicated by intersecting statuses both *prior to* and *during* the migratory journey (i.e., to be born a poor woman in Central America without family/kinship ties in the United States creates a certain migratory trajectory). This *transnational approach to intersectionality* expands the space and time settings of scholarly investigation beyond national borders—naturally against lingering "methodological nationalism" in both immigration and intersectionality literature (Wimmer & Glick Schiller, 2002). It also moves beyond purely "geographic or identity-centered models" that lose complexity and nuance in an effort to organize systems of oppression and privilege (Sanchez, 2017, p. 52).

While we consider traditional social identities such as nationality, race, gender, and legal status, we unpack how these statuses shape the lived experience of migrant women before, during, and after migratory encounters with the state. We further explore class *resources* or lack thereof to identify the simultaneous interactions with other factors that are often overlooked. Specifically, we explore the role of *parental status*, *kin ties*, and *community support* and how they are linked to critical resources that shape the experience of migrant women with crimmigration. We show how the macro-level economic and class system along with individual-level gender, class, and parental status all inform and structure the decision to migrate for the women in our sample. Although we note how gender differentially affects outcomes, we also move beyond an analysis of difference to unpack how gender interacts with the subordinating practice of the state and patriarchal systems of control. Gender not only is made forcefully salient in reaction to subordinating practices of immigration controls and policies of containment, but at times it *advantages* migrant women when compared to men in specific and temporary sites. By examining various stages of movement, *before crossing, crossing, apprehension, inspection and detention*, and *legal processing*, we not only embrace a *transnational* framework of analysis but also highlight the shifting nature of domination by the state and the multiple, simultaneous identities of migrant women that push back against subordination.

Methods

This study derives from 110 questionnaires and in-depth interviews conducted with men and women of Central American and Mexican origin between 2008 and 2016. All of the individuals were processed by U.S. immigration enforcement since 1996 and experienced different outcomes after apprehension. We identified initial participants through referrals from nonprofit organizations, community organizers, attorneys, researchers, and personal connections in El Salvador, Los Angeles, and Denver. We then performed snowball sampling until our research questions were sufficiently addressed.

Data collection was conducted in the participants' preferred language and included questions on demographics, life before migration, the migratory journey, incorporation into the United States, detention and deportation, and post-deportation outcomes and plans. During data collection, we were attuned to subjects' emotional states and adapted our line of questioning as necessary. We allowed participants the agency to share as much as they felt appropriate and avoided further probing. To leave participants empowered, we asked them for their suggestions on how to reform U.S. immigration law. To protect participants' identities, we did not retain their names or contact information but permitted them to choose their own pseudonym or have one assigned, so they might locate themselves in the findings of the project.

Results

Gendered Migratory Departures and Crossings

Our findings suggest that migratory journeys and crossings are highly gendered in ways that intersect with other key identities. Consistent with research on motivations for migration, several women in our sample left for the United States primarily for economic conditions. Ana Maria, a woman from El Salvador, explained, "I just wanted to work and have something, poverty kicks you out." Similarly, Rocio noted that she wanted "to have a better life," while Sylvia noted her economic circumstances: "I had no job. I would pray to God for him to open doors for me." All three women were motivated to migrate in part because of macro-level economic conditions of their native country but also because of their situated *class status* prior to migration. Women in developing countries, including countries in Central America and Mexico, are afforded limited opportunities to advance economically compared to men (ECLAC, 2017; but see Hite & Viterna, 2005).

Parental status is also a salient reason some women in our sample migrated *in addition to class*. Rocio's parental status as a mother further informed her decision to migrate with her children. She reportedly immigrated "because of the famous American Dream, to have a better life; and I thought more about my three kids, to give them a better future." Similarly, Sylvia Martinez grew up in Honduras separated from her mother who migrated to the United States when Sylvia was a child. Like the other women, Sylvia was pushed to migrate with her children for economic reasons, but this was underscored by trauma from being abandoned by her own mother, an experience that informs her duties to her children:

> The reason [I migrated] was because I didn't have a job in Honduras and with two kids it was very difficult. . . . I would pray to God for him to open doors for me and for him to give me something good in my life. . . . My mom left me when I was young, so it was something I couldn't tolerate and see my kids suffer the same way.

Sylvia's past trauma and her economic circumstances were further compounded by her lived reality as a woman and mother in Honduras. Like countless women in Central America facing widespread gender violence, Sylvia faced precarious and life-threatening circumstances. Growing up in the home of a woman who operated a prostitution ring, Sylvia was afraid that she would be sent to work the streets. In the absence of family ties or a state-provided safety net, she latched on romantically to the woman's son for protection. She had a child with him, but he was eventually murdered, leaving Sylvia as a single mother reliant on the generosity of friends. Sylvia eventually became romantically involved with a member of MS-13, who was also violently abusive.

After having a second child, Sylvia developed a relationship with God and planned an eventual departure in the hope she might obtain a U visa. One night after her spouse threatened to kill her, Sylvia and her children suddenly "disappeared" from Honduras and set on a journey toward refuge.

The mode of entry in the United States that women in our sample elected was determined in large part by their classed and racialized status *prior to migration*. As De Genova (2002) argues, the United States has constructed states of "illegality" to provide a steady stream of surplus low-wage labor from Latin America, such that poor men and women are more likely than wealthy and "high-skilled" migrants from other regions to be denied legal status prior to migration. Faced with few options, migrants experience dangerous and costly crossings by land, sometimes over several national contexts with limited resources. For women in particular, the process of deciding to make the journey as well as crossing the U.S.-Mexico border is replete with the heightened risk of physical and sexual violence. Gender thus intersects forcefully with both the sociolegal construction of "illegality" as well as the act and site of *border crossing* to affect whether Latinas will become further harmed en route.

Before the physical act of crossing the border, women are acutely aware of the risks associated in crossing in ways that are distinct from men. In our interviews, men's stories of crossing tended to emphasize bodily and financial risks, including fears of loss of limbs, being robbed, and being harmed by others on the journey. They adopted strategies to protect themselves including traveling with assistance, in a group, or in isolation. While sexual abuse does happen to men, men are not encouraged to openly discuss their fears of sexual assault. Not a single male migrant in our sample reported fear of sexual abuse along the migratory route. This was not the case for the women in our sample, as indicated by the following narrative from Lupe:

> [I crossed with] help from a lady that, well, she's a trafficker . . . the majority of people call them "coyotes." . . . My aunt . . . wanted it to be a woman that helped me cross over due to the fear that when [the coyotes] are men, the majority of the little girls, or young girls, they rape them on the way. . . . So my aunt was afraid of that, so she had the opportunity to meet this lady. And so she was the one that helped me cross.

An additional intersecting factor in her decision-making process resides in her *kin ties*—the aunt in this case—which are associated with potential life-saving information, such as contacting a female coyote. Lupe's aunt was able to obtain critical information regarding a woman smuggler. Although uncommon, the choice of a female extralegal human smuggler is increasingly becoming an option for not only women seeking to cross but also those seeking alternative employment (Sanchez, 2015). Though it is not impossible to locate a woman coyote, it can be difficult, and Lupe's aunt's information and ties made possible what was ultimately a successful journey.

Narratives from other women further demonstrate how gender stereotypes, such as the idea that women are weak, simultaneously make them vulnerable and serve as a protective mechanism against potential sexual and physical violence. Take the case of Elena:

> [The trip] was beautiful because nothing happened to us. We were on our journey, like an adventure, and I wasn't alone. *I was with my cousin and uncle.* We went on buses on our journey. It was adventuresome, even though I was a little bit scared because I was underage, [and] my cousin was underage. But it was a beautiful adventure and dangerous, too. Like three or four times, they assaulted us. *But since my uncle was traveling with us, he took care of us.*

Elena Ayala also described her border crossing as "beautiful, because nothing bad happened," yet throughout the interview she revealed that "bad things" did in fact happen. Not only was the group assaulted three or four times, but "they put us in a trailer for two days. It was terrible." There was a "maximum 150 people, with a small window, very small window. That's something I don't want to repeat if I was to cross again." Regardless of these experiences, Elena took great care to note that her risk of sexual and physical violence was greatly diminished by the fact that *her kin*, namely her uncle and cousin, were traveling with her. Male relatives here serve as paternalistic, benevolent, or chivalrous protectors, insulating Elena and other women we interviewed from violence. Through her gratitude, Elena not only expressed appreciation but also unwittingly helped to reproduce men's elevated status vis-à-vis her awareness of vulnerability.

Many migrant women from Central America are unable to escape such gender-based violence as they make the journey north. In the narrative below, Sylvia relates her experience of crossing, demonstrating how class, race, gender, and parental statuses are simultaneously salient in sites and interactions:

> [Crossing] was the worst. [laughs] I was with both of my kids. The first time, immigration caught me. I then was deported back to Honduras. I told myself I wasn't going to give up. . . . I crossed [again] and a lot of Mexicans helped me. [But] sometimes cops would try to take me and they would say I was their wife. I was then caught by Los Zetas. They asked me for money so that I could cross the river. I was with them for two days. I was scared, seeing them tatted with their guns. There was one who wanted me to stay with him. I told him my intention wasn't to marry a guy like him. I need a better example for my kids and plus I want to cross so that I could work.

Sylvia's experience can be understood as imprisonment by corrupt Mexican police officers who "take me and they would say I was their wife." Later, she was captured by Mexican cartel members who held her captive to extract money to *cross*, and where one of the cartel members "want[ed] [Sylvia] to stay with him." The Mexican police officers' conduct was not just because Sylvia is a woman but also likely because she's an *outsider* to Mexico. The officers' actions are one of the ways the nation-state vicariously enacts violence on women in a context where the state creates laws and policies which limit access to regularized mechanisms that enable human mobility and safe transit (Sanchez, 2015). The cartel profits by imprisoning migrants such as Sylvia and by violently converting her into sexual chattel. Sylvia's rejection of a cartel member's offer to "stay with him" is driven by her status of a mother "need[ing to be] a better example for my kids," but also her class status and personal motivation "to cross so that I could work."

Gendered Apprehensions of Migrant Women

A hallmark of the crimmigration era is its increased reliance on law enforcement to enforce immigration law through policing a vast quantity of immigration violations and nonviolent crimes (Stumpf, 2006).

The women in this study's apprehensions mapped onto this trend and in similar ways as men. They were picked up by CBP, ICE, or the police while crossing the border, during traffic stops, in home and work raids, during and after attempts to obtain lawful and fraudulent documentation, and after serving time in jail or prison. On the surface, this depicts equitable enforcement, but women are significantly less likely to be targeted; yet when they are caught, their apprehensions often reflect their subordinated structural position: by-products of men as targets.

For Alma Lopez, immigration officers raided her friend's home, seeking a man for a criminal offense. She said, "I was with some classmates. We got out early that day and we were going to get pizza. And we were asking for permission from one of my friend's mom and [ICE] got there looking for the girl's dad. And there were a few of us that were there that didn't have our papers. They got us there and sent us [to El Salvador]." Lupe experienced a similar vicarious apprehension. After residing in the United States for fourteen years, she was riding in the car with her husband, who was pulled over for a routine traffic stop for driving eight miles per hour over the speed limit. In her interview, she was unable to see how her experience connected with those of other women but noted the racialized dimensions:

> The first thing they did was ask for a driver's license . . . and since my husband didn't have one, they started to look into it a bit further. . . . When he saw that my husband was handing him *his consulate ID* card as an identification, he was able to tell that *we were Mexican*, and that's where the further investigation started. The officer called for more backup. . . . They asked us if we knew the language well, if we were here legally or illegally . . . and they told us sorry we're going to have to arrest you.

In this recollection, immigration officers infer Lupe's national origin and legal status through her male partner's lack of identification, reading onto her racialized notions of citizenship in gendered ways. In her interview we later discovered the deeply classist nature of this interaction within a broader immigration enforcement regime that serves capitalism by way of the state:

> They were making fun of us. When they arrested us they put a price on us. That's what hurts me the most. As an immigrant you have a price.

> They were saying like how much we should pay for an immigration bond.... They were telling each other, like, "You think it would be good if we charged them $2,500 for each of them?" And the other one said, "No, of course not, that's not enough. It's better if we charge them $5,000 each." And then they laughed at us.... *We had also told them that we had kids and that we didn't want anything to happen to them.* And they said, laughing, "Oh, don't worry, Obama is giving you papers.... You'll walk out of immigration with your papers." (Dingeman et al., 2017, p. 303)

Instead of garnering documentation, Lupe and her husband were separated from their five children by the private prison industry and charged five thousand dollars each in bond. They were also made to acquire thousands of dollars from family for immigration attorneys in order to fight their removal, a process that can last up to four years (Dingeman et al., 2017).

For Alejandra Hernandez, a self-declared activist, the process of getting detained by the criminal justice system demonstrates the dynamism of the politics of immigrant containment and immigration enforcement policies. Similar to Alma, Alejandra's apprehension demonstrates the links and cooperation between the criminal justice system and federal immigration enforcement apparatus since she lives in a political jurisdiction where the criminal justice system actively participates in enforcing immigration laws. The interaction and the factors precipitating apprehension demonstrate the salience of class, parental status, and perceived markers of illegality—her racialized identity of being a Latina. Alejandra states,

> I was leaving my second job. With me I had some documents that all immigrants use because I was looking for another job that day. The documents weren't false because it had my real name. On my way home, down the block there was a police car. On the street it had three lanes. As I turned, I head into the middle lane. It was at night and I had my tags expired because I didn't have money to renew them. In my head, when I turned, my instant thought was about the expired tags, but as soon as I passed the police car went right after me. So, since it was nighttime, I am sure it was hard to see the tags.

Seeing the police and knowing she had expired tags, Alejandra engaged in actions to try to evade the attention by "head[ing] into the middle lane," and figured since it was dark outside, she would avoid a police encounter. Being aware that having expired registration tags ordinarily results in a citation, Alejandra was taken aback by the officer asking about her legal status:

> I thought he was going to give me a ticket. I have always been an activist, and I have always known my rights. When the official gets closer, . . . he asks me, "Are you legally or illegally in this country?" I said, "Excuse me, I don't understand your question." He then asked me again, so I said I was going to remain silent because I knew my rights. He then asked me for my license. I didn't have one so I gave him the insurance card, the registration, and my Mexican ID. As soon as the cop went to go check my documents, I called my husband, and I told him what happened. . . . I felt like I wasn't going to go home that day. I asked him to take care of my children. Unfortunately, yes, [the officer] came and told me to get [out of] the car. I told him, "My family is waiting, I have small children."

Given that Alejandra was first asked whether she was in the country legally, her racial markers of being a Latina are associated with illegality, transforming what would have been a routine traffic stop into one of deportability. Like Lupe, Alejandra's immediate concern was her children. In asking to call her husband "to take care of my children," Alejandra called the officer's attention to her status as a mother.

As shown below, sometimes the invocation of parental status positively supports deportable women, particularly as they request alternatives to detention or relief for removal. But in moments of apprehension, such as these experienced by women like Alejandra and Lupe, emotive claims to parental status and the well-being of children are routinely overlooked, and sometimes mocked, in the service of crimmigration priorities. Unlike men's, women's migratory and crimmigration narratives were more likely to center on their children.

Gendered Inspection and Detention Experiences

Gender operates in contradictory ways for women inside immigration detention. The highly profitable system is composed of a patchwork of jails, prisons, private detention centers, "family detention" for women and children, detention centers, camps, and foster homes for minors, and various other alternatives to detention. The women we interviewed experienced a variety of placements at which their treatment varied but was typically experienced as a highly inhumane, punitive site conditioned by a dearth of resources and an assumption that migrants (technically detained through an administrative law process) are to be treated like criminal inmates, sometimes enduring worse conditions. At times they were treated by the system/law or individual officers/agents as "humanitarian exceptions," but typically their vulnerabilities and traumas were ignored or exacerbated once inside the facilities.

After being held in a local jail for twenty-three days for expired tags and not having a license, Alejandra was picked up by ICE, then transferred to another jail in Colorado. Alejandra shared how such experiences are traumatizing:

> Once we arrived, they made us wait out in the snow, and they took me and the other six women into the bathroom, and the official told us to get undressed because they were going to check us. I then responded and asked what they were going to check if they had been checking us everywhere we were being taken. He then said he had to check our private parts to see if we had drugs. For me, it felt like they had thrown a bucket of water at me. I was like, "What's wrong with you? You're not going to do that to me. You're violating my human rights. I am not going to allow you to do that to me. You don't have to violate my intimacy." He was bothered but I was the only one who did not allow it.

Alejandra was confronted by an inspection procedure that amounts to a violation of her bodily integrity, not only because the procedure involved an inspection of her "private parts" but also because it was being done by a man. The violation of Alejandra's bodily integrity is an example of how the bodies of undocumented immigrant women are violable by the actors of the state (Escobar, 2016).

Beyond inspections, migrant women are locked up in detention centers that further reveal the various ways the state subordinates women. Detention itself and the resulting forced family separation seriously impact migrant women, sometimes pushing them to seek medication to endure the lived trauma. When asked to share her experience in detention, Lupe Lopez reflected on her observation of women in detention who would cry and medicate themselves to sleep:

> Wow, it was very difficult to be there locked up in four walls where you don't even get sunlight. I felt like you can't feel the hours go by [crying], seeing so many women in there suffering, the majority of them used pills. There was a doctor, and he would give them pills; and I would ask them what's going on, like, I could see the huge line of women in there; and in Spanish the guard would tell the women that the doctor was there, and they would run to go get in line, and I didn't know why, so they told me it was because the pills were for sleeping, so a lot of the women take sleeping pills. They're desperate. For some of them, it had been four months, six months, eight months since they hadn't seen their families, so for them it was very difficult.

Similarly, when Alejandra was asked if her experience in detention was different because she was a woman, her response reflected the simultaneity of being a woman, a mother, and a person lacking financial means: "As a woman, you turn into an octopus for your children. You fight more for your children. Unfortunately, these situations also destroy families due to the stress and the lack of money. Like I tell you, our lives never go back to normal."

While Alejandra's experience speaks to the violation of her body integrity and lifelong damage to her family and Lupe's observation demonstrates migrant women seeking medication to escape the trauma in detention, other women detailed what amounts to a *situated advantage* when compared to men. According to some interviewees, their gender as migrant Latina women occasionally reflected *an advantage* due to crimmigration's particular targeting, criminalization, and harshness toward men. For example, Lupe said,

> Every case is different, but I saw that they treated the men more harshly because, like, they put chains on their feet, waist, and hands. And us? We just had them on our hands, and um, it was a little different. . . . They put us in the front of the bus, and they had them separated, like, they're a bit more harsh with the men than with the women, but every case is different. I have heard cases when they mistreat and abuse women.

Certain women experienced moments of advantage relative to men and other women from benevolence accorded to them by enforcement agents, officers, judges, and bureaucrats who took sympathy on their gendered plight or status as mothers or took a liking to them romantically or sexually. Sylvia remembered an instance in which a male ICE officer provided what might be interpreted as paternalistic care, treating her (and her children, by proxy) as a vehicle for an individuated form of humanitarian exceptionalism. Sylvia recounted his kindness affectionately:

> I then met an officer who was Puerto Rican. I would talk to him a lot and tell him my story. He asked me why I had crossed, and I told him I was running away from my daughter's dad. He [her husband] is a Mara Salvatrucha and wants to kill me. He would ask me, "Are you hungry?" and I would say "Yes, I am hungry." He would tell me he was going to give me packets of bread so that I could hide them and give them to my kids. He would only do that for me. I would then see the rest hungry so I would give them some. He would tell me to hide it under my mattress. He then advised me to get an immigration lawyer once I got out. He would tell me they were racist. He told me to never forget him. There are good people and bad people.

Sylvia highlighted the humanity that can be found in the crimmigration system, but this is rare and often complex. For example, Rocio also noted that certain agents were "nice" to her when she was caught crossing the border. One such agent took pity on her and especially her children, giving them twenty dollars for food, as he simultaneously deported them and reprimanded her for attempting to cross unlawfully. After she had been caught by CBP "five or six times," Rocio's husband was separated from the family and sent to a detention center for men. Owing to her status as woman and mother, Rocio was sent with her children to "family detention," a purportedly more humane placement, where any semblance of humanitarianism was nonexistent. She explained,

> That time I didn't like the way I was treated because they held me there until about four in the morning. They didn't separate me from the three kids, they went with me to the detention center for women. But they

didn't give us a bed or anything. It was, like, just a bed made of rock. I was there hugging my daughter, and another one on my leg, and another one over here. . . . I fell asleep sitting up and the kids, they couldn't lay down because there was no beds, so I made them sleep on me.

Rocio remembers that while she was in detention an official called her a "criminal" and a "terrorist" and that officers "would threaten me that I would get deported every day." This was despite the fact that she was eligible for and eventually granted political asylum on gendered grounds. Such an instance was echoed by nearly all our participants, who shared numerous other stories of inhumane treatment in detention, from harassment by guards to inhospitable beds, poor food, frigid air, ragged bedding, lack of medical care, coercive deportation practices, and particularly bad treatment by specific agents.

This pattern was reproduced and sometimes worse for pregnant women. According to the ACLU (2018), pregnant women receive inadequate health care in immigration detention. They are often treated as humanitarian exceptions and released on bond, but a large number are apprehended and detained, especially those who are criminalized or, increasingly common, treated as threats to national security. We interviewed one woman, Elana, who was seven months pregnant at the moment of apprehension. She was not granted bond due to a criminal history, and she was denied special treatment in spite of her child. The punitive nature of immigration detention and deportation was made irreparably tragic owing to the detention facility's gender-neutral, and likely more violent approach to Elana because of her pregnant status. Telling the story of her baby's death in detention, Elana reported,

> I had been given a bed upstairs, but they were saying lunch, we were going to eat, and I went down, and when I went down, like, I passed out. I do not know what happened, I only know that when I woke up, I was already there. They had me tied up in a stretcher and everything, and I said, "What happened?" And they told me that the girl had died inside me . . . that they were going to put me as an injection or something to cause me the pain to see if I could have it. They did not want to do a cesarean. But it is hard, hard, I had never passed that, never in my life, very hard. I needed

someone. I needed as she understands me, my mom, or my grandmother, someone with me there.

While in deportation processing, a guard further mocked Elana's miscarriage saying, "[They] told me the ugliest thing. You are going to your country and are not taking your child. . . . And I was telling him why is he doing it? And he told me to shut the fuck up. And I said, 'Okay, I'm going to shut up but why do you treat people that way?'" Elana was deported to El Salvador, where miscarriage is criminalized, where she faced domestic abuse by her partner, and from where she may emigrate one day, potentially with children.

Gendered Exceptions, Limitations, and Consequences of the Legal Process

The legal process for deportable migrants is gender-neutral on the surface but gendered in practice. Women like Sylvia entered the United States only to have the gendered violence they experienced compounded by the criminal justice and immigration systems. Sylvia fled a precarious existence in the hopes of obtaining a U visa (available to victims of violent crime who comply with law enforcement investigations) in the United States. Fortunately, she survived a dangerous crossing but immediately upon arrival was captured by immigration officials. Without the knowledge, funds, or connections to properly request a visa, Sylvia was summarily deported to Honduras. Almost immediately upon arrival, her husband attempted to murder her, and Sylvia once again fled with her children by foot. The second time they presented themselves to immigration authorities with knowledge to affirmatively request political asylum:

> I crossed and then sat down. I wanted to walk but it was all dark. An immigration officer then got there. I told him I knew no English. I then told him I was fleeing my country because I can't go back. I told him I needed their help and that I couldn't go back because my daughter's dad wanted to kill me, which is why I asked for political asylum.

Though now formally registered as an asylum seeker, Sylvia was still treated as a national security concern and sent to a family detention center in Texas where she and her children waited for two months in dilapidated conditions: "I was then detained for two months. Starving, I couldn't wash my teeth; I couldn't shower; I couldn't do my necessities. They would humiliate me. They were very racist there" (Dingeman et al., 2017, p. 307).

Like Sylvia, Rocio had experienced domestic violence at the hands of her spouse. During the family's ten attempts to arrive in the United States, he valiantly shielded her and their three children against an attack by smugglers who brutally beat him. Once in the United States the husband became abusive to her. She knew that she could seek a U visa on account of the violence but was afraid of the state's requirement that she comply with an investigation that might also lead to her vicarious deportation: "The cops had told me ten years ago that I could get help from the government if I wanted it, and I remember I had said that the last thing I wanted was to have contact with immigration." Rocio was eventually deported for a criminalized immigration violation related to fraudulent attempts to obtain a driver's license. She was unable to obtain legal aid and summarily deported without either making a claim of domestic violence or arguing for the extreme hardship her three children would face if she were removed precisely because she was poor.

Cases in which women's gendered vulnerabilities were purposefully denied because of their racialized class standing were also rampant in our sample. Before having the chance to make a case for humanitarian relief, every woman was filtered through the crimmigration system. Some of them were eventually able to garner legal status due to their gendered victimization; this was based not on eligibility or merit but on kinship ties and/or community support tied to financial resources or availability of legal aid. In Sylvia's case, she did not have access to kin ties that could provide financial resources, but she reached out to the immigrant rights agency that helped her publicly discuss her story on Telemundo. This garnered the attention of an immigration attorney who specializes in gender claims. Sylvia had in fact been ordered to be deported, but the attorney quickly filed an appeal, which ultimately led to political asylum instead of deportation to a country where a violent partner and member of MS-13 awaited her.

After her deportation, Lupe traversed Mexico again, entered the United States, and began working in a retirement home. One day she was involved in a minor collision and the police apprehended her, noted her classification as a "fugitive," and sent her into federal custody. Unlike Sylvia, Lupe had critical ties to kin, which she mobilized: "My brother paid an attorney, he told the attorney he didn't want to see me in jail so to do whatever needed to be done to get me out and either get deported or just get me out of there, whatever it took. And she got me out.... My brother paid the thousand-dollar fine to get me out."

Immediately upon release from jail, ICE apprehended Lupe, and she was transferred to detention, where she was asked to sign a voluntary return form before given a right to speak with an attorney. "ICE, they gave me a sheet of paper to sign, and I said no I'm not going to sign because the first time I didn't know, but this time my brother told me not to sign anything. He said we're going to fight this one to see what happens." Lupe's daughter, who was now old enough to assist, also reached out to several attorneys, one of whom was willing to take on her case. Lupe was soon granted asylum, for which she had always been eligible.

Not all of the women in our sample benefitted from humanitarian provisions that accounted for their gendered vulnerabilities. Like men we interviewed, they languished in legal limbo or were deported. Isabel's case was pending for years after a fraudulent attorney stole thousands of dollars and submitted her name to ICE. Unable to work, she was left relying on the financial support of her daughter who was undocumented but raised and educated in the United States. When Alejandra received an order of deportation, she relied on community support as she sought sanctuary in a church and sought a U visa for domestic violence. Ana Maria was deported after signing a voluntary return form she did not understand. Highlighting the intergenerational nature of gendered migratory circuits, she remained in El Salvador to care for her grandchildren while her daughters migrated to the United States to alleviate the family's poverty. Alma Maria faced a similar circumstance. After being deported, she decided to prioritize proximity with her son over fulfilling parental responsibilities abroad. Though worried about their financial stability, she said, "I don't want to go back [to the United States].... At least I won't leave my son because I have seen cases of mothers leaving and they don't treat their children the same—the people who they leave them with here."

Finally, we found that some women successfully receive humanitarian relief, placing them on a more secure and hopeful path. For example, Patricia was a teenager when she was apprehended after ICE raided a strip club to which she was indentured as part of a sex trafficking ring. Because of her age and status as an unaccompanied minor, she was transferred to the Office of Refugee Resettlement. There, she was placed into a series of white, English-speaking foster families, who could not relate to her situated experience. Patricia eventually obtained a T visa and green card and was able to bring her parents to the United States, but she could not escape her past. Her father was murdered in Honduras during a return visit by members of the trafficking ring who believed he was in the United States to avenge his daughter. Later on, her fiancé and father of her child was deported to El Salvador, leaving her a single working mother struggling to survive paycheck to paycheck.

When Rocio finally received asylum, she reported that her family "were all screaming and crying—my brother, my mom, my daughter, all of them were very happy. . . . They all celebrated. I jumped up and down and cried. I didn't know what to do." Being in detention for so long and witnessing many atrocities along the way made Rocio believe she was to be eventually deported. She described being in a "disturbed" state of "shock" when released from detention, as she continued to struggle with posttraumatic stress:

> When I left there, I was so disturbed because all my life has been so emotional. So much emotion—like very down, and then out of nowhere all the way up. I was so disturbed. My son-in-law picked me up at the door, and he was saying "Mom, mom come here!" But I was like "What?" He said "Come here!" The officer finally said "Go, you're free, leave!" And it was through the front door because that's how they treat you: the front door if you can go [free], the back door if you're being deported. And I couldn't make sense of it. . . . I was in shock for like a week. I remember that because I would wake up thinking I was in jail. I dreamt I was in jail. I thought something would happen. Ever since I got deported, I lived my life, like, not knowing what was going to happen. . . . [sigh] [My life] went from being down in the gutters . . . I think my life changed to like three hundred or four hundred degrees. It just, bam, turned. My emotions were the only ones that didn't realize it. They wouldn't touch the ground until

like one or two months later... I came out like dazed, mentally disturbed, like, traumatized. But because of that I consider myself a strong woman. I have been through very tough stuff and here I am standing, and still here. I'm here.

Conclusion

In this chapter we considered the ways the state shapes the contexts through which migrant identities interact to produce discrete trajectories and experiences. We developed a *transnational model of intersectionality* that pushes past binary logics that can oversimplify the lived realities of migrants. We drew on literature on "rebordering" and "crimmigration" to argue that the border is not only a physical location but a set of elastic and expanding spatial and institutional sites at which the state asserts its powers to govern migrant belonging. In the era of "crimmigration," the state asserts its sovereign power by enacting restrictionist policies via securitization and criminalization initiatives at northern and especially southern border zones and increasingly on the interior and into Mexico. This "rebordering" affects the lives of migrants as they attempt to enter and remain in the United States.

Past research has demonstrated that the effects of crimmigration are intersectional along class, race, and gendered lines. Poor, Black, and Latino migrant men are most likely to be apprehended, detained, and deported, while women and children are often left behind (Dreby, 2015). But women and girls are also entering and cycling through the system. When asked whether the system is gendered, the women in our study often mentioned that "the men have it worse" or that "it's the same for men and women." Alejandra stated, for instance, "It's not different because men suffer the same way.... When you're a good mom or a good dad you're going to do everything you can to be with your children.... Men who want to get out are suffering; [they] also cry because those feelings aren't just exclusive to women." Yet she later contradicted this initial assessment by saying, "Women do have to fight more and with more passion. We are the pillar of our families. Children need both their mom and dad, but they need their mother more."

Women's experiences with crimmigration are similar to yet unique from those of men. Like with men, there exists an intersectional nature to their experiences such that poor Latin American women are more likely to be denied legal status prior to migration, forced to cross by land, apprehended at the border, and targeted for criminalization, detention, and deportation once settled in the interior than are women of other national origins, racial groups, and class standings. As Isabel contended, her experiences cannot be attributed only to her status as a woman: "It is okay because, not because I'm a woman, simply because I'm Latina, because I'm Latina, because. . . . [crying] It's like they don't even take me into consideration . . . I feel like they don't take me into consideration *because I am Latina*." Here Isabel grasps that Latin American women enter the system both as by-products of the targeting of men and as part of a historically racialized, classed, and gendered process of ensuring a surplus source of labor for the United States (De Genova, 2002).

We examined poor Latin American women's experiences at different sites throughout their journeys, noting the power of the state in shaping the geographic and temporal nature of these spaces with which they interact. By excavating the gendered nature of these sites, we further observed that the differential experiences within the category of women are further shaped by intersections with another set of factors: in particular their parental status, their kinship ties, and the availability of community support. Thus, while our empirical analysis demonstrated that gender differentially affects immigration outcomes, we moved beyond an analysis of differences and examined the various ways gender simultaneously interacts with other social identities to shape encounters with the state.

Overall, our project found that an intersectional framework necessitates moving beyond borders and situates power in moving and temporal sites of domination and subordination. The patterns we have unearthed speak most directly to the experiences of Latinas in the Obama era. Under the Trump administration, rebordering and crimmigration accelerated at an alarming pace. Crimmigration priorities are not only superseding humanitarian concerns as they did for the women we interviewed, but are being entirely eroded. Through "zero-tolerance" policies criminalizing unlawful entry, the elimination of gender-based asylum claims that assisted women fleeing gender and sexual violence, mandatory detention, family separation, child migrant internment, attempts to eliminate DACA and TPS, and militarized tactics to prohibit asylum seekers from crossing the border, the deportation machinery is vividly and unapologetically *violando los derechos* of migrants through symbolic and direct state repression. Future research should continue to develop intersectional frameworks to explore how noncitizens differentially situated in relation to the state are impacted by these shifts.

NOTE

1 In 1924, the Border Patrol was created along with the category of "illegal entry." In 1953, the borderline expanded into a hundred-mile border zone where immigration laws could be enforced. Other major nativist efforts were instituted over time to exclude, contain, and repatriate specific national origin groups, including Chinese Exclusion (1882–1943), Mexican Repatriation (1930s), Japanese Internment (1942–1946), and Operation Wetback (1954). Various other policies limited the immigration and naturalization of the poor, women, sexual minorities, persons with health and mental health issues, radicals, and asylum seekers fleeing the regimes of political allies. Despite these efforts, Border Patrol was ineffective, interior enforcement was virtually nonexistent, and the porous borderland permitted migrants to cycle in and out relatively freely.

REFERENCES

ACLU. (2018). The constitution in the 100-mile border zone. www.aclu.org.

Andreas, P. (2000). *Border games: Policing the U.S.-Mexico divide.* Ithaca, NY: Cornell University Press.

Brigden, N. K. (2018). Gender mobility: Survival plays and performing Central American migration in passage. *Mobilities, 13,* 111–125.

Brotherton, D. C., & Barrios, L. (2011). *Banished to the homeland: Dominican deportees and their stories of exile.* New York: Columbia University Press.

Capps, R., Koball, H., Campetella, A., Perreira, K., Hooker, S., & Pedroza, J. M. (2015). *Implications of immigration enforcement activities for the well-being of children in immigrant families: A review of the literature.* Washington, DC: Migration Policy Institute.

Cervantes, W., Ullrich, R., & Matthews, H. (2018). *Our children's fear: Immigration policy's effects on young children.* Washington, DC: Center for Law and Social Policy.

Collins, P. H. (1990). *Black feminist thought: Knowledge, consciousness, and the politics of empowerment.* Boston: Unwin Hyman.

Collins, P. H. (1993). Toward a new vision: Race, class, and gender as categories of analysis and connection. *Race, Sex, & Class, 1,* 25–45.

Collins, P. H. (2000). Gender, Black feminism, and Black political economy. *Annals of the American Academy of Political and Social Science, 568,* 41–53.

Cunningham, H. (2009). Mobilities and enclosures after Seattle: Politicizing borders in a "borderless" world. *Dialectical Anthropology, 33,* 143–156.

Das Gupta, M. (2013). "Don't deport our daddies": Gendering state deportation practices and immigrant organizing. *Gender & Society, 28*, 83–109.
De Genova, N. P. (2002). Migrant "illegality" and deportability in everyday life. *Annual Review of Anthropology, 31*, 419–447.
Dingeman, K., Arzhayev, Y., Ayala, C., Bermudez, E., Padama, L., & Tena-Chávez, L. (2017). Protected, neglected, ejected: Latin American women caught by crimmigration. *Feminist Criminology, 12*, 293–314.
Dingeman-Cerda, K., & Rumbaut, R. G. (2015). Unwelcome returns: The alienation of the new American diaspora in Salvadoran society. In D. Kanstroom & B. Lykes (Eds.), *New deportations delirium: Interdisciplinary responses* (pp. 227–250). New York: New York University Press.
Douglas, K., & Sáenz, R. (2013). The criminalization of immigrants and the immigration industrial complex. *Daedalus, 142*, 199–227.
Dowling, J. A., & Inda, J. X. (2013). *Governing immigration through crime: A reader*. Stanford, CA: Stanford University Press.
Dreby, J. (2015). *Everyday illegal: When policies undermine immigrant families*. Berkeley: University of California Press.
Drotbohm, H. (2015). The reversal of migratory family lives: A Cape Verdean perspective on gender and sociality pre- and post-deportation. *Journal of Ethnic and Migration Studies, 41*, 653–670.
Eagly, I. V., & Shafer, S. (2015). A national study of access to counsel in immigration court. *University of Pennsylvania Law Review, 164*, 1–91.
ECLAC. (2017). *Social panorama of Latin America, 2016*. Santiago, Chile: Economic Commission for Latin America and the Caribbean. https://repositorio.cepal.org.
Escobar, M. D. (2016). *Captivity beyond prisons: Criminalization experiences of Latina (im)migrants*. Austin: University of Texas Press.
Fassin, D. (2011). *Humanitarian Reason: A Moral History of the Present*. Berkeley: University of California Press.
Galemba, R. B. (2018). *Contraband corridor: Making a living at the Mexico-Guatemala border*. Stanford, CA: Stanford University Press.
García, S. J. (2017). Racializing "illegality": An intersectional approach to understanding how Mexican-origin women navigate an anti-immigrant climate. *Sociology of Race and Ethnicity, 3*, 474–490.
García Hernández, C. C. (2013). Creating crimmigration. *Brigham Young University Law Review, 6*, 1457–1516.
Golash-Boza, T. M. (2015). *Deported: Immigrant policing, disposable labor, and global capitalism*. New York: New York University Press.
Golash-Boza, T. M. (2016). Parallels between mass incarceration and mass deportation: An intersectional analysis. *Journal of World-Systems Research, 22*, 484–509.
Golash-Boza, T. M., & Hondagneu-Sotelo, P. (2013). Latino immigrant men and the deportation crisis: A gendered racial removal program. *Latino Studies, 11*, 271–292.
Hallock, J., Ruiz Soto, A. G., & Fix, M. (2018). *In search of safety, growing numbers of women flee Central America*. Washington, DC: Migration Policy Institute.

Harty, A. S. (2012). Commentary: Gendering crimmigration: The intersection of gender, immigration, and the criminal justice system. *Berkeley Journal of Gender, Law, & Justice, 27*, 1–27.

Hite, A., & Viterna, J. S. (2005). Gendering class in Latin America: How women effect and experience change in the class structure. *Latin American Research Review, 40*, 50–82.

Inda, J. X., & Dowling, J. A. (2013). Introduction: Governing migrant illegality. In J. A. Dowling & J. X. Inda (Eds.), *Governing immigration through crime: A reader* (pp. 1–36). Stanford, CA: Stanford University Press.

International Crisis Group. (2018). *Mexico's southern border: Security, violence and migration in the Trump era*. Brussels: International Crisis Group.

Isacson, A., Meyer, M., & Smith, H. (2017). *Mexico's southern border: Security, Central American migration, and U.S. policy*. Washington, DC: Washington Office on Latin America.

Kagan, M. (2015). Immigrant victims, immigrant accusers. *University of Michigan Journal of Law Reform, 48*, 915–966.

Kanstroom, D. (2007). *Deportation nation: Outsiders in American history*. Cambridge, MA: Harvard University Press.

Kids in Need of Defense, Latin American Working Group, & Women's Refugee Commission. (2017, June). Sexual and gender-based violence (SGBV) & migration fact sheet. https://supportkind.org.

Macías-Rojas, P. (2017). *From deportation to prison: The politics of immigration enforcement in post–civil rights America*. New York: New York University Press.

Nevins, J. (2010). *Operation gatekeeper: The war on "illegals" and the remaking of the U.S.-Mexico boundary* (2nd ed.). New York: Routledge.

Pedroza, J. M. (2013). Removal roulette: Secure communities and immigration enforcement in the United States (2008–2012). In D. C. Brotherton, D. L. Stageman, & S. P. Leyro (Eds.), *Outside justice* (pp. 45–65). New York: Springer.

Romero, M. (2008). Crossing the immigration and race border: A critical race approach to immigration studies. *Contemporary Justice Review, 11*, 23–37.

Rosas, G. (2006). The thickening borderlands: Diffused exceptionality and "immigrant" social struggles during the "war on terror." *Cultural Dynamics, 18*, 335–349.

Sanchez, G. (2015). *Human smuggling and border crossings*. New York: Routledge.

Sanchez, G. (2017). Beyond the matrix of oppression: Reframing human smuggling through intersectionality-informed approaches. *Theoretical Criminology, 21*, 46–56.

Sanchez, G. E., & Zhang, S. X. (2018). Rumors, encounters, collaborations, and survival: The migrant smuggling–drug trafficking nexus in the US Southwest. *Annals of the American Academy of Political and Social Science, 676*, 135–151.

Slack, J., Martínez, D. E., Lee, A. E., & Whiteford, S. (2016). The geography of border militarization: Violence, death and health in Mexico and the United States. *Journal of Latin American Geography, 15*, 7–32.

Smyth, T. (2015, October 16). Abuse of migrants in Mexico rises even as number fall. Reuters. www.reuters.com.

Stumpf, J. P. (2006). The crimmigration crisis: Immigrants, crime, and sovereign power. *American University Law Review, 56*, 367–419.

UNHCR. (2006). Feminization of migration: Remittances, migrants' rights, brain drain among issues, as population commission concludes debate. United Nations. www.un.org.

U.S. Department of Homeland Security. (2017). Yearbook of immigration statistics: 2016. Washington, DC: U.S. Department of Homeland Security, Office of Immigration Statistics.

Wimmer, A., & Glick Schiller, N. (2002). Methodological nationalism and beyond: Nation-state building, migration, and the social sciences. *Global Networks, 2*, 301–334.

8

Masking Punitive Practices

Latina Immigrants' Experiences in the U.S. Detention Complex

CECILIA MENJÍVAR, ANDREA GÓMEZ CERVANTES, AND
WILLIAM G. STAPLES

Between 2003 and 2018, 90 percent of the more than 4.6 million immigrants who were deported were from Mexico, Guatemala, Honduras, and El Salvador (TRAC Immigration, 2019), but immigrants from these countries make up 67 percent of the undocumented population (Migration Policy Institute [MPI], 2019). As with deportations, Latina/o immigrants, particularly men, bear the brunt of detentions; between 2003 and 2018, 90 percent of immigrant detainees were men (Ryo & Peacock, 2018; TRAC Immigration, 2019). This targeting of Latino men has been characterized by Golash-Boza and Hondagneu-Sotelo (2013, p. 272) as a "gendered and racial removal project of the state" (see also Bosworth, Parmar, & Vazquez, 2018; Provine & Doty, 2011) with significant consequences for Latino families (Das Gupta, 2008; Dreby, 2015). However, even though the overwhelming majority of immigrant detainees and deportees are men, an examination of women's experiences highlights the gendered dimensions of the detention system. To explore Latinas' experiences of their time in confinement facilities as well as in "alternative to detention" (ATD) programs, we rely on their own accounts of their participation in these programs as well as on observations and descriptions of the system by legal professionals who assist them with their cases.

Since 1996, immigration law has made the detention of certain immigrants mandatory; this was a critical development in the expansion of the immigrant detention system that has been amplified today. The Trump administration dramatically increased the likelihood of interior apprehensions as well as "returns" from the border (Department of Homeland Security [DHS], 2017b). Latinas apprehended in the interior are sometimes released on bond (if they pose no threat to the community or are unlikely to miss future immigration hearings), and asylum seekers are typically released and placed in ATD programs if their cases are found to merit further evaluation.[1] And while the first group is composed mostly of Mexican and Central American women, the overwhelming majority of those apprehended at the border and seeking asylum originate in Central America—from Guatemala, El Salvador, Honduras—as they flee from gender-based violence in these countries (Cardoletti-Carroll, Farmer, & Velez, 2015).

In February 2018 the U.S. Supreme Court ruled that immigrants can be held in detention indefinitely (Barnes, 2018); as of this writing it is unclear how this decision will be implemented. However, the Trump administration requested a significant expansion to the bed minimum in detention facilities, from thirty-four thousand in 2016 (DHS, 2016) to fifty-four thousand in 2020 (DHS, 2018a), which, together with the Supreme Court's ruling, may signal a massive expansion in immigrant detention.

Our examination of the experiences of Latina immigrants who are detained and released on an ATD program exposes the pronounced coercive social control and surveillance policies and practices embedded in these so-called humanitarian approaches to the treatment of migrants. We see this as a form of what Agier (2010, 2011) calls "humanitarian governmentality," Fassin (2005) refers to as "compassionate repression," and Tazzioli (2016) refers to as the staging of "humanitarian real-time politics."

We find that newer, more subtle benevolence-signaling discourse (Menjívar & Kil, 2002) used in the facilities and policy narratives evoking "family," "motherhood," and the "protection" of children mask the harsh "business as usual" tactics that treat women and their children in ways that are indistinguishable from tactics used in the criminal justice system.[2] We contend that such benevolent framing does not alter the legal and bureaucratic structures that operate in these programs and that have created the conditions for increased confinements. Rather, this "humane" language serves only to conceal widespread civil and human rights violations, physical and sexual violence, and general mistreatment taking place, what Eason, Hernández, and Rubio-Goldsmith (2016) refer to as the "punitive capacity" of the immigration detention system today.[3]

In the following sections we first explore the feminized discourses that disguise strategies of control in immigration detention and in the ATD programs aimed at Latina immigrant bodies. To set the context for the current situation, we present a brief chronology of the major laws that have expanded the criminalization and consequential detention of Latina/o immigrants. Second, we offer an overview of the operation of family detention centers and other programs and introduce several concepts that we use to highlight the surveillance, control, and punitive practices used in the increasingly privatized immigrant detention complex. Third, we describe our methods and data and present our findings focusing on one illustrative case in depth from the more general pattern in our data and on interviews with lawyers who work with woman clients and who have witnessed how the system operates. Finally, we consider some of the damaging consequences for immigrant Latinas and their families brought about by their experiences with the immigration system.

The Escalation of Detention and Deportation of Immigrants

Since the 1980s, every immigration law passed by Congress has included provisions that have contributed to criminalize immigrants (Menjívar, Gómez Cervantes, & Alvord, 2018), mostly by expanding the category of behaviors labeled as crimes for immigrants (Provine, 2015), which are punishable and result in detention and later deportation for immigrants. This criminalization process has had dramatic effects on the mass detention and deportation of Latina/o immigrants. For example, the Immigration Reform and Control Act of 1986 (IRCA) and the Illegal Immigration Reform and Immigrant Responsibility Act of 1996 (IIRIRA) sought to deter undocumented migration at a time when immigrants, particularly undocumented immigrants and Latinas/os, were being blamed and held responsible for criminal behavior (Menjívar, 2014a). Among other things, IRCA increased the budget of the Border Patrol (Massey, Durand, & Malone, 2002) and created a mechanism for the immediate deportation or "expedited removal" of immigrants who were convicted of a crime (Inda, 2013).

In 1994, the Clinton administration enacted Operation Gatekeeper in an attempt to deter undocumented migration at the U.S.-Mexico border. This led to the heightened policing of traditional entrance pathways. But instead of deterring migration, it pushed immigrants to dangerous crossing environments such as deserts and rivers, leading to thousands of immigrant deaths (Massey et al., 2002). Two years later, IIRIRA broadened justifications for deportation and linked immigration offenses—previously viewed as a civil offense—to criminal ones (Menjívar, 2014b).[4] IIRIRA broadened the scope of "aggravated felony" to over twenty categories of offenses, many of which are not considered felonies for citizens (Provine, 2015). At the same time, the Anti-terrorism and Effective Death Penalty Act (AEDPA) was signed, which created mandatory detention of noncitizens with criminal offenses (Menjívar & Kanstroom, 2014). The Obama administration applied expedited removal to undocumented immigrants apprehended within a hundred miles of the border who had been in the United States for less than two weeks. However, the Trump administration made expedited removal a nationwide policy to target people who have been living in the country for under two years (American Immigration Council, 2017).

As detention strategies changed from "catch and release" to "catch and detain," today immigrants who are apprehended are sent to detention centers, jails, and prisons (Douglas & Sáenz, 2013). This new approach has affected the budgets of governmental agencies including the Department of Homeland Security (DHS), Customs and Border Protection (CBP), and Immigration and Customs Enforcement (ICE); they have increased dramatically. For instance, the total budget request for the 2005 DHS was $40.2 billion (DHS, 2004), by 2010 it increased to $60 billion (DHS, 2009), and the budget request for the DHS for 2019 was $74.5 billion (DHS, 2018a). The budgets for ICE have also increased rapidly, from $3.9 *million* in 2005 (DHS, 2006) to $8.8 *billion* in 2019 (DHS, 2018a). Similar expansions are observed with the CBP budget going from $6.1 *million* in 2005 (DHS, 2004) to $16.7 *billion* by 2019 (DHS, 2018a). These rising budgets have translated into an ever-expanding system to detain and surveil an increasing number of immigrants.

Following a series of executive orders signed in early 2017, these swelling budgets have now reached an all-time high (Menjívar et al., 2018). Enforcement tools, such as detention and deportation, are not new; however, the "punitive turn" (Garland, 2001) in the criminal justice system that has led to mass incarceration, especially for African Americans, has also transformed the tools of control into tools of criminalization for immigrants. Focusing on detention strategies, including those that take place outside formal institutions such as in ATD programs, we investigate the gendered and infantilized language used to veil social control strategies of Latina immigrant women in detention and other forms of monitoring and control.

Surveillance, Control, and Punishment of Immigrants

The immigration system operates on many of the same principles and deploys similar tactics that we see in other social control institutions such as prisons and other criminal justice programs (Foucault, 1977; Goffman, 1961; Staples, 1991, 2014). Foucault (1977, p. 135) argued that the goal of discipline in these institutions is to create "docile bodies"—mute, obedient, and pliable individuals who have been subjected, used, and transformed through a regiment of disciplinary acts. We find that such practices are likewise present in immigrant processing facilities and ATD programs, but here they operate under the guise of feminized, infantilized, and paternalistic discourses. The "mother and children" linguistic trope—what Enloe (1991) calls "womenandchildren"—serves to mask practices that criminalize women and their behaviors and control their bodies. And in an increasingly privatized immigration control complex, these bodies are frequently "commodified" (Staples, 1991) as tangible sources of profit for contractors to be controlled while in detention and disposed of through deportation. This form of humanitarian governmentality (Agier, 2011) uses "compassionate" and paternalistic tropes while simultaneously exercising systematic control of and perpetrating violence against Latina immigrants.

We have also seen forms of "humanitarian governmentality" (Agier, 2010) in the language that lawmakers have used to attempt to obscure proposed coercive control strategies. For instance, after an increase of youth fleeing violence in Central America in 2014 and entering the United States through its southern border, congressional representatives from Texas introduced a bill titled Helping Unaccompanied Minors and Alleviating National Emergency Act, or what was referred to as the Humane Act (H.R. 5114; Library of Congress, 2018a). This bill attempted to revoke the 2008 William Wilberforce Trafficking Victims

Protection Reauthorization Act of 2008, which would have prevented U.S. officials from immediately deporting youth and children from countries not sharing a border with the United States who enter without inspection. The 2014 bill aimed instead to process *all* "unaccompanied minors equally" regardless of country of origin, therefore making it easier for U.S. officials to deport non-Mexican youth (the bulk of those entering during the "surge" of 2014) faster (Downes, 2014). We see then the "humane" and "helping" language present in H.R. 5114 would have actually done the opposite and make it more difficult for youth to seek asylum and easier to deport them to life-threatening conditions. In another instance of this strategy, in the same year Senator Ted Cruz of Texas introduced Senate bill S. 2666, titled Protect Children and Families through the Rule of Law Act (Library of Congress, 2018b). This bill again deployed the compassionate-sounding language suggesting that its intent was to "protect children and families," when it actually had the same goal as the Humane Act, to speed up the deportation of unaccompanied immigrant youth applying for protection in the United States. Although these two bills did not ultimately become law, these attempts were followed in 2017 by H.R. 495, Protection of Children Act of 2017, introduced by Representative John Carter of Texas (GovTrack, 2017). Regardless of whether the flurry of proposed amendments to toughen up immigration laws, as with all bills, the titles are written by the sponsors and underscores our point. The use of terms such as "helping," "humane," and "Protection of Children" illustrates attempts to use benevolent language aimed at garnering public approval while masking the true intent and actual consequences for immigrants.

ATD programs have been in place since the early 2000s and have been quickly expanded since (Fernandes, 2017); by 2009, for instance, there were close to twenty thousand immigrants in ATDs (Schriro, 2009). Their aim has been to "provide expanded options for release of adult aliens, by assisting officers in closely monitoring aliens released into the community" (Lee, 2005). However, because these programs allow formerly detained immigrants to go live in their communities and were presented as community-based supervision strategies or as community programs (Fernandes, 2017; Schriro, 2009), they *sounded* more "humane" than outright detention. The most common of the programs that ICE operates is the Intensive Supervision Appearance Program (ISAP), which is the most restrictive and has two variations: the Technology-Only and Full Service options (DHS, 2015c).[5] The difference between these two programs is the cost and type of technology used to track immigrants, which Enforcement Removal Operations (ERO) is not monitoring directly. These programs are subcontracted to private companies that supervise and monitor immigrants outside of detention facilities to ensure their court appearances and compliance with removal orders. Strategies used to carry out this surveillance involve routine in-person meetings with case managers, unannounced home visits, electronic monitoring through ankle bracelets with GPS or radio frequency monitoring, and voice recognition software. Staples (2014, p. 42) argues that, in the criminal justice system, such tactics of social control and surveillance have, rather than operate more "humanely" as proponents claim, "inserted the power to judge and punish more deeply into the daily life of the community, 'deinstitutionalizing,' along with the offender, the disciplinary procedures and mechanisms of the prison."

Methods and Data

Our research might be characterized as a mixed-method and multiple-sources approach. Given the lack of information and transparency on the part of the U.S. government about individuals held in detention and about those who come before immigration proceedings (e.g., counts, gender, age, race, education level, etc.), we have culled material from existing documents produced by governmental offices, including DHS, ICE, Border Patrol, Government Accountability Office, nonprofit organizations, immigration law offices, advocacy groups, and private companies including Corrections Corporation of America (now CoreCivic) and the Geo Group Inc. Documents include congressional and agency statistical reports, contracts, budgets, budget requests, fiscal reports, and memoranda. Each document is likely to contain partial, incomplete, and/or limited information that we have threaded together to compose the picture we present here.

We also conducted semistructured interviews with eleven immigration lawyers who have access to women who are and/or have been detained, are in supervised ATD programs, are or were in deportation proceedings, or attempted to claim asylum. The lawyers are not subjects of research themselves but sources of information that is otherwise inaccessible. Still, we have anonymized their names in this chapter. The interview questions focus on four broad topics: (1) population of the detention centers and ATD programs, (2) role of law enforcement agents (i.e., police, judges, and immigration enforcement), (3) detention centers' infrastructure, and (4) overview and experiences of ATD programs. The lawyers interviewed have worked with immigrant women for an average of 12.3 years, ranging from 1.5 to 41 years. They have worked in a variety of detention facilities including family residential centers in Dilley, Taylor, and Karnes City, Texas, Artesia, New Mexico, and Eloy, Arizona, as well as immigration detention centers in Arizona, Colorado, and Missouri and various juvenile facilities around the country. Through the lawyer accounts of these organizations, we explore the enforcement control practices that the state and private corporations employ on Latina immigrants in detention and through various surveillance tactics when they are released.

We also draw on interviews conducted from an ethnographic project on immigration to Kansas (Alvord, Menjívar, & Gómez Cervantes, 2018; Gómez Cervantes, Alvord, & Menjívar, 2018). Eight of the immigrants in this study had been placed on ATD programs after arriving to the United States, from whom five (three women and two men) were placed on electronic monitoring (EM), having to wear ankle monitoring devices. The interviews were recorded when the participants felt comfortable; otherwise the second author wrote extensive notes during the interview. The University of Kansas Institutional Review Board approved this project.

Among our study participants, the range of time wearing an ankle monitoring device lasted between three and eighteen months and counting, since one individual has continued to have the device on his leg as of this writing. The informants who were placed on EM are Mayan Guatemalan, spoke K'iche' or Chuj as their first language, spoke no English, and had between zero and six years of schooling. All of the five informants lived in rural Kansas. The eight informants under EM turned themselves in to Border Patrol after crossing into the United States from Mexico seeking protection from violence in Guatemala. In addition to the interviews, the second author often accompanied informants to their appointments at the ISAP offices. During interviews and in informal conversations, EM informants talked openly about their feelings and experiences wearing what they refer to as *grilletes* (Spanish for shackles). These accounts, together with interviews of lawyers and government reports mentioned above, allow us to critically examine how the benevolent rhetoric of family and motherhood (Menjívar & Kil, 2002) masks a wide range of enhanced control tactics.

Privatizing Immigration Control

CoreCivic, previously known as Corrections Corporation of America (CCA), and Geo Group Inc. (GEO) are the two companies that DHS and ICE contract to house, detain, surveil, and process immigrants for deportation proceedings. CoreCivic and GEO rely on the apprehension and detention of immigrants as a key component of their business and profits; both corporations acknowledge that they would lose significant revenue if the detention of immigrants were to decrease (CCA, 2014; GEO, 2014). By 2017, 71 percent of immigrants in ICE custody were held in prisons, jails, or detention centers contracted by private corporations (Tidwell Cullen, 2018). Often, DHS and ICE contracts maintain agreements where agencies are guaranteed payment for "a number of detainees per night, no matter how many people the facilities actually hold" (Kerwin, Alulema, & Tu, 2015, p. 337).

CCA and GEO have lobbied intensely for expanding immigration detention. "CCA spent more than 8.7 million and the Geo Group spent $1.3 million to lobby Congress solely on Homeland Security appropriations between 2006 and 2015" (Gruberg, 2015, p. 3). In 2016 alone CCA spent over one million dollars on political contributions in twenty-nine states and for both Democratic and Republican associations (Core Civic, 2016). In 2016, GEO spent a total of three million dollars lobbying federal candidates, parties, committees, and state and local candidates (Core Civic, 2016). CCA and GEO also have strong ties to the American Legislative Council, which promotes restrictive immigration law by drafting restrictive legislative bills and networking around the country (Douglas & Sáenz, 2013). Both companies contributed $250,000 each to the presidential inauguration of 2017 (Burnett, 2017); after the 2016 election the stocks of both companies rose substantially, 30 percent for CCA and 20 percent for GEO (Sommer, 2017).

These lobbying efforts have paid off. There has been a significant increase of immigrants in detention or in surveillance programs beginning with the Obama administration. In 1995, there were 5,532 immigrant detention beds in the entire country (Gruberg, 2015). By 2008, there were 27,000, and by 2009 a mandated daily minimum bed quota was enacted (Chan, 2017), bringing the number of beds to 33,400 in 2009 and a slight decrease to 30,539 in 2015. However, by 2020, the average daily immigrant beds reached 54,000 (DHS, 2020). Thus, the profitable immigration detention business shows no signs of slowing down.

CCA and GEO also benefit from immigrants who are surveilled outside of detention centers. Under the ATD programs started in 2002, ICE created a series of programs to promote the supervision of immigrants not held in detention facilities during their removal proceedings (ICE, 2009). These included the Intensive Supervision Appearance Program (ISAP), started in 2004, the Enhanced Supervision/Reporting program (ESR), and EM, created in 2007 (see our discussion of the operation of these programs below). These programs rely on surveillance technologies to supervise immigrants through GPS ankle monitoring bracelets, voice recognition software for telephone reporting, radio frequency identification chipping of visas, and unannounced home visits (ICE, 2009; Koulish, 2015).

While the DHS budgets have been inconsistent in reporting the budget allocation for ATD programs, looking at DHS budget requests between fiscal years 2005 and 2019, we find that these have increased dramatically, leading to an overwhelming expansion of the surveilled population. The budget for ATD programs has increased from only $11 *thousand* in 2005 (DHS, 2004) to $6 *million* by 2012 and to an astronomical $209.9 *million* by 2020 (DHS, 2020). It is not surprising then that the number of immigrants in these programs has grown substantially, keeping pace with the budget increases. For instance, in 2008 ISAP and EM combined processed a total of 8,300 people (DHS, 2008), by 2013 ISAP supervised 40,613 individuals (ACLU, 2014), and by 2020 this number rose to 120,000 daily participants (DHS, 2020).

The evidence suggests that the partnership between governmental agencies and private corporations has enhanced the control and hypersurveillance of immigrants, while simultaneously pushing these individuals to the margins of society and generating profit for the contractors.

In 2014, ICE renewed its contract with B.I. Inc. (purchased by GEO in 2011) for five years, and GEO expected about $47 million in annualized revenue from this contract (ACLU, 2014; "GEO Group Awarded Contract," 2014).

With this broader context in mind, we move to examine the policies and practices of immigrant family detention centers and how, despite the feminized and seemingly benevolent language used to describe them, these facilities operate in a highly punitive fashion, re-creating tactics of enforcement and social control that are similar to those used in prisons (see Human Rights First, 2011; Inter-American Commission on Human Rights, 2010), with added degrees of "punitive capacity" (Eason et al., 2016).

Family Detention Centers

Although immigrant women and men are detained in over two hundred facilities across the country, in jails, prisons, and immigrant detention centers, "women and children" are often placed in family detention centers. In 2001, the Berks County Residential Center, the first detention center designated to hold immigrant children and their mothers, opened in Pennsylvania. It was managed by ICE and the county justice department and had eighty-four beds. In 2005, CCA entered into an agreement with ICE, which designated the T. Don Hutto facility, previously used as a prison, as an immigrant detention center for women and children (Detention Watch Network, 2017). Two years later, the ACLU filed a lawsuit on behalf of children claiming that the Hutto facility violated the 1997 Flores Settlement Agreement, which states that immigrant children must be released to a relative or foster care system and placed in detention only as a last resource, and if children must be detained, officials must follow certain standards of care and hold them in "least restrictive" environments (ACLU, 2007) with improved living conditions. The government announced an end of family detention at the Hutto facility the same week (ACLU, 2009), but also in 2009 Hutto entered into a new agreement with ICE to house only "adult" immigrants (Detention Watch Network, 2017). Since then, Hutto has housed only immigrant women and has remained operational under CCA, in spite of countless reports of abuses and violations.[6] In March 2018, with the support of activist groups, Laura Monterrosa, a Salvadoran asylum seeker, was released after reporting sexual assault by a facility guard and denial of medical care in the Hutto facility (Tuma, 2018). As of this writing, Hutto continues to operate.

Berks was the only family detention center in the United States prior to the 2014 increase of Central American youth entering through the U.S.-Mexico border seeking asylum. In 2014, the Obama administration increased the number of facilities that held women and their children (DHS, 2016). Artesia was created to detain women and children who were seeking asylum, and the Karnes Civil Detention Center, previously a prison, was converted into a family detention center (Costa, 2018). In December 2014, a new facility opened, the South Texas Family Residential Center in Texas. By 2015 the DHS budget requested an increase of $162 million total for CBP and ICE to address the surveillance, apprehension, detention, and "care" of unaccompanied youth and families, which also included the maintenance and expansion of family detention facilities (DHS, 2015a). As of this writing three facilities house women and children: South Texas Family Residential Center, Berks, and Karnes. This does not include facilities that house only juveniles or only adults, which include juvenile detention centers across the country as well as jails and prisons. By fiscal year 2015, ICE relied on a vast network of 630 facilities scattered throughout the country (at least two facilities in each state, with Texas and California topping the list with 115 and 70 facilities, respectively) to detain immigrants, including juveniles (Ryo & Peacock, 2018).

The women and children and gendered rhetoric of detention practices ignores the needs and abuses that transgender women in detention face (Cardoletti-Carroll et al., 2015). As Anderson (2010) finds, ICE and DHS lack guidelines to provide for transgender immigrants in adequate gender-appropriate detention. As a result, oftentimes transgender immigrants either are placed in isolation, generating vulnerabilities and psychological distress, or are held in inappropriate gender detention, thus leaving transgender immigrants at increased risk of violence and abuse by detention staff, guards, and other detainees (see Anderson, 2010). Transgender women are most often seeking asylum after fleeing gender-based violence in their countries of origin (Cardoletti-Carroll et al., 2015). Although we do not discuss the experiences of detained immigrant transgender women in this chapter, more research is needed to better understand their experiences in immigration detention.

Although detention facilities are referred to euphemistically as "residential centers," "campuses," "family" centers, and the like and policies often use rhetoric of "protection" and "care," such language masks tactics of surveillance and social control through which they operate, which closely parallel those used in prisons. According to Goffman (1961), "total institutions" are organizations that separate certain types of people from the rest of society where (1) "all aspects of life are conducted in the same place and under the same single authority"; (2) "each phase of the member's daily activity is carried on in the immediate company of a large batch of others"; (3) "all phases of the day's activities are tightly scheduled"; and (4) "the various enforced activities are brought together into a single rational plan purportedly designed to fulfill the official aims of the institution" (p. 6).

Immigration detention centers fit closely Goffman's definition of a "total institution"; they are often located in remote locations (Ryo & Peacock, 2018), making it difficult for detainees to communicate with their families and access resources outside of the centers, life is highly regimented, and all activities take place in the same location. The lawyers we interviewed, who have frequented these facilities, described the detention centers as "jail-like," "prison camps" (Allison), "indistinguishable from a prison" (Emily), or simulating "maximum-security prisons" (Celia). The lawyers described the centers as having thick concrete walls, heavy doors that are monitored by guards, small to no windows, and high levels of security including metal detectors, flood lights that stay on all night, and high fences. Visitors, including lawyers, must go through metal detectors and can talk to detainees only through glass windows. Several families are held together in one room at a time in several bunk beds and a shared bathroom, thus undermining personal privacy. And as in prisons, detainees must wear uniforms—indeed, almost undistinguishable to those worn in prison—and are sometimes color coded according to the detainee's perceived "level of threat."

Other facilities, such as the South Texas Family Residential Center in Dilley, consist of several trailers that house the detained women and their children and also serve as offices or meeting spaces. As Allison, an attorney who has been working with immigrants and immigration law since the late 1980s, explained,

> Dilley is more like a prison camp. The families live in portable trailers. Each portable trailer houses several families and there is no privacy (there is only a curtain to pull around for when the women and children need to change clothes). The families have to go outside to get to a communal bathroom. The facility is huge so the families have to walk a ways to get to the clinic or the cafeteria. It's very hot or cold much of the year and the grounds are dusty.

Within these facilities a feminized and infantilized language is used to describe the physical space. Not only are the detention centers named family residential centers, but as Celia, another attorney, explained, the different parts of the buildings, cells/bedrooms, blocks, and offices are referred to as "neighborhoods" using animal names, such as "the brown bear neighborhood, one of them can be the green turtle neighborhood . . . so they have really cute names but it is still a jail. The immigration attorneys who work there call it the 'baby jail'" (Celia). This feminized and infantilized discourse veils punitive strategies and enforcement practices while also associating Latina immigrants with stereotypical images—their fertility and motherhood—that the public has been alerted to fear (Chavez, 2013; Menjívar & Kil, 2002).

Controlling Women Inside Detention

The treatment of women inside the detention centers re-creates similar surveillance and control strategies used in prisons to control inmates (Escobar, 2016), where the goal is to create "docile bodies" (Foucault, 1977), that is, mute and obedient individuals, through the control of space and isolation, regulation of activities, and management of time and an organized system of command (Foucault, 1977; Staples, 2014). Detention facilities follow these tactics, allowing for the surveillance of detainees, making the women and children the target of constant observation, supervision, and even "micro" punishments by guards and staff if they are not disciplining themselves at all times.

As our participant lawyers told us, women and children in detention have little to no control over their lives; their time is scheduled and movements in the facilities restricted. According to Carmen, a lawyer, "They aren't free to leave, their lives are totally regimented as to times to eat, sleep, lights out. They can be disciplined/written up for infractions of rules. They can't just walk in to see a doctor, can't talk to [an] ICE officer directly without filling out a request." Moreover, withholding information about access to legal representation, even when attorneys volunteer and visit the facilities, is a tool of control and isolation that keeps them from exercising the rights they still have. As Carmen put it, "Most importantly, they cannot walk into the pro bono visitation area to request legal services, limiting volunteer lawyers' ability to access all the families. They are basically powerless." As Celia, another lawyer, noted, the women are kept separate from each other, "preventing them from sharing information and experiences, but also from letting the women know that there are attorneys available to help them." The women have little to no access to information regarding their standing in their own deportation proceedings.

With treatment similar to prisoners, women experience the emotional and physical consequences of imprisonment (see Goffman, 1961, p. 14). According to Emily, another attorney, "They face additional hurdles in terms of (1) cultural/linguistic barriers; (2) often victims of recent trauma and violence; (3) lack of knowledge about their 'sentence'—how long they will be there, what will happen to them if/when they are released; (4) extreme distances from any social connections." Grace, another lawyer, told us that the women are even referred to by their bed numbers instead of their names. Such practices strip the women's individuality and assign them new identities as "criminals" and disciplined subjects.

Given these conditions, it is not surprising that we find evidence that some of these women experience various forms of violence and maltreatment in the detention centers. In addition, the women often face direct forms of violence, including mental, physical, and sexual abuse by guards and staff. Attorney Grace offered this example:

We have heard many upsetting stories about women being mistreated, teased, and outright tortured in detention centers, including those for unaccompanied minors. I had a client tell me that when she entered at age seventeen she was pregnant. She was interrogated by an ICE official who accused her of lying about her age. When she asked for water, the ICE officers poured water on the ground in front of her and did the same with food when she was hungry.

Indeed, allegations of sexual assault by guards and staff have been made in at least twenty-five states (ACLU, 2011).[7] DHS and ICE do not make public statistics on claims of sexual abuse; however, several human rights organizations and pro bono legal agencies continue to bring these claims to DHS, CCA, and GEO (Mexican American Legal Defense and Education Fund, 2014). Complaints include guards and staff taking women out of their cells in the middle of the night to have sex in other parts of the facilities, fondling and kissing, and exchanging sexual favors for money, promises of assistance with immigration cases, and/or shelter outside of the facility (Mexican American Legal Defense and Education Fund, 2014).

Alternatives to Detention Programs

The ICE's ERO office "tracks over 1.8 million [immigrants] in immigration removal proceedings . . . [and] because ERO cannot detain all aliens who are waiting to appear in immigration courts or for removal, detention bed space is prioritized" for those immigrants who are a "risk to public safety" (DHS, 2015b). ATD programs, subcontracted to private corporations, were created to keep immigrants who are seen as not posing a threat under close supervision and to alleviate overcrowding in the detention. Adapting tactics already used in the criminal justice system, ISAP and EM were created in 2004 to track immigrants and ensure compliance with removal orders. The programs are restricted to people who live near an ISAP office or those with an Order of Release on Recognizance (ROR) or Order of Supervision (OSUP). After two major court cases, *Zadvydas v. Davis* in 2001 and *Clark v. Martinez* in 2005, the U.S. Supreme Court ruled that immigrants cannot be held in detention indefinitely awaiting deportation (Rutgers School of Law, Newark Immigrant Rights Clinic, 2012). Thus, "noncriminal" immigrants awaiting removal are given OSUP or ROR and released from the detention to be surveilled outside. Individuals must check in regularly with ICE officials, and many are placed in ATD programs.

Today ATD programs have expanded to all ICE and ERO offices (U.S. Government Accountability Office, 2014). Currently, only one ATD program is in effect, ISAP III, and various levels of monitoring are enforced, varying from electronic monitoring in the form of ankle bracelets to voice recognition software, radio frequency visa monitoring, smartphone applications to track immigrants, and face-to-face routine meetings (Koulish, 2015; Staples, 2014). Participants are required to stay within specific GPS areas; leaving restricted area results in a violation of the immigration order. The GPS ankle bracelets provide the immigrant's exact location at all times. Voice recognition software is used to verify that immigrants are at home during designated hours (DHS, 2015b; Rutgers School of Law, Newark Immigrant Rights Clinic, 2012). Although DHS provides little information about the number of immigrants or the demographic characteristics of those enrolled in ATD programs, most reports show the number of immigrants enrolled has increased astronomically, from 21,726 daily participants in 2014 to 61,664 daily participants in 2016 and over 100,000 in 2019 (DHS, 2018b; Singer, 2019). Much of the recent growth in ATD is the result of the 2017 executive orders (DHS, 2018a).

Ankle monitors—known among immigrants as *grilletes* or shackles—are increasingly used when the immigrant women cannot afford to pay bond to leave the detention centers.[8] Gender inequalities intersect with these forms of surveillance as immigrant women in general earn lower wages than men and immediately after their release from detention their financial circumstances are likely direr. They are left with few options but to wear the ankle bracelets after their release, which affects their daily lives, the kinds of jobs they can obtain, and their relations in their communities. Further, ankle bracelets can be stigmatizing and create fear among the women's family members that they are being watched as well. The experience of Daniela, a thirty-year-old woman who fled poverty and violence in her hometown in Guatemala, reflects many of the immigrant women's experiences under EM.

Daniela arrived at the U.S. border seeking asylum with her toddler, Mario. Upon arrival she turned herself in to Border Patrol officers and was placed in immigrant detention while she waited for her immigration court hearing; eventually she was released under an ATD program with an electronic monitoring device to her family in rural Kansas. Daniela shared that the immigration officer did not offer her the option to wear the grillete; instead, he only explained to her how to use it. Feeling uneasy and fearful of the consequences if she refused to wear the device, she complied. After arriving to Kansas, Daniela was to plug in the grillete every few hours so it would charge. This meant she would have to spend several hours a day next to the wall while it charged. Daniela said she felt uncomfortable wearing the grillete as it impeded her mobility around the house and hurt her ankle. She had burns on her ankle from the heat of the device, which left visible scars even months after the device was taken off. Daniela tried to cover the grillete by wearing long skirts because she also worried about what members of the community would say, especially since grilletes are often worn by people who are on parole due to a criminal record.

In addition to wearing the grillete, Daniela had to conduct monthly in-person meetings with a case manager in the ISAP office. The office was three hours away from where she lived. Given that Daniela was an undocumented immigrant in Kansas, she did not have a driver's license, which meant she had to pay coethnics with driver's licenses for the rides to the check-ins. The amount for the ride ranged between two and three hundred dollars depending on who was willing and able to drive her. The face-to-face meetings lasted less than ten minutes, during which the case management officer simply checked the grillete and updated her contact information. Daniela always brought her son Mario with her to the appointments for two reasons. First, she was fearful she could be deported at any time and be separated from her son if they were not together; and second, she was apprehensive that the case manager would report her to ICE if she was by herself. Therefore, Mario spent two years attending routine check-ins with his mother, also experiencing the surveillance of the state.

As the majority of the attorneys we interviewed explained, women are being pushed to "opt" for ankle monitors instead of trying to fight an asylum case. Rose, one of the attorneys, explained, "ICE has been pushing for ankle monitor for a long time now and depriving the women of seeing a judge by almost coercing the women to take the monitor over the bond" (a monitor is not reviewable by a judge, while a bond is).

However, as in Daniela's case, our other study participants who had been placed on EM with grilletes shared that detention officers did not explain why they were placed under such surveillance; rather, officers explained only how the surveillance system operated.

There are three types of monitoring devices that study participants described and that the second author observed through ethnographic observations: (1) a big and bulky device that must be plugged into the wall for charging for hours at a time; (2) a somewhat smaller device—preferred by most respondents—that has a reusable battery that can be charged without having to have the leg attached to the electric outlet on the wall; and (3) another big and bulky device that has its own router to be used when immigrants live in places where the GPS signal is poor. The least desirable grillete is the first one, as it requires individuals to essentially plug in their bodies to the wall for charging. This was the type most often given to the women in our study. Grace, an immigration lawyer, explained that these devices often cause rashes, redness, swelling, and even bleeding and open sores, which add to the visibility of the devices. Her clients often cry when describing the physical and social effects of these monitors.

Most of the women in these programs, particularly Central Americans, have come to the United States seeking protection from state, gender, domestic, and gang violence in their home countries (Cardoletti-Carroll et al., 2015). These forms of surveillance amplify these women's already serious trauma and add stigma to their lives as they are often viewed as criminals by members of their families and communities.

Immigrant advocacy groups had supported ATD programs in the hopes that these would be more humane and supportive of immigrant families (ACLU, 2014; Human Rights Watch, 2015). While ATD programs are presumably better alternatives to detention, given the intense surveillance and control they deploy, we find that these programs contribute to the ongoing criminalization of immigrant women through more diffused but equally potent strategies of social control. These modified control strategies do not take place in detention facilities but are transferred and adapted to operate in communities and homes. Thus, these programs blur the lines between the everyday lives of immigrants, state punishment, and social control, producing significant consequences for immigrant women, their families, and their communities. In many ways, ATD programs function like house arrest (see Staples & Decker, 2008). EM enters the everyday lives of women, managing their time and space, imposing supervision, and regulating their everyday activities, thus bringing home the coercive forms of disciplinary power found in detention facilities. ATD programs operate as appendages to the larger complex, broadening the social control functions of the system and contributing more data to the immigration "surveillant assemblage" (Haggerty & Ericson, 2000), a series of discrete individualized data flows that are reassembled as individual files in DHS information systems (Kalhan, 2013, 2014).

Conclusion

The "punitive turn" (Garland, 2001) enacted through immigration policies has amplified the "punitive capacity" (Eason et al., 2016) of the immigration detention system by increasing the number of beds available (for years into the future) and through ATD programs that work like appendages to the detention facilities. Through document analysis and interviews with immigrant women and lawyers who assist detained women with their asylum cases, we have shown that the paternalistic, feminized, and sometimes infantilized benevolent discourse that relies on "protection," "care," and "alternatives" veils the violence enacted by immigration enforcement on Latinas who are held physically inside and outside of institutional settings. This form of "humanitarian governmentality" (Agier, 2010, 2011) or "compassionate repression" (Fassin, 2005) continues to embody the legal violence (Menjívar & Abrego, 2012) of the state toward immigrants, which encroaches on women's bodies and mental well-being.

During detention, some Latina immigrants are separated for long periods from their children, who are often U.S. citizens, producing mental and emotional trauma for both the children and women (Brabeck & Xu, 2010; Chaundry et al., 2010). And when these women are detained *with* their children, they lack the resources and social and physical space to care for them (e.g., they are unable to clothe them, feed them nutritious food, or even breastfeed). As Seabrook and Wyatt-Nichol (2015, p. 360) note, "Incarcerated mothers are antithetical to the cultural concept of the ideal mother, particularly the ideology and practice of 'intensive mothering'" (see Hays, 1996). Even though the conditions of detention keep these immigrant mothers from caring for their children as they would like to, they are often labeled as "bad mothers" and blamed for their own and their children's incarceration.

ATD programs—ostensibly designed to offer less restrictive and more humane treatment and case management services—expand the reach of state and corporatized surveillance and control and are similarly disguised in the language of "family," "childcare," and "motherhood." The use of this language can be misleading even to immigrant advocates, as many immigrant rights groups initially supported ATD programs that were portrayed as humane alternatives to detention. However, these tactics of control simply blur the lines between repression and compassion (Fassin, 2005), veil the violence that women experience, and deny women's rights. At the same time, these tactics frame the government's imposition to control and surveil in benevolent rhetoric that further fuses state control and immigrants' everyday lives. Specifically, as the immigrant women described, the use of grilletes to control them hurts immigrants' mental well-being and generates physical harm.

Latinos/as from Mexico, Guatemala, Honduras, and El Salvador compose close to 90 percent of the detained population, and although women make up approximately 20 percent of the growing number of immigrants in detention (Ryo & Peacock, 2018), women's experiences offer an important empirical case to examine the expansion of surveillance and humane forms of control in the immigration system. Their experiences show the intertwined nature of race and immigration detention. As Golash-Boza and Hondagneu-Sotelo (2013) noted, it is a raced and gendered removal project. These strategies of control on which we have focused blur the lines between institutional settings, home, community, and the everyday lives of immigrants (Foucault, 1977; Staples, 2014) and between coercive state control, the interests of private corporations, and the humanitarian organizations that attempt to mediate between individuals and the state and presumably work on behalf of immigrants.

NOTES

1 This may change as former Attorney General Sessions sought to redefine who qualifies for asylum by eliminating victims of "private crimes" (e.g., gender-based violence against women), presumably to unclog courts of pending asylum

applications. This move will effectively close the door to Central American women who are fleeing gender-based violence in their countries.
2   Rabin (2009) has documented the extreme penal conditions imposed on immigrant women in detention, even when these women are not serving criminal sentences.
3   Eason, Hernández, and Rubio-Goldsmith (2016) observed that conditions are so deplorable in detention facilities that they have become predictors of death, attempted suicide, and health referrals outside the facilities. Furthermore, these researchers found that the more dangerous the facility is, the higher the likelihood of federal endorsement and continued contracting because, from ICE's perspective, the "punitive capacity" of these centers is a measure of state control over the detainees.
4   The 1986 IRCA and the 1996 IIRIRA included several major components; in this chapter we highlight only those that more directly relate to the expansion of detention and deportation.
5   For a detailed history of the development of ISAP, see Rutgers School of Law, Newark Immigrant Rights Clinic (2012).
6   In 2015 women who were held at T. Don Hutto organized a hunger strike demanding the end to violent prison-like conditions and physical and psychological abuses (Rankin, 2015; "'We Have No Rights,'" 2015).
7   See also Eason, Hernández, and Rubio-Goldsmith (2016) for additional data on these various forms of mistreatment and abuse in these facilities.
8   Immigration lawyers interviewed for this project as well as various immigrant advocacy organizations argue that bonds are often too high for these women, who do not have jobs and tend to be poor, to pay (Human Rights First, 2011).

REFERENCES

ACLU. (2007). Case summary in the ACLU's challenge to the Hutto Detention Center. www.aclu.org.
ACLU. (2009). ACLU strikes deal to continue humane conditions at Hutto Detention Center. www.aclu.org.
ACLU. (2011). Sexual abuse in immigration detention facilities. National Prison Project of the American Civil Liberties Union. www.aclu.org.
ACLU. (2014). Alternatives to immigration detention: Less costly and more humane than federal lock-up. www.aclu.org.
Agier, M. (2010). Humanity as an identity and its political effects (a note on camps and humanitarian government). *Humanity*, 1, 29–45.
Agier, M. (2011). *Managing the undesirables*. London: Polity Press.
Alvord, D. R., Menjívar, C., & Gómez Cervantes, A. (2018). The legal violence in the 2017 executive orders: The expansion of immigrant criminalization in Kansas. *Social Currents*, 5, 411–420.
American Immigration Council. (2017). A primer on expedited removal. www.americanimmigrationcouncil.org.

Anderson, L. (2010). Punishing the innocent: How the classification of male-to-female transgender individuals in immigration detention constitutes illegal punishment under the Fifth Amendment. *Berkeley Journal of Gender, Law, & Justice, 25*, 1–31.

Barnes, R. (2018, February 27). Supreme Court throws out ruling that said detained immigrants deserve bond hearings. *Washington Post.* www.washingtonpost.com.

Bosworth, M., Parmar, A., & Vazquez, Y. (Eds.). (2018). *Race, criminal justice, and migration control: Enforcing the boundaries of belonging.* Oxford: Oxford University Press.

Brabeck, K., & Xu, Q. (2010). The impact of detention and deportation on Latino immigrant children and families: A quantitative exploration. *Hispanic Journal of Behavioral Sciences, 32*, 341–361.

Burnett, J. (2017, November 21). Big money as private immigrant jails boom. In *Morning edition.* National Public Radio. www.npr.org.

Cardoletti-Carroll, C., Farmer, A., & Velez, L. (2015). Women on the run: First-hand accounts of refugees fleeing El Salvador, Guatemala, Honduras and Mexico. United Nations High Commissioner for Refugees. www.unhcr.org.

Chan, J. (2017, January 13). Immigration detention bed quota timeline. Chicago: National Immigrant Justice Center. www.immigrantjustice.org.

Chaundry, A., Capps, R., Pedroza, J. M., Castañeda, R. M., Santos, R., & Scott, M. M. (2010). *Facing our future: Children in the aftermath of immigration enforcement.* Washington, DC: Urban Institute. http://files.eric.ed.gov.

Chavez, L. R. (2013). *Latino threat: Constructing immigrants, citizens, and the nation* (2nd ed.). Stanford, CA: Stanford University Press.

Core Civic. (2016). Political activity and lobbying report 2016. http://ir.corecivic.com.

Corrections Corporation of America. (2014). 2014 annual report from 10-K. www.cca.com.

Costa, S. (2018). The detainment of families: Moral implications lacking in legal justifications. *DePaul Journal for Social Justice, 11*, 1–27.

Das Gupta, M. (2008). Housework, feminism, and labor activism: Lessons from domestic workers in New York. *Signs, 33*, 532–537.

Department of Homeland Security. (2004). Budget-in-brief fiscal year 2005. www.dhs.gov.

Department of Homeland Security. (2006). Budget-in-brief fiscal year 2006. www.dhs.gov.

Department of Homeland Security. (2008). Budget-in-brief fiscal year 2008. www.dhs.gov.

Department of Homeland Security. (2009). Budget-in-brief fiscal year 2010. www.dhs.gov.

Department of Homeland Security. (2015a). Budget-in-brief fiscal year 2016. www.dhs.gov.

Department of Homeland Security. (2015b). ICE enforcement and removal operations report fiscal year 2015. www.ice.gov.

Department of Homeland Security. (2015c). U.S. Immigration and Customs Enforcement's alternatives to detention (Revised). http://oig.dhs.gov.

Department of Homeland Security. (2016). Budget-in-brief fiscal year 2016. www.dhs.gov.
Department of Homeland Security. (2017). DHS announces progress in enforcing immigration laws, protecting Americans. www.dhs.gov.
Department of Homeland Security. (2018a). Budget-in-brief fiscal year 2019. www.dhs.gov.
Department of Homeland Security. (2018b). Department of Homeland Security U.S. Immigration and Customs Enforcement budget overview FY 2018. www.dhs.gov.
Department of Homeland Security. (2020). Budget-in-brief fiscal year 2020. www.dhs.gov.
Detention Watch Network. (2017). T. Don Hutto Residential Center: Immigration detention inspection series. www.detentionwatchnetwork.org.
Douglas, K. M., & Sáenz, R. (2013). The criminalization of immigrants & the immigration-industrial complex. *Daedalus, 142*, 199–227.
Downes, L. (2014, July 15). Beware John Cornyn's "humane" immigration act. *Taking Note.* https://takingnote.blogs.nytimes.com.
Dreby, J. (2015). *Everyday illegal: When policies undermine immigrant families.* Berkeley: University of California Press.
Eason, J., Hernández, D., & Rubio-Goldsmith, P. (2016, August). Peeking behind the veil: Exploring punitive capacity in immigrant detention centers. Paper, American Sociological Association, Seattle.
Enloe, C. (1991). "Women and children": Propaganda tools of patriarchy. In G. Bates (Ed.), *Mobilizing democracy: Changing the US role in the Middle East* (pp. 89–96). Monroe, ME: Common Courage Press.
Escobar, M. D. (2016). *Captivity beyond prisons: Criminalization experiences of Latina (im)migrants.* Austin: University of Texas Press.
Fassin, D. (2005). Compassion and repression: The moral economy of immigration policies in France. *Cultural Anthropology, 20*, 362–387.
Fernandes, J. (2017). Alternatives to detention and the for-profit immigration system. Washington, DC: Center for American Progress. www.americanprogress.org.
Foucault, M. (1977). *Discipline & punish.* New York: Vintage.
Garland, D. (2001). *The culture of control: Crime and social order in contemporary society.* New York: Oxford University Press.
The Geo Group. (2014). 2014 annual report. www.snl.com.
The GEO Group awarded contract by U.S. Immigration and Customs Enforcement for the continued provision of services under Intensive Supervision and Appearance Program. (2014, September 10). *Business Wire.* www.businesswire.com.
Goffman, E. (1961). *Asylums: Essays on the social situation of mental patients and other inmates.* Garden City, NY: Anchor Books.
Golash-Boza, T. (2012). *Due process denied: Detentions and deportations in the United States.* New York: Routledge.
Golash-Boza, T., & Hondagneu-Sotelo, P. (2013). Latino immigrant men and the deportation crisis: A gendered racial removal program. *Latino Studies, 11*, 271–292.

Gómez Cervantes, A., Alvord, D. R., & Menjívar, C. (2018). "Bad hombres": The effects of criminalizing Latino immigrants through law and media in the rural Midwest. *Migration Letters, 15*, 182–196.

GovTrack. (2017). H.R. 495—115th Congress: Protection of Children Act of 2017. www.govtrack.us.

Gruberg, S. (2015). How for profit companies are driving immigration detention policies. Washington, DC: Center for American Progress. https://cdn.americanprogress.org.

Haggerty, K. D., & Ericson, R. V. (2000). The surveillant assemblage. *British Journal of Sociology, 51*, 605–622.

Hays, S. (1996). *The cultural contradictions of motherhood*. New Haven, CT: Yale University Press.

Human Rights First. (2011). Jails and jumpsuits: Transforming the U.S. immigration detention system—A two-year review. www.humanrightsfirst.org.

Human Rights Watch. (2015). US: Trauma in family immigration detention. www.hrw.org.

Inda, J. X. (2013). Subject to deportation: IRCA, "criminal aliens," and the policing of immigration. *Migration Studies, 1*, 292–310.

Inter-American Commission on Human Rights. (2010). Report on immigration in the United States: Detention and due process. Washington, DC: Organization of American States. www.oas.org.

Kalhan, A. (2013). Immigration policing and federalism through the lens of technology, surveillance, and privacy. *Ohio State Law Journal, 74*, 1105–1165.

Kalhan, A. (2014). Immigration surveillance. *Maryland Law Review, 74*, 1–75.

Kerwin, D., Alulema, W. D., & Tu, S. (2015). Piecing together the US immigrant detention puzzle one night at a time: An analysis of all persons in DHS-ICE custody on September 22, 2012. *Journal on Migration and Human Security, 3*, 330–376.

Koulish, R. (2015). Spiderman's web and the governmentality of electronic immigrant detention. *Law, Culture and the Humanities, 11*, 83–108.

Lee, W. J. (2005). Eligibility criteria for enrollment into the Intensive Supervision Appearance Program (ISAP) and the Electronic Monitoring Device (EMD) Program. Memorandum for field directors. Washington, DC: U.S. Immigration and Customs Enforcement. www.ice.gov.

Library of Congress. (2018a, April 17). H.R. 5114—113th Congress: HUMANE Act. www.congress.gov.

Library of Congress. (2018b, April 17). S.2666—113th Congress: Protect Children and Families through the Rule of Law Act. www.congress.gov.

Massey, D. S., Durand, J., & Malone, N. J. (2002). *Beyond smoke and mirrors: Mexican immigration in an era of economic integration*. New York: Russell Sage Foundation.

Menjívar, C. (2014a). Immigration law beyond borders: Externalizing and internalizing border controls in an era of securitization. *Annual Review of Law and Social Science, 10*, 353–369.

Menjívar, C. (2014b). The "Poli-Migra": Multilayered legislation, enforcement practices, and what we can learn about and from today's approaches. *American Behavioral Scientist, 58*, 1805–1819.

Menjívar, C., & Abrego, L. J. (2012). Legal violence: Immigration law and the lives of Central American immigrants. *American Journal of Sociology, 117*, 1380–1421.

Menjívar, C., Gómez Cervantes, A., & Alvord, D. (2018). The expansion of "crimmigration," mass detention, and deportation. *Sociology Compass, 12*(4), e12573.

Menjívar, C., & Kanstroom, D. (2014). *Constructing immigrant "illegality": Critiques, experiences, and responses.* New York: Cambridge University Press.

Menjívar, C., & Kil, S. H. (2002). For their own good: Benevolent rhetoric and exclusionary language in public officials' discourse on immigrant-related issues. *Social Justice, 29*, 160–176.

Mexican American Legal Defense and Education Fund. (2014). Complaints regarding sexual abuse of women in DHS custody at Karnes County Residential Center. Los Angeles.

Migration Policy Institute. (2019). Profile of the Unauthorized Population: United States. Washington, DC: MPI. www.migrationpolicy.org.

Provine, D. M. (2015). The morality of law: The case against deportation of settled immigrants. In R. Stryker & L. Haglund (Eds.), *Closing the rights gap: From human rights to social transformation* (pp. 127–147). Berkeley: University of California Press.

Provine, D. M., & Doty, R. L. (2011). The criminalization of immigrants as a racial project. *Journal of Contemporary Criminal Justice, 27*, 261–277.

Rabin, N. (2009). Unseen prisoners: A report on women in immigration detention facilities in Arizona. *Georgetown Immigration Law Review, 23*, 695.

Rankin, K. (2015, November 9). UPDATE: 100+ women now refusing to eat in Texas immigration detention center. *Colorlines.* www.colorlines.com.

Rutgers School of Law, Newark Immigrant Rights Clinic. (2012). Freed but not free: A report examining the current use of alternatives to immigration detention. www.afsc.org.

Ryo, E., & Peacock, I. (2018). The landscape of immigration detention in the United States. American Immigration Council. www.americanimmigrationcouncil.org.

Schriro, D. (2009). Immigration detention overview and recommendations. Washington, DC: Department of Homeland Security, ICE. www.ice.gov.

Seabrook, R. L., & Wyatt-Nichol, H. (2015). Marginalization and hope: Personal narratives of previously incarcerated mothers. In J. Minaker & B. Hogeveen (Eds.), *Criminalized mothers, criminalizing mothering* (pp. 355–372). Bradford, ON: Demeter Press.

Singer, A. (2019). Immigration: Alternatives to detention (ATD) programs. Congressional Research Service. https://fas.org.

Sommer, J. (2017, March 10). Trump immigration crackdown is great for private prison stocks. *New York Times.* www.nytimes.com.

Staples, W. G. (1991). *Castles of our conscience: Social control and the American State, 1800–1985*. New Brunswick, NJ: Rutgers University Press.

Staples, W. G. (2014). *Everyday surveillance* (2nd ed.). New York: Rowman & Littlefield.

Staples, W. G., & Decker, S. K. (2008). Technologies of the body, technologies of the self: House arrest as neo-liberal governance. In M. Deflem (Ed.), *Surveillance and governance: Crime control and beyond* (pp. 131–159). London: JAI.

Tazzioli, M. (2016). Border displacements. Challenging the politics of rescue between Mare Nostrum and Triton. *Migration Studies, 4*, 1–19.

Tidwell Cullen, T. (2018, March 13). ICE released its most comprehensive immigration detention data yet. It's alarming. National Immigrant Justice Center. https://immigrantjustice.org.

TRAC Immigration. (2019). Tracking Immigration and Customs Enforcement removals. http://trac.syr.edu.

Tuma, M. (2018, March 23). Laura Monterrosa released from T. Don Hutto: Could this be a bellwether for detained immigrants? *Austin Chronicle*. www.austinchronicle.com.

U.S. Government Accountability Office. (2014). Alternatives to detention: Improved data collection and analyses needed to better assess program effectiveness. www.gao.gov.

U.S. Immigration and Customs Enforcement. (2009). Alternatives to detention for ICE detainees. www.ice.gov.

"We have no rights." 500 women go on a hunger strike at Texas immigrant holding facility. (2015, November 3). *Takeaway*. www.pri.org.

9

Adriana and Esther

Experiences of Formerly Incarcerated Migrant Women Deportees

MARTHA ESCOBAR

The creation of knowledge is heavily implicated in (re)producing relations of power. For a long time, women of Color feminist scholars have interrogated the politics of epistemology, especially the claims to objectivity and universalism of (white) Western knowledge (Anzaldúa & Moraga, 1981; hooks, 1981; Lorde, 1984; Sandoval, 1991). They have critiqued the ways dominant productions of knowledge, including white feminisms, ignore, erase, and distort the experiences and modes of knowledge of marginalized communities, and how these epistemic politics are implicated in shaping the world, often materializing in marginalization and violence (hooks, 1984; Mohanty, 1984). In response, women of Color feminists have claimed epistemic authority to bring about transformative change. A central argument is that we need to understand the world from an intersectional perspective (Collins, 2000; Crenshaw, 1991). Rather than claiming universalism, women of Color feminists maintain that knowledge is embodied and situational. In other words, depending on an individual's social positionality, they experience and know life differently in relation to others.

Attending to women of Color feminist critiques, in this chapter I present an interview conducted with Adriana and Esther, two Mexican migrant women incarcerated in California, detained, and eventually deported. I center their voices and recognize their position as producers of knowledge. As the mediator between Adriana, Esther, and the reader, I conceptualize the process of creating knowledge as an uneven yet collective endeavor to understand and transform the experiences of criminalized Latina migrants and their communities. While I privilege Adriana's and Esther's intimate knowledge of Latina migrant criminalization, it is important to contextualize their experiences within the scholarship on Latinas and the criminal legal system.

Latinas and the Carceral State

During the past four decades we have witnessed a global neoliberal shift that has resulted in increased poverty and displacement. A major response provided by the United States is the substantial use of incarceration to address social problems, including poverty, drugs, and, more recently, migration. This has resulted in what many term the "era of mass incarceration," which marks the United States as a carceral nation (Alexander, 2010). Histories of white supremacist racism have made the bodies of people of Color the principal raw material used to sustain this carceral project (Sudbury, 2010, p. 18). A review of the literature on Chicanas/os/Latinas/os and the U.S. criminal legal system reveals that mainstream society perceives them as social threats and targets them for containment (Lopez & Pasko, 2017; Morín, 2005, 2008, 2016; Oboler, 2009; Olguín, 2010; Urbina, 2012; Urbina & Álvarez, 2016; Urbina & Smith, 2007). In relation to whites, they are disproportionately arrested, face harsher sentences, and are incarcerated at higher rates.

Similar to Chicano/Latino men, Chicanas/Latinas are often racialized as "criminals" and targeted for containment. However, how individuals experience criminalization is shaped by their social positionality, including racialization, class, gender, sexuality, citizenship and migration status, language, and age (Bond-Maupin, Maupin, & Leisenring, 2002; Del Valle, Morín, Swimm, & Escalera, 2016; Díaz-Cotto, 2000, 2005, 2006; Escobar, 2016; Flores, Camacho, & Santos, 2017; Muñoz, 2004; Muñoz & Martínez, 2001; Lopez & Pasko, 2017; Pasko & Lopez, 2018; Schaffner, 2009). For example, a major tool utilized in the U.S. carceral project is the war on drugs. For Chicanas/Latinas, this war has greatly contributed to their presence in carceral spaces within the United States (Del Valle et al., 2016; Díaz-Cotto, 2000, 2006; Morín, 2005; Sudbury, 2010) and beyond its borders (Díaz-Cotto, 2005). This war funnels Latinas into prisons through their involvement in the drug trade as addicts (often using drugs to self-medicate from some form of gendered abuse), drug couriers, including being used as "decoys" in international drug exchanges to divert attention, or as a means to sustain their families. Once arrested, they have less power to plea-bargain since women often find themselves in the lower strata of this business. Thus, their involvement is racialized, gendered, sexualized, and classed.

Compounding the experiences for criminalized Chicanas/Latinas are issues of migration. A significant instrument used to criminalize Chicanas/os/Latinas/os is their association to migration and the collapsing of the identity of "immigrant" with "illegal alien." Their racialization as "foreign criminal threats" provides the ideological power to target entire communities. Since the 1990s, Latina/o migrants have experienced increased surveillance and carcerality (Dowling & Inda, 2013; Gonzales, 2014; Hernández, 2009; Lopez & Pasko, 2017; Menjívar & Kanstroom, 2013; Morín, 2005, 2016; Oboler, 2009). The global neoliberal shift has disproportionately impacted women, leading to their increased displacement and migration. Thus, women are overly affected by racist and xenophobic reactions to migration, including the intensified reliance on carceral warehousing (Díaz-Cotto, 2005; Escobar, 2016; Sudbury, 2010). Due to policy changes in 1996, especially the passing of the Illegal Immigration Reform and Immigrant Responsibility Act, migrants who are legally classified as "criminal aliens" are a priority for deportation and banned from returning to the United States. For non-English-speaking migrants, they encounter additional obstacles, including not knowing how to secure their rights, an inability to communicate with representatives of the criminal legal system throughout the criminalization process, and discrimination from carceral representatives and other people in prison (Díaz-Cotto, 2000, 2005, 2006; Escobar, 2016).

Another concern for incarcerated Chicanas/Latinas is motherhood. Some women are pregnant, and in other cases the state places their children in foster care at the time of people's arrest (Del Valle et al., 2016; Díaz-Cotto, 2000, 2005, 2006; Escobar, 2011; Olguín, 2010). Parenting is overwhelmingly unequal, with women assuming significant responsibility for their children. For incarcerated parents, captivity inherently translates into family separation. However, in the case of fathers, their children are usually cared for by the mother or other motherly figures. In the case of mothers, many are single heads of households and their children are less likely to be with the fathers or other family members, which increases the probability that the state will take their children, either temporarily or permanently. This puts women in positions where they have to struggle to remain connected to their children. For Latina migrants, this can entail a transnational process of placing their children with family, either in the United States or in their countries of origin, or trying to recuperate them after their deportation (Escobar, 2011, 2016).

Abuse prior to and during incarceration is also experienced in gendered ways (Bond-Maupin et al., 2002; Cervantes, Menjívar, & Staples, 2017; Del Valle et al., 2016; Díaz-Cotto, 2000, 2006; Olguín, 2010; Schaffner, 2009). As noted above, most incarcerated Chicanas/Latinas have faced some form of gendered violence, including sexual and domestic abuse. Many are imprisoned for engaging in criminalized actions that they were coerced into by men, or they assume responsibility for actions committed by men in their lives. Some are also incarcerated for defending themselves from men who abused them. Furthermore, during their interactions with police and carceral staff, women are more vulnerable to sexual violence.

As the review of the literature makes evident, it is important to examine the relationship of Chicanas/os/Latinas/os and the criminal legal system from an intersectional perspective. Although there is an increasing body of literature that explores the criminalization of Chicana/o/Latina/o communities as a whole, women's experiences are often made invisible if scholars are not intentional in how they consider issues of gender and sexuality in relation to other axes of power. In this chapter I draw from feminist criminologist Juanita Díaz-Cotto and her work *Chicana Lives and Criminal Justice: Voices from El Barrio* (2006), where she presents the oral histories of twenty-four formerly incarcerated Chicanas. She centers the women's voices and analyses of their lived experiences. In this work I regard the voices of Adriana and Esther as sites of knowledge. Their narratives reinforce a lot of the scholarly assertions presented in the literature review. However, they also reinforce the need to transform the conversation on the criminalization of Chicanas/Latinas to include issues that have received minimal attention, including language, migration, deportation, and deportee reintegration.

Context for Adriana and Esther's Narratives

In 2008, as I conducted ethnographic research on criminalized Latina migrants, I met Adriana and Esther, two Latina migrants impacted by the U.S. criminal legal system. Esther is originally from the Mexican state of

Oaxaca and migrated to the United States undocumented in 1989. She was convicted on drug-related charges in 2003 and spent almost three years in the California Rehabilitation Center, a state prison designated for drug rehabilitation. Esther was then transferred to Valley State Prison for Women (VSPW) to complete her five-year sentence. That is where Adriana and Esther met and became friends. Since the age of twelve, Adriana traveled consistently from her home state of Durango, Mexico, to Texas. She was a legal resident when she was arrested in 1998. She was involved in drug sales, and during an exchange, an acquaintance of hers killed another person. She was charged for second-degree murder and sentenced to fifteen years to life. She served eighteen years and in March 2015 was granted parole and deported to Tijuana, Mexico, in August of that year.

Five years ago Esther opened a small restaurant in downtown Tijuana, and when they reconnected after Adriana's deportation, Esther offered her a job. Shortly afterward I traveled to Tijuana and simultaneously interviewed Adriana and Esther on their experiences of criminalization, including the court and sentencing process, their time in jail, their imprisonment, the parole process (in Adriana's case), detention, and their eventual deportation. In the following I include excerpts of the interview, which I edited and organized to present the information based on major themes. The focus is on two main questions: What are Latina migrants' experiences in U.S. criminal legal systems? And how does their social positionality shape these experiences?

Several themes emerged throughout the interview. The first part of the chapter focuses on discrimination based on linguistic abilities and migrant status, and in the second part I include their experiences throughout the process of criminalization. Their narratives reveal that Latina migrants experience criminalization differently, and Adriana and Esther note that this is informed by race, class, gender, sexuality, and, in their case, whether they have set terms or a life sentence with the opportunity for parole.

Language as an Obstacle

During the interview, both Adriana and Esther maintained that not knowing English was the most significant obstacle they encountered. When they arrived to prison, neither Adriana nor Esther knew how to speak English. In what follows they address how this impacted the court process, the difficulty of communicating with medical staff regarding health issues, and not having an objective parole hearing because they cannot communicate their message to the Board of Parole, the state body responsible for determining individuals' readiness to reenter society. Since Adriana spent significantly more time in prison than Esther and had to do programming in English for her parole process, she took English as a second language (ESL) courses and then obtained her General Educational Development (GED) degree. She addresses some of the benefits that knowing English afford deportees in a border city like Tijuana.

Mistranslations

> AUTHOR: [Adriana], why did you decide to take [ESL] classes?
> ADRIANA: I was determined because I do not like anyone interpreting for me or saying what I wanted to say. I thought that they were not giving the right message or telling me what the other person said. So I decided to learn so that I could defend myself.
> AUTHOR: Why did you think they were interpreting incorrectly?
> ADRIANA: Because I did not understand the language and really did not know if they were giving the correct message. And now I realize that I was right in a lot of things because a translation is never exactly what you mean from one language to another.
> AUTHOR: And did you witness mistranslation in other cases?
> ADRIANA: Yes, when I started to understand a little, I started to realize that. Especially because since we were inmates . . . since we were prisoners, there was not much interest in us and everyone translated however they wanted.
> AUTHOR: And who was translating?
> ADRIANA: They had official interpreters . . . certificated . . . but they were not actually doing the work how it is supposed to be done in those places; they do not do what they are supposed to.[1]

Misunderstandings in Court

> ADRIANA: When the district attorney begins to present the case to the jury of what they are accusing you of . . . I'll never forget how

one allows oneself to be influenced by another person's words, and I learned not to judge anyone, regardless of the opinion someone else has of them. I am never going to forget that they [district attorney] stand in front [of the court] and say, "We have here this person that at her age and with her experience . . . she was easily able to manipulate these two young men [her codefendants]." And I asked myself, "Really?" And they start saying and putting stuff that has never even crossed your mind but that they are transmitting to another person so that they see you as the monster that they want to present. It's one of the first things that one leaves with . . . with that trauma. . . . "Are they really accusing me of this? Did they really make them [jury] see me like this?" I always said that I felt like a Christmas tree where you start putting ornaments on, and lights, and more, and more, and at the end, bam! They connect it and it turns on. "Let's go! Guilty!" That was traumatizing to me. It was traumatizing because I was expecting some time because I knew I was responsible, but I was not responsible for that kind of a sentence. And I don't know . . . I could never understand what exactly happened. Even the person that was interpreting for me was chastised. She tried to help me as much as she could. She told me to say that the jurors were talking about the case outside [deliberation], and that is illegal. And well, she had a microphone, and they heard her and chastised her. And when we finished, she told me, "What happened here is the most unjust thing I could have heard. I thought they were going to let you go." I don't know in reality what exactly happened. Like I told you, since then I've wondered what did they say exactly, because I could hear what they were saying, and what she [interpreter] said that I said. And that stayed with me. Because of language, it was a really difficult process for me.

AUTHOR: [Esther], how do you think not knowing English affected you in your process?

ESTHER: I think so because since they are Americans, there was no communication.

AUTHOR: But are there particular moments in your case where you think language affected you?

ESTHER: Yes, of course! When I wanted to hear something, or they were talking about my case in front of me and I could not understand anything, and I wanted to know what was going on.

AUTHOR: And that was during court?
ESTHER: It was in the court.

Difficulties of Accessing Health Care

ADRIANA: One of the biggest problems I saw was when you have health issues. If you have to go to the doctor and you can't communicate with them . . . what you are actually feeling. If they ask you if you have fever, you say yes. And if they ask you to rank your pain between one and eight, and they don't even understand what you are saying, and there is no one to say exactly what is happening.

Language and the Parole Process

ADRIANA: Those of us with a life sentence have to go through a different process than a person who has a limited time in their sentence. We have to fight for a [release] date. We have to stand before a review board where they will decide if we are remorseful of a crime, if we are accepting responsibility, and if we are prepared to leave. Whether there has been a change in us. If we cannot express ourselves with our own words, they will not receive the message. Because it's like, if I ask her [pointing to Esther] to tell you something, or she asks me to tell you something, it's not the same as if I tell you directly. We have to be in front of those people and communicate with them. An interpreter is going to reduce the intensity or emotion that you want to convey in what you are saying. It does have an effect!
AUTHOR: And did you witness any women returning from their parole hearings and say that language affected them?
ADRIANA: Yes, all of them. The first thing they ask when we go to the hearing is, "Do you speak English?" And if you say no, "And why have you not learned?" Because the opportunities [to learn] are there.
ESTHER: And they say it to you angrily.
ADRIANA: For most people, for migrants, the most difficult thing is the level of education because they can't get a GED. It's not easy. It's with great difficulty that you can sometimes take an exam in Spanish, now imagine having to do it totally in English. It's one of the most

difficult things. And the other, as in the case of one of the people that we [Adriana and Esther] know, it makes me very sad to see that she stayed behind disarmed because we are all getting out and she does not want to do anything for her life.[2]

ESTHER: Everyone has gotten out except her.

ADRIANA: She doesn't want to do anything. Absolutely nothing. And that is the hard part. That people don't want to do the things they are asking us. In school she is still in the same place since the beginning. Since she got there, she has not passed the same class. She pays to have her homework done. It's because language is such a huge barrier.

ESTHER: It's as if you did not have a leg.

ADRIANA: It's like trying to jump the border to the other side [United States] at age sixty. Imagine! That is what is difficult. The opportunities are there, and you don't take advantage of them because you do not want to. And I thank God for my determination to not let anyone be my voice, and for me to have my own voice. Maybe I would still be there [in prison] struggling because I could not tell them what I wanted.

Benefits of English for Deportees

AUTHOR: For women who are in the situation where you were, being arrested and then imprisoned, not knowing the language, migrants, what advice would you give them?

ADRIANA: For me, because this is what worked for me, it's that they try to learn the language. Because even now, when they come over here [Mexico], it will help them.

AUTHOR: In what way?

ADRIANA: Especially where we are [Tijuana]. Even to work. We are at a border where people cross every day, and not everyone speaks Spanish, although we are in Mexico. A lot of people come here from the hotel [points to a hotel in front], and Esther says, "Go ahead, those are your customers." To work here in Tijuana, in any place that you go and you speak English, they are going to pay you better than if you speak one language. Whether it's a restaurant, small business, they are going to pay you better than if you speak one language.

That's the first thing, that they learn the language. Because it's the only thing that will help them survive over there . . . the only thing that is going to help them overcome.

Limited English Skills as an Obstacle and English Language Proficiency as an Asset

This section demonstrates the considerable effect that not knowing English has on criminalized Latina migrants. Throughout their experiences, Adriana and Esther had to endure knowing that they could not defend themselves properly, and that they may have not received the best defense because of this. Charged with this understanding, Adriana made it a point to not allow anyone else be her voice. But as they discuss, not everyone has the same ability to do so, and that may mean spending the rest of their lives in prison. Adriana's experience also addresses another issue, which is her disposability in the United States, but her usefulness as an English speaker in the border city of Tijuana. Deported as a "criminal alien," she is permanently banned from returning to the United States, but the global neoliberal capitalist market finds a way of incorporating Adriana and her marketable language skills.

Discrimination

In the interview, Adriana and Esther addressed various forms of discrimination they confronted. As discussed in the previous section, language plays an extremely important role in shaping Latina migrants' criminalization experiences. In this section, Adriana and Esther discuss the issue of language again and share how women in prison that speak English discriminate against non–English speakers. They also speak about the treatment they encountered in immigration detention and the stigma that comes from having been incarcerated.

Language Discrimination among Women in Prison

ESTHER: Over there in prison, women who speak, that are fluent in English, it's as if they want to see you below them. Although at the end of the day, we are all in prison, no? But there are hierarchies and some think of themselves as higher than others. To me it seems stupid because we are all in the same [expletive] place, no? But hey, that is how it is in prison.

ADRIANA: If you do not speak English, they discriminate against you, they humiliate you, they tell you things, they do things to you.

ESTHER: They look at you as if you are worthless.

AUTHOR: Did you ever feel that way, Esther?

ESTHER: Yes. They call you *paisa*.[3]

AUTHOR: Who called you *paisa*?

ESTHER: The same ones. It's just that they think they are better.

ADRIANA: Unfortunately, the same people who are daughters of Mexican parents but born over there [United States] are the people that....

ESTHER: They call them *paisas*.

ADRIANA: [We] lived in a place where there was aggression, and sometimes people are attacking you and you don't even know it. You can answer with a yes or a no and you don't know if you got yourself into a problem. That is what made me determined, because I said, "I'm not going to let anyone," ... and like she [Esther] says, the people that speak English discriminate against the people that don't. That is one of the things ... when I could defend myself, even if I was mispronouncing or whatever, but I could communicate, I wanted to be the voice for others, the ones that could not speak [English]. To help those that had not been able to learn the language yet.

Treatment in Immigration Detention

AUTHOR: What was your experience in detention?

ESTHER: Well, nothing ... it's just that ... what I did see is that the people that work there, it's like if they feel super powerful.

AUTHOR: The people that work in detention?

ESTHER: Yes, the *migra*. What do you call them?

AUTHOR: The officers?

ESTHER: There you go, the officers. They feel super powerful. They feel like if they are super bad asses.

AUTHOR: Why?

ESTHER: Because they see you, right? And you are in their territory.

AUTHOR: How did they treat people?

ESTHER: No, they treat you really . . . they did not treat me well. They treat you badly. They laugh. They get happy if you are going to jail, or if they are going to send you back [to Mexico]. It's like a form of racism, and it's . . . how should I tell you? Arrogant. Something like that. I do not want to know anything about them ever again.

ADRIANA: In detention, even though you already served your sentence, they still segregate you. Those of us who were coming from prison, they gave us a red uniform and they put us in a different area, the others are in blue, and the people who are coming in sick, they put them in green. The days that I was in detention, I can't complain of bad treatment because they did not treat me poorly. As soon as you arrive, they give you your blanket, pillow, tooth paste, and they show you where you are going to stay, which is an open area. They have two televisions and they give you earphones so that you can listen because the televisions do not have volume. One is in English and the other in Spanish.

ESTHER: Where is that?

ADRIANA: In Mesa Verde. The detention center in Mesa Verde. That is where I spent [seven] days.

Post-incarceration Stigma

AUTHOR: One of the things that I have noticed is that not everyone in prison has the same type of support with their families or friends outside. Especially if you are a migrant, there are people that can't even communicate through letters or the phone with their families.

ESTHER: There are many inside.

AUTHOR: So how does that affect them?

ADRIANA: It affects you a lot inside because not having your family support, it's as if people see you as less than. People discriminate against you. It affects you first emotionally, but being inside, you are going to feel alone . . . the loneliness. You feel segregated. You feel . . . well, in reality, even being here, outside. To say that you have been in prison . . . forget about it. And even more if they know how much time you did. "Who knows how many . . . she was probably with the Taliban doing terrorism."

ESTHER: It's true.

ADRIANA: And still, that is a stigma. And the stigma of being alone, of not having any support. They stigmatize you.
AUTHOR: You Esther, now being outside, have you felt that stigma?
ESTHER: Not anymore. Not anymore. At first I did, but not now.
AUTHOR: How did you feel?
ESTHER: I felt shame. I felt as if they were going to see me and . . .
ADRIANA: I just said it. In fact, I just told her, "So what?"
ESTHER: That's how I felt.
ADRIANA: It doesn't take your value away. You already paid for what you did.
ESTHER: I was ashamed. Not anymore. Because now I understand a lot of things. I've seen so many people that have not needed to go to prison to . . . they are real bad.[4] And what is wrong with me if I came from prison? Do I have a virus? Do I have something? I started to think about a lot of things, and then, at the migrant shelter [the social worker], any time I had a problem with my alcoholism, I would always go ask her for help. She would say, "No, no, no! Calm down! Look, I am going to help you." She would always pick me up. "You are a very important person. You are someone." That is how I would get better. She would say that she was going to send me to a psychologist to get help. "You are well," she said, "Do you know why? Because you come and ask for my help. If not, you would throw yourself [to her addiction] and would not think about asking for help." That is why, because of all of that, I started to feel better and not deny what I am. And now I feel . . . things have gone well. I feel comfortable. I feel well as a human being.
ESTHER: When I lived in Casa Refugio Elvira there was a problem when Eliza [Esther's daughter, fifteen years old at the time] was there with me. She wanted to be in the living room. Then, Eliza, like a kid . . . rebellious . . . she wanted to watch American television. Then a [migrant] woman said, "No, I want to see the telenovela." It was a telenovela about some bakers. The woman says, "I want to watch the telenovela." And Eliza, "No mommy, I want to watch." Then I told the woman, "You know that she wants to see that program. We are going to put it on that program." My goodness, the lady got really arrogant and started to mistreat me. The woman just wanted to cross the border, and they [Border Patrol] would throw her back. She had

never been in prison... in jail... in detention. No, they would just catch her and take her out because she did not have any criminal offenses, and she knew that I was coming from prison. And she started to tell me that I was arrogant and that I had been in prison for a reason. This is when she [the director of the shelter] said "Be quiet!" She told her to not offend me in that way. She felt that the woman was offending me in a very nasty way, because she had said, "There is a reason you were in prison. Everyone who comes from prison...." Well, the worst. And she [director] told her to be quiet and that the situation that we were arguing about did not give her any right to tell me those things about prison. As I told you, until recently I did not want to address that subject, but now I don't care.

AUTHOR: When did you reach this understanding?

ESTHER: Recently. About two years ago. I even changed my physical aspect. You see me different, no? Back then you saw me more masculine. No, not now, because I know that I am in a society, and this society is harsh. So I try to avoid, to avoid comments. Like here, no one knows me here [her neighborhood]. On this street, and the people that I engage... there, in the *tortilleria* [points to the next side of the street], I supply them with tamales; in the *menuderia*, all those people treat me, "*Señora* Esther." No one has ever said anything to me. My friend next door, the dentist, knows about it because we trust each other and we share personal things. But someone coming and disrespecting me, not anymore. I am not going to allow it.

ADRIANA: ... I am not proud of having been in prison. Absolutely not. But it is not something that I should be ashamed of. The person that was arrested in 1998 for murder in the second degree is not the same person that came out of there. I don't feel less than other people. I don't feel superior to anyone either. But, like Esther was saying, just because a person was in prison, that does not make her evil, or the most detestable person in the world. There are people that have never stepped inside a jail and I wouldn't want to have them as neighbors.

An Intersectional Approach to Experiences of Discrimination

In this section on discrimination, Adriana and Esther continue the discussion of the impact of language; in this case, the discrimination non–English speakers receive from English speakers, including other Latinas. This speaks to the importance of intersectionality and understanding how people's social positionality significantly shapes their experiences. It is clear that not all Latinas in prison face the same issues. Even their detention experiences differ, and this is in part because Adriana spent only seven days in detention, and Esther, who was caught by the Border Patrol trying to reenter the United States after being deported as a "criminal alien," spent over six months in immigration detention, providing her with more time to witness the treatment of migrants in detention. The cultural climate in the detention centers may be a factor. Adriana was detained in the Mesa Verde Detention Center in Bakersfield, California, and Esther was detained at the Western Region Detention Facility in San Diego, California. Adriana maintains that although there was segregation of formerly incarcerated people, she did not receive poor treatment in detention. In contrast, Esther shares her experience and conceptualizes the treatment of migrants by immigration officers as a form of racism. Finally, they also discuss the stigma that remains with formerly incarcerated people. While Adriana appears less affected, Esther describes moments where she encountered aggression because of her history of incarceration. However, this was more prominent when she was recently deported and embodied masculinity. As she notes, she disciplined her body to conform to society's gender norms to avoid this kind of violence.

Court and Sentencing Process

In this section Adriana and Esther display a distrust of the court and sentencing process, particularly the drawbacks of having a court-appointed attorney who, as in the case of Esther, appears to compel plea bargains rather than risk going to trial. Both note that the outcomes seem predetermined and that the court process seems to be a "show," or a legal performance. While Esther seems to wonder whether a plea bargain was her best choice, in the case of Adriana, not accepting a plea bargain of seven years and going to trial resulted in spending eighteen years in prison.

> AUTHOR: The court process Esther, how was that? Do you remember?
> ESTHER: Mhmm. They already have everything ready. It's like a job, right? This is going to happen. This other thing is going to happen.

Because they tell you, "first court, second court," and you have to declare yourself guilty. It is their process. So, they are automatically telling you, "You are not going to fight. You are going to say . . . you have to declare yourself guilty."

AUTHOR: Who would tell you this?

ESTHER: The judge, the judge. They give you some paperwork.

AUTHOR: Did you have a lawyer?

ESTHER: Yes, right, the lawyer. They give you some papers and tell you, "Okay, this is going to be the second court, you are going to declare yourself guilty," . . . the lawyer that they assign you. That's it. "That is the step that we have to take. This is the next one. Declare yourself guilty, and that is it." That was your court hearing, and you go back again until your next hearing. That is how they do it.

AUTHOR: So, when you had your lawyer, you were not presented with options? They told you to declare yourself guilty? Did they tell you how many years you were going to receive?

ESTHER: They were supposedly fighting for five years, or I don't know. It's like they scare you.

AUTHOR: The lawyer?

ESTHER: Aha. They want to give you fifteen years, or something like that, but we are going to see if they will settle for four or five. But declare yourself guilty already.

AUTHOR: They scare you so you will accept. . . .

ESTHER: Yes, they scare you a lot.

AUTHOR: Your own lawyer?

ESTHER: Yes, and they tell you, "Declare yourself guilty." And they take you to the judge, you sit down, and they put on a big show there, and they say, "No, well, she just came to declare herself guilty." They declare you guilty, you return, and you wait for another court hearing. [Motions to Adriana] Yes or no?

ADRIANA: Well, in my case it was different. Now I say I should have taken the offer, but I did not. Because at the beginning they were offering seven years. I would have been out in five. But in reality, and I've always said this, all of those charges that were there were not [correct]. I'm not saying that I was completely innocent, because I was involved in something illegal, but not to the point that the charges were made. And the one that was getting the life sentence was my codefendant, who had the least to do in all of it. But to accept the deal, we all had to sign. The person who was really responsible [for killing a person] did not have a problem. He did not care if the other codefendant was sentenced or not, but I did not think that it was fair that this guy would get a life sentence and I got seven years when he was the least guilty. But they do tell you [to accept the plea bargain]. And when he [codefendant] said, "Lets fight the case," and me going to court, as she said, because I did not take the offer, I got fifteen to life.

ESTHER: So, in my case I had to back up my lawyer, who was supposedly helping me out, but he worked that way, "You are going to declare yourself guilty," and that's it. It's a process.

ADRIANA: And it is different when it's just you than when there are two or three persons involved. That's the issue. Because only you can make the decision to take the offer. But in my case, the offer was seven years.

AUTHOR: And why didn't you take it?

ADRIANA: Because the other person had to agree to a sentence of fifteen to life. They were giving him fifteen to life. Actually, the car where we gave the people a ride where it was committed . . . because we only gave them a ride . . . where the crime was committed, the car was mine but he was driving. He was just my chauffeur. We were selling drugs, so logically, as a woman, I had to have my chauffeur. And he, all he did was drive the car because I told him to give them a ride, without knowing what was going to happen. Nonetheless, we gave them a ride. So how was I going to let him go to prison for fifteen years to life for my stupidity?

AUTHOR: And how much time did he get?

ADRIANA: At the end we both received fifteen to life. He got out two years before I did. What I think about all of this . . . when they make the charges, they have to clean up the case. This is like a mafia, I imagine. They already had who was guilty of what, and they are going to prove it at any cost. And they know how much time they are going to give everyone. Because in reality, they did not make it difficult for me to get out, which is why I assume that in reality they did know what my responsibility was. Or him. He got out two years before I did, and both with fifteen to life. In the meantime, the person who is responsible is still inside.

AUTHOR: How many years did you spend incarcerated?
ADRIANA: Eighteen.
AUTHOR: How was it when they sentenced you?
ADRIANA: Before they sentence you, because I went to trial ... when they give the jury's verdict, you already know how much time you are going to get. They [district attorney] were asking for twenty-five to life for me. Just because I was older than the other two people involved.
AUTHOR: Just because you were older?
ADRIANA: Yes, that is always going to be the case. Whenever there is an older person, they assume that you are able to manipulate them because they are young.
AUTHOR: How old were the others?
ADRIANA: One was twenty-four and the other nineteen, against my thirty-eight.

The Subjectivity of the Court Process

Adriana and Esther's experiences during the court process underscore some limitations. Although they are entitled to an attorney, for Esther, not being able to afford a private attorney translates into her having an attorney who appears to not give any option other than a plea bargain. In Adriana's case, all three codefendants had to agree to the plea deal and she believed that the offer of one of her codefendants was unfair. This resulted in her going to trial and being sentenced to fifteen years to life, ultimately spending eighteen years in prison. Their experiences highlight the subjective nature of this process.

The Parole Process

As noted above, Adriana received a life sentence with the possibility of parole. In this section she describes the parole process, including the intense labor people in this situation have to engage to make their case to the Board of Parole. Programming is crucial to this and consists of obtaining an education, getting vocational training, and working on themselves through self-help courses. They also have to remain free of any behavioral problems and demonstrate through their connections to their families and communities that they are ready to reenter society.

>   AUTHOR: Adriana, you were talking a while ago about the parole process. How did you prepare to go to your first hearing?
>
>   ADRIANA: The process takes years. It was a challenge to work with my character, but it was an even bigger challenge to work with all of my emotional problems . . . with everything that I had to do to be able to present myself in front of them [Board of Parole]. In one way or another I had to justify to them what my motivation was to make bad decisions or doing things the way that I did. I had to explain why I felt one way and why I felt another and why now I saw things differently . . . why I had remorse now that I did not have before, whether it exists or not. You have to prepare. And for this, we start taking, and I say "we" because this is not just me, it's all of us. We start working with self-help programs. In prison we take classes on self-esteem, how to control our anger, how to work with our character flaws, to learn to respect ourselves and others. And it is a process. We have to go present a different person because when we arrive, they see you as "the convict," "the guilty person," "the criminal," like the person that committed the worst crime in the world. And when you present yourself in front of them, you have to demonstrate that you are not the same person they sentenced; that you are not the same person that arrived in prison. The process is to . . . prepare ourselves and to overcome.
>
>   AUTHOR: What requirements do they have to show that you are rehabilitated?
>
>   ADRIANA: As a requirement they ask, above all, that you master the language. That is one thing. Because you have to improve yourself. You have to have gotten an education inside. They want you to have a GED or a high school [diploma]. If you have not been able to get your GED or a high school [diploma] but you have consistently been in school, then that is a matter of your learning abilities, but you have been putting in your part. To participate in all self-help classes offered; that you go to Alcoholics Anonymous and Narcotics Anonymous, whether you have a drug problem or not. You have to participate in those programs because . . . and they work, they

work. I like Alcoholics Anonymous a lot, even though I don't have an alcohol problem, because that is where I learned a lot about my character flaws, and since it's a twenty-four-hour program, it helps you to survive in an emotionally healthier way. I like it because they don't concentrate on who believes in God and who does not. They concentrate on a higher power. If you believe that your pen is going to make you change, if you think that it is going to change your life, it is going to change it. And I like that, the respect. That is one of the things they require. And the other is to have a high academic level, but as a requirement, it's a GED. And that you have vocational training; to learn carpentry, to at least learn to change the oil in a car, to cut hair, simple things. Something that will open doors for you. But as I told you, maybe over there it helps, but not here [Mexico]. Those are the requirements. And the other is that you keep in contact with your family and people outside so that they know that you are prepared to reenter society. That you have economic support. The more support that you have from the outside, that is a greater guarantee for them, especially if you are going to be deported, to know that you have a way of surviving over here and you won't go back and that you won't relapse.

The Parole Process as an Uneven Experience

In a prior section Adriana spoke about the difficulties that language presents for predominantly Spanish speakers with life sentences who have to go through the parole process. If obtaining an education is a requirement, and in order to obtain that education, they have to speak English, non–English speakers are at a tremendous disadvantage. Something interesting that Adriana notes is the self-help programming that they have to participate in. She maintains that whether or not individuals have problems with addiction, they have to participate in programs such as Alcoholics Anonymous and Narcotics Anonymous. Although Adriana enjoyed and appreciates what these programs did for her, the coerciveness of this requirement deserves interrogation. Finally, Adriana notes that outside support is essential, especially for migrants facing deportation. This is another important issue. Some migrants have a difficult time remaining connected, especially if their families are outside of the United States. In the case of Mexico, there are remote areas where it is difficult to communicate, and some migrants lose connection to their families because their undocumented status prevents them from returning. These are all concerns that should be part of conversations regarding the U.S. criminal legal systems and Latina/o migrants.

Deportation Experiences

This final section focuses on Adriana's and Esther's deportation experiences. Migrants with criminal records are considered "criminal aliens" and are priorities for deportation. This is the case whether they are documented or undocumented, and regardless of when the criminalized act was committed. They are also banned from ever returning to the United States. Although they were both set for deportation after being released, the fact that Adriana had an indeterminate sentence meant that Immigration and Customs Enforcement (ICE) did not process her case while she was incarcerated, and she was held in detention for seven days to see an immigration judge.

> AUTHOR: When they deported you, Esther, how was the process?
> ESTHER: From prison they took me to the airport. From the airport they put me on an airplane to San Diego. It's their airplane, but don't think that it's an elegant airplane.
> AUTHOR: Was it on an airplane for you too [asking Adriana]?
> ADRIANA: No, they picked us up in a van . . . it depends on whether you are going to see a judge or not. They have your case open. I had to go to Mesa Verde.
> ESTHER: And from Mesa Verde, where did you go?
> ADRIANA: From Mesa Verde we came in a bus because they had to pick up people along the way. It was a lot of us. When we arrived at Mesa Verde, there were two other women besides me; the bus was already full with some other men. And when we got to another detention center, they picked up more people. And when they got on, two of them said, and I'm never going to forget . . . they had experience being deported because one of them said, "Yes, we made it!" Another man asked, "Why?" "Because there are women. They are going to

deport us through Tijuana." They had not told us where they were going to take us. Everyone says that Tijuana is the best deportation.

ESTHER: They took me from there, when I got out [from VSPW], to detention . . . they put you in a cell. From there they take you out in a little bus, and they take you to the airport. From the airport, you remain chained.

ADRIANA: Because they don't have to see a judge.

ESTHER: You remain chained.

ADRIANA: That is why they get them as close to the border as possible.

ESTHER: There they put you in a big airplane. I would say that about three hundred people fit.

ADRIANA: And all the way to the border?

ESTHER: No, to San Diego. And in San Diego, we arrived at night. We got there around one. And we waited there. They gave us blankets, pillows, put us in a room, in a cell, and we had to wait until dawn, and then the bus arrives. It picked us up and brought us to the border crossing.

ADRIANA: They just give you your deportation papers and that's it?

ESTHER: The bus arrived full. Full. It arrived, it parked. They gave you your bag . . . a paper bag where you have your shoelaces and all of your belongings that you bring from over there [prison]. And when you arrive here, they give you your bag that you are carrying all the way from over there. You have your toothpaste. . . .

ADRIANA: And you were received in an office [in Tijuana]?

ESTHER: No, there wasn't any.

ADRIANA: They just opened the door and threw you out to the other side [Tijuana]?

ESTHER: Mhmm. But wait. The bus arrives, and they put you in . . . on this side is where Grupo Beta is . . . was because they are no longer there.[5] But it was a tiny office. They just asked you, "Do you want to go to the migrant shelter? Or if you want to go, there's the door." And that was it. That is why I'm surprised about what you tell me about your experience.

ADRIANA: No, as I told [a migrant rights activist], "Why don't you go see the Chaparral so that you get to see the offices?"[6] I don't know if the men as well as the women . . . I don't know if just the women, but that was my experience.

AUTHOR: Yes, because I remember that they just let you [Esther] go, right? What time was it?

ESTHER: It was really early. That's another one. It was really early, like five in the morning. Because we arrived . . . we arrived in San Diego around eleven, one in the morning. And we just slept a little and really early the bus was there, "Let's go! Let's go!" And we all boarded the bus to drop us off here. They just open a metal door.

ADRIANA: And that was it?

ESTHER: "Go! Go! Vamonos!" That's what happened to me.

ADRIANA: No, in my case, as I said, they opened the metal door and you form a line. You don't just leave. You have to stay there. They go in small numbers. They generate a document that says you were deported, they give it to you, and with that, they open a door and you go into some offices. There they do everything. . . .

ESTHER: It's the one [document] they give you when you get deported. Because immigration gives you that one.

ADRIANA: No, no, no . . . here, where you arrive, they give you another one.

ESTHER: Now!

ADRIANA: They don't give it to you where they ask you all the questions. There they evaluate you. They check your blood pressure, they check whether you need medicine, or whatever. There they give us the document to go process the *seguro popular* [public health insurance].

ESTHER: Even that! They didn't do that before.

AUTHOR: No, because do you remember that people used to struggle with the police because you didn't have an identification?

ESTHER: Yes, they arrested me.

The Changing Conditions of Deportations

Esther was deported in 2008 and Adriana in 2015. As noted, during this time period the deportation process in Tijuana changed. Before deportees would arrive at the border and be released through a metal door. If they were lucky, they received some support from Grupo Beta. However, as Esther notes, migrants often had to fend for themselves. Now, it appears that this process has changed. Rather than just releasing deportees, they are also processed in Mexico. This includes a quick medical checkup and a discussion of the deportees' plans. There appears to be an effort to ameliorate the deportees' difficult situation. Several questions arise. What prompted these changes? To what extent is this a national project? And, as Adriana implies, women appear to receive more protection than men. Thus, to what extent is this gendered?

Conclusion

The purpose of this chapter is to center the embodied knowledge of Adriana and Esther. Their narratives produce knowledge as well as generate important scholarly and political questions regarding the criminalization of Latina migrants. The issue that both marked as a major determinant in shaping their experiences is their limited English skills. The sentencing process, their interactions with English-speaking women in prison, receiving adequate medical attention, their ability to program, the ability for people with indeterminate sentences to obtain parole, and even their reintegration into Mexican society were profoundly affected by language.

Their experiences also differed because Esther had a determinate five-year sentence, in contrast to Adriana, who had to go through the parole process that lifers with the opportunity of parole face. In addition to the anxiety and uncertainty that having an indeterminate sentence produces, this also influenced their deportation process. While Esther was immediately deported after her release from prison, Adriana had to spend additional time in detention.

Another important issue that their narratives highlight is the various forms of discrimination they endure because of their migrant status in the United States, which Esther argues stems from racism, and the stigma of having been in prison that remains with them in Mexico. Although Esther has been able to build a life for herself, including owning her own business, she observes how she had to attempt to decriminalize and discipline her body by conforming to gender norms.

Adriana and Esther also address the court hearing and sentencing process as a "show," or a legal performance, where the outcomes appear predetermined and everyone has a role to play. To what extent do their experiences reflect patterns in U.S. criminal legal systems?[7]

Another important issue that is specific to individuals with life sentences with the opportunity for parole is the difficulty of meeting all the requirements imposed by the Board of Parole. Again, language greatly influences this process, and this situation is exacerbated for individuals who do not have a formal education in any language. This is also a difficult process because of the requirement to have significant outside support; due to financial and communication issues and the distance between migrants and their home countries, for some this becomes an insurmountable obstacle.

A final concern that Adriana and Esther address is the deportation process. For migrants in general, but especially for people leaving prison, they often get deported with very little if any financial support or belongings. As Adriana's narrative reflects, this seems to be receiving some attention in Tijuana. However, how is this addressed in other deportation areas? What does this process look like for non-Mexican migrants? And of major concern is what happens when deportees have children?

Adriana's and Esther's narratives give significant insight into the questions that frame this work, specifically, what are the experiences of Latina migrants in U.S. criminal legal systems, and how does their social positionality inform these experiences? However, as I have discussed, their narratives generate additional scholarly and political questions that deserve further exploration if we are to move beyond descriptive analysis, such as what are their experiences, to asking, how do we transform this violent reality?

NOTES

1 From Adriana's perspective, part of the job of legal interpreters is to ensure that the person with limited English skills is well informed of what is being said to and about them and their cases. However, from her experience, she does not believe every interpreter does this well.
2 By "disarmed," Adriana refers to the fact that one of the Latina migrant lifers that stayed behind does not have the linguistic or academic skills necessary to present herself to the Board of Parole and make a case that she is ready to reenter society. Although she used the term *desarmada*, "disempowered" is more accurate.
3 *Paisa* is a slang term that comes from the Spanish word *paisano*, which means someone who is from the same country. In the context discussed, *paisa* is typically used by Mexicans and Mexican Americans to negatively refer to a Mexican national who embodies Mexicanness through their way of dress, customs, and/or language skills.

4 By "people that have not needed to go to prison," Esther is referring to witnessing people engage in what she deems morally wrong activities that are not prosecuted criminally.
5 Grupo Beta de Protecció al Migrante, a government agency aimed to protect migrants' human rights and to save their lives when they try to cross the border, was established by the Mexican state in 1990.
6 El Chaparral is the port of entry from San Diego into Tijuana that opened in 2012.
7 A prime example of such legal performances is Operation Streamline, which was implemented in 2005. Under this policy, undocumented migrants caught crossing in particular border regions are criminally prosecuted en masse. Usually between seventy and eighty migrants present themselves in court, often shackled at their hands and feet, and they accept plea deals for "illegal entry." Because of the large number of cases, judges "combine the initial appearance, arraignment, plea, and sentencing into one hearing" (Lydgate, 2010, p. 486). Attorneys represent multiple clients, and the hearing lasts one to two hours. At the end, the group of migrants leaves the court legally marked as "criminal aliens," which makes them ineligible for reentry. Operation Streamline highlights Adriana and Esther's argument that sentencing processes are performances since the outcome is predetermined. For further reading on Operation Streamline, see Borderlands Autonomist Collective (2012), Kerwin and McCabe (2010), and Lydgate (2010).

REFERENCES

Alexander, M. (2010). *The new Jim Crow: Mass incarceration in the age of colorblindness*. New York: New Press.

Anzaldúa, G., & Moraga, C. (Eds.). (1981). *This bridge called my back: Writings by radical women of Color*. Watertown, MA: Persephone Press.

Bond-Maupin, L., Maupin, J. R., & Leisenring, A. (2002). Girls' delinquency and the justice implications of intake workers' perspectives. *Women & Criminal Justice, 13*, 51–77.

Borderlands Autonomist Collective. (2012). Resisting the security-industrial complex: Operation Streamline and the militarization of the Arizona-Mexico borderlands. In J. M. Loyd, M. Mitchelson, & A. Burridge (Eds.), *Beyond walls and cages: Prisons, borders, and global crisis* (pp. 190–209). Athens: University of Georgia Press.

Cervantes, A. G., Menjívar, C., & Staples, W. G. (2017). "Humane" immigration enforcement and Latina immigrants in the detention complex. *Feminist Criminology, 12*, 269–292.

Collins, P. H. (2000). *Black feminist thought*. New York: Routledge.

Crenshaw, K. (1991). Mapping the margins: Intersectionality, identity politics and violence against women of Color. *Stanford Law Review, 43*, 1241–1299.

Del Valle, S., Morín, J. L., Swimm, M., & Escalera, N. M. (2016). Latinas and the U.S. criminal justice system. In J. L. Morín (Ed.), *Latinos and criminal justice: An encyclopedia* (pp. 96–118). Santa Barbara, CA: Greenwood.

Díaz-Cotto, J. (2000). The criminal justice system and its impact on Latinas(os) in the United States. *Justice Professional, 13*, 49–67.

Díaz-Cotto, J. (2005). Latinas and the war on drugs in the United States, Latin America, and Europe. In J. Sudbury (Ed.), *Global lockdown: Race, gender, and the prison-industrial complex* (pp. 137–154). New York: Routledge.

Díaz-Cotto, J. (2006). *Chicana lives and criminal justice: Voices from el barrio.* Austin: University of Texas Press.

Dowling, J. A., & Inda, J. X. (2013). *Governing immigration through crime: A reader.* Stanford, CA: Stanford University Press.

Escobar, M. (2011). ASFA and the impact on imprisoned migrant women and their children. In J. M. Lawston & A. Lucas (Eds.), *Razor wire women: Prisoners, scholars, activists, and artists* (pp. 75–92). New York: State University of New York Press.

Escobar, M. (2016). *Captivity beyond prisons: Criminalization experiences of Latina (im) migrants.* Austin: University of Texas Press.

Flores, J., Camacho, A. O., & Santos, X. (2017). Gender on the run: Latinas in a Southern California barrio. *Feminist Criminology, 12*, 248–268.

Gonzales, A. (2014). *Reform without justice: Latino migrant politics and the homeland security state.* New York: Oxford University Press.

Hernández, D. M. (2009). Pursuant to deportation: Latinos and immigrant detention. In S. Oboler (Ed.), *Behind bars: Latino/as and prison in the United States* (pp. 39–62). New York: Palgrave Macmillan.

hooks, b. (1981). *Ain't I a woman?* Cambridge, MA: South End Press.

hooks, b. (1984). *Feminist theory: From margin to center.* Cambridge, MA: South End Press.

Kerwin, D., & McCabe, K. (2010). Arrested on entry: Operation Streamline and the prosecution of immigration crimes. Migration Policy Institute. www.migrationpolicy.org.

Lopez, V., & Pasko, L. (2017). Bringing Latinas to the forefront: Latina girls, women, and the justice system. *Feminist Criminology, 12*, 193–195.

Lorde, A. (1984). *Sister outsider: Essays and speeches.* Berkeley: Crossing Press.

Lydgate, J. J. (2010). Assembly-line justice: A review of operation streamline. *California Law Review, 98*, 481–544.

Menjívar, C., & Kanstroom, D. (2013). *Constructing immigrant "illegality": Critiques, experiences, and responses.* New York: Cambridge University Press.

Mohanty, C. T. (1984). Under western eyes: Feminist scholarship and colonial discourses. *Boundary 2, 12–13*, 333–358.

Morín, J. L. (2005). *Latina/o rights and justice in the United States: Perspectives and approaches.* Durham, NC: Carolina Academic Press.

Morín, J. L. (2008). Latinas/os and US prisons: Trends and Challenges. *Latino Studies, 6*, 11–34.

Morín, J. L. (2016). *Latinos and Criminal Justice: An Encyclopedia.* Santa Barbara, CA: Greenwood.

Muñoz, E. A. (2004). Misdemeanor criminal justice: Contextualizing effects of Latino ethnicity, gender, and immigrant status. *Race, Gender & Class, 11*, 112–134.

Muñoz, E. A., & Martínez, M. R. (2001). Latinas and criminal sentencing: An exploratory analysis. *Voces: A Journal of Chicana/Latina Studies, 3*, 150–176.

Oboler, S. (Ed.). (2009). *Behind bars: Latino/as and prison in the United States*. New York: Palgrave Macmillan.

Olguín, B. V. (2010). *La pinta: Chicana/o prisoner literature, culture, and poetics*. Austin: University of Texas Press.

Pasko, L., & Lopez, V. (2018). The Latina penalty: Juvenile correctional attitudes toward the Latina juvenile offender. *Journal of Ethnicity in Criminal Justice, 16*, 272–291.

Sandoval, C. (1991). U.S. third world feminism: The theory and method of oppositional consciousness in the postmodern world. *Genders, 10*, 1–24.

Schaffner, L. (2009). Latinas in U.S. juvenile detention: Turning adversity to advantage. In S. Oboler (Ed.), *Behind bars: Latino/as and prison in the United States* (pp. 113–132). New York: Palgrave Macmillan.

Sudbury, J. (2010). Unpacking the crisis: Women of Color, globalization, and the prison-industrial complex. In R. Solinger, P. C. Johnson, M. L. Raimon, T. Reynolds, & R. C. Tapia (Eds.), *Interrupted life: Experiences of incarcerated women in the United States* (pp. 11–25). Berkeley: University of California Press.

Urbina, M. G. (2012). *Hispanics in the U.S. criminal justice system: The new American demography*. Springfield, IL: Charles C Thomas.

Urbina, M. G., & Álvarez, S. E. (2016). Neoliberalism, criminal justice and Latinos: The contours of neoliberal economic thought and policy on criminalization. *Latino Studies, 14*, 33–58.

Urbina, M. G., & Smith, L. (2007). Colonialism and its impact on Mexicans' experience of punishment in the United States. In M. Bosworth & J. Flavin (Eds.), *Race, gender, and punishment: From colonialism to the war on terror* (pp. 49–63). New Brunswick, NJ: Rutgers University Press.

10

Young Women's and Girls' Experiences in the Facilitation of Migrant Smuggling

GABRIELLA SANCHEZ

On the night of July 30, 2018, near Sasabe, a small town a few miles north of the U.S.-Mexico border in the U.S. state of Arizona, two sisters ages seventeen and eighteen were arrested under migrant smuggling charges by U.S. Customs and Border Protection (CBP). According to the official press release, CBP officers were on watch as the two young women—whose names were not publicly released—pulled to the side of the road, swiftly picked up two men, and concealed them under a blanket on the back seat of their small car. Convinced that they were witnessing an act of migrant smuggling, the officers approached the scene, alerted the women of the reason for their presence, and proceeded to search their car, finding a third man hidden in the trunk.

This short vignette may cause a bit of cognitive dissonance. Most reporting on migrant smuggling on the U.S.-Mexico border, after all, involves stories of transnationally organized criminals, frightening Central American gangsters, bloodthirsty Mexican drug trafficking "cartel" members, and even Islamic extremists—all of whom are portrayed as male. Media coverage and academic talk on smuggling depict it as a professional enterprise whose male actors rely on advanced technology and swift methods to carry out their predatory business. Male smugglers, we are told, are the sole perpetrators of what is often characterized as the evil, despicable act of smuggling. They sexually prey on women and children and do not hesitate to abandon to their fate those too weak or unable to keep up with their pace and tyrannical orders. Smuggling is in short portrayed as a male domain where women (unless as victims) do not seem to exist. Perhaps this is the reason why lacking references to death, violence, or criminal adventure, the story of the two sisters from Sasabe made only the local border newspapers.

This last sentence suggests not that migrants' irregular journeys are uneventful or safe but rather that stories devoid of references to pain, suffering, and violence are often excluded from the larger discourse of smuggling. There is in fact no shortage of scholarship and journalistic content documenting the tragedies experienced by migrants in transit. However, we have had much less to say about how migration enforcement regimes and border control mechanisms have been behind the very emergence and reliance on practices like smuggling facilitation and their highly specific forms of violence. More precisely, we have remained virtually silent concerning smuggling facilitators—unless when embracing and reproducing the monolithic narrative that depicts them as inherently criminal male predators. The focus on the graphic examples surrounding migrant suffering leaves enough room to make only passing references to the state's role in the reduction of paths for safe, dignified, and expedited forms of migration. In other words, lurid, graphic stories of migrant tragedy and death at the hand of evil male smugglers reach large readerships. Yet most references to smuggling continue to pay limited, uncritical attention to the ways in which criminalization processes related to border and immigration enforcement and control impact not only migrants but also those behind their journeys.

Despite its ubiquity in the global migration discourse, migrant smuggling is one of the least researched fields in criminology and migration studies. There have been multiple attempts toward building its presence in these fields. Yet the law enforcement and state perspectives that gave rise to its articulation as a crime, the pervasiveness of racial stereotypes and gender bias, and academic siloism have systematically limited smuggling's understanding, treatment, and discourse.

This chapter contributes to the small but growing corpus of empirical, critical smuggling research that seeks to counter these trends. It does so by privileging the experiences and perspectives of an actor often absent in smuggling narratives: the smuggling facilitator, more specifically, the young, female facilitator. I rely on in-person and in-court testimonies of three young women investigated for migrant smuggling on the U.S.-Mexico border to show that, contrary to the narratives that tend to encase it as the domain of criminally driven and organized men, the facilitation of irregular migration relies on the work performed by women and young girls.

Privileging the voice of smuggling facilitators rather than those from the state or victims alone is not an attempt to exempt the first from their responsibility in the violence experienced by many migrants in transit. What I argue is that the inclusion of the perspectives of the women who work as facilitators is pivotal toward an improved understanding and treatment of smuggling as a crime and the creation of strategies to counter migrant risk. Further, I argue that explored through the lens of intersectionality, women's testimonies concerning their participation in smuggling provide a much-needed counternarrative of border security. It recognizes women as actors but also as reliable and legitimate witnesses to the processes of criminalization that afflict them and their communities. This allows us to critically and empirically deconstruct and retell smuggling discourse that has allowed for the criminalization not only of irregular migration but also, more specifically, of its actors.

First, I briefly trace the political origins of migrant smuggling and its definition as a crime as a preface to the U.S.-Mexico border smuggling discourse mobilized today. I follow with a summary of what is empirically known about the roles of women in smuggling. I then turn to personal testimonies that attest to smuggling's role in family reunification and care, as a response to marginalization and poverty, and to its associations with different forms of violence. I conclude with a series of reflections concerning the testimonies and propose new lines of research and action.

What Is Migrant Smuggling?

While often cited in migration discourse, the term "migrant smuggling"—yet not the practices it seeks to encompass—is relatively new. In fact, it officially entered the global security lexicon only in 2000, through its inclusion in a supplemental protocol to the United Nations Convention against Transnational Organized Crime.[1] The convention was the result of an effort on the part of the United Nations General Assembly to develop "a new international legal regime to fight international organized crime" (Gallagher, 2001, p. 976). Prior to the convention's signing, migrant smuggling—defined in the protocol as "the procurement, in order to obtain, directly or indirectly, a financial or other material benefit, of the illegal entry of a person into a State

Party of which the person is not a national or a permanent resident" (UNODC, 2000)—commanded scant although growing concern among some UN member states. There had been until then not much of a push toward defining it as a stand-alone practice, and the term was in fact often used as a synonym of human trafficking.[2] Even today, and despite the now decades-long effort on the part of enforcement bodies, NGOs, policy makers, and scholars to distinguish both practices, migrant smuggling and human trafficking continue to be talked about interchangeably. This suggests not only a conceptual confusion but also the very inability in real life to cleanly distinguish practices that are after all deeply rooted in the expansion of migration controls and mobility restrictions worldwide.

To sum up, the smuggling protocol was not conceived with the intention of protecting irregular migrants who might endure victimization or exploitation in the context of their journeys. It was part of a global effort to redefine anticrime priorities. If at all, the protocol raised the provision of services conducive of irregular migration to the global level and created the ability to articulate it as a crime threatening the sovereignty and security of specific UN member states—one of them being the United States.

Over time, the discourse concerning smuggling that emerged from the signing and the ratification of the protocol has taken a specific shape, even despite significant gaps in smuggling research and data—an aspect often acknowledged by the very bodies behind the protocol.[3] The lack of empirical backing on the one hand and the weight of state and law enforcement perspectives and sources on its conceptualization on the other (Baird & van Liempt, 2016) have allowed for smuggling to be depicted as an underground and dark market under the grasp of racialized mafias, networks, and transnational criminal organizations. The story we are told is that smuggling is led by amoral and greedy ethnic kingpins whose followers prey on migrants, depicted as dispossessed, inherently vulnerable, and naïve people, desperate to entrust their lives and scant possessions to human merchants for a sole chance to reach the prosperity and freedoms of the Global North (see Salt & Stein, 1997).

It was in this sense only a matter of time before the facilitation of smuggling became also tied to the other elements of the UN convention. Anecdotal evidence of smuggling being connected to drugs and weapons trafficking, the sex trade, and, after 9/11, terrorism has helped build and consolidate its perception as a threat to the world order.[4] Furthermore, the heightened visibility of irregular migration into the United States and Europe in the first two decades of the twenty-first century—along with the growing numbers of migrant deaths—has further solidified the perception of smuggling and its facilitators as inherently evil and immoral (Achilli, 2018).

Smuggling along the U.S.-Mexico Border

The global narrative on smuggling is also present on the U.S.-Mexico border, although contextually adapted. Here smuggling is often depicted as having endured a radical transformation, the market once dominated by amateur or small-scale operators now under the control of highly organized and complex crime networks like Mexican drug trafficking organizations or cartels and transnational gangs like MS-13.[5] While interactions between drug trafficking and migrant smuggling actors cannot be denied, some of the arguments behind their ties often minimize the role state-sponsored border militarization and immigration controls have had on migrants' victimization and death (Izcara Palacios, 2017; Sanchez & Zhang, 2018). Smuggling has also been depicted as a highly sophisticated feat, relying on increasingly complex forms of technology and engineering that prevent law enforcement from dismantling criminal syndicates operating in the shadows (Andreas, 2012). Furthermore, the devastating tragedies involving the suffering and deaths of migrants traveling clandestinely in an attempt to enter the United States undetected and the visibility of the migrant caravans arriving to the border from Central America have solidified the perception of smuggling as facilitated by immoral, unscrupulous, and greedy criminals. Moreover, migrants are perceived as ignorant, infantile, and non-commonsensical people, again deflecting attention from the state's role in the creation of the conditions that lead to the demand for smuggling practices.

The predominance of criminological perspectives has led to the historical and structural conditions afflicting both sides of the U.S.-Mexico border to remain largely absent from most of the conversation on smuggling. In fact, most research on security and crime on the border seems oblivious to the ways in which, situated along the fringes of both the

United States and Mexico, the region has historically endured marginalization and poverty. Border residents have for generations faced long-standing forms of race and class-based discrimination that have constrained them to specific occupations and places (see Muñoz, 2018; Núñez & Heyman, 2007; Romero, 1992). The legacy of these practices is still visible today. Work and educational options for the people of the border continue to be scant, as well as access to health and other basic social services (Guerra, 2015). In both the United States and Mexico, border communities often rank among those with the lowest per capita income and present low levels of education and literacy (Barton, Ryder Perlmeter, Sobel-Blum, & Marquez, 2015; Gann, Bowers, & Walton, 2018).[6] Ironically, the border's location straddling both countries has also historically provided multiple opportunities for its residents to profit with varying success from contraband activities (Andreas, 2012; Díaz, 2015), including the facilitation of irregular border crossings.

While ahistorical approaches worldwide have often allowed for smuggling to be depicted as a contemporary occurrence (Ayalew, 2018; Brachet, 2018), along the U.S.-Mexico border the practice of facilitating people's mobility goes back over a hundred years. Smuggling operations first emerged as a result of the passage of the U.S. Chinese Exclusion Act of 1882, when deported and newly arrived Chinese migrants sought to re/enter the United States relying on smuggling groups operating on both sides of the border (Chao, 2011). Mexican laborers and their U.S. employers facing admission restrictions in the 1930s also relied on smuggling facilitators to secure undetected entrance into the United States (Gamio, 1971), a trend that continued well into the 1960s despite the existence of the Bracero Program—a binational agreement that granted temporary labor contracts to Mexican migrants to the United States.[7] Following the end of Bracero and until the 1980s the lack of viable paths for legal migration into the United States along with the economic crisis in Mexico ensured the continued demand for smuggling services (Spener, 2009). The 1986 passage of the Immigration Reform and Control Act (IRCA) in the United States allowed several million migrants to legalize their status, yet ensuing restrictions imposed to regularization processes translated into a continued reliance on the services of smuggling facilitators (U.S. Commission on Immigration Reform, 1997). Increasingly strict immigration enforcement laws and the deployment of technology and military-like equipment and practices to the U.S.-Mexico border in the 1990s made it harder for migrants to embark on irregular border crossings without support or guidance, and consolidated the demand for smuggling services that could improve the chances to cross the border undetected (Andreas, 2012; U.S. Commission on Immigration Reform, 1997).[8] While by the turn of the century U.S.-bound migration of Mexican nationals started to decrease (Gonzalez-Barrera, 2015), new migratory trends involving Central American and extracontinental migrants along with family migration have also allowed for the sustenance of the smuggling market, particularly in the context of a renewed wave of anti-immigrant sentiment in the era of Trump and the imposition of increasingly punitive migration controls by the Mexican government.

The persona of the migrant smuggler looms large on the border. Known colloquially as *coyotes* or *polleros*, they consistently appear in the border crossing narratives of migrants, although largely gendered as male. Perceptions concerning their actions vary widely. To some, smuggling facilitators are allies, collaborators, and even sought-after friends; for others, they are a despicable, but necessary evil. Many migrants report having experienced scams and abusive interactions with smuggling facilitators (O'Leary, 2009; Slack & Campbell, 2016; Spener, 2009) that have led to the loss of significant but ultimately replaceable financial resources (Koser, 2008). Others have heard of, witnessed, or directly endured harrowing cases of abuse, victimization, and death. Most ultimately attribute to the work of smugglers the ability to reach their destinations (U.S. Commission on Immigration Reform, 1997).

Combined, these dynamics show the historical and social complexity in which the interactions between migrants and smuggling facilitators are embedded. But this very complexity points to the need for a more nuanced approach than the one that portrays facilitators as members of organized crime, gang members, or narcos and migrants as their pusillanimous victims. Most importantly, it calls for the need of different methodological approaches that provide insights into the criminalized markets of the border. In the sections that follow, I rely on my ethnographic work on the U.S.-Mexico border among smuggling facilitators themselves and on archival research to document the experiences of women and girls who participate in the market. In particular, I shed light on smuggling's gendered dynamics, where women, despite their invisibility from the collective discourse, often play roles that shape the life and safety of migrants.

From What Is a Smuggler to Who Is Convicted for Smuggling

According to the smuggling protocol, smugglers are those who obtain a financial or material return from the provision of smuggling services (UNODC, 2017). Yet this notion clashes with the dynamics on the ground. Many migrants perform smuggling-related activities and functions during their journeys and even afterwards with the purpose of paying off their journeys (Achilli, 2018; Ayalew, 2018; Carling, 2017; Tinti & Reitano, 2018). Furthermore, many smuggling-related tasks are performed with no criminal intention (Maher, 2018; Sanchez, 2016a). My research asks a different question: in countries where the facilitation of migration has been typified as a criminal offense, who is likely to be convicted? This question is important because despite the emphasis on documenting the modus operandi of smugglers, their profits and structure, there is a dearth of data on their identities and profiles (IOM, 2016; UNODC, 2018). Most countries do not collect and/or report data on smuggling offenses, and databases concerning those prosecuted are virtually inexistent.[9] Fortunately, the United States is one of the few countries that systematically collects and reports data on smuggling prosecutions at the federal level, which allows for answering the question concerning the background of criminalized populations with some precision.

Federal data on smuggling convictions compiled by the U.S. Sentencing Commission since 1996 confirm most cases originate in five U.S. district court jurisdictions, all located in the border states of California, Arizona, New Mexico, and Texas. From 1996 to 2011, almost three-quarters of all people convicted of smuggling were Latino.[10] Since 2011, about half of those prosecuted for smuggling have been involved in the smuggling of one to five people, suggesting at least half of smuggling cases comprise small, low-key operations.[11] While between 1996 and 2011 an average of 82 percent of all convictions involved men, the annual percentage of men prosecuted had decreased from an average of 86 percent in the 1996–2003 period to 76 percent by 2017. This means not only that about 24 percent of those prosecuted in U.S. federal courts for migrant smuggling charges these days are women, but that their number has almost doubled from the 1996–2003 time range, when they constituted 13.7 percent of those convicted.[12] The lack of disaggregated data by age and the fact that people under the age of eighteen typically do not face smuggling charges if apprehended (DHIA, 2017) limit our ability to provide further insights into the women who are prosecuted for smuggling. The following section, however, relies on qualitative data to better understand the lives of women smugglers.

Young, Female, and . . . Smuggler?

Women are fundamental actors in the facilitation of migrant smuggling.[13] On the U.S.-Mexico border, they recruit migrants, cook meals for them, and house them as they transit. They also serve as decoys, lookouts, and occasionally as drivers and guides. They identify and enlist the help of other men and women who can work as drivers or guides or support the passage of migrants. Women devise logistical plans and scout meeting places and drop spots. They act as relatives or caregivers of young children being smuggled and provide first aid and recovery care for ill and/or injured migrants too sick or scared to go to hospitals for assistance. They also care for elderly migrants, newborn or infant children, and pregnant women. They negotiate fees, collect payments, and solve the all-too-common conflicts among migrants and other facilitators. They identify doctors and legal assistance and often file reports involving missing, injured, dead, and kidnapped migrants. They keep migrants' families informed and at times must also reveal tragic or negative outcomes like apprehensions, accidents, and deaths. They also enforce rules at safe houses and discipline and even dismiss migrants and other facilitators whose actions may be seen as out of line or compromising.

If this list sounds implausible, it is because security discourses and their criminological emphasis have had a tendency to depict smuggling monolithically as a single transit or journey, not as the series of steps and tasks it requires. If the roles that women assume come as a surprise, it is because smuggling has been traditionally gendered male. This is in part the result of most research on smuggling being carried out by men, whose concerns have been more centered on organized crime and mafias. To suggest migrants and those behind their journeys are engaged in close, personal, intimate interactions not only humanizes both but gives them a sense of rationality and dignity largely—and perhaps even on purpose—absent in migration and criminal justice narratives. In what follows, I map three critical elements often ignored in smuggling's dominant discourse: the role of smuggling in family reunification and care, its emergence as a response to marginalization and poverty, and the microdynamics of violence. All three are described relying on the experiences of three young women from the border. Two were interviewed in person, and the case of a third one was identified through archival research.

Rebecca

Rebecca—not her real name—is the oldest of seven children living in the city of Ciudad Juárez, on the Mexican side of the border. At age fifteen she was first returned to Mexico by CBP on the grounds of having entered the United States as an unaccompanied minor. It was determined during her screening at a Mexican welfare shelter that a smuggling group operating in her neighborhood in fact employed her on an on-call basis as a decoy. Rebecca's role involved posing as a child traveling with friends or relatives into the U.S. city of El Paso, this way justifying the crossing to the eyes of law enforcement personnel at the border checkpoint and reducing the likelihood of the car in which she rode (and which transported migrants) being inspected for contraband. "We would just get in the car, me and other kids; we would pretend we were going to White Sands, or to Walmart, and that way the [CBP] agent would not be suspicious of us and would just let us through." Rebecca did not describe her participation as a result of force or coercion. In fact, she described her experience as an invitation on the part of her neighbors to assist them. They also promised compensation—forty dollars per trip. On the border, employment and educational opportunities for teenagers are limited. Rebecca was unemployed and had dropped out of school in seventh grade. She was also the mother of an infant child. The sporadic income generated from her work in smuggling allowed her to cover basic needs. "I had to pay for diapers. My mom worked as a security guard at a hospital, and she could not provide for me and my son. I had to do something to take care of myself and not [be] a burden."

Rebecca was aware of the legal implications of her role as a decoy and often reflected on them. While she had been repeatedly told that if apprehended, she would not face criminal charges as she was underage, she still feared being detained—two of her younger siblings were in juvenile detention on the U.S. side of the border—and having to leave her son to the care of someone else in such an event terrified her. This was ultimately the reason she did not continue participating in smuggling. However, she did not consider her role unethical or immoral, compared with other prospects available to teenagers like herself: "I know passing people is not legal, but there are other jobs that are worse: you know, like crossing drugs and things like those. I wasn't doing that. What I did was not a crime. It was bad, yes, because my mom would have been very angry, because I would have made her very sad [had she found out]. But what I did was not a crime."

When asked about the lessons of working as a decoy, Rebecca explained it allowed her to be part of people's efforts to rejoin their families and to witness the consequences of migration enforcement restrictions firsthand:

> I used to get very emotional, but it was so nice to see the families reunite. You know, arrive to the place and see that they were waiting, how they were waiting for their relative. The person coming out of the car, everyone crying of happiness. People who had not been able to be together for a long time. You want to cry too; you want to be happy for them. In this job I learned that for many of the people a *coyote* was the only way they could reunite, that there was just no other way because of the law, because of how it is. In that sense it felt good to know we were helping them reunite.

Maria

Maria (a pseudonym) was arrested following a car chase with CBP, who found her transporting three migrants in her car in a remote location of the Arizona desert, not far from the Tohono O'odham Nation.[14] Court documents filed by the prosecution depict her as a conniving member of a complex human smuggling organization who profited financially and repeatedly from migrants and took advantage of their vulnerability. The legal record concerning Maria's case, however, contained no information concerning this alleged organization. At the time of the offense, she was with her cousin, who was apparently not charged, perhaps given his age. While Maria did have a record for smuggling—she had been previously convicted of a misdemeanor—police records indicated on both occasions she had worked on her own, with the sole intention of supplementing her income.

Maria's prior record suggests she worked sporadically as a smuggling driver. She was also employed by the state as a caregiver for disabled people, earning an income barely above minimum wage. The money Maria generated through smuggling supplemented her other income and was used to cover basic needs including providing for her boyfriend, who was himself disabled. Maria's attorney expressed concern for her financial precarity by indicating in court that she lived "in a house with a dirt floor and no windows." For this second offense, Maria was sentenced to eight months in prison and to one year of probation.

As Maria's and Rebecca's cases show, women who participate in smuggling facilitation often face significant financial challenges because of a systemic lack of employment and educational options. Their participation also conveys social, cultural, and gendered obligations that entrust them with the care and protection of family members. The income both women generated from their participation in smuggling was not significant in the sense that it did not provide them with financial stability but allowed them to cover basic necessities, like food, rent, and/or medication. Combined, both experiences challenge the claim that smuggling generates large returns for its participants or that it merely contributes to the wealth of transnational criminal networks.

Amanda

At age twenty-one, Amanda (also a pseudonym) was arrested under migrant kidnapping charges. She was identified by several of the migrants kept at a safe house as the person who made ransom calls to relatives demanding payment.[15] Amanda was from a small town in central Mexico. She had no formal education and was illiterate. She was also a single mother of five children and made an income performing random jobs. Faced with the inability to provide for her children financially, she decided to migrate to the United States. She lacked the financial capital to pay for the services of a smuggling facilitator but headed to the border nonetheless hoping to find a way to cross. Once at the border Amanda was approached at the bus station by a man who offered to cross her. She indicated she lacked money but that she was willing to work off her fee. In a matter of days Amanda was transported all the way to the city of Phoenix, Arizona, where she was put in charge of cleaning and cooking for the groups of migrants who continuously arrived at a safe house. Here she also became romantically involved with a man who coordinated the transportation of the migrants. She became pregnant shortly thereafter.

Amanda was not allowed to leave the safe house on her own. She was always under the watch of other men. She was also quick to realize the migrants who arrived at the house were not always allowed to leave—their release was conditioned on the payment of additional smuggling fees (that is, on top of what they had originally agreed to pay). In the beginning, Amanda's romantic partner was the one contacting the family members of migrants, but the role was eventually passed down to Amanda herself. For several months she obtained phone numbers, made calls, demanded payments, verified these were made, and ultimately authorized the release of migrants. She also threatened the families with hurting the migrants in the event payments were not made. There was no indication in the legal record that any of the threats ever materialized—in other words, there was no evidence Amanda or her codefendants inflicted any kind of physical violence on the migrants they held for payment. However, it would be amiss to suggest Amanda's calls did not cause a great deal of emotional and psychological distress to both migrants and their families. Although provided with room and board, Amanda was not financially compensated for her work. Neither did she receive prenatal care (her romantic partner feared she could alert the authorities). She miscarried a few days before the police raided the house—it was not until then that she received medical attention.

During court proceedings, Amanda was asked why she had failed to report the crime. She stated she was afraid of escaping since she did not know where she was and did not know the city and was unaware of whom to contact for help. The court sentenced her to one year in prison and barred her from reentering the United States irregularly. It was unclear who would take care of and support her children during her incarceration.

Conclusion

Reducing smuggling solely to a monolithic description of procuring or facilitating entry into a country different from one's own as outlined in the protocol's definition obscures its social practices. These commence well beyond the start of a migratory journey and can potentially surpass the successful or otherwise arrival of a migrant to a destination. Furthermore, as others have also argued, smuggling often involves the development of personal, spiritual, and even intimate exchanges between migrants and those behind their journeys (Ayalew, 2018; Maher, 2018; Vogt, 2018). These relationships are far from uncomplicated, for they emerge amid the precarity and clandestine nature inherent to smuggling journeys. In this sense, it would be amiss to understate the occurrence of violent acts like kidnapping, sexual abuse, and physical violence—acts in which migrants themselves become involved as perpetrators (Izcara Palacios, 2017; Slack & Campbell, 2016). Yet to reduce the experience of migrants to that of suffering alone minimizes and in some cases makes invisible the acts of solidarity, support, and care that are also prevalent in smuggling (González, 2018; Hagan, 2012), which are many times performed by women. While the discussion is far from gendered as such, smuggling relies on the personal, intimate, and at times unpaid labor many women perform. Smuggling does not comprise neither unidirectional interactions nor static roles. By this I mean that smuggling is not merely a financial transaction through which migrants purchase a specific service from a smuggler. Migrants often describe the quality of smuggling facilitators on the basis of their ability to connect with, interact with, and protect the people traveling with them (Achilli, 2018; Sanchez, 2018). Some researchers have gone as far as claiming that distinguishing between migrant and smuggler—as in Amanda's case, for example—is misleading, for both roles allow for individual and collective survival and mobility (Achilli, 2018; Ayalew, 2018; Sanchez, 2018). Some migrants may perform smuggling tasks to purposely offset the costs of their own journeys (Achilli, 2018; Sanchez, 2016a), while for some border residents like Maria, facilitating border crossings allows them to counter structural poverty and marginalization. For others like Rebecca, engagement in smuggling, even if sporadic, allows them to cope with the uncertainty that often characterizes border life, where employment options are limited, while also providing a close, intimate window into the impact of immigration controls.

Seen through an intersectional lens, smuggling is far from a criminal practice alone. It is also reflective of the very vulnerabilities of its facilitators—here, impoverished and marginalized Latina, Indigenous, and migrant women on the U.S.-Mexico border. The livelihoods of smuggling facilitators differ from those depicted in official discourses on transnational organized crime. Evidence shows they are people who live along the migrant trail (often rural, impoverished, marginalized communities) who while employed must supplement their income from service occupations through the provision of sporadic, on-demand, and criminalized services, relying on their very own skills and limited resources, for the sole purpose of reducing their precarity. If at all, the testimonies of Rebecca, Maria, and Amanda confirm that those convicted for smuggling are not the professional criminals some media and scholars talk about but working-class men and women, Indigenous people, irregular migrants and/or refugees, single mothers, and children, who are becoming systematically and increasingly criminalized.

NOTES

1 The supplemental protocol is called the Protocol against the Smuggling of Migrants by Land, Sea and Air.
2 The UN Protocol to Prevent, Suppress and Punish Trafficking in Persons Especially Women and Children defines trafficking in persons as "the recruitment, transportation, transfer, harbouring or receipt of persons, by means of the threat or use of force or other forms of coercion, of abduction, of fraud, of deception, of the abuse of power or of a position of vulnerability or of the giving or receiving of payments or benefits to achieve the consent of a person having control over another person, for the purpose of exploitation."
3 The UNODC report on smuggling of migrants outlines, "Data collection, analysis and research on smuggling of migrants remain at their infancy" (2018, 12). The IOM Global Review on Smuggling Data and Research also recognizes the fact that "there is currently no data available on the extent of migrant smuggling globally" (IOM 2016).
4 For examples, see Gallagher (2018), Bensman (2018), and Cornell (2009).

5   For the academic debate on the drug trafficking–migrant smuggling nexus, see Spener (2009), Slack and Campbell (2016), Izcara Palacios (2017), and Sanchez and Zhang (2018).
6   According to U.S. Census Bureau data, about a third of the population in border communities in South Texas—an area of high migrant smuggling activity—lives in poverty. These communities are also of predominantly Mexican and Mexican American origin. For a summary, see Ura and Wang (2018).
7   The Bracero Program sought to alleviate the shortage of workers in critical industries like agriculture, construction, and transportation given the U.S. involvement in world conflicts.
8   For a discussion on decision making concerning the use of smuggling facilitators, see Slack and Martinez (2018).
9   The only country known to collect data on smuggling and illicit entry in Europe is Germany. UNODC's SHERLOC database also contains a small but growing sample of smuggling convictions from UN member states.
10 Race and ethnicity were reported in official smuggling statistics only for the 1996 to 2011 year range. During these years, on average, 74.5 percent of those convicted for smuggling at the federal level were Latino. See USSC (2012).
11 In addition to these data, since 2011, 40 percent of all smuggling cases prosecuted at the federal level have involved the smuggling of six to twenty-four people. This breakdown of the data does not allow one to identify smaller and/or independent smuggling efforts but suggests, combined with data involving groups of up to five people, that about 90 percent of all cases prosecuted could effectively involve small smuggling operations, most likely facilitated by individuals or small groups, rather than networks. To access the pertinent data, see USSC (2012) and USSC (2018).
12 According to the Booker Report (USSC 2012, Part C, pp. 7–9), the percentage of women prosecuted for "alien smuggling" offenses in the 1993 to 2003 period was 13.7 percent per year, out of an average of 1,529 annual cases. By fiscal year 2017, women were named defendants in 23.2 percent of 2,733 smuggling cases (USSC 2018).
13 For an earlier analysis of the roles of women in smuggling, see Sanchez (2016b).
14 The Tohono O'odham Nation is a federally recognized tribe that includes approximately 28,000 members occupying tribal lands in southwestern Arizona.
15 A safe house or drop house is a location where migrants are kept pending transportation and/or payment.

REFERENCES

Achilli, L. (2018). The "good" smuggler: The ethics and morals of human smuggling among Syrians. *Annals of the American Academy of Political and Social Science, 676*, 77–96.

Andreas, P. (2012). *Border games: Policing the US-Mexico divide.* Ithaca, NY: Cornell University Press.

Ayalew, M. T. (2018). Refugee protections from below: smuggling in the Eritrea-Ethiopia context. *Annals of the American Academy of Political and Social Science, 676*, 57–76.

Baird, T., & van Liempt, I. (2016). Scrutinising the double disadvantage: Knowledge production in the messy field of migrant smuggling. *Journal of Ethnic and Migration Studies, 42*, 400–417.

Barton, J., Ryder Perlmeter, E., Sobel-Blum, E., & Marquez, R. (2015). Las colonias in the 21st century: Progress along the Texas-Mexico border. Federal Reserve Bank of Dallas. www.dallasfed.org.

Bensman, T. (2018, September 4). Somali smuggler brought at least 50 migrants to the Texas, California borders. Center for Immigration Studies. https://cis.org.

Brachet, J. (2018). Manufacturing smugglers: From irregular to clandestine mobility in the Sahara. *Annals of the American Academy of Political and Social Science, 676*, 16–35.

Carling, J. (2017, September). Batman in Vienna: Choosing how to confront human smuggling. https://jorgencarling.org.

Chao, R. R. (2011). *The Chinese in Mexico, 1882–1940*. Tucson: University of Arizona Press.

Cornell, S. (2009). The interaction of drug smuggling, human trafficking and terrorism. In A. Jonsson (Ed.), *Human trafficking and human security* (pp. 48–66). London: Routledge.

Derechos Humanos Integrales en Acción (DHIA). (2017). Neither criminals nor illegals: Boys, girls and adolescents in the migrant smuggling market on the US Mexico Border. Ciudad Juárez, México: DHIA. http://cadmus.eui.eu/handle/1814/50984.

Díaz, G. T. (2015). *Border contraband: A history of smuggling across the Rio Grande*. Austin: University of Texas Press.

Gallagher, A. (2001). Human rights and the new UN protocols on trafficking and migrant smuggling: A preliminary analysis. *Human Rights Quarterly, 23*, 975–1004.

Gallagher, M. (2018, June 10). Drugs, guns and people: Smuggling is a growing border problem. *Albuquerque Journal*. www.abqjournal.com.

Gamio, M. (1971). *The Mexican immigrant, his life-story: Autobiographic documents*. Chicago: University of Chicago Press.

Gann, C., Bowers, L., & Walton, T. (2018). Small area income and poverty estimates 2017, P30–04. U.S. Census Bureau. www.census.gov.

González, Y. G. (2018). Navigating with coyotes: Pathways of Central American migrants in Mexico's southern borders. *Annals of the American Academy of Political and Social Science, 676*, 174–193.

Gonzalez-Barrera, A. (2015). More Mexicans leaving than coming to the US. Pew Research Center. www.pewhispanic.org.

Guerra, S. I. (2015). La chota y los mafiosos: Mexican American casualties of the border drug war. *Latino Studies, 13*, 227–244.

Hagan, J. (2012). *Migration miracle*. Cambridge, MA: Harvard University Press.

International Organization for Migration (IOM). (2016). *Migrant Smuggling Data and Research: A global review of the emerging evidence base*. Geneva: IOM.

Izcara Palacios, S. P. (2017). Prostitution and migrant smuggling networks operating between Central America, Mexico, and the United States. *Latin American Perspectives, 44*, 31–49.

Koser, K. (2008). Why migrant smuggling pays. *International Migration, 46*, 3–26.

Maher, S. (2018). Out of West Africa: Human smuggling as a social enterprise. *Annals of the American Academy of Political and Social Science, 676*, 36–56.

Muñoz, M. M (2018). *The injustice never leaves you: Anti-Mexican violence in Texas.* Cambridge, MA: Harvard University Press.

Núñez, G. G., & Heyman, J. M. (2007). Entrapment processes and immigrant communities in a time of heightened border vigilance. *Human Organization, 66*, 354–365.

O'Leary, A. O. (2009). The ABCs of migration costs: Assembling, bajadores, and coyotes. *Migration Letters, 6*, 27–35.

Romero, M. (1992). *Maid in the USA.* New York: Routledge.

Romero, R. C. (2011). *The Chinese in Mexico, 1882–1940.* Tucson: University of Arizona Press.

Salt, J., & Stein, J. (1997). Migration as a business: The case of trafficking. *International Migration, 35*, 467–494.

Sanchez, G. (2016a). *Human smuggling and border crossings.* New York: Routledge.

Sanchez, G. (2016b). Women's participation in the facilitation of human smuggling: The case of the US Southwest. *Geopolitics, 12*, 387–406.

Sanchez, G. (2018). Portrait of a human smuggler: Race, class, and gender among facilitators of irregular migration on the US-Mexico border. In M. Bosworth, A. Parmar, & Y. Vasquez (Eds.), *Race, criminal justice, and migration control* (pp. 29–42). New York: Oxford University Press.

Sanchez, G. E., & Zhang, S. X. (2018). Rumors, encounters, collaborations, and survival: The migrant smuggling–drug trafficking nexus in the US Southwest. *Annals of the American Academy of Political and Social Science, 676*, 135–151.

Slack, J., & Campbell, H. (2016). On narco-coyotaje: Illicit regimes and their impacts on the US-Mexico border. *Antipode, 48*, 1380–1399.

Slack, J., & Martinez, D. (2018). What makes a good human smuggler? The differences between satisfaction with and recommendation of coyotes on the US Mexico Border. *Annals of the American Academy of Political and Social Science, 676*, 152–173.

Spener, D. (2009). *Clandestine crossings: Migrants and coyotes on the Texas-Mexico border.* Ithaca, NY: Cornell University Press.

Tinti, P., & Reitano, T. (2018). *Migrant, refugee, smuggler, saviour.* New York: Oxford University Press.

United Nations Office on Drugs and Crime (UNODC). (2000). Protocol against the smuggling of migrants by land, sea and air, supplementing the United Nations Convention against Transnational Organized Crime. Office of the United Nations High Commissioner for Human Rights. www.ohchr.org.

United Nations Office on Drugs and Crime (UNODC). (2017). The concept of "financial or other material benefit" in the smuggling of migrants protocol. Vienna: Human Trafficking and Migrant Smuggling Section. www.unodc.org.

United Nations Office on Drugs and Crime (UNODC). (2018). Global study on smuggling of migrants 2018. Vienna: Human Trafficking and Migrant Smuggling Section. www.unodc.org.

Ura, A., & Wang, E. (2018, September 13). Poverty in Texas drops to the lowest levels in more than a decade. *Texas Tribune.* www.texastribune.org.

U.S. Commission on Immigration Reform. (1997). Binational study: Migration between Mexico and the United States. Washington, DC.

U.S. Sentencing Commission (USSC). (2012, December). Report to the Congress: Continuing impact of *United States v. Booker* on federal sentencing. Part C: Immigration offenses. www.ussc.gov.

U.S. Sentencing Commission (USSC). (2018). Quick facts on alien smuggling offenses, fiscal year 2017. www.ussc.gov.

Vogt, W. A (2018). *Lives in transit: Violence and intimacy on the migrant journey.* Berkeley: University of California Press.

PART IV

Community Programming for System-Impacted Latinas

11

From the Streets to the Halls of Higher Education

The Case of an Undocumented Latina on the Margins of the Justice System

LISA M. MARTINEZ

Twenty-year-old Lupe Serna and I met on a chilly winter day in March 2013.[1] She was one of the first participants to respond to a recruitment email I sent to students at colleges and universities along Colorado's Front Range. I was in the early stages of a study examining the educational and occupational pathways of undocumented youth and young adults following enactment of the Deferred Action for Childhood Arrivals (DACA) program and was eager to meet her because of her emails. Every message ended with *Tlazokamati*, the Nahuatl word for "thank you," followed by her name.[2] After going back and forth, we found a time that worked with her schedule and agreed to meet at the campus library where she was a student. That day, I worked my way through the newly renovated building and past an endless number of tables with students hunched over laptops, notebooks, and coffee cups. When I finally found Lupe, she was seated at a large, round table, studying for her next class. I extended my hand to introduce myself, and Lupe returned the greeting with a handshake and warm smile, inviting me to sit down.

Thus began my interview with Lupe, one of the nearly three-quarters of a million undocumented youth and young adults who benefitted from DACA, the Obama-era executive order that deprioritized deportation and provides work authorization to those who qualify (Gonzales, Terriquez, & Ruszczyk, 2014).[3] In the interview, I learned that Lupe enjoyed writing and poetry, was an activist in the local and national immigrant rights movements, and worked part-time at a law office, all while maintaining a near-perfect GPA. I asked Lupe about her academic aspirations and how she earned a full-tuition scholarship to a prestigious private high school as well as her experiences there. She shared that while the school afforded her a quality education, she struggled with the social dynamics of being an undocumented Latina from a working-class family, which made her feel different and alienated from her mostly white and upper-class peers. Feeling marginalized, Lupe alleviated her feelings of hopelessness by "hanging out" with older cousins who were gang-involved. Due to interventions by a nonprofit organization, however, she eventually left gang life and was on the verge of graduating from college, all in the span of five years.

In the following pages, I highlight Lupe's experiences from the streets to the halls of higher education. While not typical, her case speaks to the importance of culturally responsive programs in mitigating the risk factors associated with gang involvement, which, when coupled with legal reforms that provide access and opportunity, reduce undocumented Latinas' marginalization and buffer them from system involvement. I end this chapter with suggestions for possible directions for effective change.

Segmented Assimilation and Leveled Aspirations

Within migration studies, scholars have examined the significance of social exclusion in the lives of the 1.5 generation, young people who were born elsewhere but came to the United States as children (Portes & Rumbaut, 2014; Portes & Zhou, 1993). As such, their experiences are largely rooted in this country, although they often maintain cultural and/or familiar ties to their country of origin. And while the segmented assimilation model is typically applied to the "new" second generation—that is, the children of immigrants—it is especially useful for understanding the incorporation experiences of young immigrants who face different social, economic, and political realities than those who arrived prior to 1965 (Portes & Zhou, 1993). Among the differences, post-1965 immigrants are more likely to originate from Asian or Latin American countries, particularly Mexico, and are more likely to be racialized as a result. They also face different structural barriers than before, affecting their educational and occupational prospects and ability to incorporate into society (Portes & Zhou, 1993; Zhou, 1997).

When combined with government policies that facilitate or impede incorporation, newly arrived immigrants may face a smooth or "bumpy, segmented" process. This is especially true for young immigrants whose age at arrival often means they are immersed in American culture from an early age and are educated in the public school system but, because of social exclusion, face blocked opportunities and structural barriers. Additionally, once immigrant youth lose the legal protections granting them access to K–12 education, the transition to adulthood is marked by legal exclusion as well (Abrego, 2006; Gonzales, 2015; Martinez, 2014; Silver, 2012). In response to constrained opportunities, immigrant youth may give in to an "oppositional culture," whereby they reject the values consistent with academic achievement and upward mobility (Rumbaut, 2008; Zhou, 1997) or experience leveled aspirations where their future goals are circumscribed by external circumstances (Bettie, 2014; MacLeod, 1987). It is not surprising, then, that the threat of downward assimilation (Portes & Rumbaut, 2001; Portes & Zhou, 1993; Zhou, 1997) is linked to contact with the criminal justice system, particularly when upward mobility seems improbable (Gans, 2009; Golash-Boza, 2012; Portes & Zhou, 1993).

Considering that undocumented youth are more likely to live in neighborhoods characterized by high rates of concentrated poverty and attend "majority-minority" schools, the path toward middle-class success—as defined by academic achievement—might seem especially out of reach. Prior research shows, for example, that feelings of social exclusion are linked to negative academic outcomes among Latinx youth, compelling some to construct an identity in opposition to the majority culture (Matute-Bianchi, 1991; Suarez-Orozco, 1991). More recently, Gonzales (2011) found that the transition to adulthood is especially difficult for undocumented youth as the loss of legal protections means they must learn to be "illegal," a process that requires a full-scale shift in their daily routines, survival skills, aspirations, and social patterns. Rather than viewing these responses as problematic, however, some consider the rejection of middle-class values and reoriented self-perceptions as adaptive strategies commonly employed by members of marginalized groups (Merton, 1938; Zhou, 1997).

Gang Initiation

Although scholars have found an association between marginalization, leveled aspirations, and deviance among the new second generation

(Portes & Zhou, 1993; Zhou, 1997), few studies have examined the relationship between liminal legal status (Menjívar, 2006) and deviance or criminality among Latina adolescents. One possible explanation for this gap in the literature is that undocumented status may actually be a deterrent to committing even minor crimes due to fears of being detained or deported. They may also be apprehensive about bringing unwanted attention to their immigrant family members. These arguments seem the most plausible and are supported by ample research showing immigrants are less prone to criminality than their native-born counterparts (e.g., Martinez & Lee, 2000; Martinez & Valenzuela, 2006; Rumbaut & Ewing, 2007).

Findings from studies of Latino boys might be more telling, as social marginalization has been linked to deviant behavior, including gang involvement (Howell & Egley, 2005). Rios's (2011) work, for example, provides insights about the cyclical relationship between punishment, incarceration, and limited opportunities in communities of Color. As a result of harassment, surveillance, and discipline by police and other authority figures, some Latino youth feel compelled to adopt a "fugitive life" in response to systemic inequalities and the failure of institutions to provide them with better options (Rios, 2011). The literature also suggests a strong connection between peer influence and gang membership (Walker-Barnes & Mason, 2001). According to Walker-Barnes and Mason (2001), "hanging out" with gang members and wearing colors affiliated with gangs increase the likelihood of membership. Combined with low academic performance and peer delinquency, gang membership is more likely to lead to engagement with violence later in life (Herrenkohl et al., 2000).

A significant body of work has examined the precursors to gang membership among males and, in particular, boys and men of Color. Some scholars assert that males receive the bulk of the attention because they are more likely to exhibit delinquent behavior and commit crimes than females, while others view males' delinquency and gang involvement as an affirmation of their masculinity (Messerschmidt, 2007). Nonetheless, girls and women are also gang-involved, with research showing similarities to boys but also key gender differences (Chesney-Lind, 1999; Miller, 2001). To illustrate, Archer and Grascia's (2006) study of gang-involved youth found girls join gangs for the same reasons as boys: to gain a sense of belonging and to seek protections from other forms of violence in their lives; where they differ is that girls who become involved in gangs are more likely to have experienced physical or sexual violence, pointing to the inextricable link between victimization and delinquency (Chesney-Lind, 1999). Given the greater preponderance of girls of Color in the juvenile justice system and the intersecting inequalities that place them at greater risk of contact, it is perhaps not surprising that Lupe, an undocumented Latina from a predominantly low-income community, became gang-affiliated. But her gang affiliation was not a function of being undocumented; rather, it was the result of social exclusion, marginalization, and a blocked opportunity structure, struggles she continued to face even after disassociating from gang life.

Methods

Lupe was one of sixty-two participants interviewed as part of a larger study on the mobility pathways of undocumented youth and young adults living in Colorado. The central focus of the study was to understand the impact of legal reforms—namely, Obama's executive order, DACA—on the educational and occupational trajectories of young immigrants.[4] Although the Trump administration rescinded DACA in September 2017, the program is still in effect via court order, affording more than three-quarters of a million young people relief from deportation and work authorization (Gonzales et al., 2014). It also resulted in opportunities for undocumented students, making college more accessible. And while DACA stopped short of providing legal status or a pathway to citizenship, it removed some of the structural barriers undocumented youth faced beforehand, particularly in regard to expanding employment opportunities.

The context where the study took place is also relevant: Colorado has passed a number of legal reforms affecting undocumented immigrants. For example, in 2006 the governor of Colorado, Bill Owens, signed SB 90, granting law enforcement the ability to stop persons suspected of being in the country without papers. As one of the first show-me-your-papers laws in the country, SB 90 resulted in thousands of undocumented immigrants being detained, and many were eventually deported as a result of misdemeanors such as traffic violations (White & Dwight,

2012). SB 90 was eventually repealed in 2013 when immigrant rights organizations worked successfully with sheriffs and local law enforcement agencies that opposed the bill on the grounds it was costly and made immigrants fearful and less likely to report crimes (White & Dwight, 2012). Around the same time, Colorado voted in support of an in-state tuition bill for undocumented students known as ASSET.[5] Thus, in a period of approximately seven years, Colorado instituted legal reforms ranging from antagonistic to more accommodating to undocumented immigrants (Cebulko & Silver, 2016; Martinez, 2014).

In terms of methodology, I employed a case-study approach to obtain an in-depth, multifaceted understanding of this issue in its real-life context (Feagin, Orum, & Sjoberg, 1991; Flyvbjerg, 2006). This approach complements the semistructured, open-ended format of the interviews that required participants to share their life histories from the time they were children to the present (Atkinson, 1998). It also allowed me to code interviews in such a way as to identify significant events or turning points in respondents' lives. Examples of these turning points include leaving extended family and loved ones behind in the country of origin; the loss of a parent's job or threats of violence, precipitating migration to the United States; a parent intervening on behalf of a child struggling to learn English; a parent being detained or deported; and interventions by teachers, mentors, or community groups that buffered participants from negative peer influences or system involvement. Of sixty-two participants, two participated in behavior on the margins of the criminal justice system, and of those, Lupe engaged in minor criminal activity (e.g., tagging, simple assault) as a result of her gang affiliation. Although her case cannot be necessarily generalized to others, it sheds light on the importance of social buffers—namely, nonprofit organizations that offer culturally responsive programming—that provide Latinx and undocumented youth with avenues for exiting gangs and entering college.

Case Study Findings

The interview began with a question about Lupe's ethnic identity, to which she replied, "Mexicana or Meshica . . . and I am a warrior [because] I am very tied to my roots, my history." Lupe went on to share that she was born in Mexico and brought to the United States by her parents when she was eight months old. She proceeded to share her family's migration history, childhood memories, and early schooling experiences. Throughout the interview, Lupe was amiable, doing her best to remember important details and giving thoughtful answers to my questions. After sharing her recollections about elementary school, Lupe shifted to the middle and high school years, a period that was fraught with many obstacles, first, because of her gang affiliation and, second, because of her legal status.

Early Childhood Experiences

Lupe did not recall anything about Mexico, as she was eight months old when her family migrated. The move was prompted by her grandparents who had been living and working in the United States for many years, beginning with her grandfather's participation in the Bracero Program, the post–World War II agreement designed to bring guest workers to the United States to fill labor shortages in agriculture. As Lupe explained, both of her parents had college degrees but were unable to find work back home. After settling in Colorado, her father found work in construction and her mother worked as a restaurant cook.

Because of her age at arrival, Lupe was immersed in the English language even though her family spoke Spanish exclusively at home. Even so, her mother wanted her to be proficient so that she would do well in school and enrolled her in an English-language immersion program for pre-K children. By the time Lupe was in kindergarten, she was enrolled in an English-only classroom while continuing to hone her language skills at home. The elementary school Lupe attended was diverse; the majority of students were Latinx or African American, and even though she described it as being located "in the 'hood" because of its lower socioeconomic profile, she excelled there.

History and writing were two of Lupe's favorite subjects, and in fifth grade a teacher encouraged her to hone her writing skills. Lupe noted, "My fifth-grade teacher, she was one of those really tough teachers that not a lot of people liked because she was very strict and she had a rigorous coursework, but she was always the one that inspired me to start writing and really developing my poetry which is something that up until this day keeps me sane and really empowers me." Part of what inspired Lupe's writing was her observations of things around her, things that most children were not privy to:

> Since a really young age I've noticed a lot of things around me. I notice that my parents had to work a lot. I didn't see them that much when I was younger. And I didn't understand why. And so, I would catch on to little things like that and [the teacher] would tell me to write about it. And so that was one of the biggest things was that I had this little spark of interest so she just wanted to push me to develop it and I think that really helped.

Like many immigrant families, Lupe's parents worked long hours and overnight shifts in order to make ends meet. Her father worked days and her mother worked nights, ensuring that one of them was always home to get her ready for school, stay with her after school, and supervise her homework. Lupe's hard work and her parents' support paid off as she excelled in school, won awards for perfect attendance and citizenship, and earned accolades for her poetry and writing.

The Transition to Middle School

Things started to change in middle school. Because of her academic achievements, Lupe was invited to apply to an elite private school an hour away by bus. Although the distance from home was not ideal, she agreed to shadow a student to get a better sense of the school. Ever observant, Lupe immediately noticed the student body was disproportionately white, lacking the racial diversity she was accustomed to. As Lupe described it, there were fewer than a dozen students of Color, and as far as she knew, none were undocumented. Lupe also recognized considerable class differences as the students at the private school were dressed in designer brands and the majority had cell phones, something she considered a luxury. Lupe recalled, "I showed up at that school [and] saw kids dressed in Juicy Couture and Abercrombie [& Fitch] and [they] had cell phones. . . . I was completely out of my environment and I remember the one person that I bonded that day was with the lunch lady." Despite feeling like an outsider, Lupe enrolled at the school because she could not pass up on the opportunity or the full-tuition scholarship she was offered. But soon she would begin to feel alienated, causing her to withdraw from classroom discussions out of fear she would get a question wrong. And while Lupe had mostly positive things to say about her elementary school, she felt it did not adequately prepare her for the rigors of an elite institution:

> I was kind of scared because you get a kid from the 'hood and stick them in the middle of [neighborhood where school is located], that was crazy to me. So I was scared to speak up because I didn't want to be wrong and then I think more than anything it was my academics just kind of went down because of the rigorous work.... It was a completely different level and that's when I realized that my elementary school was good but it didn't prepare me to the level that [school] was at.

Feeling alienated and unprepared took a toll on Lupe's confidence and, eventually, her grades. Because she once earned straight As, received awards and recognition from her teachers, and could see the pride in her parents' eyes because of her academic successes in elementary school, Lupe expressed feeling "devastated" when she began earning Bs and Cs, saying, "When I got to middle school and I started getting Bs and Cs it was devastating to me because I was no longer the good student but I was failing. To me that was failing." Whereas Lupe once prided herself on being a high academic achiever, the context of the new school combined with her struggling performance contributed to feelings of isolation, pushing her further to the margins.

The second year of middle school began to improve when Lupe sought out support and resources from the foundation that awarded her the scholarship. Not only did she receive tutoring, but she also became more involved in extracurricular activities and sports. Nonetheless, she continued to struggle with the social dynamics at school as Lupe felt she had little in common with her classmates. Instead, Lupe began spending more time with her cousins who were older and gang-involved.

Lupe described feeling as though she was two people, one who attended private school by day and one who was gang-affiliated by night: "Since I was one of the younger [cousins], I hung out with a lot of the older ones. So, a lot of the older ones were in gangs and all that, and so when I wasn't in school, I was hanging out with them, so I had that influence." Of her time in the gang, Lupe said, "I felt I was more in my environment because I was with people that looked like me. I was with people that grew up in the same place with me. I was with family. And being at [school], I was just here to do what I needed to do and not interact because I didn't fit in."

Lupe's parents were not aware she was hanging out with her gang-involved cousins, a fact she worked hard to conceal from them. Adding to her alienation at school were other family members who chided Lupe for caring about school, telling her, "You think you're all that because you're going to this school," and trying to convince her that she was wasting her time when she should be helping her parents financially instead. Although Lupe recognized her cousins' taunts for what they were, they nonetheless affected her. She explained, "I didn't want that because that's not how I was trying to be. I was just trying to get educated but at the same time I didn't want to lose my cred with my family."

By all accounts, Lupe lived a double life. When asked how she managed, she gave me a rundown of a typical day: get up, go to school, come home, do homework for three to four hours, "go off and do stuff" with her cousins, come home around midnight, finish homework. All the while, Lupe claimed her grades did not suffer. Yet when asked how she kept up such a grueling pace, she admitted, "I was trying to balance both being a kid in a private school and hanging out with my cousins and it was hard, it was a struggle." Also around this time, Lupe became friends with another Latina at school who grew up in a similar neighborhood and also had gang ties via her older brother. Unlike Lupe, however, the other student eventually became more heavily involved in gang life. As Lupe explained, the other student had "family issues" and "things started to go downhill fast," causing her to withdraw from school. She and Lupe eventually lost touch.

The Transition Away from Gang Life

Lupe was gang-affiliated from middle school through the first year of high school. Her decision to leave was precipitated by two pivotal events. First, one of her cousins was killed as a result of gang violence. This prompted Lupe to question her involvement:

> That really had me questioning what I wanted to do and what I was doing with my life, and it really hit me, and so it got me into this, trying to

figure out what I wanted to be. And being at [school], being in [that] environment, it was kind of difficult because during my whole life, I usually associate more with guys because I feel like I really bond with them more than girls. And so it was difficult. I didn't want to be there either.

Gang life provided Lupe with a sense of belonging and purpose at a time when school was alienating. And because she was the only child until high school, Lupe's older cousins were "like brothers" to her; to lose one to gang violence was devastating. She said, "They were my big brothers and so to lose a brother to me was a turning point in my life. I lost family."

Lupe's decision did not go over well with her cousins. They teased her, telling her she was scared, she "wasn't down," and that her cousin had died with honor. But Lupe was not convinced:

> To me, someone got shot and that wasn't really an honor. And, so to me that was the hardest thing trying to figure out if I did leave this lifestyle and try to get away from it, it wasn't going to happen because my family was the influence. Which also meant that if I stayed in it, what was I going to end up doing with my life? What if the next person to go through that was me?

Lupe eventually made the decision to stop socializing with her cousins. A few of them would go on to be imprisoned or deported, while others were raising children as single parents as a result of gang violence.

The transition out of gang life did not happen all at once, nor did Lupe do it alone. She immersed herself in schoolwork and sports, activities that took up a lot of time and kept her at school until late at night. These commitments gave her cover such that, if her cousins went looking for her at home, she either was not there or had excuses for not going out. Lupe did not say so directly, but she was able to avoid contact with the justice system for several reasons, including the value she and her parents placed on education. That is, despite feeling marginalized and sometimes struggling academically, school provided not only an avenue to escape gang affiliation but also a pathway to higher education. Additionally, Lupe's vicarious involvement likely served as a deterrent, particularly after witnessing gang violence. Finally, as a girl, she found it easier to avoid a deviant label and resume life as a high school student instead.

The second pivotal event occurred when Lupe reached out to a nonprofit organization for gang-involved youth. Situated in a predominantly Latino neighborhood, the organization serves as an intervention program for youth at risk of joining gangs or those who are currently gang-involved. Focusing on programming and intervention strategies, the organization endeavors to provide youth with a "curing culture," advocacy, mentoring, and resources for exiting gangs. For Lupe, the emphasis on Mexican culture and history was especially compelling. The organization's mission had such an effect on Lupe that she decided to participate voluntarily rather than doing so as part of a court-ordered program as others were doing. When asked what it was about the program that resonated with her, Lupe explained,

> I remember hearing this story of one of the guys there and talking about how he lost so many friends and how he lost so many things to [gang] violence. So it was what began the program and how it was the experience of all of them that was able to create a change in more youth and that to me was something inspiring. That off of someone's experience you're able to change the lives of so many others. And the way that I was approached was through my history, which was something that, going to [elementary school] I was surrounded by Latinos, but I never learned *my* history.

She elaborated,

> So when I got to [the organization], the first thing [the founder] told me was about my history. "Your people, you come from warriors, you come from kings, you come from royalty. And those guys that are fighting over their own streets, they're killing their own brothers and sisters," and he starts talking about bloodline and all those things that our ancestors have done and the spiritual side to it, and I was like, "What are you talking about? I never learned this." So the way that I was approached just gave me a whole different perspective about humanity and something that I didn't know. And by giving me a little lesson in the history of my people, it was such a changing thing.

The organization proved to be life changing to Lupe, prompting her to seek out books about Mexican history and culture, subjects she was not taught throughout her schooling even in her racially diverse elementary school. This not only motivated Lupe to participate in community service projects but also gave her a sense of belonging and newfound purpose. It also provided a connection to other Latinx youth—a connection she had previously sought among her gang-involved family and friends.

The Road to Higher Education

Things were going fairly well for Lupe until her junior year of high school. That was the period Lupe's undocumented status would present additional barriers, making her dream of attending college seem almost improbable. As her classmates discussed SATs and college applications, Lupe realized that, without a social security number, it would be difficult for her to apply. Her mother's reasons for why she was unable to get a driver's license or why her neighborhood friends' families qualified for Medicaid when hers did not finally began to make sense: Their status rendered them ineligible for government support, including financial aid.

Undeterred, Lupe met with officials at the scholarship foundation that financed her education since middle school. Rather than helping Lupe explore options to attend a four-year college or university, however, they encouraged her to consider community college instead. This was not the advice she was hoping for. Lupe explained, "To me going to community college wasn't being successful. To me community college wasn't living up to my potential. So I was devastated, like why do I even want to be here, why do I want to keep on going to school if that's the only alternative you guys are going to give me?" Lupe's status became even more of an issue when, as part of a class activity, students were directed to fill out financial aid (FAFSA) forms. Not knowing what to do, Lupe pretended to fill out the form before revealing to her counselor in private that she was undocumented. This information caught the counselor by surprise, and rather than helping Lupe identify private scholarships, she echoed others' suggestions that Lupe apply to community college instead. Disheartened, Lupe questioned why she went to private school, why she left gang life, and why she recommitted herself to academics and sports when her status was the biggest obstacle standing in her way.

Realizing she might be out of options, Lupe informed her counselor about plans to drop out of school and instead get a vocational degree. The counselor and Lupe's mom eventually convinced her to stay in school, and she continued to explore different options, including applying to a university in New Mexico known for accepting undocumented students at in-state tuition rates as well as contacting private scholarship foundations. One foundation took an interest in Lupe's application, but as before, she faced another roadblock when she was asked to provide a social security number on an application form. Unable to provide one, Lupe contacted the foundation office only to be told there was nothing they could do. Feeling like she was out of options, Lupe applied to a local public university as an international student. While tuition was almost double the cost for in-state students, Lupe learned her parents had been putting money into a college fund, which helped pay a portion of her expenses. But it was not enough.

Around this time, higher education administrators and elected officials in Colorado were debating whether or not to pass an in-state tuition bill for undocumented students. As one of many undocumented students who would be affected, Lupe was invited to speak about the merits of the proposed bill known as ASSET:

> I spoke that day and told them, "I want to be here. There's been so much up and down that now I just want to be here. I have a 3.8 GPA, I have credits from high school, I pretty much skipped over my freshman year and the only thing that was different between me and the other student was nine digits [a social security number]." And thankfully that day it passed and my tuition got cut . . . it was the most amazing thing.

After ASSET was implemented, Lupe's tuition was reduced by nearly half, and with an additional private scholarship, she was better able to afford school and was thriving academically. It was also around this time that Lupe became more interested in social justice issues, joining Campaign for the American Dream, a group of undocumented student activists who traveled across the country in support of immigration reform. And once she applied for and received deferred action, Lupe began working at a law firm part-time and contemplating a teacher training program for DACA recipients. Asked about her future goals, Lupe expressed interest in opening an arts center in an underserved community for children to learn poetry, spoken word, painting, and music while also learning about their history and culture.

Reflecting on her experiences and the long, tumultuous road she navigated to higher education, Lupe attributed her parents' decision to migrate as the reason she prevailed in the face of adversity:

> I think a lot of it has to do with my family. I understood finally why it is that they came. I understood finally why it is that my mom chooses to be in a restaurant cooking when she's an engineer. I understand why my dad decided to be in construction and going through all that hardship when he's also an engineer. I finally understood that their struggle and their sacrifice comes with the need and want to give me something better and to give me those opportunities that maybe for a minute I felt were denied.

Unlike the parents of most participants in the study, Lupe's parents were college educated, but without legal status, they worked low-wage jobs to support their family. Nonetheless, having educated parents was another protective factor, giving Lupe the resolve to stop hanging out with gang-involved family members and instead work toward obtaining a college degree.

Policy and Practice Implications

Lupe's case study reveals several insights. First, she could have easily become a statistic, succumbing to the pull of delinquent and, perhaps eventually, criminal behavior. Given the factors that increase the risk of juvenile delinquency, she could also have found herself among the growing number of Latinas in the criminal justice system (Lopez & Pasko, 2017; Pasko & Lopez, 2018a, 2018b). Second, Lupe transitioned away from gang life with the support of others, namely, a nonprofit organization for at-risk youth. The organization not only had roots in her community but also engaged Lupe through a "culture of care" that emphasized Mexican history and heritage. Finally, she benefitted from the implementation of state (ASSET) and federal (DACA) reforms that made it possible for her to access higher education at a crucial time in her life. Without these reforms and the avenues they afforded, by her own admission, Lupe was unlikely to have graduated from high school and even less likely to be in college.

In terms of recommendations for effective change, the importance of culturally responsive interventions cannot be overstated. While advocates of criminal justice reform have attended to the growing needs of female offenders with the implementation of gender-responsive programming (Bloom & Covington, 2001; Treskon & Bright, 2017), those targeting girls and women of Color could stand to be enhanced, acknowledging that the developmental stages of delinquency are responses to racism and structural barriers (Federle & Chesney-Lind, 1992). Culturally responsive interventions must also occur in early adolescence, preferably in connection with schools (Martinez & Salazar, 2018). Doing so increases the likelihood of engaging Latinas before the risk of contact with the justice system increases and before their academics begin to suffer. Moreover, emphasis on strengths—rather than deficits—will do more to engage Latinas, particularly if done in a way that places a high value on culture (Martinez & Salazar, 2018). The nonprofit organization for gang-involved youth taught Lupe to value her history, traditions, and culture, which heightened her consciousness and compelled her to get involved in social justice efforts locally and nationally. This shows the importance of decolonizing knowledge and providing access to curricula and prosocial programming so that youth of Color can develop the social skills and tools to challenge systemic inequalities they and others face (Hounmenou, 2012; Martinez & Salazar, 2018). Thus, unless intervention programs are tailored to meet Latinas' intersecting identities and multiple risk factors, they will continue to represent a larger share of system-involved girls and women.

In addition to culturally responsive programming, structural barriers to immigrant incorporation must also be addressed. This may be accomplished through mechanisms operating at different levels. For example, comprehensive immigration reform can build upon the successes of federal policy measures, such as DACA, by not only expanding educational and occupation opportunities for immigrant youth but also providing a pathway to legalization and citizenship (Martinez, 2014). Because many of the barriers immigrant youth face are a direct result of their legal status, legalization will go a long way toward eliminating their legal liminality (Menjívar, 2006) and social exclusion. As well, enhancing state-level policies such as ASSET to include more financial assistance will ensure undocumented students not only have access to higher education but are able to finish once there. Internship opportunities while in college would also prove beneficial, giving undocumented students valuable work experiences that can serve as bridges to employment opportunities once they graduate (Gonzales et al., 2014). And K–12 schools can provide additional support by funding future centers where undocumented students have access to information about scholarships, private foundations, and academic institutions that accept them. Counselors and school administrators can be more attentive to the needs of undocumented students and work to eliminate the school-to-prison pipeline by exploring positive alternatives to existing disciplinary practices (Welch, 2017), particularly in majority-minority schools. Finally, teachers can contribute by incorporating humanizing and inclusive pedagogies in the classroom when teaching youth of Color the arts, humanities, and social sciences as well as the natural sciences (Martinez, Salazar, & Ortega, 2016; Salazar, Martinez, & Ortega, 2016). This multipronged approach will go a long way toward supporting undocumented youth such that they no longer have to engage in patchwork, haphazardly piecing together various resources in order to achieve educational goals (Enriquez, 2011). While Lupe proved resourceful in exploring countless options when applying to college, the elimination of structural and financial barriers would have made the path to higher education much smoother and her schooling experiences more positive.

Admittedly, the likelihood of any of these recommendations becoming reality is slim, especially at a time when undocumented immigrants are being maligned as criminals by elected officials at the highest levels of office, despite research showing fears about immigrant criminal involvement are unfounded (Dingeman et al., 2017; Ewing, Martinez, & Rumbaut, 2015). This narrative appears to be more popular than attending to the structural barriers facing immigrant communities, many of which could be minimized with more accommodating policies (Cebulko & Silver, 2016; Martinez, 2014). While Lupe never had contact with the justice system, her gang affiliation heightened the risk. Nonetheless, she exited gang life due to the social buffer provided by a nonprofit organization for at-risk youth and her embeddedness into education. Five years later, she was on the verge of graduating from college, something she never imagined possible before ASSET and DACA and certainly not before connecting to her roots.

NOTES

1 As in the larger study, I use pseudonyms to protect participants' identities.
2 Nahuatl is one of the Indigenous languages of Mexico. It was widely spoken at the height of the Aztec Empire until the Spanish conquest.
3 In early 2018, U.S. Citizenship and Immigration Services resumed processing DACA renewals as a result of a federal court order, but the program is closed to first-time applicants.
4 For information about the methodology and participants' demographic profiles, see Martinez (2014).
5 The Advancing Students for a Stronger Economy Tomorrow (ASSET) bill grants in-state tuition to undocumented students at public universities in Colorado.

REFERENCES

Abrego, L. J. (2006). "I can't go to college because I don't have papers": Incorporation patterns of Latino undocumented youth. *Latino Studies, 4*, 212–231.

Archer, L., & Grascia, A. (2006). Girls, gangs and crime: Profile of the young female offender. *Journal of Gang Research, 13*, 37–48.

Atkinson, R. (1998). *The life history interview.* Thousand Oaks, CA: Sage.

Bettie, J. (2014). *Women without class: Girls, race, and identity.* Berkeley: University of California Press.

Bloom, B., & Covington, S. (2001). Effective gender-responsive interventions in juvenile justice: Addressing the lives of delinquent girls. Center for Gender and Justice. www.centerforgenderandjustice.org.

Cebulko, K., & Silver, A. (2016). Navigating DACA in hospitable and hostile states: State responses and access to membership in the wake of Deferred Action for Childhood Arrivals. *American Behavioral Scientist, 60*, 1553–1574.

Chesney-Lind, M. (1999). Girls, gangs, and violence: Reinventing the liberated female crook. In M. Chesney-Lind & J. M. Hagedorn (Eds.), *Female gangs in America: Essays on girls, gangs and gender* (pp. 295–310). Chicago: Lakeview Press.

Dingeman, K., Arzhayev, K., Ayala, C., Bermudez, E., Padama, L., & Tena-Chávez, L. (2017). Neglected, protected, ejected: Latin American women caught by crimmigration. *Feminist Criminology, 12*, 293–314.

Enriquez, L. E. (2011). "Because we feel the pressure and we also feel the support": Examining the educational success of undocumented immigrant Latina/o students. *Harvard Educational Review, 81*, 476–500.

Ewing, W., Martinez, R., Jr., & Rumbaut, R. (2015). The criminalization of immigration in the United States. Washington, DC: American Immigration Council. www.americanimmigrationcouncil.org.

Feagin, J., Orum, A., & Sjoberg, G. (1991). *A case for the case study*. Chapel Hill: University of North Carolina Press.
Federle, K., & Chesney-Lind, M. (1992). Special issues in juvenile justice: Gender, race, and ethnicity. In I. M. Schwarz (Ed.), *Juvenile justice and public policy: Toward a national agenda*. New York: Macmillan.
Flyvbjerg, B. (2006). Five misunderstandings about case-study research. *Qualitative Inquiry, 12*, 219–245.
Gans, H. J. (2009). First generation decline: Downward mobility among refugees and immigrants. *Ethnic and Racial Studies, 32*, 1658–1670.
Golash-Boza, T. (2012). *Due process denied: Detentions and deportations in the 21st century*. New York: Routledge.
Gonzales, R. G. (2011). Learning to be illegal: Undocumented youth and shifting legal contexts in the transition to adulthood. *American Sociological Review, 76*, 602–619.
Gonzales, R. G. (2015). *Lives in limbo: Undocumented and coming of age in America*. Berkeley: University of California Press.
Gonzales, R. G., Terriquez, V., & Ruszczyk, S. (2014). Becoming DACAmented: Assessing the short-term benefits of Deferred Action for Childhood Arrivals (DACA). *American Behavioral Scientist, 58*, 1–21.
Herrenkohl, T., Maguin, E., Hill, K. G., Hawkins, J. D., Abbott, R. D., & Catalno, R. F. (2000). Developmental risk factors for youth violence. *Journal of Adolescent Health, 26*, 176–186.
Hounmenou, C. (2012). Black settlement houses and oppositional consciousness. *Journal of Black Studies, 43*, 646–666.
Howell, J. C., & Egley, A. (2005). Moving risk factors into developmental theories of gang membership. *Youth Violence and Juvenile Justice, 3*, 334–354.
Lopez, V., & Pasko, L. J. (2017). Bringing Latinas to the forefront: Latina girls, women, and the justice system. *Feminist Criminology, 12*, 195–198.
MacLeod, J. (1987). *Ain't no makin' it: Leveled aspirations in a low-income neighborhood*. Boulder, CO: Westview.
Martinez, L. M. (2014). Dreams deferred: The impact of legal reforms on undocumented Latina/o youth. *American Behavioral Scientist, 58*, 1873–1890.
Martinez, L. M., & Salazar, M. (2018). The bright lights: The development of oppositional consciousness among DACAmented Latino youth. *Ethnicities, 18*, 242–259.
Martinez, L. M., Salazar, M., & Ortega, D. M. (2016). Dehumanizing and humanizing pedagogies: Lessons from U.S. Latina/o and undocumented youth through the P–16 pipeline. In F. Tuitt, C. Haynes, & S. Stewart (Eds.), *Race, equity, and the learning environment: The global relevance of critical and inclusive pedagogies in higher education* (pp. 131–148). Sterling, VA: Stylus.
Martinez, R., Jr., & Lee, M. (2000). On immigration and crime. *Criminal Justice, 1*, 485–524.
Martinez, R., Jr., & Valenzuela, A., Jr. (Eds.). (2006). *Immigration and crime: Ethnicity, race, and violence*. New York: New York University Press.

Matute-Bianchi, M. E. (1991). Situational ethnicity and patterns of school performance among immigrant and non-immigrant Mexican descent students. In J. Ogbu & M. A. Gibson (Eds.), *Minority status and schooling: A comparative study of immigrant and involuntary minorities* (pp. 205–247). Boca Raton, FL: Garland.

Menjívar, C. (2006). Liminal legality: Salvadoran and Guatemalan immigrants' lives in the United States. *American Journal of Sociology, 111*, 999–1037.

Merton, R. (1938). Social structure and anomie. *American Sociological Review, 3*, 672–682.

Messerschmidt, J. W. (2007). Crime and masculinities. In *The Blackwell encyclopedia of sociology*. Hoboken, NJ: John Wiley.

Miller, J. (2001). *One of the guys: Girls, gangs, and gender*. New York: Oxford University Press.

Pasko, L. J., & Lopez, V. (2018a). All the rage: Contextualizing intersectionality and violence in delinquent girls' lives. In K. Mcqueeney & A. A. Girgenti-Malone (Eds.), *Girls, aggression, and intersectionality: Transforming the discourse of "mean girls" in the United States* (pp. 109–129). Philadelphia: Taylor & Francis.

Pasko, L. J., & Lopez, V. (2018b). The Latina penalty: Juvenile correctional attitudes toward the Latina juvenile offender. *Journal of Ethnicity in Criminal Justice, 16*, 272–291.

Portes, A., & Rumbaut, R. G. (2001). *Legacies: The story of the immigrant second generation*. Berkeley: University of California Press.

Portes, A., & Rumbaut, R. (2014). *Immigrant America: A portrait*. Berkeley: University of California Press.

Portes, A., & Zhou, M. (1993). The new second generation: Segmented assimilation and its variants. *Annals of the American Academy of Political and Social Sciences, 530*, 74–96.

Rios, V. M. (2011). *Punished: Policing the lives of Black and Latino boys*. New York: New York University Press.

Rumbaut, R. (2008). The coming of the second generation: Immigration and ethnic mobility in Southern California. *Annals of the American Academy of Political and Social Science, 620*, 196–236.

Rumbaut, R., & Ewing, W. (2007). *The myth of immigrant criminality and the paradox of assimilation*. Washington, DC: American Immigration Council. www.americanimmigrationcouncil.org.

Salazar, M., Martinez, L. M., & Ortega, D. M. (2016). Sowing the semillas of critical multicultural citizenship for Latina/o undocumented youth: Spaces in school and out-of-school. *International Journal of Multicultural Education, 18*, 88–106.

Silver, A. (2012). Aging into exclusion and social transparency: Undocumented immigrant youth and the transition to adulthood. *Latino Studies, 10*, 499–522.

Suarez-Orozco, M. M. (1991). Migration, minority status, and education: European dilemmas and responses in the 1990s. *Anthropology & Education Quarterly, 22*, 190–220.

Treskon, L., & Bright, C. L. (2017). Bringing gender-responsive principles into practice: Evidence from the evaluation of the PACE Center for Girls. Research brief. MDRC. www.mdrc.org.
Walker-Barnes, C. J., & Mason, C. A. (2001). Ethnic differences in the effect of parenting on gang involvement and gang delinquency: A longitudinal, hierarchical linear modeling perspective. *Child Development, 72,* 1814–1831.
Welch, K. (2017). School-to-prison pipeline. In *The encyclopedia of juvenile delinquency and justice.* https://doi.org/10.1002/9781118524275.ejdj0102.
White, K. A., & Dwight, L. (2012). Misplaced priorities: SB 90 and the costs to local communities. Denver: Colorado Fiscal Institute. www.coloradofiscal.org.
Zhou, M. (1997). Growing up American: The challenge confronting immigrant children and children of immigrants. *Annual Review of Sociology, 23,* 63–95.

12

Maternal Racial and Ethnic Strategies as a Protective Factor against Delinquency among Latina Girls

An Exploratory Study

VERONICA E. CANO

Due to their disadvantaged structural positions, many Latina/o youth must contend with stressors, such as negative ethnic stereotypes, discrimination, and acculturative stress (Pérez, Jennings, & Gover, 2008; Scott, 2018). Such stressors or strains have been associated with increased risk for delinquency among this population (Pérez et al., 2008); however, the impact of these stressors has been found to vary by youth acculturation. Less acculturated Latina/o youth are less likely to engage in delinquent activity than more acculturated Latina/o youth (Samaniego & Gonzales, 1999). Research on acculturation indicates that Latina/o youth who are able to successfully navigate belonging to both their ethnic culture and larger U.S. mainstream culture are less likely to engage in delinquency than youth who reject their own ethnic culture in favor of U.S. mainstream culture (Sullivan et al., 2007).

Parents play a powerful role in helping children navigate the stressors related to being a member of a stigmatized ethnic minority group in the United States (Hughes, Witherspoon, Rivas-Drake, & West-Bey, 2009). Parental racial and ethnic socialization (RES) strategies can potentially offset some of the negative ramifications of dealing with stressors such as discrimination (Wang, Henry, Smith, Huguley, & Guo, 2020). Research specific to African American youth indicates that parental cultural socialization practices can significantly decrease the impact of discrimination on crime (Burt, Lei, & Simons, 2017; Burt, Simons, & Gibbons, 2012).

To date, most research examining the relationship between stressors (e.g., discrimination, acculturative stress) and delinquency has focused on Latino boys. Scant attention has been paid to Latina girls. Further, no study to date has examined the potential role that maternal RES strategies play in offsetting the risks associated with structural position risk factors such as discrimination and acculturative stress. Thus, the aim of this study was to qualitatively examine how Latina girls experience discrimination and deal with acculturative stress as well as the role that mothers (and maternal figures) play in facilitating RES strategies to help their daughters deal with these stressors. A related aim was to examine how Latina girls' experiences vary by generation status and youth system involvement.

Structural Position Stressors among Latina/o Youth

Discrimination

Prejudice and discrimination are sources of stress that are particularly relevant for Latinos in the United States. Of Latinos between the ages of eighteen and twenty-nine, 65 percent say they have experienced unfair treatment because of their race or ethnicity. U.S.-born Latinos (62 percent) are more likely than immigrants (41 percent) to report they have experienced discrimination or unfair treatment (Krogstad & Lopez, 2016). Previous studies have found that discrimination is associated with risky behaviors (Delgado, Updegraff, Roosa, & Umaña-Taylor, 2011), violence (Hoskin, 2013), gang involvement (Barrett, Kuperminc, & Lewis, 2013), and substance use among Latino youth (Kulis, Marsiglia, & Nieri, 2009; Okamoto, Ritt-Olson, Soto, Baezconde-Garbanati, & Unger, 2009). The one quantitative study to date focused on Latina girls failed to find a significant relationship between discrimination and offending among a general sample of youth (Scott, 2018); however, other studies specific to system-involved Latina girls indicate that they are well aware of the damaging stereotypes that youth professionals have of them (Lopez & Chesney-Lind, 2014).

Acculturative Stress

Acculturation refers to the cultural changes resulting from intergroup contact (Berry, 1997). According to Berry's fourfold model, the acculturation process is characterized by four strategies. Some individuals affiliate exclusively with their culture of origin (separation) or with members of the dominant or host culture (assimilation). Others affiliate with members of both cultures (integration) or with neither (marginalization). Individuals may shift between these four strategies as a result of their interactions with their environment. Individuals with a bicultural or integrated profile fare better across a number of social and emotional indicators (Berry, Phinney, Sam, & Vedder, 2006).

Acculturative stress occurs when conflict between an individual's ethnic identity and acceptance of the dominant culture is experienced (Berry, 2006). For youth, acculturative stress can arise during the process of acculturation when they begin developing their identities. Acculturative stress can also occur when youth and parents acculturate at different rates (Frazer, Rubens, Johnson-Motoyama, DiPierro, & Fite, 2017). When families immigrate to the United States, the levels of acculturation are not the same across all family members (Portes & Rumbaut, 2001). In most instances, children learn the new culture more quickly than their parents, and this involves learning a new language and a new set of values and behaviors associated with the host culture (Kam & Lazarevic, 2014). When children learn the U.S. culture more rapidly than their parents, parents might become dependent on their children to help navigate and interpret the new culture. This process not only contributes to stress felt by the adolescent but might also undermine parental authority and lead to family conflict and inconsistent parental discipline and monitoring, increasing the risk of involvement in problem behaviors (Biafora, Warheit, Zimmerman, & Gil, 1993; Portes & Rumbaut, 2001; Samaniego & Gonzales, 1999). Such dissonance can be particularly detrimental for Latina girls growing up in traditional homes where women are expected to be chaste, self-sacrificing, and submissive to their male partners, but who face a different set of gender expectations outside the home (Zayas, 2011). Caught between two worlds, Latina girls must either learn to successfully navigate both sets of cultural messages or run the risk of clashing with their parents, which can place them at increased risk for social and emotional problems (Zayas, 2011).

Maternal Racial and Ethnic Socialization Strategies

Mothers play a significant role in helping their children prepare for acculturative stress via positive RES. RES is defined as "the process by which families teach children the social meaning and consequence of ethnicity and race" (Brown, Tanner-Smith, Lesane-Brown, & Ezell, 2007, p. 14). Researchers have identified several types of RES strategies, but the strategy that has been studied most as a potential protective factor is cultural socialization, which has been defined as "parental practices that promote children's knowledge about their history and heritage and that instill group pride" (Hughes et al., 2009, p. 113). Positive RES places ethnic culture in high esteem, leading to a strong sense of self and positive ethnic identity. Research suggests that when parents provide strong RES, youth fare better against discrimination and prejudice (Hughes et al., 2006). Youth with a negative ethnic identity are more susceptible to the ecological strain of identifying with a stigmatized ethnic group (Scott, 2018). This strain can increase the propensity for deviancy as they attempt to find coping strategies to alleviate the effects of acculturative stress. Coping mechanisms can manifest in acting out their anger and frustration through property damage, assault, and drug and alcohol abuse (Phinney, Horenczyk, Liebkind, & Vedder, 2001).

The Current Study

The data presented in this chapter are part of a larger comparative study examining the effects of culture on Latina youth delinquency in the United States and United Kingdom. This chapter focuses on the influence of culture and RES as a protective factor for delinquency. Specifically, it centers on the variations in influence between first and later generations of Latina girls. The findings primarily focus on the U.S. cohort of mother-daughter dyads in Tucson, Arizona, but data from one father-daughter dyad are included. The cohort is further stratified into a group of girls involved in the juvenile justice system and a comparison group of girls without a history of system involvement, referred to in this chapter as the community group.

The overall aim of the study was to bring to light the role of protective factors from the shadow of risk factors used so readily in the juvenile justice system and to highlight their influence on Latina girls. There is limited research on the protective factors of culture among Latina youth and even less research addressing the varying degrees of protection traditional cultural practices have across generations of Latina girls. This chapter addresses these gaps by exploring the lived experiences of young Latina girls and their mothers.

Methods

Tucson was the recruitment site for the U.S. cohort. Tucson is the second largest city in the state of Arizona, located in Pima County, approximately a hundred miles north of the U.S.-Mexico border. It is often referred to by natives as the Old Pueblo due to its deep roots in Mexican culture. Despite a strong Latino presence in Pima County, the remainder of the state has historically leaned conservative politically. However, Pima County has traditionally exhibited a more progressive stance on policy issues around education, immigration, law enforcement, juvenile justice, and delinquency.

Using a mixed-methods design, this study examines the differences and similarities between system-involved Latinas with regard to the quality of the mother-daughter relationship and maternal racial and ethnic social strategies. Both random sampling and snowball sampling methods were used to recruit study participants. The system-involved group of twenty-one girls and their parents/caregivers was selected using random sampling from the juvenile court case management database. The selection criteria were set to specifically pull active court cases of the young women who fit the study criteria in terms of age, race/ethnicity, and guardianship status. (Girls who were classified as wards of the state by the child welfare system and girls who were not living with a maternal figure of the same ethnicity were excluded from this study.) The community group of six girls and their parents/caregivers was selected based on contacts made at local school meetings and religious institutions that catered to the Latino population in the area.

Of the twenty-one girls in the system-involved group, approximately two-thirds lived in single-parent/caregiver households, which were usually headed by either their mother or grandmother. The average annual income for families in the system-involved group was approximately $23,000, which falls slightly below the federal poverty line for a family of four (U.S. Department of Health and Human Services, 2014). Most of the Latina girls in the community group also resided in poor communities of Color. All but one of the six youth interviewed in the com-

TABLE 12.1. Youth Participant and Comparison Group Demographics

	System-Involved Group	Community Group
Ethnic heritage		
Mexican	19	5
Guatemalan	0	1
Mixed	2	0
Place of birth		
United States	16	6
Mexico	5	0
Guatemala	0	0
Generation level		
Foreign-born/first generation	5	0
Second generation	12	6
Third generation or later	4	0

munity group lived in two-parent households. The young woman who lived in a single-female-headed household spent an equal amount of time with extended family members who lived in the same community. The average income for families in the community group was approximately $4,500 higher than that of the system-involved group. (See Tables 12.1 and 12.2 for more information on youth and parent participant demographics.)

Despite the variance in income and family structure, Latinas in both groups were exposed to similar environmental strains. The neighborhoods where the families resided were composed of a mix of immigrant/first-generation, second-generation, and later-generation Mexican and Central American families. Given the low income of most Latino immigrants, settlement in high-poverty neighborhoods, with access to low-cost housing and higher crime rates, is common (Jarkowsky, 2009).

The first part of the data collection involved a structured survey that was administered separately to the participants and their parents. The youth survey included items related to demographics, acculturation, ethnic identity, perceived discrimination, peer relationships, mother-daughter relationships, school bonding, and risk-taking behaviors. The parent survey addressed demographics, acculturation, perceived discrimination, and the mother-daughter relationship. The second part of the interview was semistructured. This part of the interview allowed

TABLE 12.2. Parent Demographics

	Parent of System-Involved Girls	Parent of Girls in Community Group
Ethnic heritage		
Mexican	21	5
Guatemalan	0	1
Place of birth		
United States	16	0
Mexico	5	5
Guatemala	0	1
Generation level		
Foreign-born/first generation	5	5
Second generation	15	1
Third generation or later	1	0
Education level		
Elementary	15	5
High school	5	1
University credits	1	0

the participants to deviate from the survey questions and contextualize some of their answers by delving deeper into their lived experiences. Interviews lasted on average sixty minutes.

The location of interviews varied between the system-involved and community groups. All twenty-one interviews for the system-involved group were conducted at the juvenile court center. For youth housed in detention, interviews took place in an interview room, and the parent was called to complete the interview. Otherwise, all Latina youth on probation or diversion were interviewed at the court in probation interview offices. All youth preferred their interviews to be conducted in English. All parent interviews, except one, were conducted in Spanish. Interviews for the community group families primarily took place in their homes.

Findings

Perceived Discrimination

In the structured survey part of data collection, youth participants were asked to respond to whether they had personally experienced or witnessed racial/ethnic discrimination in school, while socializing, and/or in the media. The aim was to explore the experiences of inclusion and exclusion from the perspectives of girls in both the system-involved and community groups as well as examine any differences by generation status. Of the twenty-seven youth participants, 52 percent reported either personally experiencing or witnessing discrimination. Nine (33 percent) reported perceived discrimination at school, eleven (52 percent) reported perceived discrimination while socializing, and fifteen (71 percent) reported observing perceived discrimination in the media. A greater proportion of foreign-born/first-generation and second-generation youth reported experiencing discrimination than did later-generation youth.

Many of the girls in the sample experienced discrimination irrespective of whether they were system-involved. Indeed, Lisa, a fourteen-year-old system-involved girl who identified as Mexican and African American, recalled an incident of explicit discrimination that she experienced at the mall. "Well, like, the looks you get, you know what I mean? Like, it takes [salespeople] forever to do something, but when someone else asks them from a different race, they do it quickly. Like, you ask them to do something, and they think that you are going to steal something." Lisa had deduced that the disparate treatment from sales representatives was a result of stereotypes held against members of her ethnic group categorizing Latino and Black people as criminals. Evelyn, a first-generation Mexican girl who was also system-involved, shared a similar story about experiencing discrimination in a public setting. Only in this instance, Evelyn almost got into a fight. "Me and my friend were in the mall and this girl, she was white, she was with her other little friends. And she turned around and told my friend, 'Mojada,' you know people that cross the border [illegally] you know. And my friend went at her, and she's like, 'Tell me that to my face.' We were going to get into a fight when they, like, walked away."

The effects of stereotypes and discrimination carry real-world implications for Latina girls, as these assumptions about cultural deficiencies serve as the fulcrum for institutional racism and disparate treatment (Pasko & Lopez, 2018). Research on Latina/o youth echoes Lisa's and Evelyn's feelings of stigmatization via societal assumptions of their propensity for criminality (Lopez & Chesney-Lind, 2014; Rios, 2011). While Latinos tend to experience more subtle acts of discrimination than do

Black people, there are instances when individuals who do not possess obvious physical characteristics reflective of their ethnic minority group experience overt racism, targeting members of their ethnic group as opposed to them directly. Jess, from the community group, discussed an incident where she encountered discrimination and racism toward members of her Mexican ethnic group when her local school closed down and she was required to attend a more affluent school composed of predominantly white students.

> Well, I had to move schools because our school closed down and our new school . . . well, no offence, but it is full of white kids. Well, they wouldn't say it directly at me, but they would be talking about Mexican kids and be like, "Oh, a bunch of Mexican kids in this school, because their school is so ghetto, they had to close it down, and they were poor and stuff." Yeah, they would make fun of that. They would say, "It looks like they got sunburned or something." That is messed up right there. So, I get mad. I don't hang out with them.

Jess was highly aware of the stigmatization of her ethnic group, despite not being the direct recipient of discrimination, and this awareness was reflected in how she perceived others' treatment of her ethnic group. Scholars contend that indirect forms of discrimination can be just as cognitively and emotionally taxing as blatant discrimination for members of the stigmatized groups (Sue et al., 2007). Researchers have also found that even slight but constant disparities in treatment can have cumulative effects for Latina/o youth in terms of their emotional well-being (Finch, Kolody, & Vega, 2000), social adjustment (Greene, Way, & Pahl, 2006), and educational and professional aspirations (Devos & Torres, 2007).

Acculturative Dissonance

Youth participants shared narratives about two types of acculturative stressors: language brokering and clashes with parents over values. Each of these stressors is discussed below.

LANGUAGE BROKERING. Growing up with a sense of being not only different but substandard can be stressful for Latina/o youth going through the acculturation process. While studies have found that the effects of negative messages are relative to the individual's degree of acculturation (Guyll, Madon, Prieto, & Scherr, 2010), the promotion of assimilation in the United States paints Latino youth in a corner where they are encouraged to reject their parents' culture and language while simultaneously embracing a culture that perpetuates negative messages about their ethnicity. The implications of these conflicting messages were clearly expressed by many of the respondents irrespective of whether they were system-involved. Charlotte, from the system-involved group, was aware of the negative reactions from the majority culture when she had to use Spanish to translate for her mother. She began by describing how uncomfortable she felt and how she perceived others judged her and her family because of her mother's inability to speak English.

> Well, for me it is embarrassing. I don't know why it's embarrassing. I am just not comfortable with it. I feel that she's been here quite some time. I feel that she slacks, like she could have gone to some types of classes to know a little bit, the basics. I feel that people view us as Mexicans you know like umm, the stereotype. I am not comfortable with it. I mean I try to help her with it, like we speak to her in English, I feel she understands it because that is what we [siblings] speak at home other than when we are speaking to her. I feel like she is really insecure . . . not comfortable with it, like she feels like a fool or like people don't understand her.

Quintana and Scull (2009) highlight how important social consequences can be associated with identifying or being identified as Latina, as Latinos are affected by the group's stigmatized status in the United States. Charlotte expressed shame in translating for her mother not necessarily because she did not want others to know she is Mexican but because her mother's inability to speak Spanish fit the stereotype that Mexicans fail to make an effort to fit into American culture and/or are inferior because they cannot speak English. Qualitative studies with college-aged Latinos who served as language brokers during their youth revealed similar reactions as Charlotte's. These youth felt annoyed and sometimes burdened by their responsibility, while younger children reported a mix of satisfaction and stress (DeMent, Buriel, & Villanueva, 2005; Love & Buriel, 2007). Villanueva and Buriel (2010) found that a youth's reaction to language brokering was directly related to the environment, with most participants reporting the school setting as the most stressful, especially parent-teacher conferences. Since Charlotte had been involved with the juvenile justice system for a few years, most of her language brokering involved translating for her mom in meetings with probation officers and judges, making the interactions increasingly stressful for her, as she had to communicate to her mother all the negative comments regarding her behavior.

While some youth are proud to be language brokers and do not find it stressful, other youth struggle with having to translate for their parents (Kam & Lazarevic, 2014). The same was true in the current study. For some Latinas, language brokering was just something they did as part of their role in the family. As Alice explained, "I usually have to translate for my parents because my dad doesn't speak any English and my mom is okay with English but not as well as Spanish. I'm used to it really. I don't really feel anything about it; I am just used to it."

CLASH OF VALUES. Another stressor related to acculturative dissonance involves parent-child differences with regard to how daughters should be raised, with more traditional parents believing that girls should be closely monitored (Zayas, 2011). Abigail, for example, prefers that her granddaughter have more native Mexican than Anglo friends because she believes that the liberal customs implemented in raising children in the United States distance children from their family support system and inhibit the protective elements of the Latin American culture, which keeps them on track. "The girls in this country believe that they need to leave the home at eighteen years regardless of whether they are ready and this puts them at risk for many risk behaviors. I know it is perhaps considered old fashioned, but in my day, females stayed home until they were married, and the men too, and we didn't see these types of problems with youth and crime." Traditional Latino values have been described as primarily restrictive on females and encouraging exploration in males (Neimann, 2001). However, Abigail's views were gender-neutral with respect to allowing Latino youth freedoms accorded by the white American culture. Value conflicts seemed to plague many of the parents in the system-involved group whose daughters or female relatives chose to leave behind traditional Latin American norms in lieu of the values of their peer culture. Gonzalo, a fifty-five-year-old Mexican immigrant monolingual father, attributed his daughter Christina's long history with the juvenile justice system to the poor influences in her life. He claimed that although her friends were primarily Latinas, they were second and later generation and lacked the traditional upbringing of first-generation Latina girls.

> I blame her Mexican American friends for all her troubles. Look at her sister. She is properly married with a young child and a responsible husband. She never got into trouble and went to university. Cristina started hanging out with these girls that were not brought up right and try to be independent and free and think that by doing drugs and stealing cars they are asserting their independence. I just wish I could send my daughter back to Mexico to get her away from these influences.

Studies have found that first-generation youth demonstrate greater levels of educational achievement (Perriera, Fugligni, & Potochnick, 2010), perceive fewer barriers to reaching their goals (Hill, Ramirez, & Dumka, 2003), and demonstrate lower levels of problem behaviors (Sampson, 2008) than second and later generations. One explanation for differences between generations is the protective pattern of being surrounded by culture within the immediate family and primarily immigrant Latino communities.

RES Strategies within the Context of Strong Mother-Daughter Relationships

Ethnic affiliations can have positive effects on ethnic minority youth as they provide for an interchange of shared experiences, culture, and language. These shared experiences offer a bond that for girls creates an investment in and influence on their behaviors. While positive ethnic affiliations can lead to positive influences and outcomes, negative ethnic ties can be just as influential, ultimately limiting the opportunities of the young women invested in those negative relationships. However, as evidenced by the narratives of both the system-involved and community group families, there are many significant influences on girls' behaviors. Structural disadvantage, discriminatory practices, and acculturative dissonance all seemed to exacerbate conditions ripe for delinquent activity for the system-involved girls. Although the girls in the community group also experienced strain from structural disadvantage, perceived discrimination, and acculturative stressors, their positive relationships with mothers who used RES strategies appeared to buffer the effects of adversity. Despite a similar degree of exposure to perceived discrimination across the system-involved and community groups, the girls in the community group consistently exhibited a strong ethnic identity and shared a strong bond with their mothers. Survey responses revealed that all of the community group girls said they had a moderate to strong relationship with their mothers. For these young women, maternal support appeared to function as a buffer from discrimination and adversity. Greta, for example, recounted how past experiences with discrimination motivated her to dispel the set stereotypes of her ethnic group while highlighting the significance of family support in helping her through that process.

> It is just certain people [that] really try to emphasize and make me realize that I am not like them. I am something else. I feel that sometimes they highlight that I am not as good. I feel like I want to show them that I can be just as good as they are, even though we are obviously different. I just want to show them, to know, that no matter what color of skin you are, what kind of race you are, we're all the same, and we can be just as good as each other. I have to push myself harder maybe to prove that the stereotypes are incorrect. I feel that for those youth that do not have family support it is harder to be proud 'cause I feel that you need that family support to tell you, "you can do this. I believe in you." I feel that is a huge impact on how well they do in life.

Research suggests that, in addition to strong parental bonds, parents with a strong ethnic identity are more likely to engage in ethnic practices at home (e.g., speaking Spanish, observing Mexican celebrations and holidays, serving Mexican food, listening to Mexican music, and watching TV and films in Spanish) and connect with members of their ethnic group outside the home (Quintana & Scull, 2009). Parents send implicit and explicit messages to their children through these practices, promoting self-pride and enhancing their abilities to overcome the stigmatization that comes with being Latina in America.

While all of the mothers in the community group used RES strategies, this was true for only four of the twenty-one mothers in the system-involved group. Upon closer examination of the four system-involved group families, findings suggest a pattern between strong parental socialization and offending severity: girls who committed less severe offences and were given diversion or standard probation as a consequence were more likely to have mothers reporting strong parental socialization practices in the home than girls with more serious offending histories. Erin, one of these mothers, shared how she attempts to promote ethnic pride in her daughter Evelyn: "I try to explain the Mexican culture to my daughter. She tells me that it is a beautiful culture and she likes watching Spanish television with me and the food and the music. I understand that because we live here now, she will adapt to American culture but I want her to stay connected to both sides so she can feel proud. I don't want her to feel discrimination like I have." Evelyn's mother was actively engaged in socializing her daughter in all things Mexican to ensure that she retained her Mexican identity in the midst of a developing American identity. Studies suggest that Latina mothers prepare their children for the discrimination and stigmatization they are anticipated to face by promoting academic achievement, ethnic identity, and self-confidence to help them manage the effects (Hughes et al., 2006; Hughes et al., 2009). Evelyn's narratives suggest that her mother's actions were effective at promoting a positive ethnic identity and buffering her from feelings of inferiority. "I like [Mexican culture] 'cause it's more adventurous and talks more, more details. I feel good that I am Mexican because I speak Spanish and my nana [grandmother] also teaches me about the culture. I have never felt that because I am Latina, I am not good enough. I am Mexican and no one is going to change me."

The narratives from the mothers in the community group indicated consistent socialization of Latin American culture in the home, including celebrating traditional holidays with Latin American food and Spanish music and teachings of humility and honor, characteristics promoted in Latin American cultures (Olmeda, 2003). Not only did parenting practices emphasize experiences of discrimination, but there were practices that revolve around promoting egalitarian views toward all racial and ethnic groups (Hughes et al., 2006). Egalitarian parenting practices are reflective of Latino teachings of humility and respect toward others. Inez, Jess's mother, promoted such teachings in conjunction with ethnic socialization. She explained how the children were allowed to speak only Spanish in the home as a means of keeping them connected to their native tongue and culture. "We only speak Spanish in the house. If you conducted the interview with Jess in English it was because my husband was not home. If he is home, she knows that she needs to speak Spanish. Also when watching television, if my husband is here, it is in Spanish." Yet she also acknowledged the negative effects of Mexican stereotypes and that these stereotypes will follow her children but felt that a strong ethnic identity was important to maintain a positive sense of self in the face of adversity. For Inez, it was important that her children maintain a sense of humility by being proud of who they are but not at the expense of others.

> Well, one of the things that is really important for me is that they are proud of who they are, that they are not ashamed, but also that they not put on airs. We are all the same, that is what we teach them. We don't want them to be those people that do not have an identity. I tell them, "You have to have your identity but keep your feet on the ground . . . know that we are all at ground level."

Inez's socialization of her children illustrated an egalitarian approach where she promoted the Mexican culture in the home but promoted acceptance of other cultures and races, pointing out that as long as they were not bad influences that conflicted with her teachings in the home, she was comfortable letting her daughter choose the race of her social networks.

Greta's mother Bethany also exhibited strong ethnic socialization practices in combination with egalitarian views in an attempt to balance the development of pride and self-worth with respect for others. Bethany described her socialization practices with regard to race and ethnicity and how others' unfair treatment of her and her daughters made her feel; however, she emphasized the importance of leading by example and providing her daughters with a positive role model.

> There are times it makes me very angry, impotent at times. There have been some ugly experiences, but I can't change everyone's beliefs. I can

however influence the beliefs of my daughter, that those people are wrong. There is no need to treat people badly. I tell her that she needs to be an example, that there should be equality because we are all equal. It doesn't matter what color you are or language you speak. I cannot influence the entire world but I do have influence on my daughters so they are better people. That they treat everyone equally and not believe they are inferior to anyone because they are different.

Research on gendered strains or stressors has highlighted females' affinity for relationship maintenance and development (Broidy & Agnew, 1997), explaining why culture transfer typically occurs between generations of women and girls. Studies suggest that despite the presence of cumulative risk factors in Latinas' lives, a strong bond with the mother or maternal figure functions as a protective factor against negative external influences and experiences (Corona, Lefkowitz, Sigman, & Romo, 2005). Factors such as high maternal assimilation, weak culture transfer, and a strained mother-daughter relationship may increase the likelihood of poor Latina youth outcomes.

Conclusion

The current study qualitatively examined how both system-involved and non-system-involved Latina youth experienced discrimination and acculturative stressors as well as how their mothers used RES strategies as a way of enhancing their daughters' ethnic identities. Findings highlight the importance of a strong mother-daughter relationship to promote parental RES practices, which prepare young Latinas for incidences of discrimination and exclusion that accompany membership within a stigmatized group. The girls with a strong bond considered their mothers' teachings when faced with decisions regarding risk-taking behaviors. They also incorporated these teachings as a means of empowerment and support when they themselves encountered discrimination and prejudice. Aspects of their shared culture in the home functioned as a protective factor for deviancy among Latina youth who exhibited a strong sense of ethnic identity. Yet mothers also encouraged their daughters to be bicultural by respecting U.S. mainstream culture. In the absence of bicultural competence, ethnic minority individuals may be more likely to personalize negative reactions and embrace what some have referred to as an oppositional frame of reference (Fordham & Ogbu, 1986). As illustrated by the narratives presented in this chapter, RES can offset this risk. Without such parenting practices, Latinas may be left to navigate the strain stemming from discrimination and prejudice, internalizing these negative messages and increasing their propensity for deviancy as a means of coping with the effects of acculturative stress. Programs such as Xinachtli, discussed in chapter 14 of this volume, have the potential for enhancing system-involved (and other) Latina girls' sense of ethnic pride and identity within the context of supportive, caring relationships with other girls and women.

REFERENCES

Barrett, A. N., Kuperminc, G. P., & Lewis, K. M. (2013). Acculturative stress and gang involvement among Latinos: US-born versus immigrant youth. *Hispanic Journal of Behavioral Sciences, 35*, 370–389.

Berry, J. W. (1997). Immigration, Acculturation, and Adaptation. *Applied Psychology: An International Review, 46*, 5–68.

Berry, J. W. (2006). Contexts of acculturation. In D. L. Sam & J. W. Berry (Eds.), *The Cambridge handbook of acculturation psychology* (pp. 27–42). New York: Cambridge University Press.

Berry, J. W., Phinney, J. S., Sam, D. L., & Vedder, P. (2006). Immigrant youth: Acculturation, identity, and adaptation. *Applied Psychology: An International Review, 55*, 303–332.

Biafora, F. A., Warheit, G. J., Zimmerman, R. S., & Gil, A. G. (1993). Racial mistrust and deviant behaviors among ethnically diverse Black adolescent boys. *Journal of Applied Social Psychology, 23*, 891–910.

Broidy, L., & Agnew, R. (1997). Gender and crime: A general strain theory perspective. *Journal of Research and Crime and Delinquency, 34*, 275–306.

Brown, T. N., Tanner-Smith, E. E., Lesane-Brown, C. L., & Ezell, M. E. (2007). Child, parent and situational correlates of familial ethnic/race socialization. *Journal of Marriage and Family, 69*, 14–25.

Burt, C. H., Lei, M. K., & Simons, R. L. (2017). Racial discrimination, racial socialization, and crime: Understanding mechanisms of resilience. *Social Problems, 64*, 414–438.

Burt, C. H., Simons, R. L., & Gibbons, F. X. (2012). Racial discrimination, ethnic-racial socialization, and crime: A micro-sociological model of risk and resilience. *American Sociological Review, 77*, 648–677.

Corona, R., Lefkowitz, E. S., Sigman, M., & Romo, L. F. (2005). Latino adolescents' adjustment, maternal depressive symptoms, and the mother adolescent relationship. *Family Relations, 54*, 386–399.

Delgado, M. Y., Updegraff, K. A., Roosa, M. W., & Umaña-Taylor, A. J. (2011). Discrimination and Mexican-origin adolescents' adjustment: The moderating roles of adolescents', mothers', and fathers' cultural orientations and values. *Journal of Youth and Adolescence, 40,* 125–139.

DeMent, T., Buriel, R., & Villanueva, C. (2005). Children as language brokers: A narrative of the recollections of college students. In R. Hoosain & F. Salili (Eds.), *Language in multicultural education* (pp. 255–272). Greenwich, CT: Information Age.

Devos, T., & Torres, J. A. C. (2007). Implicit identification with academic achievement among Latino college students: The role of ethnic identity and significant others. *Basic and Applied Social Psychology, 29,* 293–310.

Domènech Rodriguez, M. M., Donovick, M. R., & Crowley, S. L. (2009). Parenting styles in a cultural context: Observations of "protective parenting" in first-generation Latinos. *Family Process, 48,* 195–210.

Eamon, M. K., & Mulder, C. (2005). Predicting antisocial behavior among Latino young adolescents: An ecological systems analysis. *American Journal of Orthopsychiatry, 75,* 117–127.

Finch, B. K., Kolody, B., & Vega, W. A. (2000). Perceived discrimination and depression among Mexican-origin adults in California. *Journal of Health and Social Behavior, 41,* 295–313.

Fordham, S., & Ogbu, J. (1986). Black students' school success: Coping with the burden of acting white. *Urban Review, 18,* 176–206.

Frazer, A. L., Rubens, S., Johnson-Motoyama, M., DiPierro, M., & Fite, P. J. (2017, February). Acculturation dissonance, acculturation strategy, depressive symptoms, and delinquency in Latina/o adolescents. *Child & Youth Care Forum, 46,* 19–33.

Greene, M. L., Way, N., & Pahl, K. (2006). Trajectories of perceived adult and peer discrimination among Black, Latino, and Asian American adolescents: Patterns and psychological correlates. *Developmental Psychology, 42,* 218–238.

Guyll, M., Madon, S., Prieto, L., & Scherr, K. C. (2010). The potential roles of self-fulfilling prophecies, stigma consciousness and stereotype threat in linking Latino/a ethnicity and educational outcomes. *Journal of Social Issues, 66,* 113–130.

Hill, N. E., Ramirez, C. L., & Dumka, L. E. (2003). Adolescent's career aspirations: A qualitative study of perceived barriers and family support among low income ethnically diverse adolescents. *Journal of Family Issues, 24,* 934–959.

Hoskin, A. W. (2013). Experiencing prejudice and violence among Latinos: A general strain theory approach. *Western Criminology Review, 14,* 25–38.

Hughes, D., Rodriguez, J., Smith, E. P., Johnson, D. J., Stevenson, H. C., & Spicer, P. (2006). Parents' ethnic-racial socialization practices: A review of research and direction for future study. *Developmental Psychology, 42,* 747–770.

Hughes, D., Witherspoon, D., Rivas-Drake, D., & West-Bey, N. (2009). Received ethnic-racial socialization messages and youths' academic and behavioral outcomes: Examining the mediating role of ethnic identity and self-esteem. *Cultural Diversity and Ethnic Minority Psychology, 15,* 112–124.

Jarkowsky, P. A. (2009). Immigrants and neighbourhoods of concentrated poverty: Assimilation or stagnation? *Journal of Ethnic and Migration Studies, 35,* 1129–1151.

Kam, J. A., & Lazarevic, V. (2014). The stressful (and not so stressful) nature of language brokering: Identifying when brokering functions as a cultural stressor for Latino immigrant children in early adolescence. *Journal of Youth and Adolescence, 43,* 1994–2011.

Krogstad, J. M., & Lopez, G. (2016). Roughly half of Hispanics have experienced discrimination. Pew Research Center. www.pewresearch.org.

Kulis, S., Marsiglia, F. F., & Nieri, T. (2009). Perceived ethnic discrimination versus acculturation stress: Influences on substance use among Latino youth in the Southwest. *Journal of Health and Social Behavior, 50,* 443–459.

Lopez, V., & Chesney-Lind, M. (2014). Latina girls speak out: Stereotypes, gender and relationship dynamics. *Latino Studies, 12,* 527–549.

Love, J., & Buriel, R. (2007). Language brokering, autonomy, parent-child bonding, biculturalism, and depression: A study of Mexican American adolescents from immigrant families. *Hispanic Journal of Behavioral Sciences, 29,* 472–491.

Marin, G., & Marin, B. V. (1991). *Applied social research methods: Vol 23. Research with Hispanic populations.* Newbury Park, CA: Sage.

Neimann, Y. F. (2001). Stereotypes about Chicanas and Chicanos: Implications for counselling. *Counseling Psychologist, 29,* 55–90.

Okamoto, J., Ritt-Olson, A., Soto, D., Baezconde-Garbanati, L., & Unger, J. B. (2009). Perceived discrimination and substance use among Latino adolescents. *American Journal of Health Behavior, 33,* 718–727.

Olmeda, I. (2003). Accommodation and resistance: Latinas' struggle for their children's education. *Anthropology & Education Quarterly, 34,* 373–375.

Pasko, L., & Lopez, V. (2018). The Latina penalty: Juvenile correctional attitudes toward the Latina juvenile offender. *Journal of Ethnicity in Criminal Justice, 16,* 272–291.

Pérez, D. M., Jennings, W. G., & Gover, A. R. (2008). Specifying general strain theory: An ethnically relevant approach. *Deviant Behavior, 29,* 544–578.

Perriera, K. M., Fugligni, A., & Potochnick, S. (2010). Fitting in: The role of social acceptance and discrimination in shaping academic motivations of Latino youth in the U.S. Southeast. *Journal of Social Issues, 66,* 131–153.

Phinney, J. S., Horenczyk, G., Liebkind, K., & Vedder, P. (2001). Ethnic identity, immigration, and well-being: An interactional perspective. *Journal of Social Issues, 3,* 493–510.

Portes, A., & Rumbaut, R. G. (2001). *Legacies: The story of the immigrant second generation.* Berkeley: University of California Press.

Quintana, S., & Scull, N. (2009). Latino ethnic identity. In F. A. Villaruel, G. Carlo, J. M. Grau, M. Azmitia, N. J. Cabrera, & T. J. Chahin (Eds.), *Handbook of U.S. Latino psychology: Developmental and community-based perspectives* (pp. 81–98). Thousand Oaks, CA: Sage.

Rios, V. M. (2011). *Punished: Policing the lives of Black and Latino boys.* New York: New York University Press.

Samaniego, R. Y., & Gonzales, N. A. (1999). Multiple mediators of the effects of acculturation status on delinquency for Mexican American adolescents. *American Journal of Community Psychology, 27,* 189–210.
Sampson, R. J. (2008). Rethinking crime and immigration. *Contexts, 7,* 348–383.
Scott, D. I. (2018). Latina fortitude in the face of disadvantage: Exploring the conditioning effects of ethnic identity and gendered ethnic identity on Latina offending. *Critical Criminology, 26,* 49–73.
Sue, D. W., Capodilupo, C. M., Torino, G. C., Bucceri, J. M., Holder, A., Nadal, K. L., & Esquilin, M. (2007). Racial microaggressions in everyday life: Implications for clinical practice. *American Psychologist, 62,* 271–286.
Sullivan, S., Schwartz, S. J., Prado, G., Huang, S., Pantin, H., & Szapocznik, J. (2007). A bidimensional model of acculturation for examining differences in family functioning and behavior problems in Hispanic immigrant adolescents. *Journal of Early Adolescence, 27,* 405–430.
U.S. Census Bureau. (2010). QuickFacts: United States (Table PST045219). www.census.gov.
U.S. Department of Health and Human Services. (2014). Office of the Assistant Secretary for Planning and Evaluation. https://aspe.hhs.gov.
Villanueva, C. M., & Buriel, R. (2010). Speaking on behalf of others: A qualitative study of the perceptions and feelings of adolescent Latina language brokers. *Journal of Social Issues, 66,* 197–210.
Wang, M. T., Henry, D. A., Smith, L. V., Huguley, J. P., & Guo, J. (2020). Parental ethnic-racial socialization practices and children of Color's psychosocial and behavioral adjustment: A systematic review and meta-analysis. *American Psychologist, 75,* 1–22.
Zayas, L. H. (2011). *Latinas attempting suicide: When cultures, families, and daughters collide.* New York: Oxford University Press.

13

Mi Hermana's Keeper

Empowering Latina Youth to Improve Services That Prevent Juvenile Justice System Involvement

DEANA SWAN, JOHANNA CRESWELL BÁEZ, AND
DIANDREA GARZA

Research has clearly outlined the value of implementing evidence-based programming for all system-involved youth (Henggeler & Schoenwald, 2011). Several organizations and agencies, such as the Substance Abuse and Mental Health Services Administration, the Coalition for Evidence-Based Policy, Child Trends, and the Department of Justice, recommend evidence-based programs (Blueprints for Healthy Youth Development, 2018). Blueprints, one evidence-based registry for prevention and intervention programs, provides a list of violence prevention programs "whose effectiveness has been scientifically demonstrated" (Mihalic, Irwin, Elliott, Fagan, & Hansen, 2004, p. 1). The registry provides online tools for programs to identify evidence-based programming by program outcome (e.g., delinquency and criminal behavior, violence), targeted participants (e.g., age, gender, race), and type of program (e.g., juvenile justice, mentoring). Blueprints rigorously vets programs that can be replicated with high confidence in the outcomes they will produce. While there is a lack of evidence-based, gender-specific, culturally responsive delinquency prevention programs focused on Latina youth (Chesney-Lind, Morash, & Stevens, 2008; Foley, 2008), Blueprints identifies one promising program for Latino youth and families, Familias Unidas (Pantin et al., 2009). The lack of rigorously vetted programs for Latinos highlights the need for more evidence-based prevention and intervention programs for this population.

Prevention interventions are more effective when grounded in culturally competent approaches (Furman et al., 2009; Marsiglia & Booth,

2015). Research suggests the need to be purposeful and strategic when implementing evidence-based programming to ensure it is culturally appropriate and relevant (Holleran Steiker et al., 2008) through the adoption of a "culturally grounded approach" (Marsiglia & Booth, 2015, p. 423). By definition, culturally grounded approaches offer opportunities to assess and adapt methods so they can be both effective and relevant to clients from diverse cultural backgrounds (Marsiglia & Booth, 2015). When pursuing cultural adaptations of evidence-based program models, Holleran Steiker et al. (2008) recommend inviting participants to give feedback through a pilot of the interventions. Though these processes have been proven both significant and necessary, their application can be quite challenging for program staff. In fact, even with the literature to support the importance of including culturally relevant approaches, there are few resources aimed at equipping practitioners with culturally adapted programming.

Organizational Commitment to Serving Latina Youth in the Juvenile Justice System

In a correctional system that has historically overlooked women and girls (Foley, 2008), racially and ethnically diverse women and girls experience an added layer of inequity (Chesney-Lind et al., 2008). Gender-specific delinquency prevention programs are seldom culturally tailored, and none focus specifically on Latina youth at risk for delinquency (Chesney-Lind et al., 2008; Foley, 2008). With a lack of program models and very few resources to help program staff address the gaps in providing culturally responsive prevention programming for Latina youth, Southwest Key Programs developed the MHK Toolkit based on the voices of Latina youth and their caregivers (Báez & Garza, 2017). The My Brother's Keeper Initiative (Obama, 2014) along with other calls to action for the inclusion of women and girls (Morris, 2014) inspired the timely, research-informed MHK Toolkit to support Latina youth in juvenile justice prevention programs. Southwest Key Programs conducted a community-based participatory action research study highlighting the voices and experiences of Latina youth in prevention programs.

Southwest Key Programs is a national nonprofit organization that has positively impacted the lives of children and their families for over thirty years. In 2017, the organization served over a hundred thousand individuals, 87 percent of whom were Hispanic or Latino, in eighty-seven programs across seven states. As a community-based and community-informed organization, Southwest Key has made a concerted effort to build holistic programming informed by Latina/o youth and their caregivers. Southwest Key has a vested interest in the needs and experiences of Latina/o youth because of its identity as a Latino-led organization working to fill the gap in services that consider this group's distinctive experiences and needs. As one of the nation's largest Hispanic-led nonprofits, Southwest Key Programs is uniquely qualified to champion the MHK Toolkit recommendations.

The MHK Toolkit was developed through a community-based participatory research study aimed at understanding the perspectives and experiences of at-risk and system-involved Latina youth and their caregivers. The community-based participatory design is an advanced mixed-methods intervention and social justice exploratory sequential design (Creswell, 2013) that allowed the researchers to work directly alongside Latina youth and include them in each phase of the research process. Participatory action research incorporates an emancipatory aim to improve and empower individuals (Creswell & Guetterman, 2019). Therefore, the research design was an intentional effort to engage Latina youth as experts of their lives and experiences. The research priority throughout the study was to promote social justice by developing culturally responsive services for Latina youth, and in the process the Latina youth themselves emerged as citizen scientists with assured voices, codeveloping focus group questions and guiding program recommendations based on qualitative data. These efforts unfolded in three phases described below and detailed in prior publications (Báez & Garza, 2017, 2018).

Methods

Using Tongco's (2007) purposive sampling technique, Southwest Key Programs staff recruited former Latina clients (ages ten to seventeen), their caregivers, and key community stakeholders (e.g., social workers, educators, case managers, probation officers, and nonprofit leaders) from three different Family Keys program sites in Austin, Laredo, and

San Antonio, Texas.[1] Staff contacted individuals via phone and email offering personal invitations to participate in the research study, framing it as an opportunity for participants to share their experiences and suggest improvements to program services. Because staff invited only Latina youth who had previously participated in the Family Keys program, youth were positioned as expert informants, one well-regarded consequence of purposive sampling (Tongco, 2007). Purposive sampling is described as "a type of non-probability sampling that is most effective when one needs to study a certain cultural domain with knowledgeable experts within" (Tongco, 2007, p. 147). Because the study aimed to understand the experiences of Latina youth in order to provide them greater support, purposive sampling aligned directly with the research goal.

Data were collected via nine focus groups and eleven supplemental interviews with twenty-two Latinas youth formerly served by Southwest Keys, eighteen of their caregivers, and forty-two stakeholders in Austin, Laredo, and San Antonio. Each youth participant received a ten-dollar gift card for their involvement; no similar incentive was offered to caregivers and stakeholders. The focus groups and interviews took place at various community agencies, including the Southwest Key offices.

While the research steps are outlined in greater detail in the MHK Toolkit (Báez & Garza, 2017, p. 11), an overview of the phases is also included here. Researchers developed interview questions in partnership with participants, including Latina youth. The qualitative data were audio-recorded and transcribed verbatim. Words were translated to English when necessary, although all data were primarily collected in English. Researchers then uploaded all transcripts into MAXQDA software (Kuckartz, 2007) and used it to analyze the data by grouping topics into categories (codes) and then into broader themes. The use of software for data analysis provided a more efficient way to access data and a way to visualize the relationships among themes (Creswell, 2013).

From these qualitative data, eight key themes emerged from the questions based on Latino cultural values, how best to support Latina youth and enhance programming, and Latina youths' involvement in various systems (school, juvenile justice, and community-based programs) to better understand changes that could lead to success. Southwest Key staff checked the accuracy of the themes in a follow-up focus group of program staff, stakeholders, and Latina youth. After consensus was met, these themes guided the development of nine program recommendations and corresponding action steps for supporting Latina youth and their caregivers in community-based programs.

Findings

The MHK Toolkit outlines six program-level and three system-level recommendations with corresponding action steps that are culturally responsive, gender-specific, trauma-informed, strengths-based, and developmentally appropriate (see Table 13.1).

Findings from the focus groups and interviews revealed that Latina youth, caregivers, and community stakeholders' experiences with prevention and intervention programming are strongly influenced by systemic barriers, creating a need to address necessary changes within both program services and the systems themselves.

Systems can inherently hinder the progress of Latina youth simply by failing to consider the way in which culture influences their experiences. For example, when discussing systemic barriers to services for Latina youth, one stakeholder asserted, "There is a disconnect between the education system and our culture.... If we're not doing it in a culturally competent way, to where we acknowledge the culture that they bring with them and their family, then we are putting these students at a disadvantage" (Báez & Garza, 2017, p. 22). Latina youth also shared feelings about the ways some of the larger systems felt unsupportive to their needs and culture. When talking about her experience in school, one Latina stated, "Like, you know, how they just say 'Good Morning' and then they start the lesson. No, like 'How's your day?' Stuff like that. Make [me] feel comfortable" (Báez & Garza, 2017, p. 22). It was evident that Latina youth had a desire for staff to take more of a relational-cultural approach through the use of cultural concepts like *personalismo*, *simpatía*, and *empatía* (Báez & Garza, 2017). This type of direct feedback led to the recommendations and actions steps in the MHK Toolkit.

At the programmatic level, Latina youth expressed a strong need to feel respected by staff. Therefore, this theme led to recommendation 2, "Provide services that value *respeto* and teach respectful practices." The notion of *respeto* requires that Latinas are given voice to state concerns or questions and that their opinions are validated. One Latina youth

TABLE 13.1. Nine Recommendations for Supporting Latina Youth in Juvenile Justice Prevention Programs

Nine Recommendations Based on Key Themes

1. Provide services that are respectful and reflective of shared and individual Latino cultural heritage
... Speak to families in their preferred language
... Learn about family cultural values and discuss these interactions
... Incorporate services that are specifically focused on teaching cultural heritage
... Factor in each family's strengths and characteristics, rather than applying the same approach to all families

2. Provide services that value *respeto* and teach respectful practices
... Train staff to uphold key cultural values with Latino families, such as *familismo*,[1] *personalismo*,[2] *respeto*,[3] and *espiritualismo*[4]
... Support staff and families in validating the opinions of Latina youth
... Ask Latina youth how they want to be respected and validated
... Hold individual check-ins with Latina youth and remind them that they are part of the process and in control

3. Provide services that utilize a relational approach
... Provide services with a relational-cultural lens that upholds Latino values, such as *simpatía*[5] *y empatía*[6]
... Use relational strategies such as listening, empathic responding, and being authentic
... Focus on Latina youths' strengths

4. Provide case management services for the entire family
... Help access essential resources and provide one-on-one counseling, as part of case management services with the entire family
... Support open discussions on family matters between Latina youth and their caregivers
... Support families in times of crisis and develop a referral resource manual to connect caregivers with local resources
... Develop or use referrals for "intensive case management" services when needed, such as wrap-around services, linkages, home visits, and parent workshops

5. Support cross-generational services to instill values
... Hold collaborative discussion groups between caregivers and Latina youth on acculturation and transmitting cultural values (e.g., discussing technology use and practices)
... Planning cross-generational projects
... Establish cross-generational programming (e.g., youth serving elders)

6. Develop caregiver-specific services
... Use a trauma-informed framework, train staff in this framework
... Provide school-based parental involvement programs that include parent-teacher partnerships
... Create a space for caregivers to come together in the school such as "*platicas de padres*"
... Provide intensive case management and build supportive rapport with caregivers
... Develop program recruitment strategies and marketing that is relational, clear, and avoids when possible the words "juvenile justice"

7. Build culturally responsive school practices
... Provide opportunities to support familiarity, welcome students, and ask about their day
... Advocate for school staff to use Spanish or translation services when necessary
... Support access to cultural capital by promoting communication between caregivers and school staff
... Encourage school staff to support Latina youth with curricula and teaching that incorporates relatable aspects of their daily lives

8. Support effective systems advocacy
... Partner with stakeholders and advocate for equitable resource distribution (resources equal to those in other neighborhoods), high-quality teachers, supportive school culture, active parent involvement, and intervention/prevention programs for Latinos
... Advocate for more bilingual social workers and counselors in the schools
... Collaborate with other agencies serving Latina youth
... Partner with stakeholders to inform key government allies of "crisis" in providing funding and training for juvenile justice prevention programs that are gender-specific and trauma-informed
9. Promote the dismantling of systemic racism and bias
... Develop interventions aimed at reducing implicit racial bias
... Use anti-discriminatory strategies: learn about individuals and see the potential for success in each Latina
... Develop and host consciousness-raising workshops on undoing racism
... Hold collaborative discussion groups between caregivers and Latina youth on how racism is experienced to bridge differing views

1. *Familismo* is an emphasis and priority on family relationships involving a strong sense of loyalty, solidarity, and reciprocity (Ruiz, 2005).
2. *Personalismo* is an important value within Hispanic culture that expresses appreciation for the uniqueness of individuals, which creates a sense of worth, and it also reflects the importance of personal contact and social interactions (Ruiz, 2005).
3. *Respeto* is a cultural value that prioritizes respect and honors hierarchical roles in the family and community, and it emphasizes one's responsibilities to family and community (Ruiz, 2005).
4. *Espiritualismo* allows for decision making to be highly reliant on spiritual and religious beliefs (Delgado, 2007).
5. *Simpatía* is a cultural value related to being easy to get along with and likeable (Ruiz, 2005).
6. *Empatía* describes the cultural value that expects individuals to express mutual empathy (Delgado, 2007).

expressed it clearly when she stressed the way that staff can engage with Latinas while offering respect: "Actually listen and not have like a smart comment to say about it, or like laugh at it . . . just sit there and listen" (Báez & Garza, 2017, p. 16). Because of the common Latino family hierarchical structure that places greater value on thoughts of family elders, the opinions and voices of Latina youth can easily be silenced if staff members are not intentional to create a space for them (Báez & Garza, 2017). Therefore, one of the action steps corresponding to this recommendation is to "support staff and families in validating the opinions of Latina youth." This process of listening to the voices of Latina youth, their caregivers, and stakeholders while also considering Latina cultural norms and values led to the creation of three additional actions steps under recommendation 2 (for the full list, see Table 13.1).

The second phase focused on piloting the MHK Toolkit with direct service providers at three Southwest Key program sites in Texas to create a tailored practice toolkit specific to the program sites. With input from program staff, a shorter practice-centered toolkit was developed to further operationalize the recommended action steps for practical use in their programs as outlined below (Báez, Swan, & Garza, 2017). The third and final phase is still under way and involves the development of an interactive training curriculum. As detailed below, Southwest Key is training its own staff in these recommendations and has presented at conferences nationwide, including an Office of Juvenile Justice and Delinquency Prevention training webinar that can be accessed at https://www.youtube.com/watch?v=dSrsLBuTvKU. The MHK Toolkit can be downloaded free of charge at https://nationalmentoringresourcecenter.org/index.php/component/k2/item/431-mi-hermana's-keeper-toolkit-promising-practices-for-juvenile-justice-prevention-programs-supporting-latina-youth.html.

Application of the Mi Hermana's Keeper Toolkit in Direct Practice

Additional resources that are simple and can be tailored to fit various program models and agencies to improve services for Latina youth are needed. One distinct challenge faced by service organizations that are committed to research-driven practices is the frequent disconnect between research-based resource guides and direct care work. The absence of culturally competent approaches in direct practice can lead to negative outcomes, such as clients terminating early (Marsiglia & Booth, 2015) or clients being misunderstood or mislabeled (Lee, 2010; Pasko & Lopez, 2018). Marsiglia and Booth (2015) assert that many practitioners are aware of the importance of integrating culturally competent approaches, though they often struggle with how to prioritize and integrate the client's culture into the application of evidence-based practices.

When thinking about how to incorporate recommendations and action steps into direct practice, context is critical. Because the vast majority of the participants in the MHK Toolkit research study were Mexican American, when applying the toolkit staff must consider the cultural cues of the Latina clients. For example, recommendation 1 advocates that staff "provide services that are respectful and reflective of shared and individual Latino cultural heritage." Corresponding action step 2 contends that this can be accomplished if staff intentionally learn about family cultural values and discuss them in interactions. One example of how staff might discuss cultural values is to ask about holiday celebrations. Southwest Key Program staff working in South Texas may choose to ask Latina youth and their caregivers about their experiences during Día de los Muertos, a traditional Mexican holiday, as a sign of interest in shared cultural values. Since many Latina youth in South Texas programs come from Mexican and Mexican American backgrounds, mentioning the holiday would be appropriate in this context, though it would be less appropriate for staff in programs that enroll primarily Cuban girls.

Bridging research and practice is a focus of the MHK Toolkit—to make research findings usable and relevant for program staff. In sharing Southwest Key Programs' process for incorporating these recommendations and actions steps into tangible results for Latina youth, the hope is that other organizations can also think creatively about how to invest in the future of Latina youth by adapting practice recommendations that best fit their program models.

To better empower service providers to utilize these toolkit findings in their own work, additional training models are needed. The following is a description of the training model used by Southwest Key Programs to ensure that program staff incorporate the MHK Toolkit findings into their direct practice. Upon completion of the MHK Toolkit, program staff from three different program locations came together to participate in an in-depth training process with the goal of improving services for Latina youth. The training began by providing the toolkit to participants and training staff in the recommendations and action steps during a three-hour, in-person training. During the training, a short presentation also described the research design to provide staff with context about how the information was gathered, and program staff were asked to respond to the following three questions:

(1) What recommendations and actions steps are you already applying in your work with Latina youth?
(2) What action items are missing from the recommendations, but are applicable to your work with Latina youth?
(3) What action items are not feasible for you in your work with Latina youth?

Staff were encouraged to apply the toolkit recommendations and action steps to their own contexts as well as think about what was missing from the recommendations and action steps. Staff then discussed their answers together and created actions steps unique to their own programs based on the MHK Toolkit recommendations.

This discussion and the action steps tailored to the staff members' own programs were then used to create a practice toolkit (Báez et al., 2017). The practice toolkit provides a way to sustain the conversation around services and approaches to use with Latina youth and their families and offers a medium for staff members to reflect on their work. The practice toolkit contains space for field notes and serves as a workbook to apply the recommendations and their unique action steps in direct practice. This approach aligns with Arya, Villarruel, Villanueva, and Augarten's (2009) suggestion of modifying practices to meet the specific cultural, language, and contextual realities of clients when applying evidence-based practices to specific communities. Program staff were thoughtful with regard to how recommendations and action steps did or did not apply to their exact contexts.

To illustrate, the first recommendation in the MHK Toolkit proposes that staff "provide services that are respectful and reflective of shared and individual Latino cultural heritage" (Báez & Garza, 2017, p. 15). It includes four corresponding action steps, including one suggesting that staff "speak to families in their preferred language." During the training with program staff, some members took the idea of speaking to families in their preferred language a step further by suggesting ideas such as "being flexible to switch back and forth between languages, by mirroring the language of the family/Latina youth." Many of the ideas shared by staff were also consistent with the research literature. As Santiago-Rivera, Altarriba, Poll, Gonzalez-Miller, and Cragun (2009) assert, mental health workers who are able to switch between English and Spanish in sessions with Latina/o clients hold an advantage when it comes to creating bonds and strong relationships with their clients. Thus, rather than using the action steps from the MHK Toolkit as a checklist, staff expanded on ways in which they accomplished action items that were applicable to them, often discussing best practices along the way.

As a second illustration, findings from the MHK Toolkit stressed the importance of considering family dynamics and needs in providing services to Latina youth. During the training, staff gave examples of ways that they involved and considered family members in their program services, such as increasing their availability to meet with Latina youth during

TABLE 13.2A. Mi Hermana's Keeper Training Model

Learning Objectives

1. Articulate the experiences and desires of Latina youth in prevention youth justice programs
2. Engage in a dialogue around culturally specific, gender-responsive service and care for Latina youth in prevention and/or intervention programs
3. Apply the recommendations and actions steps to your program and with your Latina youth

TABLE 13.2B. Mi Hermana's Keeper Training Model

Program Staff Action Steps

Before Training	After Training
Read through the full MHK Toolkit	Schedule a team meeting
	Review the practice toolkit template and the notes from the live training
	Create a practice toolkit

times when family members were also available, even if that meant after business hours. In addition, staff described being intentional in identifying and highlighting the strengths not only of the Latina youth but also of their family during interactions. Holding the family as central is reflected in the action step that encourages training "staff to uphold key cultural values with Latino families, such as *familismo*" and is also supported in research on Latino families. Skogrand, Riggs, and Huffaker (2008) specify *familismo*, or family closeness, as a source of strength in many Latino families, suggesting that service providers remain intentional in involving family members in community-based services for Latina youth and continuing to build upon that value. The staff's examples of how they consider the relationship of the family were directly aligned with the needs expressed by both Latina youth and their caregivers in the toolkit.

The initial process of training program staff on the MHK Toolkit took around six hours, with three hours for the in-person exercises and three hours to write up the practice toolkit. Staff also spent additional time reflecting on their opportunities to apply the action steps in their practice toolkit beyond the initial in-person training. This follow-up is also a critical part of using resources like the MHK Toolkit because of the constantly evolving needs of the Latina youth that Southwest Key Programs serves. Cultural adaptations to programs must be sustainable and woven into everyday practice, with frequent revisiting of ideas and approaches.

TABLE 13.2C. Mi Hermana's Keeper Training Model

Training Summary

Provide an introduction and a 5–6 slide PowerPoint overview of the project *(30 minutes)*

Discuss the following questions in relation to each of the nine recommendations *(90 minutes)*
- Which of the MHK recommendations/action steps are you already using in your program?
- What action steps are missing that you are already using in your work or want to use in your work?
- What recommendations/action steps will not work well for your program?

Bring the entire group back together to share the staff's thoughts and ideas followed by a discussion on the practice toolkit more broadly *(60 minutes)*

For a snapshot of the dynamic Southwest Key Programs training model, see Table 13.2a–c.

Conclusion

The next generation of Latina youth is influential. Their contributions will have a significant impact on our nation's future. When systems that are designed to serve these youth fail to do so, it is a disservice both to the individual and to society. It is critical that leaders take time to consider the needs and experiences of Latina youth to create change and more effectively serve this growing population. Failure to invest in the well-being of Latina youth in prevention and intervention programming is a major missed opportunity for our communities. Related to this, more work needs to be done to identify and develop program models and resources that are culturally responsive, gender-specific, and can be integrated into direct practice with Latina youth.

Evidence-based programs have garnered more attention in recent years, yet they are lacking culturally relevant, gender-specific approaches. Service providers must be willing to supplement and individualize programming with available tools to ensure that Latina youth are treated justly and effectively. Resources are necessary but must also be accessible to direct service providers who often have limited funding and time to devote to training and individual reflection on the job. Therefore, there is a clear need for simple tools that can produce immediate results. The MHK Toolkit is seminal and offers an open-access resource that can be tailored to any prevention program model. The toolkit is one way to provide Latina youth the support they need and deserve.

However, there is still much work to be done in advocating for the resilient and powerful women whom the White House Initiative on Educational Excellence for Hispanics (2015b) identified as the "linchpin of the next generation." Despite recent tension around the political support for Latinas/os in the Trump administration, the White House Initiative on Educational Excellence for Hispanics (2015a) has been renewed by all five serving presidents of the United States since its launch in 1990. This suggests a consensus among political leaders that the success of Latinas is vital to the future of the nation. However, with the political climate placing Latinas/os at risk of increased discrimination, continued support for service providers, program administrators, researchers, policy analysts, and key stakeholders is imperative.

Note

1 The Family Keys program is a three-month prevention and intervention program aimed at decreasing the number of youth referred to and engaged in the juvenile justice system. The program model has been recognized by OJJDP as a deinstitutionalization of status offenders (DSO) best practice program and combines wraparound case management, crisis prevention planning and intervention, youth- and family-driven service planning, skills development, and community collaborations and linkages at no cost.

REFERENCES

Arya, N., Villarruel, F., Villanueva, C., & Augarten, I. (2009, May). America's invisible children: Latino youth and the failure of justice. National Criminal Justice Reference Service. www.ncjrs.gov.

Báez, J. C., & Garza, D. R. (2017). Southwest key programs: Mi Hermana's Keeper. Unpublished manuscript. http://www.swkey.org.

Báez, J. C., & Garza, D. R. (2018). Las hermanas on "being heard": Promising practices for Latina youth in juvenile justice prevention programs. Unpublished manuscript.

Báez, J. C., Swan, D., & Garza, D. R. (2017). Southwest key programs: Mi Hermana's Keeper practice toolkit—Family keys. Unpublished manuscript.

Blueprints for Healthy Youth Development. (2018). Resources. www.blueprintsprograms.com.

Chesney-Lind, M., Morash, M., & Stevens, T. (2008). Girls' troubles, girls' delinquency, and gender responsive programming: A review. *Australian & New Zealand Journal of Criminology, 41*, 162–189.

Creswell, J. (2013). *Qualitative inquiry and research design: Choosing among five approaches* (3rd ed). Thousand Oaks, CA: Sage.

Creswell, J. W. (2014). *A concise introduction to mixed methods research.* Thousand Oaks, CA: Sage.
Creswell, J. W., & Guetterman, T. C. (2019). *Educational research: Planning, conducting, and evaluating quantitative and qualitative research* (6th ed.). Saddle River, NJ: Pearson.
Delgado, M. (2007). *Social work with Latinos: A cultural assets paradigm.* New York: Oxford University Press.
Foley, A. (2008). The current state of gender-specific delinquency programming. *Journal of Criminal Justice, 36,* 262–269.
Furman, R., Negi, N. J., Iwamoto, D. K., Rowan, D., Shukraft, A., & Gragg, J. (2009). Social work practice with Latinos: Key issues for social workers. *Social Work, 54,* 167–174.
Henggeler, S. W., & Schoenwald, S. K. (2011). Evidence-based interventions for juvenile offenders and juvenile justice policies that support them (Dataset). Washington, DC: American Psychological Association.
Holleran Steiker, L. K., Castro, F. G., Kumpfer, K., Marsiglia, F. F., Coard, S., & Hopson, L. M. (2008). A dialogue regarding cultural adaptation of interventions. *Journal of Social Work Practice in the Addictions, 8,* 154–162.
Kuckartz, U. (2007). MAXQDA: Qualitative data analysis. Berlin: VERBI Software.
Lee, E. (2010). Revisioning cultural competence in clinical social work practice. *Families in Society, 91,* 272–279.
Lopez, V., & Nuño, L. (2016). Latina and African American girls in the juvenile justice system: Needs, problems, and solutions. *Sociology Compass, 10,* 24–37.
Lopez, V., & Pasko, L. (2017). Bringing Latinas to the forefront: Latina girls, women, and the justice system. *Feminist Criminology, 12,* 195–198.
Marsiglia, F. F., & Booth, J. M. (2015). Cultural adaptation of interventions in real practice settings. *Research on Social Work Practice, 25,* 423–432.
Mihalic, S., Fagan, A., Irwin, K., Ballard, D., & Elliott, D. (2004). Blueprints for violence prevention (NCJ 204274). Washington, DC: Office of Juvenile Justice and Delinquency Prevention.
Morris, M. (2014, June 4). 5 things that a "My Sister's Keeper Initiative" must include. *Ebony.* www.ebony.com.
Obama, B. H. (2014). About My Brother's Keeper initiative. https://obamawhitehouse.archives.gov.
Pantin, H., Prado, G., Lopez, B., Huang, S., Tapia, M. I., Schwartz, S. J., Sabillon, E., Brown, C. H., & Branchini, J. (2009). A randomized controlled trial of Familias Unidas for Hispanic adolescents with behavior problems. *Psychosomatic Medicine, 71,* 987–995.
Pasko, L., & Lopez, V. (2018). The Latina penalty: Juvenile correctional attitudes toward the Latina juvenile offender. *Journal of Ethnicity in Criminal Justice, 16,* 272–291.
Ruiz, E. (2005). Hispanic culture and relational cultural theory. *Journal of Creativity in Mental Health, 1,* 33–55.
Santiago-Rivera, A. L., Altarriba, J., Poll, N., Gonzalez-Miller, N., & Cragun, C. (2009). Therapists' views on working with bilingual Spanish-English speaking

clients: A qualitative investigation. *Professional Psychology: Research and Practice*, 40, 436–443.

Skogrand, L., Riggs, K., & Huffaker, S. (2008). Latino youth participation in community programs. *Journal of Youth Development*, 3, 126–134.

Tongco, M. D. C. (2007). Purposive sampling as a tool for informant selection. *Ethnobotany Research and applications*, 5, 147–158.

White House Initiative on Educational Excellence for Hispanics. (2015a). Fulfilling America's future: Latinas in the U.S., 2015. U.S. Department of Education. https://sites.ed.gov.

White House Initiative on Educational Excellence for Hispanics. (2015b). A national education blueprint: Investing in Hispanics to fulfill America's future. https://obamawhitehouse.archives.gov.

14

Xinachtli

A Healing-Informed, Gendered, and Culturally Responsive Approach with System-Involved Latinas

SARA HASKIE-MENDOZA, JOSEPHINE V. SERRATA, HERIBERTO ESCAMILLA, AND CHRISTIAN JAIMES

Xinachtli encourages self-recognition, accountability, social awareness, self-love, healthy relationships, respect for others, cultural and spiritual development, and allows for the creation of safe spaces. Girls participating in the program will be motivated to continue with their education; be more informed on women's health and human rights; will work through scenarios involving personal boundaries, dating and community violence; and will strengthen the use of their voice. When finished, the young women will have created artwork reflective of their past, present, and future selves. They will graduate from Xinachtli with their heads held high, proud of the work they have accomplished, proud of who they are and where they come from, and proud to now be a part of a wider network of sisters that have completed the curriculum across the country.
—Daniela Macias, Xinachtli program facilitator

Almost all system-involved girls report some form of emotional, physical, or sexual abuse prior to interactions with the juvenile justice system, with over 60 percent of girls reporting trauma before the age of five (Dierkhising et al., 2013). Research examining racial/ethnic differences in trauma exposure among girls in the juvenile

The authors are affiliated with the National Compadres Network.

justice system is both limited and mixed. A large-scale study of female juvenile detainees, for example, found that while few racial/ethnic differences in self-reported victimization existed among white, African American, and Latina female detainees, there were some differences (Abram et al., 2004). While Latina detainees experienced traumatic events at high levels and on par with African American and white female detainees, they reported a significantly higher rate of physical victimization—as measured by "ever been attacked physically, or beaten badly"—than African American girls. Approximately 47 percent of Latina detainees endorsed this item, compared to only 26.7 percent of African American girls. Other research has found that system-involved Latina girls are either just as likely or more likely than white girls to be exposed to multiple forms of victimization (Pasko & Dwight, 2010).

Although feminist scholars have called for more gender and culturally responsive trauma-informed programming for system-involved girls, the majority of contemporary programming continues to focus primarily on gender and interpersonal forms of trauma without looking at the ecosystemic forms of traumas that generations of Latinos and other communities of Color have endured (Chesney-Lind, Morash, & Stevens, 2008; Day, Zahn, & Tichavsky, 2015; Foley, 2008). Examples of ecosystemic trauma include both directly experienced and intergenerational effects of racism and sexism (Goodman, 2015). Such systemic root causes have been left out of traditional programming discourse to avoid naming our nation's painful history of white supremacy and gender domination that, to this day, persists and is embedded in our institutions, including educational, health, and law enforcement delivery systems. Scholarship has shown that for Latina girls, intervention and programming must center healing the devastating effects of the trauma created by systems of oppression and center cultural realities in healing frameworks (Haskie-Mendoza, Tinajero, Cervantes, Rodriguez, & Serrata, 2018). Such an approach "asks that we consider trauma as the direct result of systemic forces (e.g., heterosexism, racism, discrimination), as well as transgressional systems of oppression (e.g., children of those who have experienced racism)" (Karcher, 2017, p. 123). As we have seen in other chapters in this volume, Latina girls and women endure high rates of both interpersonal and systemic traumas.

Trauma-informed frameworks for responding to the needs of individuals in juvenile justice have pushed for an understanding of the impact of trauma and healing in the context of system involvement (Olafson et al., 2018). Critical race and culturally responsive frameworks call for increased understanding and responses to the unique experiences of trauma and oppression for adolescent youth of Color, especially adolescent girls (Crosby, 2016; Lopez & Nuno, 2016). These frameworks coupled with decades of practice-based expertise lend evidence for approaches that center both gender and culture when working with Latina girls in the juvenile justice system. This chapter describes such a program. Rooted in a racial justice, anti-oppression framework, Xinachtli (germinating seed) is a gender and culturally responsive rites of passage philosophy and curriculum that promotes healing, resilience, and leadership capacity of Latina and Indigenous girls. In this chapter, we provide a description of Xinachtli's development and content, a presentation of process data in the form of a program facilitator's reflections and observations, and a discussion of preliminary evaluation data. In doing so, we join other feminist researchers and practitioners in the call for more trauma-informed programming to better meet the needs of girls of Color in the juvenile justice system.

Xinachtli: Promoting Healing through Culture

The Xinachtli (germinating seed) curriculum is a cultural and gender-responsive "rites of passage" program that was developed by the first author. The original *chispa* (spark) for the Xinachtli curriculum occurred in 1996, during the first author's community work with community-based organizations in the Boyle Heights community of East Los Angeles. Implementation of the earliest version of the current curriculum was through the Los Angeles Indigenous People's Alliance (LAIPA) with funding from the California Wellness Foundation. In 2000, the original version was created and implemented with eleven teen girls ages fourteen to eighteen. The inaugural group created the logo for the curriculum/program. For the next eleven years, Xinachtli was implemented with previously system-involved girls and high school teens in local continuation schools and city recreation centers in Northeast Los

Angeles. International human rights work, conducted by the first author, influenced the social justice framework, guiding the meaningful service component of the curriculum.

Xinachtli is currently located and administered within the culturally rooted and healing-informed organization National Compadres Network (NCN). NCN recognizes the value of cultivating the capacity of those who are most impacted by systemic inequities as they are the closest to the solution. In doing so, NCN supports interested communities and organizations to fill the significant gap in culturally competent services to families and communities of Color. NCN strives to strengthen, rebalance, and redevelop the traditional "Comadre/Compadre" or extended family system of Chicanas/os, Latinas/os, and Indigenous Latinos.[1]

At the foundation of all NCN's work is an ideology that builds on Indigenous practices, which involves incorporating culturally grounded physical, emotional, mental, and spiritual principles and practices referred to as la cultura cura (LCC), or culture-based healing (see Myers et al., 2005, for more on Indigenous healing practices). The core tenet of LCC is an understanding that within Latina/o individuals, families, and communities exist cultural values, traditions, and Indigenous practices that promote natural pathways toward healthy development, community safety, and lifelong well-being (Tello & Acosta, 2012). LCC employs a multigenerational process of learning and/or remembering one's true and positive cultural values, principles, customs, and traditions. NCN's programming, including Xinachtli, reflects this cultural healing philosophy.

While a thorough discussion of the Xinachtli philosophy and its foundation in an Indigenous worldview is beyond the scope of this chapter, it is important to note that the curriculum is embedded in what Native Americans call the Medicine Wheel, a powerful symbol that embodies relationships, interconnectedness, and growth (see McCabe, 2008, and Twigg & Hengen, 2009, for more information on how the Medicine Wheel can be used in counseling and healing). Consistent with its focus on relationships, interconnectedness, and growth, one of the central objectives of Xinachtli is the development of *palabra*. This term literally translates to "word" in English and conceptually refers to something similar to integrity.

Xinachtli: Description

Curriculum Structure

The Xinachtli curriculum consists of sixteen modules or sessions. Xinachtli sessions are approximately two hours long. Experienced facilitators may be able to implement a module over two shorter sessions, but this is not recommended. Girls cannot participate if they are under the influence of alcohol or other mind-altering drugs. *Respeto* (respect) is a vitally important concept in the Xinachtli curriculum. Attendance at eleven of fourteen *círculo* sessions is required for formal graduation. The ideal size of the Xinachtli círculo is twelve participants, but no more than fifteen. Even with a cofacilitator, we have found it very challenging to effectively devote the necessary time and attention to more than fifteen girls. Consistent with gender-responsive programming recommendations, we find that smaller groups also foster connections, trust, and confidence among girls (Kerig & Schindler, 2013).

During the first session of Xinachtli, parents or other guardians are included and provided with an orientation to the program. The orientation is not only informative but also participatory in that parents actually go through the experience of an actual círculo. This session is very important in terms of buy-in. The young women who have the support and encouragement of parents or guardians are more likely to complete the program.

Sessions 2 to 15 of the Xinachtli program typically begin with a *conocimiento*, or check-in time, during which participants share something personal about themselves (e.g., a significant event in their lives). This is done in a círculo so that the young women face each other. As they become more comfortable and confident, the extent of their sharing becomes deeper and more heartfelt. Each session focuses on trust, relationship building, and working with participants to develop a sense of belonging. The *enseñanza* or teaching anchors each session around important aspects of daily life such as relationships, family life, and progress at school. Participants learn important LCC concepts such as trust, dignity, integrity, and respect. Each session also includes a kinesthetic component, which involves creating an artistic project that represents the session's lessons/teachings. These *manualidades* or creations reinforce the teaching.[2] For example, in the session that talks about masks, participants create their own masks. Each session concludes with the *comparto* or sharing. During this time, participants share how they felt about that particular session. Similar to the conocimiento, the depth of exploration and sharing increases with time and practice.

The last session is a celebration of accomplishment. The actual celebration may be as simple as handing out certificates of completion to more formal ceremonies. Ideally, it includes parents, relatives, and other significant people who help validate and support the participants' transition into adulthood. Some program facilitators provide necklaces, bracelets, or other symbols of accomplishment. Others construct actual bridges across which the girls walk. It is important that there be some kind of community recognition of the accomplishment.

Curriculum Content

Through participation in Xinachtli, participants learn to clear away myths, stereotypes, and misconceptions about gender and ethnicity to discover their own values and identity. During the earlier sessions, the young women take ownership of the círculo, learn about "asking permission," not as an indication of submission but as an acknowledgment that they occupy space and have a relationship with people around them. Participants discover and exercise their own creativity in applying themselves. In later sessions, participants raise their awareness to a higher purpose related to interconnectedness and community service. In the final sessions of Xinachtli, the participants finalize and implement a community action plan designed to address a social justice issue. The Xinachtli program uses very basic cultural anchors to "reorient" young women. It helps them to remember and reinforce their reference points, their values, and what is important to them in their lives.

Critical Pedagogy

A key component of Xinachtli is its inclusion of critical pedagogy—an understanding of oppressive social conditions to empower girls to become social justice change agents. Specifically, as noted by Thomas, Davidson, and McAdoo (2008, p. 290), critical pedagogy "focuses on the development of critical consciousness that enables learners to recognize connections among their individual problems and the experiences and social contexts in which they are embedded." The hope is that participants or learners can then build upon this knowledge to transform oppressive societal structures and conditions. For example, one recent community project focused on Xinachtli participants working with program facilitators to examine the perceived impact of race and gender on Latinas in the juvenile justice system. The youth participants conducted focus groups with other system-impacted Latina youth to learn about their perceptions of biased treatment, their interactions with juvenile justice professionals, and their recommendations for ways the juvenile justice system could better meet the needs of Latina girls (Haskie-Mendoza et al., 2018).

Facilitating Xinachtli

We believe that any adult or elder woman can serve as a Xinachtli facilitator, as long as she exhibits the *ganas* (spirit, desire, and willingness) to do so. The primary characteristic of a Xinachtli facilitator is a deep sense of self-awareness and the capacity to learn—to change their perceptions, understanding, and delivery. The facilitator training process begins with a three-day, highly participatory experience. Active facilitators are expected to have a strong commitment to their integrity. In other words, they should live by the principles and values they seek to instill in the young women. They are encouraged to participate in their own self-discovery through therapy, self-help groups, or some other activity that promotes self-care and growth. We define an experienced facilitator as one who has been trained and certified and has implemented Xinachtli círculos for at least three years.

We believe that facilitators for Xinachtli should be adult women with backgrounds similar to the young women in the círculo that they are working with. When working with system-involved girls, we find most success when facilitators have things in common with the girls. Previously incarcerated women with a deep sense of meaningful service have been successful in implementing Xinachtli. For maximum effectiveness, we strongly recommend cofacilitation for Xinachtli. True kinship is developed in trusting spaces. This modeling allows the girls to see a real example of what it looks like when two women can respectfully share space and be supportive of each other. Such modeling is also key to gender-responsive programming (Kerig & Schindler, 2013). The building of trust is foundational to the success of Xinachtli, and the facilitators play an instrumental role in the success of the program (Haskie-Mendoza et al., 2018).

A Facilitator's Reflections and Observations

The lived experiences of Xinachtli facilitators are central to their ability to facilitate Xinachtli and the development of an environment of trust and respect in order for young Latina participants to engage in healing and change. This reflection serves to highlight the unique experience of Xinachtli facilitators. Christian Jaimes, a thirty-two-year-old Mexican American woman, reflects on her experience of facilitating Xinachtli in a juvenile justice facility. Christian has facilitated Xinachtli for two and a half years in the southern region of Santa Barbara County. In the following excerpt, she describes the first time she facilitated a Xinachtli group with a new group of girls.

> It was late August and the meeting room felt stuffy and a bit warm. It was much hotter than expected when filled with teenage girls, their after-school attitudes, and heavy eye-rolling. This group of girls had been mandated to attend this group as part of their disciplinary action plan. They were expected to attend all sessions, arrive on time, listen to an adult they didn't trust, and share stories with girls they didn't roll with in a location they associated with punishment. Needless to say, this was not the perfect start, but it was in fact, a start.

Christian then described how an important part of Xinachtli is to help girls uncover the "masks" that system-involved young women often wear to hide their "true selves." Key to this unmasking is developing trust-based relationships that focus on girls' strengths. Still, as Christian noted, it can be quite challenging for young women with histories of trauma and fractured relationships to develop these types of trust-based relationships.

> I believe that one of the most challenging hurtles to overcome throughout the Xinachtli process and working with girls who have been incarcerated

or are involved in the juvenile justice system is the lack of trust the young girls have with adults. When they walk into group, they are walking in with not only seven generations of their great grandmothers' and mothers' burdens, but also with a preconceived and valid notion that they are not welcomed as they are. Xinachtli is unique in that before we begin our strength-based character-development teachings, we dive deep into discovering and revealing the girls' vulnerable, true selves. Because they see us, the adult, being vulnerable, they too can let down their guard. This is where the mascaras break down and the healing begins, and it is in this state that we see the shift in the dynamics of the group, from a punitive place to a safe and trusting space that allows for the healing to begin.

Still, as Christian noted, this transformative process "does not happen overnight," nor does it always happen, as illustrated in the following reflection.

> It was not a surprise to me when all the young women trickled in and were guarded, especially a young girl who sat in complete silence, who looked clocked out and ready to fight at the same time, I will call her Brenda. As my cofacilitator and I began to explain the process, direction, and first session of Xinachtli, Brenda slouched back in defiance and seemed irritated at the whole process. I made two observations that day that would later impact the group dynamics: (1) Brenda was stoic (throughout the session) and the first one out the door; and (2) there was a "shot caller" in the group who I will call Luna. She definitely had influence over the other three young women in the group.

After four weeks of facilitating Xinachtli, Christian noted, "the group was getting more comfortable with each other with the exception of Luna." Ultimately, to the dismay of Christian, Luna did not continue with the program due to her removal by the Probation Department. Reflecting on this removal, Christian noted,

> If there is one lesson that I have continually looked to for direction from our Xinachtli and LCC teachings, is that as facilitators we are here to plant seeds and provide a space for self-reflection and healing; however, some people, and many youth are not in the frame of mind to receive,

much less harvest those seeds. Luna's words and actions in our Xinachtli group reflected what she could not verbally express: She was battling many problems on all fronts, and she was not able to take in the lessons at that point in her journey. Probation decided it would be best if Luna was reassigned a new disciplinary action plan.

Brenda, on the other hand, ultimately began to share more in group and became an active participant: "Brenda was able to share much more of herself, which forced her to reexamine the relationship with her mother and estranged father. She also shared that she connected to the Indigenous approach of Xinachtli because her family is Native American and practices the custom and tradition of circle gathering and was able to find comfort in this process." Christian also noted that there were "many small and big breakthroughs among the young women" who participated in that first Xinachtli group. Reflecting specifically on Brenda's experience, she shared,

> Brenda went on to be successfully terminated from probation. She completed her probation requirements and was able to participate in the probation graduation and also the Xinachtli Young Women's Ceremony, where we ask the young girls who have completed the program to recommit their palabra and integrity to their selves, each other, and to all their relations with their family, friends, and partners. Through the platicas, lessons, and resources Xinachtli brings forth, Brenda's beautiful journey is one example of how Xinachtli ultimately creates a place for positive change to manifest within the self and, in turn, within the community.

Xinachtli: Creating Change
Preliminary Outcome Data

While the Xinachtli program has been recognized as an effective community-based program for the past two decades, formal attempts to document and reinforce program fidelity and assess effectiveness began in late 2016. We recently implemented a one-group, pretest/posttest pre-experimental design to examine changes in attitudes and behaviors related to program participation. The self-report questionnaire used for the pretest/posttest was developed with input from program staff. The questions were formatted into open-ended, multiple-choice, and four-point Likert-scaled items. Xinachtli participants were asked to self-report on behaviors and attitudes over the past two weeks prior to instrument administration and immediately posttest. Although preliminary, data analysis to date provides some promising results.

In 2017, we collected a total of forty-two matching pre-post questionnaires from Xinachtli círculos in Denver, Santa Barbara, and Salinas, California. Young women in the sample ranged in age from 12 to 19, with an average age of 14.87. All of the girls self-identified as Latina or of more than one ethnic/cultural group that included Latinos. Fewer than half of the sample (42.5 percent) lived in intact homes with both biological parents. The remaining 57.5 percent were from blended, single-parent, or some other household structure. Approximately 20 percent of the young women were involved with the juvenile justice system.

Chi-square analysis was used to test the significance of nonparametric data, while repeated measures t-tests were used to examine pre-post differences for all scaled items. Pre-post data were compared for the following variables: importance of ethnic identity, attitudes and behaviors related to caring relationships, and attitudes and behaviors related to resiliency and self-care. We also compared pre-post differences concerning the importance of community connection and the overall importance of Xinachtli in program participants' lives. Table 14.1 presents these differences, which are discussed below.

Importance of Ethnic Identity

A critical component of the Xinachtli curriculum is developing and nurturing positive ethnic identity development. Comparing participants' responses to items regarding their ethnic identity, one can see how participants grew in regard to their attitudes about the importance of ethnic identity development. There was a statistically significant increase in the importance that the young women ascribed to their ethnic identity before and after the program. While not statistically significant, there was also a pronounced decrease in the frequency that participants thought about belonging to another ethnic group,

TABLE 14.1. Pre-Post Comparisons

	Pretest Mean Score	Posttest Mean Score	Significance
Importance of ethnic identity	2.43	3.62	***
Thought about belonging to another ethnicity	2.62	2.14	N.S.
Know people to depend on	2.86	3.67	***
Know special person that cares	2.95	3.67	***
Get along with others	2.70	3.43	***
Being a friend is important	3.05	3.60	**
Know how to care for self	3.09	3.57	**
Can handle pressure	2.71	3.24	***
Comfortable asking for help	2.62	3.43	***
Express self-confidence	2.62	3.52	***
People can make the community better	3.05	3.57	**
Need to be involved in positive activities	2.90	3.52	**
How much did you learn from Xinachtli?	2.67	3.81	***

Note: N.S. = not significant.
**$p < .01$. ***$p < .001$.

indicating that after the program, participants compared their own ethnic group to others less.

Attitudes and Behaviors Related to Caring Relationships

Participants were asked to indicate how much they agreed with each of the following items: (1) know people to depend on, (2) know a special person that cares, (3) get along with others, and (4) being a friend is important. There were significant positive differences across all four items from pre- to posttest.

Attitudes and Behaviors Related to Resiliency and Self-Care

Participants were asked to indicate how much they agreed with each of the following items: (1) know how to care for self, (2) can handle pressure, (3) comfortable asking for help, and (4) express self with confidence. There were significant positive differences from pre- to posttest for all four items.

Importance of Community Connection

As indicated earlier, one of the "products" of the Xinachtli curriculum is a community action project that connects the young women's experience in Xinachtli with the broader community. In accordance with the project, we saw corresponding changes in the participants' attitudes regarding community connection. This is an important finding, as it indicates that Xinachtli participants became more connected with their communities and more confident in their own ability to create change.

Importance of Xinachtli

Important to our program is to hear from participants about their expectations of the program, where we can improve, and where we can grow. We asked participants to tell us how participation in Xinachtli had influenced their lives. The response rates for open-ended questions, especially for long questionnaires such as this one, typically are not very high. Nonetheless, eighteen of the forty-two participants (42.8 percent) told us how Xinachtli had influenced their lives. A few of these responses are presented below:

> I have better friendships, me and my dad are getting along better, teachers [are] easier [to get] along with because I have palabra and walk away when they piss me off.

> I learned about my culture and my ancestors and to honor my relations even though I am having a bad day.

> Realize that what I do affects people around me. Take all relationships more seriously.

The findings of our evaluation match anecdotal evidence that we have collected over the past two decades on the positive impact that the Xinachtli program has for its participants. These results are especially important in the context of working with system-involved Latinas who face multiple risk factors (e.g., low academic achievement, substance abuse). The program shows promising potential in curtailing the added layer of risks for system-involved Latinas while promoting protective factors, such as positive ethnic identity, resilience, positive self-care, and increased community connection.

Conclusion

Despite multiple calls for culturally and gender-responsive programming for system-involved girls, few such programs exist. Instead, most gender-responsive programs focus only on gender (Chesney-Lind et al., 2008; Day et al., 2015; Foley, 2008). Xinachtli is unique because it focuses on both gender and culture to address the needs of system-involved Latina and Indigenous girls. In doing so, Xinachtli acknowledges both the interpersonal and the intergenerational ecosystemic traumas that these young women face. Consistent with gender-responsive tenets, Xinachtli focuses on relationships and social connections (Kerig & Schindler, 2013), but goes one step further to also consider participants' interconnectedness with their communities.

Unlike programs that focus primarily on individual and family-level changes, Xinachtli adopts a critical pedagogical approach to raising participants' critical consciousness. Consistent with this goal, program participants undertake a community action project. As mentioned earlier, one such project employed a youth participatory action research approach to provide system-involved Latinas with the opportunity to develop their own project related to addressing the specific needs of other Latina girls in the juvenile justice system (Haskie-Mendoza et al., 2018). Our commitment to such projects stems from our beliefs that changing current oppressive policies and practices in various systems, including juvenile justice, will not come about without Latinas who are directly impacted sitting in their rightful place at the decision-making table. We further believe that to participate, system-involved Latinas need to have not only strong but also healthy and balanced voices—voices that come from hearts that are solidly connected to the families and communities they speak for or represent. They should be "rooted" and "oriented" in the healthy values of that culture and not myths and misconceptions promoted by the dominant culture. In order for this to happen, system-impacted Latinas should be engaged in programming that is rooted in a racial justice, anti-oppression framework that is gender responsive and culturally responsive.

As our preliminary evaluation data indicate, Xinachtli is well received and catches the interest of young Latinas. Latinas who participate in the program exhibit important changes in both attitudes and behaviors. They also demonstrate appreciation for their place among peers and a belief that they can contribute to their communities and make a difference, a finding that has promise for larger community-level change. Nevertheless, it is important to note that while our preliminary results are promising, we acknowledge the limitations of our pre-experimental design with a short-term follow-up. A longer-term follow-up is needed to determine whether changes associated with program participation dissipate over time. It also would be ideal to compare Xinachtli with a comparison or randomized control group to determine the program's effectiveness (Foley, 2008). Still, we believe that programs such as Xinachtli are critically important because they respond to the loud outcry from academic researchers and practitioners looking for community-based programming that centers cultural and gender understandings of system involvement and responds to the unique experiences of trauma and oppression for Latina teens (Crosby, 2016; Lopez & Nuno, 2016).

NOTES
1. Chicana/o refers to the chosen identity of a Mexican American person who values a social-political identity and Indigenous diaspora. The spiritual homeland of Chicanas/os is Aztlan. Latina/o refers to an individual with roots in Latin America. Even though many who identify as Latina/o have direct Indigenous roots, they choose to discard an Indigenous identity and use a broader term to identify their Latin American roots.
2. *Manualidad* is derived from the Spanish word for "hand." To Indigenous Mesoamericans the hand is a very important limb. When referring to a person's skills, we say he or she has a good hand for planting, healing, and so on. The hands manifest or make real dreams that originate in the heart. The *manualidades* (crafts) that the girls produce are very important for personal development.

REFERENCES

Abram, K. M., Teplin, L. A., Charles, D. R., Longworth, S. L., McClelland, G. M., & Dulcan, M. K. (2004). Posttraumatic stress disorder and trauma in youth in juvenile detention. *Archives of General Psychiatry, 61*, 403–410.

Chesney-Lind, M., Morash, M., & Stevens, T. (2008). Girls troubles, girls' delinquency, and gender responsive programming: A review. *Australian & New Zealand Journal of Criminology, 41*, 162–189.

Crosby, S. D. (2016). Trauma-informed approaches to juvenile justice: A critical race perspective. *Juvenile and Family Court Journal, 67*, 5–18.

Day, J. C., Zahn, M. A., & Tichavsky, L. P. (2015). What works for whom? The effects of gender responsive programming on girls and boys in secure detention. *Journal of Research in Crime and Delinquency, 52*, 93–129.

Dierkhising, C. B., Ko, S. J., Woods-Jaeger, B., Briggs, E. C., Lee, R., & Pynoos, R. S. (2013). Trauma histories among justice-involved youth: Findings from the National Child Traumatic Stress Network. *European Journal of Psychotraumatology, 4*. https://doi.org/10.3402/ejpt.v4i0.20274.

Foley, A. (2008). The current state of gender-specific delinquency programming. *Journal of Criminal Justice, 36*, 262–269.

Goodman, R. (2015). A liberatory approach to trauma counseling: Decolonizing our trauma-informed practices. In R. Goodman & P. Gorski (Eds.), *Decolonizing "multicultural" counseling through social justice* (pp. 55–72). New York: Springer.

Haskie-Mendoza, S., Tinajero, L., Cervantes, A., Rodriguez, J., & Serrata, J. V. (2018). Conducting youth participatory action research through a healing-informed approach with system-involved Latinas, *Journal of Family Violence, 33*, 605–612.

Karcher, O. P. (2017). Sociopolitical oppression, trauma, and healing: Moving toward a social justice art therapy framework. *Art Therapy, 34*, 123–128.

Kerig, P. K., & Schindler, S. R. (2013). Engendering the evidence base: A critical review of the conceptual and empirical foundations of gender-responsive interventions for girls' delinquency. *Laws, 2*, 244–282.

Lopez, V., & Nuno, L. (2016). Latina and African American girls in the juvenile justice system: Needs, problems, and solutions. *Sociology Compass, 10*, 24–37.

McCabe, G. (2008). Mind, body, emotions and spirit: Reaching to the ancestors for healing. *Counseling Psychology Quarterly, 21*, 143–152.

Myers, L .J., Obasi, E. M., Jefferson, M., Anderson, M., Godfrey, T., & Purnell, J. (2005). Building multicultural competence around Indigenous healing practices. In M. G. Constantine & D. W. Sue (Eds.), *Strategies for building multicultural competence in mental health and educational settings* (pp. 109–128). Hoboken, NJ: John Wiley.

Olafson, E., Boat, B. W., Putnam, K. T., Thieken, L., Marrow, M. T., & Putnam, F. W. (2018). Implementing trauma and grief component therapy for adolescents and think trauma for traumatized youth in secure juvenile justice settings. *Journal of Interpersonal Violence, 33*, 2537–2557.

Pasko, L., & Dwight, L. (2010). *Understanding and responding to female juvenile offenders in Colorado*. Denver: Colorado Division of Criminal Justice.

Tello, J., & Acosta, F. (2012). Lifting Latinos up by their "root-straps": Moving beyond trauma through a healing-informed model to engage Latino men. National Compadres Network. www.nationalcompadresnetwork.org.

Thomas, O., Davidson, W., & McAdoo, H. (2008). An evaluation study of the Young Empowered Sisters (YES!) program: Promoting cultural assets among African American adolescent girls through a culturally relevant school-based intervention. *Journal of Black Psychology, 34*, 281–308.

Twigg, R. C., & Hengen, T. (2009). Going back to the roots: Using the medicine wheel in the healing process. *First Peoples Child & Family Review, 4*, 10–19.

Conclusion

VERA LOPEZ AND LISA PASKO

My blood, the very substance that pumps through my veins every day, keeping me alive, is just like family. It was there in the beginning, and it will be in the end. So, I've learned to love it and cherish it in my heart because without it, you can't live.
—Liana, system-impacted fifteen-year-old, on her reflections of "being Latina"

Latinas in the Criminal Justice System is a book reflective of our commitment to bring the experiences of system-impacted Latinas to the forefront of feminist criminological research. Employing different methodologies, every chapter in this volume is dedicated to understanding how Latinas experience victimization and the juvenile justice, criminal justice, and immigration systems. All too often, policy makers, scholars, and practitioners have ignored the needs of Latina women and girls and rendered their presence invisible. We believe that ignoring system-impacted Latina girls and women does a disservice to the many who are caught up in one or more of the various interlocking justice systems.

A central theme running through many of the chapters in this volume is the conflicted relationship between the various justice systems and Latino communities in the United States. Many of the Latina women whose stories are presented in this volume did not trust police officers, probation officers, and other state actors even when they were victims in need of support. This distrust is not surprising given that the U.S. criminal justice system has inflicted grave harms on Latinos. The war on drugs, for example, had a devastating impact on Latinos (Díaz-Cotto, 2000, 2005, 2006). Gang surveillance ordinances have likewise disproportionately impacted Latinos (Durán, 2009; Rios, 2007). Today, the war on immigration demonizes and criminalizes Mexican and Central American immigrants. Both of these so-called wars position Latinas/os as deviant "others" in need of heightened surveillance, control, and punishment. Politicians and conservative political pundits fuel this rhetoric, even in the absence of supportive empirical data, and the media give them a platform to air these views. These negative social constructions of Latinas/os are then used to rationalize punitive policies and social control practices that further criminalize Latinas/os. Not surprisingly, certain entities and corporations financially benefit from the surveillance, detention, and incarceration of Brown and Black bodies (Urbina & Peña, 2019). Yet the very people whose lives are sacrificed in the name of justice rarely have a forum to share their voices and interpretations of their experiences, without being reduced to ethnic stereotypes of hypersexual, entitled, culturally parasitic criminals (see Pasko & Lopez, 2018).

In this volume, our goal was to share how these larger so-called wars against Latinas/os have impacted the lives of Latina women. In heartbreaking detail, the chapters in this volume demonstrate that who is constructed as a victim versus an offender is often based on gender, ethnicity, class, nationality, and past histories of drug use and gang affiliations. Such thinking can potentially impact how decision makers respond to Latinas. In the juvenile justice system, for example, decision makers relying on negative social constructions and stereotypes of Latina girls run the risk of further criminalizing them. Such views have real-world consequences for system-involved Latina girls, as powerfully illustrated by the words of one juvenile judge from one of our earlier publications:

> I know we are particularly harsh on Hispanic girls. Not just the assumptions . . . but without alternatives for them, without having a proper placement or even knowing the full extent of what is going on with them . . . it's tough. I do feel like they just sit in detention way more than the Caucasian girls I send [to detention]. I feel like I get more of the story from the Caucasian girls. I also feel like Caucasian girls have more medical and psychiatric problems, whereas Hispanic girls . . . I see more family problems, young families . . . gangs, drugs . . . cannot send that to treatment. That requires more security. (juvenile court judge, Pasko & Lopez, 2018, p. 286)

The chapters in this volume also illustrate why many Latinas are hesitant to call upon state actors even when they are clearly victims of intimate partner violence. Again, intersecting identities and histories of oppression play a role. As we saw in the chapter by Vega, Durfee, and Messing, many women, particularly those who are undocumented, fear calling law enforcement for a number of reasons, including fear of deportation, which is not an unfounded fear given the overlap between the criminal justice and immigration systems in the United States (see Menjívar et al. and Dingeman and Rosales chapters in this volume.) Yet even Latina women who have been in the United States for many generations are reluctant to call upon law enforcement due to intergenerational histories with law enforcement. Such reluctance to call law enforcement was certainly the case for the young Mexican American women growing up in San Antonio whose life histories were presented in the chapter by Cepeda and colleagues in this volume.

Even when Latinas are involved in the commission of crimes, their roles are often gendered, as we saw in Sanchez's chapter on female human smugglers. These women, as Sanchez notes, are not hardened criminals, but rather young women struggling to survive by acting as decoys, drivers, and cooks. As further illustrated by Adriana's story in Martha Escobar's chapter, Latina women continue to play subordinate roles to men when it comes to the commission of crime (see also Díaz-Cotto, 2005). That is, contrary to popular images of gang-involved criminals.

Because this book is a project of social justice, we end it with a call to action. In order to address the many issues system-involved Latinas face, multilevel interventions are needed that address Latinas' intersecting social identities. How do we do this? First, we must recognize that certain private and political parties benefit from the prison-industrial complex as well as the treatment-industrial complex that profit from the surveillance, detainment, and incarceration of Black and Brown bodies (Urbina & Peña, 2019). Second, understanding how these same parties benefit from the immigration-industrial complex is necessary. Third, grassroots efforts are needed to advocate on behalf of system-impacted Latinas. In short, we advocate for a shift in social consciousness in terms of how key stakeholders responsible for policy and practice decisions think about system-involved Latinas. Understanding how and why Latinas become entrenched within the various justice systems is necessary for true reform that moves beyond pathologizing individuals, families, and cultures. Instead, state- and institutional-level reforms are needed.

In an era of "fake news," we echo the chorus of scholars, activists, and community members who call for the better collection of county, state, and national data that account for gender, ethnicity, and nationality (Eppler-Epstein, Gurvis, & King, 2016; Villarruel et al., 2002). Such data are needed to create and develop data-informed policies and practices. At the policy level, we recommend decriminalizing Latina girls' and women's survival-related behaviors, including drug use, sex work, and immigration-related offenses. Resources should be allocated toward education and treatment and community-based caring approaches, as opposed to punitive practices such as detention and incarceration. This includes more humane approaches in the immigration system that take into account the past traumas many of these women have faced in their countries as well as current trauma experienced when policies separate them from their children at our borders.

Consistent with the Mi Hermana's Keeper Toolkit, which was presented in the Swan et al. chapter of this volume, we argue that such programs should build upon Latinas' cultural strengths and not be deficit focused. Thus, in line with Veronica Cano (see chapter 12), we believe that programs targeting system-impacted Latinas should focus on strengthening their racial and ethnic identities. Xinachtli, presented in chapter 14, is a powerful example of what can happen when programs are both gender and culturally responsive to the needs of Latinas. We saw firsthand in chapter 11 how Lupe identified her participation in such a program as "life changing."

While programs such as Xinachtli are exemplars of the transformative work that is being done in our communities, they do not yet meet the standard stamp of approval designating them as "evidence-based." Yet what they do demonstrate is that community members are already doing the work needed to transform the lives of system-impacted Latinas and their communities. As researchers entrenched in the academic domain, we need to take a step back and learn from our community partners and collaboratively work with them to test the many promising programs already in place to meet the needs of system-impacted youth. Of course, this requires trust on both sides, but we believe that such partnerships can be established and support the development of more funding opportunities dedicated to researcher-practitioner collaborations. If programming is to "speak" to Latina girls and women in trouble with the law, it must embrace them from the start.

Building upon Vega and colleagues' work presented in chapter 1, we also advocate for the development of gender and culturally responsive outreach and intervention efforts for Latina victims of intimate partner violence. As discussed by Vega et al., promotora programs represent a promising approach that builds upon Latinas' already existing network of comadres. Such efforts can complement existing formal services already present in the nonprofit sector.

Although we covered many topics related to Latinas' experiences with the various U.S. justice systems, more research is needed to address existing gaps. One notable gap, even in this volume, is the dearth of research on the collateral consequences to work, family, and education that many system-impacted Latinas experience as well as a focus on Latina women on probation, in prison, and on parole. Additionally, more work on Latinas from other ethnic groups and regions is needed to complement what we already know about Mexican-origin and Central American Latinas whose stories were presented in this volume. In our current era of aggressive anti-immigration enforcement, health and economic crises, and protests on police brutality and lethal force, we cannot forget the Latina girls and women who are once again barely visible in media representations and academic analyses. Last, we recommend that future researchers adopt a feminist intersectional approach to truly bring the lives and experiences of Latinas to the forefront of criminological research and to create effective policy for girls and women like Liana and the many Latinas we met in this volume. We end with the words of Juanita Díaz-Cotto (2006, p. 301):

> While some say it is useless to dream of reforms, much less wide-spread structural changes, others guide our actions by just such dreams.... Each one of us has to be willing to change ourselves for the better and join others committed to changing oppressive conditions. There are solutions; the question is, are we willing to work toward them?

REFERENCES

Díaz-Cotto, J. (2000). The criminal justice system and its impact on Latinas (os) in the United States. *Criminal Justice Studies*, 13(1), 49–67.

Díaz-Cotto, J. (2005). Latinas and the war on drugs in the United States, Latin America, and Europe. In J. Sudbury (Ed.), *Global lockdown: Race, gender, and the prison-industrial complex* (pp. 137–154). New York: Routledge.

Díaz-Cotto, J. (2006). *Chicana lives and criminal justice: Voices from el barrio*. Austin: University of Texas Press.

Durán, R. J. (2009). Legitimated oppression: Inner-city Mexican American experiences with police gang enforcement. *Journal of Contemporary Ethnography, 38*, 143–168.

Eppler-Epstein, S., Gurvis, A., & King, R. (2016). *The alarming lack of data on Latinos in the criminal justice system*. Washington, DC: Urban Institute.

Pasko, L., & Lopez, V. (2018). The Latina penalty: Juvenile correctional attitudes toward the Latina juvenile offender. *Journal of Ethnicity in Criminal Justice, 16*, 272–291.

Rios, V. M. (2007). The hypercriminalization of Black and Latino male youth in the era of mass incarceration. In M. Marable, K. Middlemass, & I. Steinberg (Eds.), *Racializing justice, disenfranchising lives* (pp. 17–33). New York: Palgrave Macmillan.

Swavola, E., Riley, K., & Subramanian, R. (2016). *Overlooked: Women and jails in an era of reform*. New York: Vera Institute of Justice.

Urbina, M. G., & Peña, I. A. (2019). Crimmigration and militarization: Policing borders in the era of social control profitability. *Sociology Compass, 13*, e12654.

Villarruel, F. A., Walker, N. E., Minifree, P., Vazquez, O. R., Peterson, S., & Perry, K. (2002). Donde esta la justicia? A call to action on behalf of Latino and Latina youth in the US juvenile system. East Lansing: Michigan State University, Institute for Children, Youth, and Families.

ABOUT THE CONTRIBUTORS

ARIANA OCHOA CAMACHO specializes on the intersections of gender, race, migration, and nationalism in the United States. She has published her work in *Feminist Criminology, Feminist Media Studies, Emerging Perspectives in Health Communication*, and *Progress in Community Health Partnerships: Research, Education, and Action* and has been published by Demeter Press. She has also collaborated with visual artists to produce a video, "Elizabeth's Story," now housed at the National Museum of Mexican Art. She holds a doctorate and MPhil degree in American Studies from New York University and also earned an MA in Communication Studies from San Francisco State University. An Assistant Professor, she teaches gender and Latino studies at the University of Washington, Tacoma.

VERONICA E. CANO is Assistant Professor in the Law and Justice Department at Central Washington University, where she has been a faculty member since 2017. She completed her PhD at the University of Sheffield in the United Kingdom. In addition to her doctorate, she holds an MA in social work from Arizona State University and two undergraduate degrees, in sociology (BA) and physiology (BS), from the University of Arizona. Her research interests include youth justice, Latin American culture, gender, and comparative research with a focus on intersectionality. Her research has focused on exploring the impact of ethnic identity on risk-taking behaviors among Latina youth in the United States and United Kingdom.

ALICE CEPEDA is Associate Professor in the School of Social Work at the University of Southern California. She received her doctoral degree in sociology from the City University of New York, Graduate Center. Her work focuses on the social epidemiology of drug use and the related health risk behaviors that disproportionately affect urban

Mexican-origin minority populations, including violence, HIV/STI infection risks, and mental health conditions. Her research has also highlighted the unique gendered experiences encountered by females within this cultural context.

ANDREA GÓMEZ CERVANTES received a PhD in sociology from the University of Kansas. She is Assistant Professor of Sociology at Wake Forest University. She specializes in international migration, families, race and ethnicity, and Latina/o sociology. Her research has been funded by the National Science Foundation, Ford Foundation, and American Sociological Association.

JOHANNA CRESWELL BÁEZ is Director of Research and Evaluation at Southwest Key Programs and Adjunct Assistant Professor at the Columbia University School of Social Work. Her research focuses on adolescents, trauma, and social-emotional learning using mixed-methods research. She received a BS from Colorado College, an MS from Columbia University, and a PhD from Smith College.

JEAN DENIOUS is CEO of the OMNI Institute in Denver, Colorado, and leads strategic visioning as well as the development of new business areas and services. She also provides oversight to OMNI's Justice Reform Division. Before joining OMNI, she was Faculty Associate in the Departments of Psychology and Gender Studies at Arizona State University.

KATIE DINGEMAN is Assistant Professor of Sociology at California State University, Los Angeles. Her research examines detention, deportation, and the criminalization of migrants in the United States and Central America.

ALESHA DURFEE is Professor of Women and Gender Studies in the School of Social Transformation at Arizona State University. Her research and teaching focus on social policy and domestic violence using quantitative and qualitative methods; her work has been published in journals such as *Gender & Society*, *Violence Against Women*, and *Feminist Criminology*. Her research includes legal mobilization and the use of protection orders by domestic violence survivors, the effects of mandatory arrest policies, the social construction of domestic violence victimization, and how gender influences the interpretation of survivors' narratives of violence by the justice system. Her work has been funded by both the National Science Foundation and the National Institute of Justice.

HERIBERTO ESCAMILLA received his doctorate in clinical psychology from the California School of Professional Psychology San Diego Campus in 1993. He delivered direct clinical services through several community-based organizations and health centers in San Diego. He has taught psychology and Chicano history classes at the university level. In addition to community organizing, he has participated in the evaluation of several community- and school-based health, crime, and teen pregnancy prevention initiatives. He has been part of multidisciplinary teams evaluating multisite and component initiatives such as the Border Health Initiative, the Juvenile Crime Prevention Project, the Male Involvement Program, the Teen Pregnancy Prevention Initiative, the Partnership for the Public's Health, the California First Five Initiative, and the Community Action to Fight Asthma Initiative. He is Director of Evaluations and Program Improvement for the National Compadres Network, a culture-based technical assistance and capacity-building organization.

MARTHA ESCOBAR is Associate Professor in the Department of Chicana/o Studies at California State University, Northridge. She obtained her doctoral degree in ethnic studies from the University of California, San Diego and is the author of the award-winning book *Captivity Beyond Prisons: Criminalization Experiences of Latina (Im)migrants*. Her interests focus on gender and transnational (im)migration, citizenship and nation building, incarceration, racialized and gendered state violence, and women of Color feminisms.

JERRY FLORES is a Ford Foundation Fellow, UC President's Post Doc, and Assistant Professor in the Sociology Department at the University of Toronto. He is also the author of *Caught Up: Girls, Surveillance and Wraparound Incarceration*.

HOLLY FOSTER is Professor of Sociology and Chancellor EDGES Fellow at Texas A&M University. She is also an Affiliated Scholar with the American Bar Foundation in Chicago. She has published extensively on the topic of mass incarceration influences on children and families. Her research on women in prison appears in *Women & Criminal Justice, Journal of Ethnicity in Criminal Justice, Journal of Gender, Race and Justice*, and *Journal of Criminal Justice* as well as an edited volume. Her research with a large national longitudinal study on maternal and paternal incarceration influences on children over the life course (with John Hagan) is published in *Social Problems, Sociology of Education, Law & Society Review, Social Science Research*, and *Annual Review of Sociology*. She also investigates influences of different types of violence exposure over the life course (with Jeanne Brooks-Gunn) with articles appearing in *Journal of Health and Social Behavior* and *Journal of Youth and Adolescence*.

JESSICA FRANKEBERGER is Project Specialist at the University of Southern California (USC) Suzanne Dworak-Peck School of Social Work. She currently works on an ongoing NIH-funded longitudinal research study focused on drug use and intimate partner violence among gang-affiliated Mexican American women. She has been working in the fields of substance use and public health research for over five years. She received a master's of public health from USC in 2016.

DIANDREA GARZA is Research Coordinator at UT Health San Antonio in the Department of Family and Community Medicine and a dual-degree master's student in clinical social work and public health at the University of Texas at Austin and UT School of Public Health, Austin Campus. Her research interests include communities of Color, trauma and resilience, and community-based participatory research.

SARA HASKIE-MENDOZA has worked twenty-five years as a grassroots community organizer, trainer, and outreach specialist. She developed Xinachtli–an innovative healing-informed rites of passage curriculum for girls—in which she has trained hundreds of facilitators nationally. She is a Fellow of the California Women's Policy Institute and a recipient of the 2007 AFSC L.A. Peace Maker Award. She worked as a fundraising trainer for the Grassroots Institute for Fundraising Training and has served as a field representative for the International Indian Treaty Council, working at the UN Commission for Human Rights in Geneva, Switzerland. Her work is focused on disseminating the Xinachtli Rites of Passage Curriculum, grassroots fundraising training, and Indigenous leadership and capacity building for women and girls. As Manager of Women and Girls Programs at the National Compadres Network, her work focuses on lifting up the strengths, needs, and issues of Chicana, Latina, and Indigenous women and girls. She has extensive experience working with communities and organizations.

CHRISTIAN JAIMES is a Xinachtli facilitator who has facilitated this program in the southern region of Santa Barbara County, which includes the cities of Goleta, Santa Barbara, and Carpinteria. Today, she serves as the Xinachtli Comadres National Colectiva (XCNC) Coordinator for the National Compadres Network, where she works alongside Xinachtli young women and Xinachtli facilitators to create a community of agencies nationwide.

LINDSAY KAHLE is Teaching Assistant Professor of Criminology in the Department of Sociology and Anthropology at West Virginia University. She is also affiliate faculty of the WVU Research Center on Violence and the Laboratory for Youth Inequality and Justice. She received her BA in psychology and her MA in sociology from Indiana University of Pennsylvania, before pursuing her PhD in sociology at Virginia Tech. Her preliminary areas of specialization are in criminology and women's and gender studies. Thus, her areas of teaching include criminology, gender and crime, youth violence, and juvenile delinquency. Her research interests focus primarily on the intersections of race, ethnicity, gender, and sexual orientation in youth inequality, and violence and victimization. Her dissertation, titled "Examining Victimization in the Lives of Lesbian, Gay, Bisexual and Questioning Youth," assessed the effects of bullying, homophobic bullying, dating violence, and sexual assault on school avoidance, substance use, and poor mental health outcomes in LGBQ youth. Her research has been published in outlets such as *Criminal Justice Studies, Journal of Child and Family Studies, Victims and Offenders, Sociological Spectrum, Violence and Victims, Gender, Place, and Culture, Journal of Interpersonal Violence, Journal of Criminology, Sociology Compass, Encyclopedia of Research Methods and Statistical Techniques in Criminology and Criminal Justice,* and *The Handbook of Race, Ethnicity, Crime, and Justice.*

LISA M. MARTINEZ is Professor of Sociology and Criminology and a Core faculty member of the DU Latino Center for Community Engagement and Scholarship (DULCCES)—an interdisciplinary program dedicated to conducting research on Latina/o communities in Denver and the Rocky Mountain West. In terms of scholarship, she studies the impact of immigration policies on the social, economic, and political well-being of Latina/o communities as well as educational, health-related, and job market outcomes among Latinas/os and immigrants. She is currently working on an interdisciplinary project with her DULCCES colleagues on the pathways to mobility among Latino and immigrant youth.

CECILIA MENJÍVAR holds the Dorothy L. Meier Chair and is Professor of Sociology at the University of California, Los Angeles. Her immigration-related research focuses on the effects of legal status classifications, enforcement practices, the legal production of "illegality," social networks, family dynamics, the workplace and schools, family separations, religious participation, and citizenship and belonging. Her publications include the books *Fragmented Ties: Salvadoran Immigrant Networks in America* (2000), *Enduring Violence: Ladina Women's Everyday Lives in Guatemala* (2011), and *Immigrant Families* (with Leisy Abrego and Leah Schmalzbauer, 2016). She recently co-edited *The Handbook of Migration Crises* (with Marie Ruiz and Immanuel Ness, 2019). She is a John Simon Guggenheim fellow, an Andrew Carnegie fellow, and past Vice-President of the American Sociological Association.

JILL MESSING is Professor in the School of Social Work at Arizona State University. She specializes in intimate partner violence risk assessment. She has evaluated the predictive validity of several forms of the Danger Assessment, including the DA-5 and the Lethality Screen. She has created risk assessment instruments for use in risk-informed collaborative interventions, including the Danger Assessment for Law Enforcement (DA-LE) and the Arizona Intimate Partner Risk Assessment Instrument System (APRAIS). As a social worker, she is particularly interested in the use of risk assessment in evidence-based practice and with the development and testing of innovative interventions for victims of intimate partner violence. She was the Principal Investigator on the National Institute of Justice–funded Oklahoma Lethality Assessment Study, an examination of the effectiveness of the Lethality Assessment Program (LAP), a collaborative police-social service response to intimate partner violence. She is also a co-investigator on two studies examining the utility of internet-based decision aids for women in abusive relationships funded by the National Institutes of Health.

CHANTREY J. MURPHY is Assistant Professor of Sociology at California State University, Long Beach. She received her PhD in sociology from Texas A&M University. Her primary research focuses on developing interpersonal and structural interventions to reduce the inequality that occurs in interactive and demographically diverse small-group contexts. Her research also focuses on the interpersonal and structural consequences of incarceration and on applying interdisciplinary and mixed-methods approaches for understanding (negative) emotion management and physical health outcomes within historically marginalized populations. She has a forthcoming publication with John Hagan and Holly Foster in *Social Science Research* on the multilevel influences of incarceration on adult educational attainments and another forthcoming publication with Jane Sell and Katie Constantin in *Advances in Group Processes*.

KATHRYN M. NOWOTNY is Assistant Professor at the University of Miami Department of Sociology. Her research explores how mass incarceration contributes to health inequalities, the intersections of crime and health behaviors, and the contextual influences on health more broadly for vulnerable populations. These complementary "streams" of research center on understanding the health of disadvantaged and underserved populations using both quantitative and qualitative methods. She is a Fellow in the NIDA-funded Lifespan/Brown Criminal Justice Research Training (CJRT) Program on

Substance Use, HIV, and Comorbidities. She received her PhD in sociology (2016) from the University of Colorado Boulder.

ANTHONY PEGUERO is Professor of Sociology and Criminology. He is also Director of the Laboratory for the Study of Youth Inequality and Justice and Research Affiliate of the Center for Peace Studies and Violence Prevention at Virginia Tech. His research interests fall into the areas of youth inequality and justice, race/ethnicity, immigration, and social inequities and how these factors socialize and affect the life course of youth in our society. More specifically, he investigates the intersection of race/ethnicity, immigration, and gender in relationship to youth marginalization, particularly within the educational system. Mentoring and facilitating the success of underrepresented junior scholars, including undergraduate and graduate students, is of the utmost importance to him. He mentors underrepresented scholars in two broad ways. First, as Director of the Laboratory for the Study of Youth Inequality and Justice, he funds as well as collaborates with undergraduate and graduate students on lab research projects. Second, he is a member of the Racial Democracy, Crime, and Justice Network and co-founder of the Latina/o/x Criminology group. These two groups hold the goals of advancing research by underrepresented junior scholars on the intersections of race, crime, and justice and of promoting racial democracy within the study of these issues.

ESMERALDA RAMIREZ has an MA in media studies from the University of Texas. She previously taught at the North East School of the Arts, Northwest Vista College, and San Antonio College. She is Field Director for Alice Cepeda's NIDA-funded Health Consequences of Drug Use and IPV Trajectories for Young Latinas study in San Antonio, Texas.

WILLIAM ESTUARDO ROSALES is Assistant Professor of Sociology at California State University, Los Angeles. His research examines immigrant civic and political integration, social trust, and the educational pathways of undocumented students in higher education.

GABRIELLA SANCHEZ is Research Fellow at the European University Institute's Migration Policy Centre. Her research (carried out in the Americas, North Africa, the Middle East, and Europe) documents the perspectives of migrants and the people behind their journeys to strengthen the empirical and conceptual base of "crimes of mobility," establishing the practices known as smuggling as part of community life to document the impact of their criminalization on women, young people, and Indigenous communities. She is the author of *Human Smuggling and Border Crossings* (2016) and co-editor of the 2018 special issue on Migrant Smuggling of *Annals of the American Academy of Political and Social Sciences*.

XUAN SANTOS is Associate Professor at California State University, San Marcos. His research interests are on the informal economy/political, gangs, convict criminology, prison-to-school pipeline, body modifications, race/class/gender, and transnational migration. He currently works with formerly incarcerated and system-impacted students through Project Rebound and the Transitions Collective, programs that help reduce recidivism rates and increase graduation rates.

JOSEPHINE V. SERRATA is a clinical and community psychologist. She is co-owner and licensed psychologist at Prickly Pear Therapy and Training, where she shares her expertise in trauma-informed and culturally relevant approaches to healing and organization development. She also serves as a research evaluation consultant and former director of research and evaluation at the National Latin@ Network for Healthy Families & Communities, a national domestic violence organization. Her research and evaluation work are embedded in participatory research and action-oriented evaluation.

WILLIAM G. STAPLES is Professor of Sociology and Founding Director of the Surveillance Studies Research Center at the University of Kansas. He is the author, most recently, of the second edition of *Everyday Surveillance: Vigilance and Visibility in Postmodern Life*, winner of the 2015 Surveillance Studies Network Book Prize. He is also Associate Editor of the international journal *Surveillance & Society*.

DEANA SWAN is a doctoral student in educational leadership and policy at the University of Texas at Austin. She explores Latina/o student experiences and is interested in culturally competent program evaluation. She received a BS from the University of Wisconsin–Madison and an MSEd from the University of Pennsylvania.

AVELARDO VALDEZ is Professor in the School of Social Work and the Department of Sociology at the University of Southern California. He obtained his PhD in sociology at the University of California, Los Angeles. A primary focus of his research has been on the relationship between substance abuse and violence and health issues among high-risk groups. His research projects have been among "hidden populations" such as youth and prison gang members, heroin users, sex workers, aging drug users, and crack users. He is a nationally and internationally recognized scholar with an extensive publication record in his field of research. His most recent book is *Mexican American Girls and Gang Violence: Beyond Risk*.

SUJEY VEGA is Associate Professor of Women and Gender Studies and Affiliate Faculty in the School of Transborder Studies and Religious Studies at Arizona State University. Her research explores the everyday lived experiences of Latinas/os in the United States. Her book, *Latino Heartland: Of Borders and Belonging in the Midwest* (2015), places in dialogue ethnoreligious practices, comadrazgo (female social networks), ethnic solidarity, and community organizations. This scholarly emphasis on the lived realities of Latinas/os as they confront larger structural systems of inequality has led to publications in *City and Society* (2012) and a book chapter in *The Criminalization of Immigration: Contexts and Consequences* (2013). Whether working with Latinas/os in the Midwest, Mormon Latinas, or Latina survivors of domestic violence, her work has always centered on the lived experience of immigrant communities whose lives and bodies become racialized, gendered, and classed in contemporary U.S. politics.

ABOUT THE EDITORS

VERA LOPEZ is Professor of Justice & Social Inquiry in the School of Social Transformation at Arizona State University. Her research areas include adolescent delinquency, substance use, and prevention research. Her work has been featured in a number of journals including *Journal of Family Issues, Journal of Youth and Adolescence, Latino Studies, Journal of Adolescence, Youth & Society, Feminist Criminology, Family Relations,* and *Criminal Justice & Behavior*. Her book *Complicated Lives: Girls, Parents, Drugs, and Juvenile Justice* was published in 2017.

LISA PASKO is Associate Professor of Sociology and Criminology and Affiliated Faculty in the Gender and Women's Studies Program at the University of Denver. In addition to numerous articles, book chapters, and technical reports, she is co-author of *The Female Offender: Girls, Women, and Crime* and of *Girls, Women, and Crime: Selected Readings*. Her research examines the intersectionality of race, gender, and sexualities in the lives of justice-involved girls. With Dr. Jean Denious, she recently finished an Office of Juvenile Justice and Delinquency Prevention grant titled "Characteristics and Predictors of Juvenile Diversion Program Success for Girls: A Focus on the Latina First-Time Offender."

INDEX

Page numbers in *italics* indicate Tables and Figures.

academic achievement: DACA and, 259, 266–68; gang membership and, 262; immigrant youth rejection of, 261; majority-minority schools and, 261; mother-daughter relationship and, 293; prison opportunities for, 227–28; risk factor of low, 328; school marginalization and, 93–94; social exclusion and negative, 261

acculturation-related stressors, 13, 280; assimilation strategy for, 281–82; integration strategy for, 282; language brokering, 288–90; of Latina youth, 281–82; marginalization strategy, 282; separation strategy for, 281; values clash, 290–91

acculturative dissonance: clash of values, 290–91; language brokering, 288–90

ACLU lawsuit, against T. Don Hutto facility, 192

Advancing Students for a Stronger Economy Tomorrow (ASSET), for in-state tuition, 264, 272, 273–75, 276

AEDPA. *See* Anti-terrorism and Effective Death Penalty Act

African Americans: census data on, 144n1; incarceration rates, 127; juvenile justice system and victimization of, 316; mass incarceration of, 185–86; maternal efficacy among imprisoned women, 128, 130, 137, 141–42; mother-child residences before imprisonment, 128; mothers integrated family ties, 128; parental socialization practices and, 280

alternative to detention (ATD) programs, 182; for asylum seekers placement, 183; CCA and GEO benefits from, 191; DHS budget allocation for, 191; EM ankle monitors in, 188, 189–90, 197, 198–201; ERO technology, 188, 197; ICE ISAP program, 187–88, 197; ISAP III program, 198; for ROR or OSUP immigrants, 197–98; significant growth of, 198; subcontracting of, 197; surveillance in, 188

American Legislative Council, restrictive immigration law promoted by, 190

anti-immigrant initiatives, 337; asylum seekers protections elimination, 151; CBP and ICE expansion, 151, 178n1; DACA revocation as, 151, 263; Muslim travel ban, 151; TPS suspension, 151, 177; U.S.-Mexico border wall, 151

anti-immigrant legislation: IPV and ripple effects, 21; POs barriers from, 23

anti-immigrant sentiment, Trump and, 151, 243, 312

Anti-terrorism and Effective Death Penalty Act (AEDPA), noncitizens criminal offenses mandatory detention, 185

Arizona: detention centers in, 189; Latinas population in, 4; maternal racial and ethnic strategies study in, 283–84; migrant smuggling in, 237, 244, 249

Artesia family detention center, 193

351

ASSET. *See* Advancing Students for a Stronger Economy Tomorrow
assimilation, 289; immigrant youth downward, 261; segmented, 260–61; strategy for acculturation-related stressors, 281–82
asylum seekers, 202n1; ATD programs placement of, 183; from El Salvador, 183; Guatemala immigrants as, 183, 189, 198; Honduras immigrants as, 161–62, 183; protections elimination for, 151
ATD. *See* alternative to detention

benevolence framing, in detention complexes, 183, 194, 201
Berks County Residential Center, for family detention, 192, 193
bilingual services, 99
Blacks: Goffman on fear of capture of, 104; Rios on criminalized lives of, 103; terminology for, 9. *See also* African Americans
Blueprints for Healthy Youth Development (Blueprints): on Familias Unidas, 300; on violence prevention programs, 300
bonds, in criminal justice system, 166; detention release with, 183; EM and, 198, 199; immigration lawyers on, 203n8; for pregnant women, 171
Booker report, on migrant smuggling, 252n2
Border Control, 189
borderlands: challenges within, 13; otherness and, 7
Border Patrol. *See* Customs and Border Patrol
Boyles Heights community of East Los Angeles, Xinachtli and, 317
boys, Latino: deviant behavior and social marginalization of, 262; gang involvement and masculinity of, 262; interpersonal victimization of, 43

Bracero Program, 242, 252n7, 265
Brewer, R. M., 104
bullying, as interpersonal victimization, 46, 50–51

California: family detention centers in, 193; Latinas population in, 4; Mesa Verde Detention Center in, 223; migrant smuggling in, 244; migrant women incarceration in, 209; Southern California barrio "on the run" experiences, 102–23; Western Region Detention Facility in, 223
California juvenile probation: community-based corrections, 104; El Valle Detention Center and, 104–6; gang restrictions, 105; probation violations, 105; requirements of, 105; secure confinement in, 104; Youth Authority detention centers, 123n1
California Rehabilitation Center state prison, 213
California Wellness Foundation, Xinachtli funding from, 317
Campaign for the American Dream, 272
carceral state, 6, 210–12
caregiver services development recommendation, of MHK, 305
caring relationships attitudes and behaviors, Xinachtli on, 326
catch and detain policy, 185
CBP. *See* Customs and Border Patrol
CCA. *See* Corrections Corporation of America
CDC. *See* Centers for Disease Control and Prevention
census data, on African Americans and Latinas, 144n1
Centers for Disease Control and Prevention (CDC): sexual minority youth definition by, 46; YRBSS of, 45
Central America: asylum seekers from, 183; gendered violence in, 161–62, 164,

INDEX | 353

183; migrant women from, 157–60; migration control attempts, 155–56, 157; youth fleeing violence in, 186. *See also specific countries*
Chicana feminism, 3; intersectional perspective of, 7
Chicana Lives and Criminal Justice (Díaz-Cotto), 212
Chicana/o terminology, 329n1
children: DCS removal of, 13; deportation of, 186–87; imprisoned women and residential placement of, 129–30, 131, *136*, 141–43, 144n5; IPV and DCS removal of, 24, 71, 75; mother incarceration and DCS removal, 211–12
Child Trends, 300
Chinese Exclusion (1882-1943), 178n1; migrant smuggling and, 242
churches, linkpersons in, 37
Citizenship and Immigration Services DACA processing, 276n3
Clark v. Martinez (2005), 197
Clinton, Bill, 184–85
CMM. *See* concurrent mixed-method
Coalition for Evidence-Based Policy, 300
coethnic best friendships, 21–22
collective efficacy, 144n2
Colorado: ASSET bill for in-state tuition, 264, 272, 273–75, 276; court-involved Latina and white girls comparisons in, 11, 83, 87–90, *88*, *89*, 94–95; undocumented immigrants legal reforms, 263
comadrazgo (sister of the heart) bond, 32, 37
comadres (co-mother), 21–22, 37
community: IPV nondisclosure in minority, 61–62; juvenile diversion programming study on, 92–95; nondisclosure of IPV in context of, 64; Xinachtli on connection importance, 327
community-based programming, 14, 336; delinquency prevention from, 13; lay advocates training by, 37; of MHK Toolkit, 302; for system-impacted Latinas, 10, 12–13; of Xinachtli, 317
co-mother (*comadres*), 21–22, 37
concurrent mixed-method (CMM) design, 63
controlling images, of Latinas, 8
conviction, of migrant smuggling, 244–45
CoreCivic: DHS and ICE contract with, 190–92; previously CCA, 190
Corrections Corporation of America (CCA): as CoreCivic previous name, 190; detention lobbying efforts by, 190–91; surveillance benefits for, 191; T. Don Hutto facility contract of, 192
court and sentencing process, for migrant women deportees, 223–25, 232, 233, 234n7; court process subjectivity, 226; language misunderstandings, 214–16; parole process, 216–17, 226–29, 233
Crenshaw, Kimberlé: on identity politics, 52; on intersectionality, 6–7, 52
Criminal Alien and Secure Communities programs, 155
criminal aliens classification, 223; deportation and, 211, 229; Operation Streamline court, 234n7
criminality: among immigrant youth, 262; poverty and female, 62
criminalization: identities intersections with, 103–4; IIRIRA increased, 185, 211; of immigrants, 184, 210; from immigration laws, 184; migrant women experience of, 212; of trauma experiences, 62; war on immigration and, 334
criminal justice systems, U.S.: females as offenders in, 3, 4–5; good women narrative sympathetic response in, 11; immigration enforcement merging with, 12; immigration punitive turn, 185–86; oppression within, 104; othering in, 2; U.S.-Mexico border crossing and, 3

criminal records, IPV victim nondisclosure due to, 62
criminological research, on Latino males or white females, 2
crimmigration system, 12; immigration and criminal justice systems combination, 151–52; migratory departures and crossing, 160–64; undocumented Latina women and, 3, 10
crimmigration system study, 151–78; inspection and detention experiences, 167–72; legal process exceptions, limitations and consequences, 172–76; methods, 160; migrant women apprehensions, 164–67; migration and border reconfiguration, 154–56; migration and deportation feminization, 156–57; transnational intersectional approach, 153–54, 157–60, 176
cross-generational services recommendation, of MHK, 305
cultural-deficit approach, 13
culturally grounded approach, for evidence-based programs, 301
culturally responsive interventions, 274; risk factor reduction and, 260
culturally responsive school practices recommendation, of MHK, 305
cultural socialization, as RES strategy, 283
culture: -based healing practices, 318; education disconnect with, 304; immigrant youth oppositional, 261; values strength in, 13; Xinachtli on healing promotion through, 317–18, 328
curriculum: content, in Xanchtli, 320; LCC practices in Xinachtli, 319; MHK Toolkit interactive training, 307; NCN Medicine Wheel and, 318; *respeto* in Xinachtli, 319; Xinachtli on structure of, 319–20
Customs and Border Patrol (CBP): catch and detain budget impact on, 185; expansion of, 151, 178n1; IRCA budget increase of, 184

DA. *See* district attorney
DACA. *See* Deferred Action for Childhood Arrivals
data: African Americans and Latinas census, 144n1; in detention complex study, 188–90; Germany UNODC SHERLOC database, 252n9; in juvenile diversion programming study, 85, 86, 98; on juvenile justice system, 14n4; in maternal efficacy among imprisoned women study, 130–31; MAXQDA software for analysis of, 303; system-impacted Latinas challenges, 3–4, 14n1; U.S. federal, on migrant smuggling, 244–45, 252n11; Xinachtli preliminary outcome, 324–25; YRBSS use in LGBQ girls study, 42, 44–45
dating violence, as interpersonal victimization, 46, 50
DCS. *See* Department of Child Safety
Deferred Action for Childhood Arrivals (DACA), 177; academic achievement and, 259, 266–68; Citizenship and Immigration Services processing, 276n3; Obama executive order for, 259, 263; revocation as anti-immigrant initiative, 151, 263; Trump rescinding of, 263; undocumented youth education and occupation, 259, 273–76
delinquency: community-based programming for, 13; gender-specific prevention programs for, 301; maternal racial and ethnic strategies and, 13; RES as protective factor for, 283; victimization link with, 263
Department of Child Safety (DCS), 13; IPV and children removal by, 24, 71, 75; mother incarceration and children removal, 211–12

Department of Homeland Security (DHS): ATD programs budget allocation by, 191; catch and detain budget impact on, 185; CoreCivic and GEO contracts with, 190–92
Department of Justice, on evidence-based programs, 300
deportation, 12, 13–14, 156–57; Criminal Alien and Secure Communities programs for, 155; criminal aliens classification and, 211, 229; to El Salvador, 172, 175, 182; escalation of, 184–86; gender and racial disparities in, 152; gendered legal process of, 172–76; of Guatemala immigrants, 182; of Honduras immigrants, 172, 182; increase of, 151–52; IPV and fear of, 335; of males, 152–53; mass incarceration compared to, 152–53; migrant women deportees experiences, 229–32; POs and, 30; to Tijuana, Mexico, 213, 214, 230–31, 233; of youth and children, 186–87
detention: barriers in, 196; bond release for, 183; catch and detain budget impact, 185; CCA and GEO expansion lobbies, 190–91; of El Salvador immigrants, 202; escalation of, 184–86; of Guatemala immigrants, 202; of Honduras immigrants, 202; of males, 182; punitive capacity of, 183, 192, 201, 203nn2–3. *See also* alternative to detention programs; family detention centers
detention centers: ICE on, 193; immigration lawyers on prison-like appearance of, 194; juvenile, 193; maltreatment in, 196–97, 203n7; privatization of, 184, 190–92; sexual assault in, 197; transgender women and, 193–94; violence in, 196–97
detention complex study, in U.S.: ATD programs, 182–83, 187–88, 197–202; benevolence framing in, 183, 194, 201; detention and deportation escalation, 184–86; family detention centers, 192–95, 201–2, 203n6; female control inside detention, 195–97; government documents for, 188, 202; immigrants surveillance, control and punishment, 186–88, 194, 195–201; immigration control privatization, 184, 190–92; immigration lawyers interviews for, 188–89, 194–97, 203n8; Kansas subjects in, 189, 198–99; methods and data, 188–90; on violence and maltreatment, 196–97
detention experiences, of women migrants, 12, 167; forced family separation, 168; inhumane treatment in, 170–71; inspection procedures, 168; medication and, 168–69; placement variety, 168; pregnancy and, 171–72; transgender women and, 193–94
DHS. *See* Department of Homeland Security
Díaz-Cotto, Juanita, 212
discrimination, 8; LGBQ girls experience of, 53; maternal racial and ethnic strategies and perceived, 286–88; of migrant women deportees, 218–23, 232; race and class-based, of U.S-Mexico border residents, 242; of second generation, 287; stereotypes and, 287; system-impacted Latinas influenced by, 13; as youth structural position stressor, 281
discrimination, in incarceration: detention treatment, 219–20; intersectional approach to experiences of, 222–23; language discrimination, 218–19; post-incarceration stigma, 220–22
district attorney (DA), juvenile diversion programming and, 85
domestic violence shelters, 19, 32–33; promotora training in, 37, 337
domination sites, 158

downward assimilation, of immigrant youth, 261
drug trafficking, 106, 120, 132, 237, 241, 252n5

economic conditions, migration as reason for, 160–61
Economic Innovation Group, 64
ecosystemic forms, of trauma experiences, 316
education, 312; culture disconnect with, 304; DACA for undocumented youth, 259, 273–76; public IPV, 34–35. *See also* academic achievement; higher education of undocumented Latina study; schools
effective systems advocacy recommendation, of MHK, 306
El Chaparral port of entry, into Tijuana, 234n6
electronic monitoring (EM) ankle monitors: in ATD programs, 188, 189–90, 197, 198–201; CCA and GEO benefits from, 191; criminal justice system bonds and, 198, 199
elementary schools experiences, 93, 265–67, 271
El Salvador immigrants, 5, 160, 165, 174; asylum seekers of, 183; deportation of, 172, 175, 182; detention of, 202
El Valle Detention Center: background of, 105–6; California juvenile probation and, 104–6; Legacy Community School and, 106–8
EM. *See* electronic monitoring
Enforcement Removal Operations (ERO): ATD programs in, 188, 197; immigrants tracking by, 197
English as second language (ESL), 214
English language: benefits, for migrant women incarceration, 217–18; immersion program, 265
Enhanced Supervision/Reporting program (ESR), 191

ERO. *See* Enforcement Removal Operations
escalation, of detention, 184–86
ESL. *See* English as second language
ESR. *See* Enhanced Supervision/Reporting program
ethnic identity: maternal racial and ethnic strategies and positive, 13; Xinachtli on importance of, 325–26
evidence-based programs: Blueprints as, 300; Child Trends on, 300; Coalition for Evidence-Based Policy on, 300; culturally grounded approach for, 301, 311; Department of Justice on, 300; SAMHSA recommendation for, 300
expansion, of CBP, 151, 178n1

facilitators: in migrant smuggling, 238–39, 243–44; migrant smuggling and female, 238–39, 245–50; reflection and observation in Xinachtli, 322–24; in Xinachtli program, 321–22
Familias Unidas, Blueprints on, 300
family: in juvenile diversion programming study, 90–92; rejection in "on the run" avoidance study, 112–15; separation, 168, 177, 211
family case management services recommendation, of MHK, 305, 309–10
family detention centers, 201–2; Artesia, 193; Berks County Residential Center, 192, 193; in California and Texas, 193; Karnes Civil Detention Center, 193; Obama increase of, 193; South Texas Family Residential Center, 193, 194–95; T. Don Hutto facility, 192–93, 203n6
Family Keys program, 302–3, 312n1
federal prisons: drug offenders in, 126; Latinas in, 126; racial and ethnic disparities in, 126–27
females: of Color LGBQ victimization, 11; control inside detention, 195–97; as criminal justice systems offenders, 3,

4–5; criminological research on white, 2; migrant smuggling facilitation by, 238–39, 245–50; multiple marginalization of, 2; U.S. imprisonment rates, 126, 127; as violence victims, 3, 8. *See also* girls; juvenile offenders; migrant women

feminist pathways theory, 62

Flores Settlement Agreement, of 1997, ACLU on T. Don Hutto facility violation of, 192

formal resources: barriers to, 20–21; informal resource networks prior to, 31; IPV and, 27; Latina women distrust of, 333; of medical services, 20; of social services, 11, 20. *See also* police interactions

gangs: academic achievement and membership in, 262; California juvenile probation restrictions on, 105; culturally responsive programs and, 260; exposure to, 93; gender differences, 262–63; higher education of undocumented Latina study and initiation to, 261–63, 267–68; intervention program, 270–71, 273–74; masculinity affirmation and, 262; MS-13 transnational, 161, 173, 241; peer influence and, 262; surveillance ordinances, 333; transition to higher education from, 268–71

gender differences, in gangs, 262–63

gendered violence: in Central America, 161–62, 164, 183; incarcerated Latinas and, 212; in Northern Triangle, 156; in schools, 103

gender-responsive programming, for interpersonal victimization, 55

gender-specific prevention programs, for delinquency, 301

general strain theory (GST), prisons and, 142

Geo Group Inc. (GEO): detention lobbying efforts by, 190–91; DHS and ICE contract with, 190–92; surveillance benefits for, 191

Germany UNODC SHERLOC database, 252n9

germinating seed. *See* Xinachtli program

girls, Black, in juvenile justice system, 4–5, 14n4

girls, Latina: bullying of, 42, 44; dating violence of, 42, 43; interpersonal victimization impact on, 42–43; in juvenile justice system, 4–5; juvenile justice system and physical victimization, 316; sexual assault of, 42, 43; violence exposure, 42–44; white girls juvenile diversion program comparisons, 11, 84, 86–90, *88, 90,* 94–95

girls, white: in juvenile justice system, 4–5, 14n4; juvenile justice system and victimization of, 316; Latina girls juvenile diversion program comparisons, 11, 84, 86–90, *88, 90,* 94–95; victimization concerns, 54

Global Review on Smuggling Data and Research, IOM, 251n3

Goffman, A., 104, 120; Latinas "on the run" research, 110, 122; on total institutions, 194

good women narrative, criminal justice system sympathetic response, 11

government, IPV prevention funding, 27

grilletes. *See* electronic monitoring ankle monitors

grounded theory, IPV study use of, 23

Grupo Beta de Proteccio al Migrante, 224n5, 230, 231

GST. *See* general strain theory

Guatemala immigrants, 5; as asylum seekers, 183, 189, 198; deportation of, 182; detention of, 202; at Mexico-Guatemala border, 155

hand (*manualidades*) crafts, in Xinachtli, 319, 329n2
Helping Unaccompanied Minors and Alleviating National Emergency Act (Humane Act) bill, 186–87
hermana (sister), 21–22
hermanadad (sisterhood bond), 22
higher education of undocumented Latina study, 259; case study findings, 264–73; early childhood experiences, 265–66; gang initiation, 261–63, 267–68; methods, 263–64; middle school transition, 266–68; policy and practice implications, 273–76; road to higher education, 271–73; segmented assimilation and aspirations, 260–61; transition from gang life, 268–71
Hispanic terminology, 9
Honduras immigrants, 5, 164, 175; asylum seekers of, 161–62, 183; deportation of, 172, 182; detention of, 202
Humane Act. *See* Helping Unaccompanied Minors and Alleviating National Emergency Act
humanitarian immigration mechanism, U.S., 152; benevolence framing of, 183, 194, 201; immigration laws language, 186–87; social control and surveillance practices in, 183, 186
human trafficking, migrant smuggling and, 240
Hurtado, Aida, 9

ICE. *See* Immigration and Customs Enforcement
identities, criminalization intersections with, 103–4
identity: criminalization intersections with, 103–4; ethnic, 13, 325–26; politics, Crenshaw on, 52
Illegal Immigration Reform and Immigrant Responsibility Act (IIRIRA), of 1996, 184, 203n4; increased criminalization from, 185, 211
immigrants: criminalization of, 184, 210; indefinite detention hold of, 183; IPV and institutional, structure inequalities, 20; mass incarceration of, 185–86. *See also* El Salvador immigrants; Guatemala immigrants; Honduras immigrants
immigrant youth: academic achievement rejection by, 261; criminality among, 262; downward assimilation of, 261; gang initiations of, 261–63, 267–68; levels aspirations of, 261–62; oppositional culture of, 261; social exclusion of, 261; systemic barriers for, 304
immigration: control privatization, 190–92; gendered reasons for, 5; Latina women and, 5; system processing of women migrants, 12; U.S. humanitarian policies on, 152. *See also* migration
Immigration and Customs Enforcement (ICE): catch and detain budget impact on, 185; CoreCivic and GEO contract with, 190–92; on detention centers, 193; expansion of, 151; IPV and police reporting to, 24; ISAP program of, 187–88; at U.S.-Mexico border, 155
immigration enforcement: anti-immigration rhetoric and, 151; criminal justice system merging with, 12; IPV survivors concern with, 29–31; victims of, 14n5
immigration-industrial complex, 335
immigration laws: American Legislative Council promotion of, 190; anti-immigrant legislation, 21, 23; criminalization from, 184; Humane Act bill, 186–87; humanitarian language n, 186–87; IIRIRA, 184, 185, 203n4, 211; IRCA, 184, 203n4, 242; Protect Children and Families bill through Rule of Law Act, 187; Protection of Children Act bill, 187

immigration lawyers: on criminal justice system bonds, 203n8; on detention centers prison-like appearance, 194; interviews with, 188–89, 194–97, 203n8; on South Texas Family Residential Center, 194–95
Immigration Reform and Control Act (IRCA), of 1986, 203n4; CBP budget increase from, 184; migrants status legalization, 242
incarceration, 5; African Americans mass, 185–86; gender-sensitive alternatives to, 14; Latinas gendered violence and, 212; mass, 126, 152–53, 185–86, 210; poverty addressed by, 210; rates of African Americans, 127. *See also* maternal efficacy among imprisoned women study; migrant women deportees incarcerated experiences study; prison
incarceration "on the run" avoidance study, 102; California juvenile probation and El Valle Detention Center, 104–6; El Valle Detention Center and Legacy Community School, 106–8; family rejection and, 112–15; Goffman research and, 110; identities and criminalization intersections, 103–4; of Latinas, 110–12; living on streets and, 118–20; methods, 108–9; practice implications, 122–23; sample demographics, *109*; street negotiation and, 115–18
inclusive policies, for juvenile justice system, 54–55
Indigenous practices, NCN and, 318
inequalities, 9, 20
informal resource networks, for IPV, 19, 23–26, *27*; coethnic best friendships, 21–22; *comadrazgo* bond for, 32; *comadres* and, 21–22; of *hermana*, 21–22; of neighbors, 33–34; prior to formal supports, 31; promotora programs use of, 37, 337

inhumane treatment, of detention experiences, 170–71
institutional contact, as IPV nondisclosure reason, 70–72, 74
institutional inequalities, for IPV and immigrants, 20
integration: African American mothers family ties, 128; strategy for acculturation-related stressors, 282
integrity (*palabra*), Xinachtli objective of, 318
Intensive Supervision Appearance Program (ISAP), of ICE, 191; in ATD programs, 187–88, 197
interaction sites, 158
International Organization for Migration (IOM), Global Review on Smuggling Data and Research of, 251n3
interpersonal victimization, 55; of boys, 43; of bullying, 46, 50–51; of dating violence, 46, 50; gender-responsive programming for, 55; juvenile justice system involvement and, 53–54, 315; Latina girls impact from, 42–43; LGBQ Latina girls study, 44–54; mental health and, 52; of psychological violence, 46; of sexual assault, 46; sexual orientation and identity, 43–44; of youth, 42–43
intersectionality: Crenshaw on, 6–7, 52; LGBQ girls study and importance of, 52–53; matrix of domination, 157–58
intersectional perspective, 2, 5; of Chicana feminism, 7; importance of, 6–9; inequalities and, 9; on IPV nondisclosure, 61–62
intervention programs: culturally responsive, 260, 274; for gangs, 270–71, 273–74; juvenile diversion programming, 88–89; social justice multilevel, 335; for undocumented immigrants risk factors, 274

interviews: with immigration lawyers, 188–89, 194–97, 203n8; in juvenile diversion programming study, 86–87
intimate partner violence (IPV), 3; abusers isolation use, 20, 29, 35; anti-immigrant legislation ripple effects, 21; DCS and children removal, 24, 71, 75; domestic violence shelter and, 19, 32–33; formal resources aid barriers, 20–21, 335; gender and culturally responsive outreach for, 337; government prevention funding for, 27; ICE reporting by police, 24; informal resource networks and survivor safety, 24; informal resource networks for, 19, 21–26, 27, 31, 33–34, 337; institutional and structural inequalities impact, 20; Latina women complicated situations of, 19; life course victimization pathway, 61; linkpersons for, 20, 22; National Intimate Partner and Sexual Violence Survey on, 4; public education on, 34–35; safety barriers for, 19; social networks for, 19. *See also* nondisclosure
intimate partner violence (IPV) study: abusers control and citizen status, 30; abusers linguistic seclusion control, 33–34; abusers social networks denial, 30; abusers surveillance and, 31; existing and denied informal networks, 26–31, 27; grounded theory use in, 23; immigration status concerns, 29–31; isolation and, 28, 28–29; methods for, 23–24; participants in, 24–26, 25; police interactions and, 26–28, 27, 35–36; on public IPV education, 34–35; social networks and linkpersons, 31–35
intimate partner violence (IPV) survivors, informal resource networks and safety of, 24
IOM. *See* International Organization for Migration

IPV. *See* intimate partner violence
IRCA. *See* Immigration Reform and Control Act
ISAP. *See* Intensive Supervision Appearance Program
ISAP III program, 198
isolation: IPV abusers use of, 20, 29, 35; IPV study on, 28, 28–31

Japanese Internment (1942-1946), 178n1
justice reinvestment programs, 76–77
juvenile detention centers, 193
juvenile diversion programming study, 83; bilingual services and, 99; on community and school, 92–95; DA office programs, 85; data and analysis in, 85; on family and relationships, 90–92; intervention program findings in, 88–89; interviewing process in, 86–87; juvenile justice system experiences, 95–97; methods, 84–87; participants of, 84–85; policy and practice implications, 97–99; POs and, 96–97; questionnaire research in, 86; recidivism data in, 86, 98; results, 87–90; state funding programs, 85; white and Latina girls comparisons in, 11, 84, 86–90, 88, 89, 94–95
juvenile justice system: African Americans and victimization, 316; California community-based corrections, 104; control and surveillance of, 11; data on, 14n4; inclusive policies for, 54–55; interpersonal victimization impact on, 53–54, 315; Latinas negative social constructions and, 334; LGBQ girls involvement in, 53–54; MHK and, 300–312; offense statistics, 4; risk factors and, 11, 283; women and girls in, 4–5. *See also* delinquency
juvenile offenders, female, 10; coexisting mental health of, 84; growing population of, 83; interconnected difficulties

of, 83–84; Latina and white comparisons, 11; in residential facilities, 83; social stressors of, 84; substance abuse disorders of, 84

Kansas subjects in detention complex, 189, 198–99
Karnes Civil Detention Center, 193
Kinsey, Alfred, 50

la cultura cura (LCC) practices, 318; in Xinachtli curriculum, 319
LAIPA. *See* Los Angeles Indigenous People's Alliance
language: brokering, 288–90; discrimination, in incarceration, 218–19; English, 217–18, 265; ESL, 214; immigration laws and humanitarian, 186–87
language obstacles, of migrant women deportees incarceration, 213, 228, 232; court misunderstandings, 214–16; English benefits, 217–18; ESL courses and, 214; health care access difficulties, 216; legal interpreters, 215–16, 233n1; limited English skills, 218; mistranslations, 214; parole process and, 216–17
Latinas: census data on, 144n1; controlling representational images of, 8; incarceration of, 110–12; incarceration rates, 127; terminology of, 9; war on drugs impact on, 126, 127, 210–11, 333
Latina youth: acculturation-related stressors of, 281–82; MHK juvenile justice system commitment to, 301–2; structural position stressors among, 281–82; systemic barriers for, 304
lay advocates, community-based programming for training of, 37
LCC. *See* la cultura cura
legal interpreters, for migrant women deportees incarceration, 215–16, 233n1
legal process, of deportation, 172–76

legal reforms, 14
legal resident/citizens, 21
lesbian, gay, bi-sexual, or questioning (LGBQ) girls: discrimination experience of, 53; identification of, 50–51; victimization experiences, 11, 48, 48–49, 49; youth violence experiences, 43–44
lesbian, gay, bi-sexual, or questioning (LGBQ) girls study, 50–51; analytic strategy in, 46; descriptive statistics, 47, 47; intersectionality importance, 52–53; on justice system involvement, 53–54; logistic regression of victimization, 48, 48–49, 49; methods of, 45–46; practice and policy implications, 54–55; results in, 47–49; sexual orientation description, 45–46; YRBSS data use for, 42, 44–45
levels aspirations, of immigrant youth, 261–62
LGBQ. *See* lesbian, gay, bi-sexual, or questioning
life course victimization pathway, for IPV, 61
linguistic seclusion, by IPV abusers, 33–34
linked lives, maternal race/ethnicity and, 127–28
linkpersons: in churches, 37; IPV social networks and, 20, 22–23
living on streets, "on the run" study and: length of time for, 120; sex work and, 118–19; substance abuse and, 118
lobbying, by CCA and GEO for detention expansion, 190–91
Los Angeles Indigenous People's Alliance (LAIPA), Xinachtli and, 317

majority-minority schools, academic achievement and, 261
males, Latino: criminological research on, 2; deportation of, 152–53; detention of, 182. *See also* boys, Latino

maltreatment, in detention centers, 196–97, 203n7
manualidades (hand) crafts, in Xinachtli, 319, 329n2
marginalization: academic outcomes and school, 93–94; Latino boys behavior and social, 262; migrant smuggling as poverty response and, 239, 246, 247–48, 251, 252n6; people of Color position in, 103, 209; of second generation, 260–61; strategy for acculturation-related stressors, 282; women and girls multiple, 2
mass incarceration: of African Americans and immigrants, 185–86; deportation compared to, 152–53; U.S. as world leader in, 126, 210
maternal efficacy among imprisoned women study, 11, 126; analytic plan, 133; children school-related problems and, 130, 131, 138–39, *139*, *140*, 142; for child residential placement, 129–30, 131, *136*, 141–43, 144n5; data in, 130–31; dependent variables in, 131–33; descriptive statistics on, 133–36, *135*; of Latinas and African American mothers, 128, 130, 137, 141–42; maternal childhood trauma, 132; maternal drug histories, 132, 141; maternal efficacy defined, 128–30; maternal race/ethnicity and linked lives, 127–28; measures in, 131–33, 144n4; multivariate analyses, 136–41; OLS regression of, 136–37, *137*; practice and policy implications, 143; sociodemographics, 132–33
maternal racial and ethnic strategies: acculturation related stressors and, 280; girls positive ethnic identity and, 13; RES strategies, 291–95; structural position stressors, 281–82
maternal racial and ethnic strategies study, 280, 292–96; acculturative dissonance findings, 288–91; acculturative stress, 281–82; background on, 283–84; discrimination, 281; methods, 284–86; participants in, 283–85, *285*, *286*; perceived discrimination findings in, 286–88; role of, 282–83
matrix of domination, intersectionality, 157–58
MaXQDA software, for data analysis, 303
media: on migrant smuggling, 237; stereotyped representation by, 8, 334
medical services, 20
medication, detention experiences and, 168–69
Medicine Wheel, Native Americans, 318
mental health: female juvenile offenders and coexisting, 84; interpersonal victimization and, 52
Mérida Initiative, of Mexico, 155
Mesa Verde Detention Center, in California, 223
methodological nationalism, 159
Mexican American Girls and Gang Violence (Valdez), 62
Mexican Repatriation (1930s), 178n1
Mexico: cartel in, 164, 241; Mérida Initiative of, 155; Plan Sur program in, 155; Programa Frontera Sur in, 155–56; southern border militarization, 155–56
Mexico-Guatemala border, 155
MHK. *See* Mi Hermana's Keeper
migrant smuggling, 163, 335; Booker Report on, 252n12; conviction of, 244–45; defined, 239–41; facilitators in, 238–39, 243–44; family reunification and, 246–47; females facilitation of, 238–39, 245–50; Germany UNODC SHERLOC database, 252n9; human trafficking and, 240; IOM Global Review on Smuggling Data and Research, 251n3; IRCA and, 242; as marginalization and poverty response, 239, 246, 247–48, 251, 252n6; media on, 237; perception of, 237, 241; safe house and, 248–49,

252n15; technology use and, 242–43; Transnational Organized Crime on, 239–40; UNODC report on, 251n3; UN Protocol for, 251; U.S. federal data on, 244–45, 252n11; along U.S.-Mexico border, 12, 241–44; violence microdynamics and, 246, 248–50
migrant women deportees incarcerated experiences study, 209; carceral state, 210–12; court and sentencing process, 216–19, 223–29, 232, 233, 234n7; deportation experiences, 229–32; discrimination, 218–23, 232; language obstacles, 213–18, 228, 232, 233n1; narratives context, 212–13, 233; outside support for, 228–29; self-help programming, 228
migration: border reconfiguration and, 154–56; Central America, 155–56, 157; criminalization and, 212; deportation feminization and, 156–57; economic conditions as reason for, 160–61; gendered departures and crossings, 160–65; migrant women apprehensions, 164–67; parental status reason for, 161–62; poverty reason for, 156, 160, 174, 198; unlawful entry zero-tolerance policies, 177; xenophobic reactions to, 211
Mi Hermana's Keeper (MHK) Toolkit study, 336; caregiver services development recommendation, *305*; cross-generational services recommendation, *305*; culturally competent approach for, 307; culturally responsive school practices recommendation, *305*; direct practice application, 13, 307–11; effective systems advocacy recommendation, *306*; family case management services recommendation, *305*, 309–10; findings, 304–7; interactive training curriculum, 307; juvenile justice system commitment to Latina youth, 301–2; methods for, 302–4; phases of, 303; pilot program of, 306–7; program-level recommendations, 304, *305–6*; relational-cultural approach recommendation, 304, *305*; respect of Latino cultural heritage recommendation, *305*, 307–9; *respeto* value and respectful practices recommendation, 304–5, *305*, 307; systemic racism and bias dismantling recommendation, *306*; system-level recommendations, 304, *305–6*; Texas location of, 302–3; training models, 308–11, *310*, *311*

militarization: Mexico southern border, 155–56; of U.S.-Mexico border, 154, 241, 243

minority communities, IPV victimization nondisclosure in, 61–62

Monterrosa, Laura, 192–93

mother-daughter relationship: academic achievement and, 293; RES strategies and strong, 291–95

MS-13 transnational gang, 161, 173, 241

mujeristas spaces, for IPV survivors, 37

multiple marginalization, of women and girls, 2

Muslim travel ban, 151

My Brother's Keeper Initiative, 301

National Compadres Network (NCN): culture-based healing practices, 318; Indigenous LCC practices, 318; Medicine Wheel and curriculum of, 318; Xinachtli administration by, 318

National Institute on Drug Abuse Proyecto SALTO study, 61, 63

National Intimate Partner and Sexual Violence Survey, on IPV, 4

National Longitudinal Study of Adolescent to Adult Health, 131

National Violence Against Women Survey, on victimization, 14n3

Native Americans Medicine Wheel, 318

Natural History Interview (NHI) technique, 63
NCN. *See* National Compadres Network
negative perceptions, of police interactions, 70, 75
neighbors, as informal resource, 33–34
New Mexico, migrant smuggling in, 244
NHI. *See* Natural History Interview
nondisclosure, of Latina young adult IPV study, 60; analysis of, 63–64; CMM design use in, 63; community context, 64; intersectional perspective, 61–62; justice reinvestment programs and, 76–77; methods in, 63; NHI technique for, 63; partner loyalty reason for, 65, 67; police response reason for, 73–75, 335; practice and policy implications, 76–77; retaliation fear reason for, 68–70; sample characteristics, 64–65, 66; social ambivalence and aversion reason for, 67–68; unwanted institutional contact reason for, 70–72, 74; victim criminal records and, 72
Northern Triangle: gendered violence in, 156; violence against women in, 156

Obama, Barack: DACA executive order, 259, 263; family detention centers increase by, 193; My Brother's Keeper Initiative, 301; undocumented immigrants expedited removal, 185
Office of Juvenile Justice and Delinquency Prevention (OJJDP) training webinar, 307, 312n1
Office of Refugee Resettlement, 175
OJJDP. *See* Office of Juvenile Justice and Delinquency Prevention
1.5 generation, social exclusion of, 260
Operation Endgame, at U.S.-Mexico border, 155
Operation Streamline, 234n7

Operation Wetback (1954), 178n1
oppositional culture, of immigrant youth, 261
oppression: within criminal justice system, 104; IPV and, 335; racialized, 8
oppressive policies and procedures, 8
Order of Release on Recognizance (ROR), for ATD participants, 197–98
Order of Supervision (OSUP), for ATD participants, 197–98
othering, in criminal justice systems, 2
otherness, borderlands and, 7
overt racism, 288

paisa, 219, 233n3
palabra (word, integrity), Xinachtli objective of, 318
parental socialization practices, of African Americans, 280
parental status: detention experience and, 167; as migration reason, 161–62
parole process, for migrant women deportees, 216–17, 226–29, 233
participatory action research, 302
partner loyalty, as IPV nondisclosure reason, 65, 67
peers, gangs and influence of, 262
people of Color: carceral state and, 210; female juvenile offenders, 84; justice system impact on, 102; marginalization positions of, 103, 209; terminology of, 9; violence and neighborhood disadvantage, 61–62
personal efficacy, in imprisonment, 128, 143; global perceptions of, 129; task-specific forms, 129
Plan Sur program, in Mexico, 155
PO. *See* probation officer
police interactions, 3, 20; IPV and ICE reporting, 24; IPV nondisclosure reasons, 73–75, 335; IPV study and, 26–28, 27, 35–36; negative perceptions of, 70, 75; POs and, 26

policies and practices: data-informed, 336; discriminatory, 8; higher education of undocumented Latina study on, 273–76; incarceration "on the run" avoidance study on, 122–23; juvenile diversion programming study on, 97–99; juvenile justice system inclusive, 54–55; LGBQ girls study on, 54–55; maternal efficacy among imprisoned women study on, 143; MHK Toolkit study on, 13, 307–11; nondisclosure of Latina young adult IPV study on, 76–77; oppressive, 8; stakeholders social consciousness for, 335–36; U.S. humanitarian immigration policies, 152; zero-tolerance policies, 102, 177
political asylum, 172
POs. *See* protection orders
post-incarceration stigma, 220–22
poverty: female criminality and, 62; incarceration to address, 210; migrant smuggling response to, 239, 246, 247–48, 251, 252n6; migration due to, 156, 160, 174, 198; in San Antonio, 64; system-involved Latinas and, 284; undocumented youth, 261; at U.S.-Mexico border, 242
pregnancy, detention experiences and, 171–72
prison: academic achievement opportunities in, 227–28; GST and, 142; -industrial complex, 335; racial and ethnic disparities in, 126–27
privatization, of immigration control, 184; by CoreCivic, 190; by GEO, 190–92
probation officer (PO), juvenile diversion programming study and, 96–97
Programa Frontera Sur, for Mexico southern border militarization, 155–56
program-level recommendations, of MHK, 304, 305–6
promotora programs, in domestic violence shelters, 37, 337

Protect Children and Families bill, through Rule of Law Act, 187
Protection of Children Act bill, of 2017, 187
protection orders (POs): anti-immigrant legislation barriers to, 23; deportation fears and, 30; police interactions and, 26
Proyecto SALTO study, 61, 63
psychological violence, as interpersonal victimization, 46
public IPV education, 34–35
punitive capacity, of detention, 183, 192, 201, 203nn2–3
purposive sampling technique, in MHK study, 302–3

questionnaire research, in juvenile diversion programming study, 86

racial and ethnic socialization (RES) strategies, 280; cultural socialization, 283; as delinquency protective factor, 283; for risk factors, 281, 295; strong mother-daughter relationships and, 291–95
racialized oppression, 8
racism, overt, 288
recidivism data, in juvenile diversion programming study, 86, 98
recommendations, in MHK Toolkit study: caregiver services development, 305; cross-generational services, 305; culturally responsive school practices, 305; effective systems advocacy, 306; family case management services, 305, 309–10; program-level, 304, 305–6; relational-cultural approach, 304, 305; respect of Latino cultural heritage, 305, 307–9; *respeto* value and respectful practices, 304–5, 305, 307; systemic racism and bias dismantling, 306; system-level, 304, 305–6

relational-cultural approach recommendation, of MHK, 304, *305*
relationships: in juvenile diversion programming study, 90–92; RES strategies and strong mother-daughter, 291–95; Xinachtli on caring, 326
representational images: Latinas controlling images, 8; oppressive policies and procedures, 8; stereotyped media representations, 8, 334
RES. *See* racial and ethnic socialization
research: Goffman Latinas "on the run," 110, 122; juvenile diversion programming study questionnaire, 86; on Latina women in criminal justice system, 337; Latinos and white criminological, 2; participatory action research, 302; on system-impacted Latinas, 337. *See also* data; *specific study*
residential facilities: for children of imprisoned women, 129–30, 131, *136*, 141–43, 144n5; female juvenile offenders in, 83
resiliency, self-care attitudes and behaviors, Xinachtli on, 327
respect. See *respeto*
respect of Latino cultural heritage recommendation, of MHK, *305*, 307–9
respeto (respect): MHK on value of, 304–5, *305*, 307; in Xinachtli curriculum, 319
retaliation fear, as IPV nondisclosure reason, 68–70
Rios, Victor, 103–4
ripple effects, IPV and anti-immigrant legislation, 21
risk factors: culturally responsive interventions and reduced, 260; juvenile justice system and, 11, 283; of low academic achievement, 328; maternal RES strategies for, 281, 295; undocumented Latinas intervention programs and, 274; victimization and juvenile justice system, 11

rites of passage program, of Xinachtli, 317
ROR. *See* Order of Release on Recognizance
Rule of Law Act, 187

safe house, migrant smuggling and, 248–49, 252n15
SAMHSA. *See* Substance Abuse and Mental Health Services Administration
San Antonio, Texas: MHK program, 303, 335; poverty in, 64
schools: academic outcomes and marginalization by, 93–94; gendered violence in, 103; juvenile diversion programming study on, 92–95; majority-minority, 261; MHK on culturally responsive practices in, *305*; middle school transition, 266–68; -related problems, imprisoned maternal efficacy and, 130, 131, 138–39, *139*, *140*, 142; sexual minority youth bullying in, 51; zero-tolerance policies in, 102
second generation, 285; discrimination of, 287; marginalization and leveled aspirations of, 260–61; segmented assimilation model and, 260–61
Secure Border Initiative, 155
securitization efforts, at U.S.-Mexico border, 154, 155
segmented assimilation model, 260–61
self-help programming, 228
separation: family, 168, 177, 211; strategy for acculturation-related stressors, 281; women migrants detention and forced family, 168
sex trafficking, 119, 120, 175
sexual assault, 212; in detention centers, 197; as interpersonal victimization, 46
sexual minority youth: CDC description of, 46; LGBQ girls study and, 49–50; school bullying of, 51
sexual orientation: LGBQ study description of, 45–46; youth violence and, 43–44

sister (*hermana*), 21–22
sisterhood bond (*hermanadad*), 22
sister of the heart (*comadrazgo*) bond, 32, 37
social ambivalence and aversion, as IPV nondisclosure reason, 67–68
social control: in detention complexes, 186–88, 194; in humanitarian immigration mechanisms, 183
social exclusion: of immigrant youth, 261; negative academic outcomes and, 261; of 1.5 generation, 260
social justice, 3; multilevel interventions for, 335; Xinachtli framework for, 318, 320–21
social marginalization, boys deviant behavior and, 262
social networks: as assistance sources, 22; emotional and instrumental support of, 22–23; for IPV, 19, 22–23; linkpersons, 20, 22; as survival mechanism, 36; unhelpful and abusive, 31–32
social service providers, 20; victimization response from, 11
social stressors, of female juvenile offenders, 84
Southern California barrio, incarceration "on the run" experiences in, 102–23
South Texas Family Residential Center, 193; immigration lawyer on, 194–95
Southwest Key Programs: MHK study recruitment, 302–3; MHK Toolkit of, 301
state prisons: drug offenders in, 126; racial and ethnic disparities in, 126
stereotypes, discrimination and, 287
stigmatized behavior-related statuses, 62
street negotiation, for "on the run": physical, psychological, sexual violence exposure, 115; for place to stay, 116–18, 121; for ride transports, 115–16, 121; substance abuse and, 116–18

structural position stressors among Latina youth: acculturative stress, 281–82; discrimination, 281
subcontracting, of ATD programs, 197
Substance Abuse and Mental Health Services Administration (SAMHSA), 300
substance abuse disorders, of female juvenile offenders, 84
Supreme Court, U.S.: *Clark v. Martinez*, 197; immigrants indefinite detention, 183; *Zadvydas v. Davis*, 197
surveillance, 102, 103; in ATD programs, 188; CCA and GEO benefits from, 191; detention complex study on, 186–88, 194, 195–201; in humanitarian immigration mechanisms, 183; IPV abusers, 31; juvenile justice system control and, 11; ordinances and gangs, 333
systemic barriers, for Latina youth: education and culture disconnect, 304; relational-cultural approach absence, 304
systemic racism and bias dismantling recommendation, of MHK, 306
system-impacted Latinas, 2; community-based programming responses, 10, 12–13; in criminal justice system, 4–5; data challenges, 3–4, 14n1; discrimination impact on, 13; immigration, 5; IPV and, 4; in juvenile justice system, 4–5; terminology of, 10; understanding of, 3–5
system-involved Latinas: MHK Toolkit for youth, 301–2; multiple forms of victimization, 316; poverty and, 284; stereotypes impact on, 334; terminology of, 10; trauma-informed programming for, 316–17; Xinachtli approach, 315–29
system-level recommendation, of MHK, 304, 305–6

T. Don Hutto facility, 203n6; ACLU lawsuit for Flores Settlement Agreement violation, 192; adult immigrant housing at, 192–93; CCA contract for, 192; Monterrosa on violations of, 192–93

Temporary Protected Status (TPS) suspension, 151, 177

Texas: family detention centers in, 193; migrant smuggling in, 244; San Antonio, 64, 303, 335; South Texas Family Residential Center, 193–95

Tijuana, Mexico: deportation to, 213, 214, 230–31, 233; El Chaparral port of entry into, 234n6; English language benefit in, 217, 218

Tohono O'odham Nation, 247, 252n14

total institutions, Goffman on, 194

TPS. *See* Temporary Protected Status

trafficking, 186–87; defined, 251n2; drug, 106, 120, 132, 237, 241, 252n5; human, 240; sex, 119, 120, 175; weapons, 241

transgender women, detention centers and, 193–94

transnational intersectional framework, for crimmigration system, 153–54, 160, 176; intersectionality matrix of domination, 157–58; methodological nationalism, 159; sites of domination, 158; sites of interaction, 158

Transnational Organized Crime, UN Convention against, 239–40

trauma experiences: criminalization of, 62; ecosystemic forms of, 316; juvenile justice system involvement and, 315–16; maternal childhood, 132; systemic forces in, 316

trauma-informed programming, 316–17

treatment-industrial complex, 335

Trump, Donald: anti-immigrant sentiment and, 151, 243, 312; crimmigration acceleration and, 177; DACA rescinding by, 151, 263; interior apprehensions support, 182; undocumented immigrants expedited removal, 185; U.S.-Mexico border wall, 151

T visa, 175

undocumented immigrants, 21; Colorado legal reforms and, 263; intervention programs for risk factors, 274; Obama expedited removal of, 185; social networks importance for, 36

undocumented Latina women, crimmigration system and, 3, 10

undocumented youth: Colorado ASSET in-state tuition bill, 264, 272, 273–75, 276; DACA and, 259, 263, 273–76; poverty and, 261

United Nations Office on Drugs and Crime (UNODC), on migrant smuggling, 251n3

United States (U.S.): female imprisonment rates, 126, 127; humanitarian immigration mechanisms, 152; humanitarian immigration policies, 152; as mass incarceration world leader, 126, 210; migrant smuggling federal data, 244–45, 252n11; Supreme Court on immigrants indefinite detention, 183

UNODC. *See* United Nations Office on Drugs and Crime

UN Protocol to Prevent, Suppress and Punish Trafficking in Persons Especially Women and Children, 251n2

U.S. *See* United States

U.S.-Mexico border: criminal system response to crossing, 3; ICE initiatives and, 155; migrant smuggling trade along, 12, 241–44; migrants risk of life at, 12; migration reconfiguration at, 154–56; militarization of, 154, 241, 243; Operation Endgame at, 155; Operation Gatekeeper and, 184–85; physical and sexual violence risk at, 162–63; poverty at, 242; residents race and class-based discrimination, 242; Secure Border

Initiative and, 155; securitization efforts at, 154, 155; wall at, 151
U.S. Sentencing Commission, 244
U visa, 162, 172, 173, 174

Valdez, A., 62
values: acculturative dissonance and clash of, 290–91; MHK on *respeto*, 304–5, 305, 307; strength of cultural, 13
VAWA. *See* Violence Against Women Act
victimization: criminalization and, 13; delinquency link with, 263; as juvenile justice system risk factor, 11; Latina juvenile justice system physical, 316; LGBQ girls experiences of, 11, 48, 48–49, 49; National Violence Against Women Survey on, 14n3; social service providers response to, 11; women and girls of Color LGBQ, 11. *See also* interpersonal victimization
violence: Blueprints on prevention programs, 300; in detention centers, 196–97; Latina women as victims of, 3; micro-dynamics and migrant smuggling, 246, 248–50; Northern Triangle and women, 156
Violence Against Women Act (VAWA), 25 visa, 156, 191; T, 175; U, 162, 172, 173, 174; VAWA and application for, 25

war on drugs, Latinas impacted by, 126, 127, 210–11, 333
war on immigration, criminalization and, 334
weapons trafficking, 241
Western Region Detention Facility, in California, 223
white: female criminological research, 2; terminology for, 9; women detainees, 316
White House Initiative on Educational Excellence for Hispanics, 312
white supremacy, 210, 316

William Wilberforce Trafficking Victims Protection Reauthorization Act, of 2008: on youth and children deportation, 186–87
women of Color feminists, 209
word (*palabra*), Xinachtli objective of, 318

xenophobic reactions, to migration, 211
Xinachtli (germinating seed) program, 13, 315–16, 329, 336; Boyle Heights community of East Los Angeles and, 317; on caring relationships attitudes and behaviors, 326; on community connection importance, 327; critical pedagogy, 320–21; curriculum content, 320; curriculum structure in, 319–20; on ethnic identity importance, 325–26; facilitation of, 321–22; facilitator reflection and observation, 322–24; healing promotion through culture, 317–18, 328; LAIPA and, 317; *manualidades* crafts in, 319, 329n2; NCN administration of, 318; *palabra* objective of, 318; preliminary outcome data, 324–25; pre-post comparisons, 326; on resiliency, self-care attitudes and behaviors, 327; as rites of passage program, 317; social justice framework for, 318, 320–21

youth: Central America violence and, 186; deportation of, 186–87; interpersonal victimization of, 42–43; LGBQ girls' experience of violence, 43–44. *See also* immigrant youth; Latina youth; sexual minority youth; undocumented youth
Youth Control Complex, Rios on, 103–4
Youth Risk Behavior Surveillance System (YRBSS), 42, 44; description of, 45

Zadvydas v. Davis (2001), 197
zero-tolerance policies: in migration unlawful entry, 177; in school, 102

www.ingramcontent.com/pod-product-compliance
Lightning Source LLC
Chambersburg PA
CBHW020239030426
42336CB00010B/547